The NEW AMERICAN CUISINE

The NEW AMERICAN CUISINE

by the Editors of
Metropolitan Home

Greenwich House

Distributed by Crown Publishers, Inc.
New York

Acknowledgments

Many cookbooks are the results of one cook's vision, the triumphs of a single mind as it collects recipes, tests, modifies and finally comes out with a fresh pronouncement. This book is the absolute opposite—it's the product of a group of editors who, for almost ten years have offered inspiration to a whole generation. *Metropolitan Home* is the grown-up evolution of a magazine entitled *Apartment Life*—and to capsulize quickly what that change means, the magazine and its readers went from the Pepsi generation to the Perrier generation in a decade.

The New American Cuisine, while weighted to the food attitudes of the last several years, combines the best of *Apartment Life*'s talent for teaching and demystifying with *Metropolitan Home*'s global food sensibility.

Who are the people responsible for this huge effort? The magazine has two widely traveled, well-read editors with an intense interest in food. Carol Helms has superb editorial sense, incisive food ideas and a discriminating eye for making the best food pictures in the business; a vision shared with Donna Warner who creates fine pictures herself with intensive research and writing. Joining these two *Metropolitan Home* editors in constant dialogue is Contributing Editor Helen Feingold—the food professional whose credentials, overwhelmingly extensive recipe archives and ample test kitchen make sure our food ideas are doable, thoroughly accurate and foolproof. Her rich and instinctive understanding of food is unflappable, moving with ease from Middle Eastern mezze to a New England clambake; from layering a chocolate torte to baking a two-foot bagel (don't ask). Helen, unlike other food stylists, has always equated food with love and is generous in dispensing both, with more than a pinch of wisdom added. There is a certain type of chemist/scientist food practitioner who goes to literally inhuman lengths to make food look gorgeous, and unattainable, rendering it totally inedible in the process. Helen brings love to our pictures in the form of very real, eminently edible and visually satisfying food.

This book represents the second effort in an unusually happy collaboration between book publishers and magazine editors. The first was *The Apartment Book* (Harmony, 1979). With a rare respect for the imperatives of each others' disciplines, these two teams worked in almost daily contact for well over two years to produce a book that satisfied both. Original publisher Bruce Harris, who, as the chief cook in his family, needed this book fast to figure out what to make for dinner next week—but never backed off once from his commitment to making a definitive volume with the extra attention to detail that it requires. Editor Harriet Bell managed with intelligence, equanimity and a firm hand on potential chaos. She skillfully interpreted deadlines for us and still retained her good humor and enthusiasm. After a long editing session she still wanted to go home and try that day's favorite recipe. Ken Sansone, Art Director for the original publisher, is a creative rock who thoroughly understands editorial design. He remained flexible, sure and hungry all the way.

The staff of *Metropolitan Home,* itself undergoing editorial changes, never had a day they forgot there was a cookbook afoot. Bob Furstenau and Marcia Andrews, our Art Director and Executive Editor, respectively, were always ready to shelve a magazine crisis for a book one. Similar thanks to other senior editors Joanna Krotz and Ben Lloyd for their patience and assistance. Carol Helms and Donna Warner had a full load of magazine story production to handle at the same time they took on this book. That we got both printed is a testimony to their devotion, energy and weekends. To Charla Lawhon, who was promoted to Assistant Editor just in time to assume total book coordination duties (which resulted in more than one all-nighter) we say "welcome to the glamorous world of publishing" and "we literally couldn't have done it without you." The helpfulness of Pam Hanks, Francine Matalon-Degni and Dayna Dove are likewise praised.

Thanks, too, to Nancy Shuker, a writer with a slew of Time/Life books to her credit including work on the "Foods of the World" series. Nancy did much of the background organizing and new research necessary to turn a vast catalogue of magazine articles into a substantial, responsible book.

This is a book of pictures as well as words and photographers like Bill Helms and Tom Hooper have, together with our editors, developed a signature style of photographing food. Particularly significant is Bill Helms, who photographed the major portion of this book with an unprecedented eye for food in a way that makes the ordinary special. His energy, talent and devotion to this project are so intense, it's a relief to be treated to a barrage of food puns, like: "what foods these morsels be." No wonder we call him a man for all seasonings.

To contributors and readers alike, we hope *The New American Cuisine* brings you joy aplenty.

Dorothy Kalins
Editor, *Metropolitan Home*

Introduction

We call this cookbook *The New American Cuisine* because a whole new way of cooking and eating has developed in this country over the last thirty years. This cuisine is the sum of all our travels, all our restaurant forays, all our cooking experiences, and yet it is tempered by everyday realities. There are three singular characteristics of the New American Cuisine: the *freshest ingredients* in the most *stylish presentation* with the most *ingenious and efficient use of time.*

The New American Cuisine defines for the first time a truly American food sensibility. It is neither chauvinistic, regional nor diluted international, but the sum of our food experiences over the last three decades.

If we were to characterize the American home of the Eighties, it would be at least half kitchen, in the same way that the home of the Fifties was half family room, the tempestuous Sixties home was half bedroom and the Seventies house was half status living room. For many of us, the kitchen is the soul of our home life.

Obviously, food followed these same social trends. The Fifties saw convenience foods with a vengeance. The thrill for Mom was in not having to cook at all, so the family could spend more time gathered around the television set. Breaded frozen fish filets were of indistinguishable origin and stamped into uniform shapes. Spaghetti—mushy and oversauced—came in cans; Minute Rice was a miracle; frozen vegetables were a status symbol. "Just heat and serve" was the selling point; shelf life was all. While *The New American Cuisine* skips many packaged products, it does incorporate the Fifties notion of saving time.

The Sixties saw a more worldly palate develop as travel increased, especially to Europe. The first fumbling coq au vins, veal parmigianas, lasagnes, fondues and ducks à l'orange came from cooks trying to be "Continental." The Sixties back-to-the-land movement brought the equation of food with health, an awareness of freshness of ingredients and the potential dangers of food additives—all attitudes that have become a cornerstone of the New American Cuisine.

The early Seventies saw pretentiousness run rampant, with well-meaning but intimidated cooks slavishly following dogmatic recipes such as beef wellington, chicken kiev and anything flambé. For the first time, however, the freshness found in a spinach salad became standard fare. With it came omelets and quiche, eggplants and artichokes. The Seventies ushered in the beginning of the electronic kitchen, replete with excessive gadgetry, food processors, electric woks, crêpe makers and crock pots.

The late Seventies saw the rise of Nouvelle Cuisine, the French revolt against the tyranny of classic haute cuisine. The New American Cuisine has been influenced by some, but not all, Nouvelle Cuisine principles. It adopted the notion of inventive combinations of ingredients: duck with figs, goat cheese with salad greens, pasta with vinaigrette. We learned that rapid preparations—such as a chicken with rosemary—could be as elegant as an elaborate all-day ordeal. Nouvelle Cuisine refined presen-

Pasta Primavera

Chicken Breasts with Ginger Sauce

tation as a simple art: edible garnishes of fresh vegetables, herbs and fruits, and sauces that enhance instead of smother.

And there is no question that Julia Child's formal French and Marcella Hazan's classic Italian cuisines have had an enormous influence on the American cook. But today, few people cook exclusively from one or the other.

Having survived this culinary history, Eighties cooks are more knowledgeable, more relaxed and thus more stimulated and creative about food. There is a feeling of joy, of celebration, of well-being about preparing and eating. Today's cooks are more instinctive and—this is key—understand basic cooking methods instead of only specific recipes. They have a repertoire of cooking styles including both regional and national specialties and feel completely at home with any of them. The best European and Asian cooks excel at what they do—but we do it *all:* one day a stir-fry, the next a sauté.

Sophisticated confidence and innovative joy is what the New American Cuisine is all about. What it is not is a snobbish rejection of the heritage of American food—there's as much love in a good bowl of chili as in a cassoulet. Peanut butter is with us still, in crumbly cookies and pork saté. Tuna, rescued from bland noodle casseroles, has new life in mousse and *vitello tonnato.*

The New American Cuisine respects the abundance of this land. What's new is that we're finally learning how to use and appreciate it all. We anticipate the first tiny zucchini or tender yellow squash that appears in the market. We have a new reverence for herbs. From waving fields of grain we are now making bread at home in gratifying quantities. In our search for new ways to handle fish, mussels and squid, scallops and sushi are becoming as everyday as sole.

Essentially American, too, is not having enough time to deal with this rich abundance. The New American Cuisine cuts through doctrinaire preparation methods without losing legitimacy. It's realistic about the availability of ingredients and possible substitutions, never assuming, for example, an endless supply of homemade chicken stock on hand. Indeed, many recipes in this book need less than a half hour of preparation time.

This is the perfect cookbook for cooks of all levels. For the beginner, every vital ingredient and cooking method (including how to boil water) is carefully detailed in pictures and words, in sections covering Techniques and Basics and in the Glossary. We show the competent cook how to experiment fearlessly with a whole vocabulary of ingredients, from new ways with pasta to the bottomless stewpot. The experienced cook will delight in ingenious ways to shortcut tedious preparation procedures, such as food processor puff pastry.

For days when cooking becomes our favorite indoor sport, there are menus and strategies for feasts and special holidays. The kid cook in all of us will revel in comfort foods, those nourishments for the soul, such as homemade vanilla ice cream and, of course, chicken soup.

The New American Cuisine is nothing short of a movement—an American style come into its own. So, here it is all in one book, the best of everything we love.

Saffron Mussels   **Poached Eggs with Asparagus**

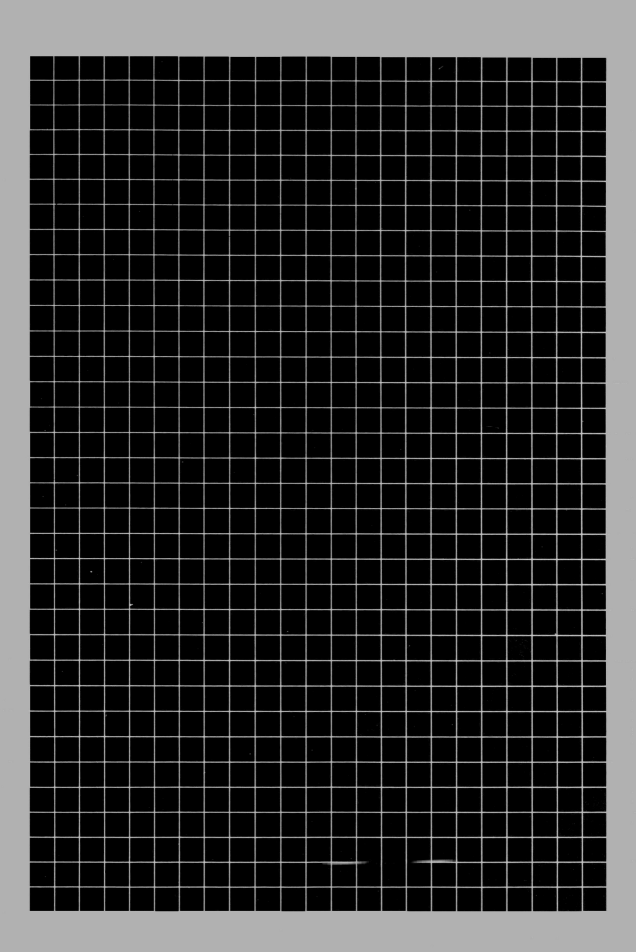

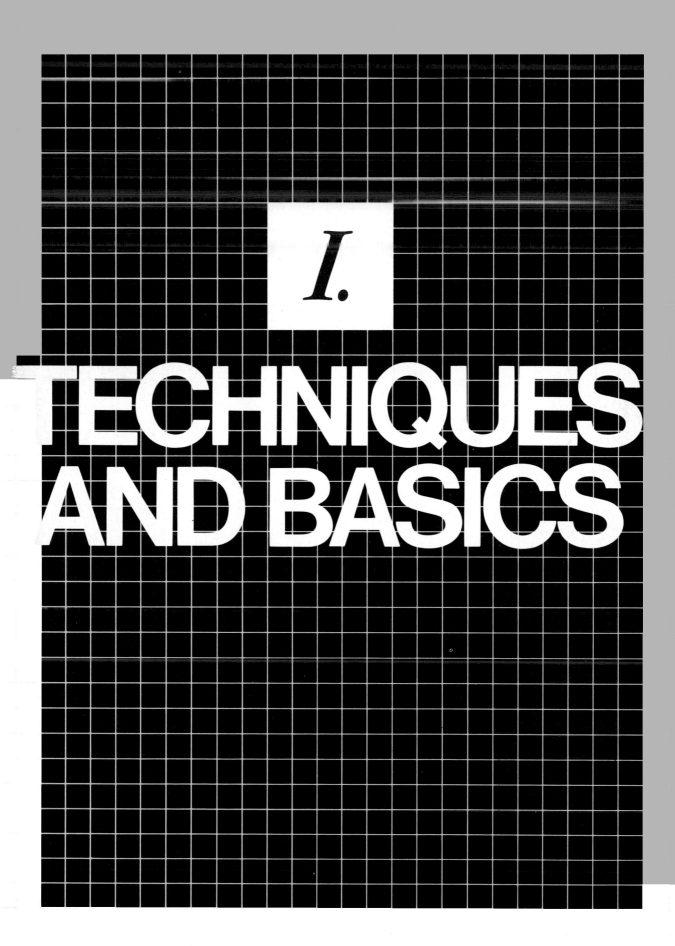

I.

TECHNIQUES AND BASICS

Cooking Techniques

Poach. The great advantage to poaching is that it cooks food without changing the shape—a lazy simmer in a small amount of seasoned liquid, such as wine or stock. Usually, the pan is covered so the flavor won't escape—the food is steam-enveloped and simmered in the liquid.

Use the liquid for sauces or soups later on. Fruit, fish and vegetables all take well to poaching and to seasonings like lemon, celery, cloves, leeks and onions.

To prepare a 2-pound poached red snapper, sprinkle with salt inside and out. Put it in a large skillet, roasting pan or fish poacher and add 2 cups of water, 1 cup dry white wine, 2 tablespoons white wine vinegar, 4 sliced scallions, 1 sliced lemon, 4 whole cloves, 1 bay leaf and 1 teaspoon salt. Cover and simmer gently for 30 minutes.

While keeping the fish warm in the poaching liquid, melt ¼ cup of butter in a saucepan and stir in 1 tablespoon Dijon mustard. Put the fish on a serving platter and serve it with the mustard butter.

Steam. The reason for steaming's popularity: increasingly, vegetables fill up more room on our plates, and even are being served as entire meals. No longer do we boil tiny pieces of food until they emerge limp and anonymous in looks and taste. Steaming produces crisp vegetables that look like vegetables and preserves nutrients. Food is steamed in a perforated basket set just above an inch or so of boiling water and tightly covered. The result is the vegetables (or fish or rice) emerge from the pot with their essence intact.

To prepare steamed broccoli, trim the tough ends of 1 bunch broccoli. Break the broccoli into flowerets. Put the vegetables into a perforated basket or a colander, cover with 1 sliced lemon, 1 sliced medium onion and sprinkle lightly with salt. Put the basket over boiling water, cover and steam approximately 12 minutes or until the vegetables are tender but crunchy.

While the vegetables are steaming, melt ¼ cup butter in a saucepan and stir in the juice of 1 lemon and ½ teaspoon paprika. Remove the lemon and onion slices; serve topped with lemon butter.

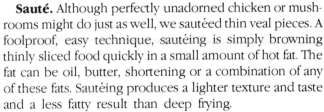

Sauté. Although perfectly unadorned chicken or mushrooms might do just as well, we sautéed thin veal pieces. A foolproof, easy technique, sautéing is simply browning thinly sliced food quickly in a small amount of hot fat. The fat can be oil, butter, shortening or a combination of any of these fats. Sautéing produces a lighter texture and taste and a less fatty result than deep frying.

Using an open skillet and moderate heat, you shake or toss the food occasionally so everything browns evenly. Two things to remember: excess moisture and crowding produces steam and the food won't brown.

To make the sautéed veal in wine, pound 8 slices of veal until ¼-inch thick. Sprinkle the veal with salt and pepper, dredge with flour and then shake off the excess flour.

In a large skillet, heat 2 tablespoons each of butter and oil. Brown the veal quickly on both sides, then put it on a serving platter and keep warm. In the same pan, sauté ½ cup finely chopped fresh mushrooms until they are golden brown. Then stir in 1 tablespoon of lemon juice and ⅓ cup dry white wine. Boil for 1 minute, scraping up all the brown particles. Spoon the pan juices over the meat and sprinkle with chopped parsley.

Stir-fry. Stir-frying is an Oriental method that is suited to just about any food. Vegetables, meats, fish—cut up in fairly even, small pieces—are cooked in a small amount of very hot oil over high heat. Constantly stirring the food ensures fast, low-fat, uniform cooking and nutritious eating.

The wok shown here is efficient and authentic fun, but a deep skillet does the job as well.

To prepare the stir-fry beef and vegetables, heat ¼ cup peanut oil in a wok or large skillet over very high heat. Add 1 clove garlic, chopped, 1½ pounds round steak or sirloin, sliced paper thin, and stir-fry until the beef is brown. Add 1 bunch scallions, diagonally sliced, ½ pound fresh pea pods and ½ pound sliced mushrooms. Stir-fry these for 5 minutes. Add 1½ cups Brown Stock (see page 57) that has been mixed with ¼ cup cornstarch and ⅓ cup soy sauce. Stir until the sauce has thickened and the vegetables are tender but still crisp. Serve spooned over rice or vermicelli

TECHNIQUES AND BASICS

Boil. There are many stages of a boil—from a gentle simmer over the lowest setting on your burner to a great bubbling, rolling boil over high heat. Rapid boiling in an open pot over high heat is used to cook pasta, rice and shellfish. To keep the temperature of the water high, use the largest pot you have and plenty of water—6 to 8 quarts—so the addition of the cold food doesn't stop the action. Real boiling means very fast cooking, so check the food frequently for doneness. Keep the pot covered whenever possible for faster cooking. Boiling is also used to reduce and concentrate stocks and sauces, this time uncovered.

Braise. Braising is a gentle way to cook foods in a small amount of simmering liquid after an initial browning in fat. Braising means long slow cooking that enhances the less tender but often more flavorful cuts of meat, like beef pot roasts and stews. Frequently a mélange of chopped aromatic vegetables—onions, shallots, leeks, garlic, carrots, celery—is added. Vegetables also braise to a beautiful richness. Braising liquid can be water, wine, stock or a combination. A braising pot should be heavy to spread the heat evenly and should have a tight-fitting lid to retain all the moisture.

To braise a 4-pound boneless chuck roast, brown it well on both sides in 3 tablespoons vegetable oil or 1½ tablespoons oil and 1½ tablespoons butter. Remove the meat and add 1 cup dry red wine or Beef Stock (see page 57) to the pan, stirring all the brown particles. Return the meat to the pan and add ½ cup each chopped onions, carrots and celery and a bouquet garni (see page 26). Cover tightly and simmer for 1½ to 2 hours.

Fry. Deep-fat frying is done in very hot oil (360° to 375° F) at least 2 inches deep to sear the outside of the food and cook the inside. Some foods (potatoes) need only be cut up before frying; others, especially those with high moisture content (zucchini and chicken), require a coating of flour, crumbs or batter. If possible, use a deep-fat fryer fitted with a wire basket to lift out the cooked food all at once. Fry in small quantities; never overcrowd. Cooking too many pieces of food at one time causes the temperature of the fat to drop, and you'll end up with soggy, limp food. Thoroughly dry raw foods or they will spatter and steam. Preheat the oil. Drain fried foods on paper towel.

To make perfect French-fried potatoes, cut Idaho potatoes into strips and soak them for 1 hour in cold water. Drain off all the water and thoroughly dry the potatoes. Fry them for 12 to 15 minutes in at least 2 inches of vegetable oil at 375° F.

Shallow frying is done in a skillet with fat ¼- to ½-inch deep. Preheat the fat or oil and fry foods such as breaded veal cutlets and potato pancakes until brown on both sides.

Broil. Broiling is cooking directly under a heat source. It is a fast method of cooking fish, tender pieces of meat and fowl, but foods with no fat must be brushed with butter or oil to keep them from drying out. Excess fat drains through the broiling rack into the pan. The heat for broiling is controlled in two ways—by regulating the heat itself, which must be fairly high to be effective, and by putting the food at different distances from the heat source. For example, sprinkle trout with salt, pepper and lemon juice and brush with butter, then place 6 inches below the heat source to cook for 4 to 5 minutes; turn over and cook another 4 to 5 minutes to achieve crisped skin and a perfect, moist interior. Broiling is also used to brown the tops of sauced dishes and gratins.

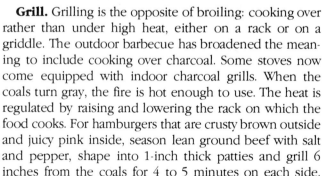

Grill. Grilling is the opposite of broiling: cooking over rather than under high heat, either on a rack or on a griddle. The outdoor barbecue has broadened the meaning to include cooking over charcoal. Some stoves now come equipped with indoor charcoal grills. When the coals turn gray, the fire is hot enough to use. The heat is regulated by raising and lowering the rack on which the food cooks. For hamburgers that are crusty brown outside and juicy pink inside, season lean ground beef with salt and pepper, shape into 1-inch thick patties and grill 6 inches from the coals for 4 to 5 minutes on each side.

Bake. Baking uses dry heat in the oven—a controlled, even heat environment. Bake cakes, bread, muffins, soufflés and all mixtures that rise when exposed to steady heat. Custards and mousses are also baked to make them firm. Vegetables and meats layered with sauce, such as moussaka, are baked to marry their flavors. The important thing in baking is to let the hot air circulate freely, surrounding the food with constant heat. Stagger cake pans; never let two pans touch each other or the sides of the oven. Two different dishes—cake layers and a lasagne, for example—can bake at the same time as long as there is plenty of space between them and they require the same temperature. Because few ovens have perfect circulation, it's a good idea to rotate pans halfway through the cooking time to allow the food to cook more evenly. Use an oven thermometer to check your oven's temperature.

Clay baking. Poultry and meats are splendidly succulent when baked in an unglazed container of porous, fired clay. Roasts and vegetables baste in their own juices with the juices of whatever vegetables and seasonings have been added for flavoring. Soak the pot in water for 10 minutes. Trim the meat of fat and put it in the clay pot, making sure the lid fits tightly. Put the pot in a cold oven, turn the heat to 450° F and bake 1½ hours for a 3- to 4-pound chicken. Brown a roast by removing the lid, pouring off the juices for sauce and letting the meat cook uncovered for an additional 10 minutes. A few guidelines on clay pots—clean only with hot water, no soap; leave open when not in use to stay fresh; and never bring from one temperature to another too quickly.

Roast. Roasting means cooking with dry heat in an oven. Meats with natural marbling of fat inside and a layer of fat on the outside are the easiest to prepare. Others, particularly veal, require added fat to prevent drying out. Sometimes this fat is a thin layer wrapped around the outside; other times it is pushed into the meat with a larding needle. Rub a 6- to 7-pound leg of lamb with salt, pepper, garlic and rosemary and put it on the rack of a roasting pan with a meat thermometer stuck into the thickest part of the flesh. Roast for 1½ hours in a preheated 350° F oven until the meat thermometer reads 135° F. The roast will be crisp and brown on the outside and tender and pink on the inside. Roasts produce natural juices that may be used as is or as the base for other sauces.

The New Larder

Beyond flour and sugar, the New Larder is an enlightened cook's library. It's a stockpile of edible reference material for the many times when *any* preparation seems too much; when friends show up, welcome but unannounced; when all you can do of an evening is manage to bring home the bacon—and nothing else. The intelligently stocked larder can make a meal of itself; it can embellish the simplest fresh ingredients. Put together properly, looking at it can, like a fine library, cause inspirational combinations to dance in your head.

It's all in the shopping and it comes with practice: knowing that this caviar tastes wonderful on those special crackers from England; that a certain pâté is smooth, herb-flavored and delicious when stuffed in artichoke bottoms; that an imported mustard complements a certain spicy sausage.

Here's the shopping list for the New American Cuisine.

INGREDIENTS IN PACKAGES, CANS, JARS

Whole Italian plum tomatoes. Enrich sauces, stews and soups.

Tomato paste. Thickens and flavors sauces, stews and soups.

Chicken broth. With a little doctoring, it can be used instead of homemade for soups, creamy risottos and a fast white sauce.

Tuna. For *salade niçoise* and sauce for *vitello tonnato.*

Salmon. For soufflés, mousses, simple salads.

Sardines. Dress with oil and lemon.

Anchovy filets and anchovy paste. Blend with tuna and oil for *tapénade* or with capers and oil for a quick pasta sauce.

Clams and clam juice. Emergency fish stock for soups and sauces, and a very acceptable base for white clam sauce for linguine.

Caviar and lumpfish roe. Savor simply with chopped egg or a squeeze of lemon or, more substantially, to glorify an omelet with sour cream.

Imported canned ham. Wrap slices around asparagus or use in a gratinée with leeks.

Canned pâté. For instant hors d'oeuvres or to enrich sauces.

Roasted red peppers. Add to cooked vegetable, fish or meat salads.

Capers. Enhance smoked salmon and salads. Use in a quick caper and lemon sauce.

Cornichons. Little sour pickles to team with crusty bread, strong Dijon mustard and a good pâté.

Olives. Add to *salade niçoise* and a chicken provençal.

Chilies. Add to guacamole, soups, eggs and sauces.

Bread crumbs. Coat food for sautéing or sprinkle on gratinées.

Dijon mustard. Makes a fast mustard mayonnaise and goes into vinaigrette and sauces.

Soy sauce. Flavors sauces, marinades, dressings and stir-frys.

Hoisin sauce. Add to shellfish, pork and poultry when prepared in the Chinese style.

Worcestershire and Tabasco sauce. Add spice to soups and stews.

Water chestnuts. Add to any stir-fry or salad.

Oils. Use imported *olive* oil to make salads, pasta, ratatouille, or drizzle it on a chèvre or smoked mozzarella. Oil from Provence has a fruity flavor; Italian olive oil tastes nutty. Strong and fragrant *walnut* oil can dress a salad of the stronger, darker salad greens. *Corn, peanut* and *vegetable* oil are all-purpose; with little taste of their own, they are good for sautéing and deep-frying. *Oriental sesame* oil is used sparingly, as a seasoning and for sautéing.

Vinegars. *Wine* and *herb* vinegars blend with the best oil, coarse salt and freshly ground pepper to dress delicate greens. Use *fruit* vinegar —such as raspberry—in a sauté of chicken and fresh raspberries.

Horseradish. Serve plain or blended with whipped cream to accompany a beef roast.

Chutney. Mix with yogurt or serve as is with curries.

Pasta. A near-instant dinner with sauce or add to soups or salads.

Cellophane noodles. Soak and cook with stock or broth or as part of a meat and vegetable stir-fry.

Beans. *Garbanzo* (chickpeas) make hummus, fill out a minestrone or are dressed with oil, vinegar and herbs. *Kidney* and *pinto* make red beans and rice or a salad. Toss *canellini* with tuna, lemon juice and olive oil. *Flageolets* accompany lamb or delicate greens and vinaigrette. Dried *lentils* make soup and add to a salad or a stew.

Rice. *Long-grain* rice is used for soups and salads, jambalaya and paella. *Arborio* rice makes the best possible risottos. *Wild* or *brown* rice accompanies game and fowl and makes a quick and interesting beef and rice salad.

Bulghur wheat. Soak in water and mix with onions, olive oil, lemon juice and mint to make tabbouleh.

Couscous. Team with fruit or lamb or make a salad with peas, pimentos and vinaigrette.

Herbs and spices. See Seasonings, pages 20–26.

Bouquet garni. Herb bunches flavor soups, stews and braised meat.

Kosher (coarse) salt. Use whenever salt is needed—for drawing out liquid, cooking or in salads; plain salt is an alternative.

Dried mushrooms. French, Italian or Oriental; reconstitute for soup, stews or pasta.

Dry white wine. Create a quick sauce for fish or chicken or moisten a veal stew.

Red wine. For marinades or to baste braised beef.

Dry vermouth. See Dry white wine.

Baking powder. For baking.

Baking soda. For baking.

Flour. For quick breads and biscuits, sauce making, *beurre manié* and lightly coating food to be sautéed.

Granulated and brown sugar. For baking, flavoring and caramelizing.

Cornstarch. Thickens sauces.

Gelatin. To make aspics and molded desserts.

Yeast. For bread making. Keep the yeast refrigerated until ready to use; check the date on the package for freshness.

Nuts. Mix *walnuts* with tender greens and dress with walnut oil and herb vinegar. Use *pine nuts* to make pesto and stuffed grape leaves; add to rice and pasta. *Almonds*, plain or toasted for fish, vegetables or fruits.

Chocolate. Semisweet, unsweetened or milk squares, bits or bars to melt for cakes, mousses and soufflés.

Cocoa. Lightly dust over cakes or dessert mousses.

Honey. Sweeten tea, muffins and yogurt.

Preserves. Glaze fruits and fruit tarts, fold into whipped cream.

Dried fruits (raisins, dates, apricots, prunes). Eat as is or add to compotes, tarts and stuffings.

Brandied fruits. Complement roasted birds and game.

Toast and crackers. Accompany caviar, pâté, sardines and cheese.

Bread sticks. Wrap in freshly sliced prosciutto.

Tea. Black (fermented), green (unfermented), spiced and herbal.

FRESH INGREDIENTS

Eggs. Boil, poach, scramble or fry. Use the yolks to thicken sauces, beat the whites for soufflés and meringues.

Butter. For sautéing, sauce making and baking.

Milk and cream. Make sauces, puddings, soups.

Plain yogurt. Make sauces, soups and dressings.

Cheeses. Team *mozzarella* with tomatoes, basil and a fine olive oil. Melt over veal, eggs, tomatoes. Fold *Parmesan* into risotto, grate over pasta and broth and use in gratinées.

Sour cream or *crème fraîche*. Enrich sauces and soups and fresh fruits.

Bacon or ham. Make frittatas and pasta sauces; use in stews and sautées.

Bread. Make croutons or *croque monsieur*.

PRODUCE

Yellow, white or red onions, shallots, garlic. Use in soups, stews, sautés or salads.

Celery. Braise in stock or flavor a risotto.

Lemons. Squeeze over veal sauté, smoked salmon, a silky sauce or a seafood salad.

Limes. Use in place of lemons and to make delicate ices and soufflés.

Salad greens. Tear long-lasting *escarole* or *romaine* into salads or soups or turn into a purée. Dress *chicory* with a good strong mustardy vinaigrette.

Potatoes. Steam, boil, fry or bake—alone or with a roast or stew. Sauté with thyme, or mix with shellfish and lightly steamed green beans for a wonderful salad.

Carrots. Cook with roast veal or make a light purée or soup.

Apples. Bake, or slice and sauté, or combine with cream, Calvados and pork or fowl.

Oranges. Make compotes and frozen ices; sauté with fowl or braise with veal.

FROZEN

Artichoke hearts. Make a salad of them or team with rice and seafood or meat.

Peas. Add to salads, soups and vegetable stews.

Stocks. To make soups and sauces, risottos and vegetable braises.

Coffee. Roasted or ground beans keep much longer in the freezer.

Puff pastry, homemade or commercial. For quick tarts or hors d'oeuvres.

Phyllo dough. Wrap around spinach and feta cheese or make a curried mushroom strudel.

Pasta, especially stuffed. Tortellini, agnolotti.

Fresh tomato sauce. To sauce a pasta, enrich a sauce, thicken a stew.

Pesto. Spoon onto pasta or a salad of chicken and vegetables.

Egg whites. For soufflés and meringues.

Breads. Enjoy crusty loaves or sauté as the base for tournedos or French toast.

Steaks. Sauté and sauce with butter and shallots; slice paper-thin for a stir-fry.

Chicken breasts. Sauté in butter and herbs; slice for stir-frying.

Veal scallopini. Sauté in butter with lemon juice or dipped in egg and crumbs.

Sausage meat. Make a stuffing or enrich a sauce.

Seasonings

More than any single ingredient or cooking method, herbs and spices are the stuff the New American Cuisine is made of. It's not simply that more seasonings are being used: their flavors have assumed a preeminence.

We want to taste something with, say, basil or rosemary, and the flavor we seek is as important as the vehicle—the tomatoes or the chicken—it is prepared with.

If this sounds sophisticated, it is not without its naive delights. The preparation part of seasoning is unabashedly sensual. Olive oil heated with a clove of garlic, a sprinkling of thyme, a crackle of coriander is sublime nose food even before anything really edible is added to the pan.

The choices are endless as we discover the cuisines of more nations and incorporate them into our American repertoire. We make new taste liaisons: sprigs of savory in warm apple soup; freshly grated nutmeg on pasta; wood mushrooms sautéed with sage; cardamom seeds popping in rice; star anise's licorice scent in a beef stir-fry.

Here's *The New American Cuisine*'s guide to some of the world's best seasonings and how to make use of them. Read from top to bottom, right to left. Whenever possible, we show fresh herbs as well as dried. Two *caveats:* the amount of herbs and spices we show is merely a basis on which to build. Seasoning is a very personal matter, so feel free to increase or decrease amounts as your palate dictates. Seasonings tend to lose their flavor when cooked too long, so before serving taste and correct if necessary

1. Allspice. The berry of the allspice tree—native to Central America—is packaged whole or ground. It smells and tastes of cloves, cinnamon, pepper and nutmeg, which explains its name. Allspice is used in pâtés, pickling, spice cakes and marinades.

2. Aniseed. These tiny seeds with a strong licorice flavor come from a bush of the hemlock family. Baked in bread by the ancient Greeks and used in candies and wedding cakes by the Romans, today aniseed is also used in cookies, cakes and liqueurs such as anisette and ouzo. Star anise, an Oriental spice from a tree in the magnolia family, has an even stronger licorice flavor.

3. Basil. Sweet basil, so special to the New American Cuisine, has a lengthy history. It was a sacred plant in its native India, a lover's emblem in Rome, an offering to the gods in Egypt. Despite its regal background, basil enhances all kinds of salads, soups and stews; it has a love affair with tomatoes, zucchini and eggplant, and its aroma reminds us of the south of France, especially when it is added to ratatouille. It is the base of the beloved Pesto (see page 187), which we use lavishly on pasta and salads. Vegetable soup becomes *soupe au pistou* with the addi-

tion of a pungent oil, garlic and basil mixture. A simple favorite is torn leaves on a mozzarella and tomato salad. Basil is a warm-weather plant and easy to grow in a sunny spot. While lovely used fresh, it can also be kept in a jar in the refrigerator, covered by olive oil, leaving no air space.

4. Bay leaf. A strong, distinctive and classic herb from the Mediterranean, bay leaf is an essential ingredient in a bouquet garni and an almost universal flavoring in meat, fish, stews and stocks. Bay leaves retain their flavor longer than most dried herbs, and a single leaf is usually sufficient in any recipe.

5. Capers. An essential in the New Larder, these piquant beads of flavoring are the pickled, unopened flower buds of a desert shrub native to the Sahara but now grown commercially all around the Mediterranean. The smallest, least-developed buds are considered the choicest, and the handpicking of the buds at just the right stage contributes to the high cost of the best capers, which come from France. Capers are marvelous with fish in particular, but are used in sauces and salads as well. They are delicate with lemon juice and butter on lightly sautéed veal scallopini, perfect with pasta as part of a pungent Puttanesca Sauce (see page 190), and classic with thinly sliced smoked salmon. Black butter and capers are essential to calves' brains.

6. Caraway seed. These aromatic, spiky seeds were found at the site of Neolithic lake settlements in Switzerland, where they may have been man's first herb. Most commonly known as the flavoring for rye bread, they are used in cheese making and are added to noodles, cabbage and salads in northern European cuisines. They can also flavor the Alsatian choucroûte garnie, a warming braised sauerkraut and pork.

7. Cardamom. An Indian spice, cardamom is the dried pod of a perennial plant in the ginger family. The white pods—most readily available here—are bleached. Green cardamom is oven-dried and black cardamom is sundried. It is the seed inside the pod that gives cardamom its lemony flavor, most pungent in the green pods. It is a basic in the spice mixtures used in curry, and can be added to cookie and sweet bread recipes.

8. Celery seed. Much like a concentrate of celery flavor, these dried seeds grow on wild celery plants called smallage. They add bite to pickles, cold salads, soups and stews and are particularly good in crab or shrimp boils.

9. Chervil. A native of southwestern Russia and western Asia, chervil is a cousin to parsley, which it greatly resembles. It is somewhat sweeter, more subtle and more flavorful, and is a part of the classic mix known as *fines herbes*. The French are now the major growers (and users) of chervil, but it can be grown from seed as an annual in a sunny location. At its best fresh, it can be used rather generously. The trick to chervil is adding it at the last

minute to cooked fish, sauces or salads—as with all herbs, cooking diminishes the taste.

10. Chives. Also a component in the *fines herbes* mix, chives are a member of the onion family with a delicate but distinct flavor. They are wonderful snipped fresh into salads and in creamy puréed soups. Chives are a perennial in summer gardens, and will grow in a tiny pot on a sunny windowsill all winter. It's lovely to have them always at hand—and the more you cut, the more they grow.

11. Cinnamon. The dried bark of an evergreen tree native to Ceylon, cinnamon was known to the Chinese as early as 2700 B.C. It was more than worth its weight in gold to the Romans, who used it to flavor wine. After Magellan's expedition discovered the Spice Islands in the sixteenth century, cinnamon became the most widely used spice in Europe. Cinnamon sticks—curled quills of dried bark—give a spicy aroma to mulled cider and wine. We've grown up with ground cinnamon on apple pies and on toast. We're learning the Indian and Middle Eastern way with cinnamon in sauces, redolent, long-cooking stews and phyllo pies of chicken or meat.

12. Cloves. The most aromatic spice, cloves were known and treasured in Western Europe for almost fifteen hundred years before their source—five tiny islands in the Moluccas—was discovered by one of Magellan's men in 1511. First the Portuguese and then the Dutch tried to protect and monopolize the production of cloves (and eventually killed off all the plants), but a clever Frenchman had smuggled out seed; thanks to him, today cloves grow profusely on Zanzibar—where smuggling clove seed is a capital offense still—and Madagascar. Whole cloves are the dried, unopened flower buds of the clove tree; they must be handpicked at just the right moment and sun-dried, which makes them expensive. Ground cloves should include only the head of the whole clove. Cloves season meats, baked goods, hot drinks and, stuck into whole onions, French stews and soups.

13. Coriander. A relative of parsley, but with a more startling bite, coriander leaves have a suprisingly sharp citrus-rind taste—lemony to some, more like orange to others. Used in salads and as an herb in Middle Eastern, Latin American and Chinese cooking, fresh coriander is also called Chinese parsley or cilantro. Coriander seed, which tastes much sweeter than the leaf, is basic to pickling, and ground coriander is used in curries, sausages and baked goods. Ground coriander does not keep well, so for the best flavor grind your own as you need it—an extra pepper mill works fine.

14. Curry powder. A blend of spices usually including cumin, coriander, fenugreek, peppers and ginger and dominated by turmeric in taste and color, curry powder in this country is a fairly standard, commercially mixed spice that can vary in degree of hotness. Experiments with your own versions of the above can yield an authentic Indian "signature blend"—in India, there is no one version of ground spice curry. Curry is splendid used in less traditional ways such as in mayonnaises for poached fish, shellfish or artichokes.

15. Dill. A favorite herb in Northern and Eastern Europe, dill is superb in mayonnaise or vinaigrette for vegetable salads and cold poached fish. Dill and crisp chilled cucumbers bound with a fresh cream or sour cream sauce is a summer classic. It also works beautifully in cool creamy soups, as well as in hot soups. Dill has a delicate, slightly bitter flavor vaguely related to caraway. It mixes well with other herbs in breads, salad dressings and omelets. Fresh dill, frequently seen in markets now, is also easy to grow in a sunny place. Dried dill weed is a winter substitute.

16. Fennel. Fennel seed has a licorice flavor, much milder and sweeter than anise, that especially complements fish, pork and vegetables. The fennel plant has celerylike stalks and is prepared and eaten much like celery—the tender stalks eaten raw and the more mature ones sautéed in butter or quickly stewed in oil. In France fennel leaves are used in salads. Bunches of dried fennel stalks are added to fish to make a superb summer grill.

17. Garlic. A bulbous member of the onion family, garlic was used as a vegetable by the ancient Greeks, but has served mainly as an herb since. It is the cornerstone of many Mediterranean cuisines. The cooking of southern France and southern Italy is dependent on garlic with its heady, pungent aroma and almost sweet flavor. Once looked down on in this country as lower class and unrefined, garlic has become one of America's most popular seasonings in the last forty years—the New Larder should never be without it. It is sold fresh, dried and powdered, but fresh garlic is the best—the bigger, fatter bulbs are the sweetest.

18. Ginger. For cooking we use the root of this native of tropical Asia. Fresh ginger root—the gnarled object at the top of the photograph—when peeled and grated has a pungent, spicy flavor. We're beginning to use this staple as Orientals and Indians do. Fresh ginger root, carefully wrapped, will keep for weeks in the refrigerator and months in the freezer, so you can slice off just what you need. Often thought of as an ingredient in complex recipes, fresh ginger root is wonderfully fragrant grated or sliced on crisp steamed vegetables. It offers new flavor on crab, chicken, duck and pork. Dried ginger pieces are used in canning fruits and preserves. Dried ground ginger is used in baking; it is not a substitute for the fresh root in cooking.

19. Horseradish. The grated outer part of the root of the horseradish plant has a strong, stinging flavor that goes well with cold meats. Usually sold in a vinegar brine, prepared horseradish comes in a white version (shown) and a red version. Fresh horseradish is good mixed with butter and mustard or in a sauce bound with whipped cream. Horseradish needs liquid to release its flavor.

20. Juniper berries. These bittersweet, aromatic berries from a wild European shrub are used in sauces and marinades for game and pork, pork pâtés, sauerkraut or braised red cabbage and some preserves.

21. Lemon rind. The yellow outer skin of the lemon —carefully peeled away from the bitter white membrane underneath it—has a refreshing, tart, concentrated flavor similar to that of the fruit itself, but more intense. For recipes requiring a really distinct lemony taste, like lemon pudding, sauce or sherbet, fresh, minced or grated lemon rind is a necessity. Fresh is always preferred, but dried works well. Candied lemon rind is available for use in fruitcakes and cookies.

22. Orange rind. As with lemon rind, the usable part of orange rind is the bright outer peel and not the white membrane. It has a tangy, orange flavor much more potent than the fruit or its juice and is used to intensify orange flavor in a variety of desserts. Orange marmalade is made of orange rind rather than the fruit itself. Candied orange rind (also called candied orange peel) is a common confection, eaten by itself or used in spice cakes and puddings and as a garnish. Fresh orange rind has a better flavor than dried and when slivered adds a lovely flavor to a wine and tomato laden veal stew.

23. Mace. The reddish, weblike outer part of nutmeg is a thin skin that is dried in flat blades and called mace. Sold whole or, more usually, ground into a powder, mace is used in cakes, cookies and puddings and has a mild, delicate nutmeglike flavor.

24. Marjoram. Frequently confused with oregano, the herb is often called sweet marjoram to distinguish it from wild marjoram, another name for oregano. Marjoram is the more delicate of the two herbs, with a spicy, sweet fragrance that makes it popular in potpourris and sachets as well as in stuffings and soups and with meat and fish. The fresh leaves are good in salads and on grilled lamb and are a wonderful addition to sauces, soups and stews when tomatoes are a main ingredient.

25. Mint. The Greeks used mint to sweeten bathwater, and the Elizabethans planted paths of it in their gardens so it would be crushed as they walked and release its fresh, sweet smell. Of the many varieties, spearmint, a hardy perennial, is believed to be the oldest and is still the most useful to cooks in jellies, sauces and fruit preparations. Peppermint, with its stronger menthol taste, is used in candies and crème de menthe liqueur. Fresh mint leaves are best, but dried mint has adequate flavor. Mint also is an important flavoring in Middle Eastern cuisine and is often added to yogurt there as well as in India.

26. Mustard. Second only to pepper in world spice trade, mustard is made from the ground seeds of two related plants—white mustard, which is yellow, and so-called black mustard, which is really brown. All prepared mustards are from these seeds. The ground powder is used to season and bind mayonnaise and other sauces. White mustard seeds are mild but distinctive in flavor, and have enzymes that discourage mold and bacteria (hence their use in preserving brines). Black mustard seeds have the hot pungency that gives bite to Chinese, English and Dijon mustards. This hotness is created by the interaction of cold water with the oils released by grinding the seeds. To make the hottest mustard, mustard powder is mixed into a paste with cold water and allowed to stand for ten minutes. Heat inhibits this sharpness, so the mustard paste is added to hot dishes after they have been cooked. Most commercial mustard powder is a combination of white and black seeds. Dijon mustard is basic to some vinaigrettes, mayonnaises and cream sauces for pork and kidneys. A good coarse mustard enhances a country pâté, sausages and meat pies. Flavored mustards are available, with added tarragon, green peppercorns or lemon.

27. Nutmeg. Like cloves, nutmeg is native to the Moluccas, dubbed by Magellan the Spice Islands. Also the subject of trade wars between the Portuguese and the Dutch, nutmeg trees were finally smuggled out of the islands by a Frenchman. In this case, the environmental transplant wasn't successful. Even now the trees grow in only one area besides their original home: the West Indies. Nutmeg trees are harem plants—female plants must be fertilized by male plants. Nutmeg is the seed of the tree and has a warm, sweet, fragrant flavor that enhances the taste of vegetables and sauces as well as pastas and desserts. Nutmeg is also an aromatic addition to gnocchi, gratins and potato purées. Since ground nutmeg loses its strength quickly, the spice is better bought whole and grated fresh as needed, with a nutmeg grater or the smaller holes of a standard grater.

28. Oregano. Stronger and spicier than marjoram, with which it is often confused, oregano is a hearty herb known as shepherd's thyme in some regions. A favorite seasoning in Mediterranean cooking from Italy to the Middle East, oregano is used with tomatoes, eggplant and lamb dishes. It is basic to pizza. Dried oregano can become stale, changing color and flavor, so buy small quantities that will be used up quickly. The packages will be clearly marked so you can tell where your oregano originates, but most packaged oregano is a blend of many kinds. Oregano grown here not only differs from the Mediterranean variety, but also from region to region.

29. Paprika. Ground from a variety of chili pepper, paprika is as sweet or hot as the peppers used, which range from very mild to cayenne intensity. The best paprika comes from Hungary, where it is considered the national spice and is never used simply as a decoration. Spanish paprika is excellent, but coarser in texture and flavor. Paprika is very perishable and keeps best in a metal container in a cool place. Heating paprika in hot oil brings out its flavor. Recipes that call for paprika mean sweet paprika unless otherwise specified.

30. Parsley. Fresh parsley, like lemon juice and salt, is more a flavor enhancer than a definitive seasoning, although it has its own special tangy, sweet taste. That is why a bouquet garni almost always has parsley, whatever the other ingredients may be, and *fines herbes* always include parsley with any combination of other aromatics. Curly parsley is more delicate in flavor than the flat-leaf, Italian variety preferred in Mediterranean recipes. Both are available year-round in markets and are hearty plants in the garden. Dried parsley is a poor substitute. Parsley shows up as a key ingredient in jambon persillé, green sauces, mayonnaises and butters for fish and grilled meats.

31. Pepper flakes. These red and yellow dried flakes of hot chili peppers add zest to pasta sauces, stews and eggs. Because they are dehydrated, they need at least five minutes in liquid to develop their flavor and should be used sparingly until their strength is fully appreciated.

32. Black peppercorns. Many times during the Middle Ages black peppercorns were considered a more stable means of exchange than gold or silver. Rents, bribes and dowries were paid in peppercorns, and noblemen who married commoners for their wealth were known as "pepper bags." A native of India, and the first Oriental spice to reach Europe, black pepper is the most widely used spice in the world today. Its major production area is Indonesia. A single vine produces all the true peppers (genus *Piper*)—black, white and green peppercorns. The chili-type peppers (*Capsicums*) native to the New World were called peppers by Columbus in a moment of wishful thinking. Black peppercorns are the unripened berries of the pepper vine which have been dried in the sun. Whole peppercorns are used in stocks and brines and should be slightly crushed to release their flavor.

33. White pepper. For white pepper, the berries of the pepper vine are allowed to ripen before being picked. They are then soaked in water to loosen their skins, which are removed before the berry is dried. The core does not darken much in drying. More expensive than black pepper because of its processing, white pepper is also milder. Tradition calls for its use in white sauces because its grains are less visible than those of black pepper.

34. Freshly ground black pepper. The most spicy pepper flavor comes from freshly ground black peppercorns; commercially ground pepper loses its potency very quickly. Many pepper mills can be adjusted from fine to a very coarse grind to suit different purposes.

35. Cayenne pepper. Bright red and red hot, cayenne is a ground form of dried chili pepper. When used delicately, it enhances marinated or grilled shrimp, shellfish stews and mayonnaise. Buy cayenne in small quantities because it loses its potency with age.

36. Green peppercorns. The immature berries of the true pepper vine, green peppercorns are preserved in brine, frozen or air-dried for export. Soft in texture and very perishable, they have a wonderful, pungent flavor quite different from that of black peppercorns. Good in butter sauces for meat, fish and poultry, they can be preserved by freezing in butter or water. They combine well with shellfish and duck, fish terrines and pâtés. Also gaining popularity are pink peppercorns with a mild pepper flavor, especially prized in France.

37. Pickling spice. A mixture of whole spices—usually coriander, mustard seed, bay leaves, allspice, dill seed and pepper—is packaged as the essential seasoning for a pickling brine or good shellfish boil. Dried chili peppers are often added for hotness. The spices differ from one manufacturer to another, so read the labels carefully. Pickling spices are a convenience if you find a mix you like. If not, you can create your own combination.

38. Pimento. Mild sweet chili peppers, pimentos are peeled (by roasting until the skins are black), cored and put up in jars commercially. Buy whole pimentos and chop them yourself (the canned chopped pieces are soaked in water and have no flavor). Add them to rice, pasta and vegetable salads.

39. Poppy seeds. Tiny seeds with a nutty flavor, poppy seeds have Eastern European origins. They fill pastries and season noodle dishes. East Indians prefer white poppy seeds, which taste much like the black.

40. Rosemary. A beautiful Mediterranean herb with a strong, almost incenselike aroma that comes from oil of camphor in its spiky leaves, fresh rosemary, like basil, has become one of our favorites, loved for its ability to enhance and marinate a substantial range of foods. Rosemary goes well with roasts of lamb, veal, pork and chicken, and especially grilled fish, but its flavor is just as sumptuous released in buttery sautées.

41. Saffron. The most expensive seasoning in the world, saffron is the stigma of the autumn crocus. Picked laboriously by hand, saffron was probably equally costly in ancient Crete, where its cultivation was depicted on palace walls four thousand years ago. Saffron imparts a unique, spicy, almost bitter flavor and brilliant yellow color to rice dishes such as risotto Milanese and to breads and cakes, as well as fish soups like bouillabaisse. It is a natural with fish, shellfish, fennel and garlic. Always buy saffron in threads, as pictured; a few go a long way. Powdered saffron loses flavor, and because of its high price, it invites adulteration with other ingredients by

Herbs in vinegar add a special flavor—whether in cooking or simply on a green salad.

unscrupulous spice dealers. Turmeric is often confused with saffron because of its color.

42. Sage. An ancient herb native to the Mediterranean, sage was first used for its medicinal powers, ingested more for healing than for seasoning. Very strong in aroma and taste, it reached its peak of popularity in Europe during the Middle Ages, when heavy flavoring was preferred (probably to mask less-than-fresh ingredients). The English are still very partial to sage and lace cheese with it as well as baked tomatoes, roasts and leek pies. Sage used to be limited to stuffings and sausages, but the Italians are showing us new ways of preparing sage with meat and pasta. Sage is a hearty herb to grow in the garden. A milder variety, pineapple sage, can be grown in a sunny window.

43. Savory. Winter savory, a perennial, is a bit strong for most cooks. A more delicate relative, summer savory, is a spicy herb that is frequently used in bean dishes and more recently in stewed fruits and soups. It has a sweet peppery quality and mixes well, fresh or dried, with other herbs in stews and meat dishes. Summer savory is easy to grow from seed as an annual.

44. Sesame seed. The dried seeds of the sesame plant, which is native to India, are chiefly used for oil. The seeds have a wonderfully nutty flavor, particularly when they have been toasted in the oven or skillet. In Middle Eastern cooking sesame seeds are ground into a paste called tahini, which is used as the base for many hors d'oeuvres such as hummus, a creamy, smooth paste of tahini and chickpeas that's eaten with warm pita bread. We use sesame seeds, also known as benneseeds, in stir-frys, sautées, breads, cookies and pastries.

45. Shallots. Small reddish or green-white members of the onion family, shallots have a sweet and nutty flavor all their own that distinguishes sauces such as béarnaise. Much used in French cooking, red shallots are becoming more available in groceries here. Buy the green (sometimes called gray) variety if you have a choice; they are more flavorful than the red. Shallots are most important in delicate sauces where their particular flavor is not overwhelming. Shallots grow in clustered cloves like garlic.

46. Tarragon. Brought to Europe by the Crusaders, tarragon comes from the steppes of Central Asia. The French in particular took to this amazing herb for its tart but subtle flavor and slight licorice aroma. A seasoning that can enhance natural food flavors while adding its own, it is recommended to people on salt-free diets. Americans are at a disadvantage with tarragon because dried tarragon, unlike most herbs, is less intense than

TECHNIQUES AND BASICS

BAKING PANS

Don't be discouraged by this long list—choose those pans that will satisfy your personal baking needs.

* Casseroles and gratin dishes, of porcelain, glass or earthenware. Start with one or two: 1-quart, 1½-quart, 2-quart, 3-quart.

  Angel food cake pan: 10-inch tube

  Bundt pan: 3-quart

  Terrine: 1½-quart

* Ring mold: 1½-quart. Good for cake, pâté, fish mousse, etc.

  Soufflé dish: start with a 6- or 8-cup size and then individual dishes

  Quiche or tart pan

* Pie pans: start with the 9-inch size, then add 8-inch and 10-inch

* Two loaf pans: 9 × 5 × 3-inch. Good for bread, cake, meat loaf.

* Two baking sheets: 12 × 16-inch, heavy-duty metal

  Cake pans: start with two or three 8-inch pans, add 9-inch and 10-inch later

  Spring-form pan: 8-inch diameter, 3-inch sides

* Baking and/or jellyroll sheets: 10 × 15 × 1-inch. A heavy, nonwarping jellyroll pan can double as a baking or roasting pan

  Two muffin tins: 2½-inch cups. Two make 24 muffins, the usual recipe yield.

  Pastry bag and tips: start with a plain ½-inch tip or a small set with at least one small (8-inch), one medium (10-inch) and one large (12-inch) bag

  Two square cake pans: 8-inch and 9-inch

* Two or three oblong cake pans: 9 × 13 × 2-inch. These are very versatile—use for lasagne and small roasts.

OTHER BAKING EQUIPMENT

* Rolling pin—best bet is heavy hardwood with ball bearings
* Wire cooling racks

  Pastry board. A marble slab is preferred, since it stays 10 degrees cooler than room temperature, but any large surface at least 20 × 24 inches will do.
* Sifter
* Pastry brush with soft bristles that can be easily washed

  Pastry wheel

  Ruler or tape measure for measuring dough, etc.

  Pastry blender

  Pastry scraper, oversized stiff plastic or wood and metal

  Cake tester (toothpicks work fine, too)

  Aluminum baking pellets (or you can use rice or dried beans instead)

  Biscuit, cookie and doughnut cutters

FOOD PROCESSING EQUIPMENT

  Food mill

  Rotary egg beater

  Salt mill
* Pepper mill
* Food processor or blender

  Mortar and pestle
* Potato masher or ricer
* Juicer or juice reamer

  Drum sieve

  Chinois or conical sieve with a wooden pestle
* Strainers: small, medium or large, depending on your needs; one fine sieve, one coarse sieve
* Colander

  Meat grinder with sausage stuffer

* Heavy standing electric mixer with dough hooks. Attachments may include grater, slicer, meat grinder, juicer, even pasta maker.
* Toaster

  Pasta machine
* Coffeepot. Choose from top-of-stove, electric, drip, espresso models—simple or complex.

  Coffee grinder (hand or electric)

  Tea ball

  Ice cream machine

MISCELLANEOUS

* Potholders, washcloths, sponges
* Cheesecloth

  Parchment paper

  Dish drainer

  Vegetable brush
* Linen or cotton dish towels

  Rack for paper towels, foil, plastic wrap
* Plastic bags for storing vegetables and salad greens.
* Canisters (clear glass or plastic are best) that close tightly for flour, sugar, tea, pasta, beans, etc.
* Garbage pail

  Salad spinner
* Serving spoons, forks, etc.

  One or two gelatin, aspic or mousse molds: 1½-quart

  Spice and herb jars
* Lidded containers for storing leftovers, cheese, cut vegetables, etc.: 1-cup, 2-cup, 1-quart

  Oil and vinegar cruets

  Pots of herbs—tarragon, chives, dill, chervil, sage
* Storage bins for onions and potatoes

  Glass jars with lids for storing liquids, soups, etc.
* Cord, twine or heavy sewing thread for trussing, tying, etc.

Preparation Techniques

In many of our recipes, we tell you to use a certain technique: mince instead of chop; julienne instead of slice. In many instances, the actual cooking of the food calls for a certain technique, whether it is to achieve a certain texture or to make sure that the foods blend together correctly.

Always start off with a very well-sharpened knife. Not only does a sharp knife make cutting faster and easier, but the end result is clean and neat (example: no more mushy tomato slices). Good carbon or stainless steel knives should be sharpened with every use (the cheaper, nonprofessional knives don't respond to sharpening). If you have been lax in keeping your knives sharpened, it is a good idea to have them sharpened professionally before you develop your own routine for sharpening them at home.

To sharpen your knives, hold the knife firmly by the handle in one hand and grasp the sharpening steel in the other. Draw the knife along the steel, starting at the knife's base. Keep the cutting edge of the blade at a 45° angle to the steel. Repeat this action alternating sides of the blade until the knife is sharp, about 5 or 6 times on each side.

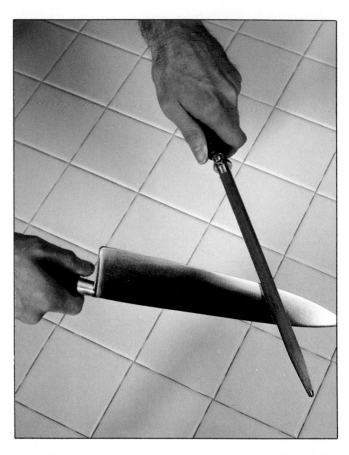

Slice. To slice a cucumber for garnishing, score the peel with the tines of a fork. Hold the cucumber against a cutting board, and firmly draw the knife down and through.

Chop. To chop an onion or clove of garlic, peel but leave the root end intact. Slicing toward the root but not through it, makes a series of parallel cuts. At right angles to these, make

another series of cuts. Holding the knife parallel to the root end, slice the bulb and the chopped pieces will fall onto the board.

To chop fresh herbs, hold the leaves together in a tight bunch and slice through with a sharp knife. You'll have coarse, rather than fine, pieces.

Mince. To mince fresh herbs, hold the chef's knife securely. Move the knife up and down (with a rocking motion) first in one direction, then in the other.

Julienne. To julienne, slice carrots in half first and lay them flat side down. Cut each half into ¼-inch slices, then lay the slices flat and cut into strips.

Shred. To shred cabbage or lettuce, cut the head into quarters. Lay the quarter flat side down and cut into thin slices or shreds.

Peel. To peel garlic, mash the clove with the broad side of a large knife or cleaver. This loosens the skin enough to let you pull it off easily. Try this with shallots, too.

Flute. To flute a mushroom, use the tip of a small sharp knife to cut out tiny slivers of the cap at even intervals all around the edge.

Calculated Cooking

Two important components of the New American Cuisine are a dedication to quality, no matter how simple the preparation, and an unflagging curiosity—the desire to be infinitely adventurous and creative. We are bound only by the limits of time. Although the very thought of a weekly round of seven precisely planned meals may be discouraging, with a little strategic planning we can reconcile our gastronomic needs and hectic lifestyles for days. It goes like this: when you have the time, prepare something like a turkey, ham or brisket, then divide what is left for several equally satisfying meals over the next few days. The options are endless and you can proceed with ingredients from the New Larder. The point is, be flexible.

LEFTOVER	MAIN COURSE	SOUP/STEW	SALAD
Poultry	Quenelles à la Crème (see page 130)	Turkey/Chicken Stock (see pages 136/58)	Chicken Pesto (see page 319)
Fish	Cold Salmon Mousse (see page 103)	not recommended	Seafood Dill Salad (see page 104)
Shellfish	Peking Crab and Vegetables (see page 106)	not recommended	Mussels with Ravigote Sauce (see page 109)
Beef	Corned Beef Hash (see page 298)	Vegetable Beef Soup (see page 60)	Cold Sliced Beef with Mustard Vinaigrette (see page 80)
Pork	Cassoulet (see page 330)	Ham and Lentil Soup (see page 63)	Ham and Beet Salad (see page 236)
Vegetables	Julienne of Vegetable Omelet (see page 88)	Cream of Any Vegetable Soup (see page 59)	Vegetables Vinaigrette (see page 41)
Pasta	Vegetable Pasta Salad (see page 194)	Minestrone (see page 60)	Japanese Noodle Salad (see page 197)
Rice	Stir-fry of Rice and Vegetables (see page 207)	Vegetable Rice Soup (see page 60)	Brown Rice Salad (see page 207)

Create three meals from one preparation. Baked Ham
(see page 173) becomes a Frittata (see page 89) one day
and Ham and Leeks au Gratin (see page 173) the next.

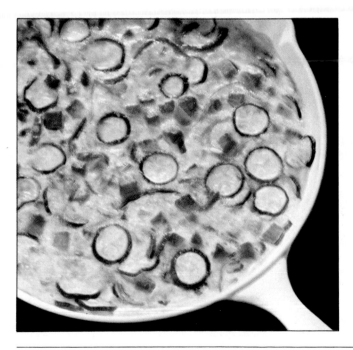

II.

COOKING

First Courses

□□□□

Beyond the broiled grapefruit and the lone glass of tomato juice, first courses have come into their own. The French first labeled them *hors d'oeuvres,* or "outside the main work," i.e., the main course. But they were wrong. In our culinary lexicon the beginnings are every bit as important as the middle and the end, if not a meal in themselves. Luckily, much of the rest of the world agrees, and we have an entire international repertoire to choose from. Forget the miniature hot dogs and Swedish meatballs of yesteryear. Today's hors d'oeuvres draw heavily on the ingredients and combinations that define the New American Cuisine: seafood, fresh vegetables, fresh herbs, light cheeses, inventive mixings and matchings.

Hors d'oeuvres should have elegance and beauty, taste and freshness; they must be easily prepared, presented with wit, warmth and style; appropriate as party fare or an elegant supper.

The new first courses tempt tired palates with jewellike eyefuls—small collages of the freshest ingredients. They are generous with vegetables, and ingenious with delectable tastes.

SHRIMP AND SCALLOPS WITH GREEN SAUCE

Serves 6 to 8

1½ pounds medium-size raw shrimp
1½ pounds sea scallops
1 tablespoon whole pickling spice
1 cup sour cream
2 tablespoons grated Parmesan
1 clove garlic, mashed
3 tablespoons minced watercress
2 tablespoons minced spinach leaves
1 tablespoon chopped chives
1 tablespoon chopped fresh parsley
1 tablespoon chopped fresh dill
salt

1. In a large pot, bring 2 quarts of water to a rolling boil over high heat. Add the shrimp, scallops and pickling spice. Cook over high heat for a few minutes, just until the water returns to a boil and the shrimp are pink. Drain in a colander and plunge the shellfish into a bowl of cold water to stop the cooking and cool. Drain.

2. Shell and devein the shrimp (see page 108). Cut the scallops into thin slices. Chill both in a covered dish for at least 2 hours.

3. To make the sauce, combine the remaining ingredients in a bowl, mix, season with salt to taste and chill. To serve, put the shrimp and scallops on a serving platter, garnish with lime wedges and serve the sauce in a bowl.

TAPENADE

Serves 6 to 8

A Mediterranean fish purée most often made with tuna.

1 cup olive oil
2 large cloves garlic, chopped
3 sprigs fresh parsley
3 sprigs fresh or ½ teaspoon dried thyme
12 black olives, pitted, preferably Italian, Greek or French
3 tablespoons drained capers
1 2-ounce can flat anchovy filets, drained
juice of 1 lemon
1 7-ounce can water-packed tuna, drained

Clockwise from top left: **Shrimp and Scallops with Green Sauce, Curried Mushrooms with Red Bell Peppers, Croque Monsieur, Radis au Beurre, Smoked Salmon with Horseradish Cream, Vegetables Vinaigrette, Herbed Goat Cheese, Tapénade and Carpaccio**

6 hard-cooked eggs, halved
1 9-ounce package frozen artichoke hearts, cooked, drained and chilled
2 red onions, sliced and separated into rings
3 navel oranges, peeled and sliced
pitted black olives for garnish

1. Combine olive oil, garlic, parsley, thyme, olives, capers, anchovies, lemon juice and tuna in a blender or food processor and purée. Pour the mixture into a dish, cover and chill until ready to serve.

2. Arrange a platter with the egg halves, artichoke hearts, onion rings and orange slices. Garnish the tapénade with black olives and serve with crusty bread.

CARPACCIO

Serves 6 to 8

As elegant as smoked salmon, these paper-thin slices of raw beef are similarly served, but with a mustard sauce.

1 pound beef filet or sirloin steak, 1½ inches thick
½ cup olive oil
⅔ cup lemon juice
1 tablespoon minced onion
2 tablespoons drained capers
2 tablespoons Dijon mustard
salt

1. Trim the beef of excess fat and wrap in freezer paper or foil. Freeze until just hard—this should take about 30 to 40 minutes. Freezing allows you to make very, very thin slices easily with a very sharp knife. Cut into diagonal slices and arrange in an overlapping pattern. Chill.

2. Make the sauce by combining the remaining ingredients in a bowl and beating until thick. Let stand for 30 minutes for the flavors to blend, beat again and pour into a serving dish. Drizzle dressing on beef slices.

SMOKED SALMON WITH HORSERADISH CREAM

Serves 6 to 8

A creamy, biting sauce for the venerable salmon.

1 cup heavy cream
2 tablespoons prepared white horseradish, drained
salt
¾ pound smoked salmon, thinly sliced
12 to 16 thin slices pumpernickel or other dark bread
1 bunch scallions, washed and trimmed

1. In a bowl, whip the cream until soft peaks form. Fold in the horseradish and season with salt to taste. Chill until ready to serve.

2. Arrange the salmon, bread and scallions on a platter with the sauce on the side.

RADIS AU BEURRE
Radishes with Butter

Serves 6

2 bunches red or white radishes
whipped sweet butter
12 thin slices pumpernickel
coarse salt

1. Wash the radishes and leave some of the greens attached for handles. Chill.

2. Serve the radishes, butter, bread and salt in a large shallow bowl or arrange on a platter.

CROQUE MONSIEUR

Serves 6

A miniature version of the classic grilled ham and cheese sandwich served in French cafés.

12 slices firm white bread
½ cup soft butter for spreading
1 tablespoon Dijon mustard
6 slices smoked or boiled ham
6 slices Fontina
3 eggs
½ teaspoon salt
1 cup milk
¼ cup butter for frying

1. Spread one side of each slice of bread with ½ cup butter mixed with mustard. Top 6 of the slices—butter side up—with ham and cheese and another slice of bread, butter side down.

2. In a shallow bowl beat the eggs with the salt and milk. Melt the remaining butter over medium heat on a large griddle or in a heavy skillet.

3. Soak each sandwich in the egg mixture and brown slowly in butter on both sides. Drain on paper towels and cut into 4 squares. Keep warm until ready to serve.

HERBED GOAT CHEESE

Serves 6

Classy cheese shops have the costlier version, but it's easy to roll your own chevre in fresh herbs and olive oil.

1 11-ounce Montrachet log
½ cup chopped fresh herbs (a mixture of any of these: parsley, dill, rosemary, chives, thyme, basil, chervil and tarragon)
¼ cup olive oil

1. Chill the cheese to firm it for easy slicing. Unwrap and cut with a sharp, wet knife into 6 slices.

2. Mix the chopped herbs in a bowl and roll each cheese slice in the mixture until it is completely covered. Place the herbed cheese on a serving platter and drizzle the olive oil over the top. Let the cheese warm to room temperature and serve with crusty bread.

VEGETABLES VINAIGRETTE

Serves 6 to 8

Blanched or steamed tender-crisp, then marinated in a vinaigrette and served cold, any vegetable is fair game, from baby artichokes to zucchini.

½ pound snow peas, strings removed
2 zucchini, cut into ½-inch slices
2 yellow squash, cut into ½-inch slices
1 cauliflower, broken into flowerets
½ pound green beans
1 head broccoli, cut into flowerets
½ pound Brussels sprouts
1 cup olive oil
⅓ cup red wine vinegar
1 clove garlic, mashed or minced
salt
1 teaspoon sweet paprika
freshly ground black pepper
1 tablespoon chopped fresh or 1 teaspoon dried oregano
1½ teaspoons chopped fresh or ½ teaspoon dried summer savory
3 tablespoons chopped chives

1. Blanch or steam each of the vegetables until tender but crisp. Drain and chill, covered, in the refrigerator for at least 2 hours.

2. Make the dressing by combining the olive oil, vinegar, garlic, salt, paprika, pepper, oregano and savory in a bowl

and beating until thick. Arrange the vegetables on a platter and pour the dressing over them. Turn them to be sure they are well coated. Cover the platter and let the vegetables chill in the dressing for at least 2 hours. Sprinkle with chives before serving.

CURRIED MUSHROOMS WITH RED BELL PEPPERS

Serves 6

Mushrooms can take on myriad flavorings, especially evident in this delicious yogurt-based curry.

¼ cup butter
1½ pounds button mushrooms
3 red bell peppers, seeded and cut into strips
1½ cups plain yogurt
1 teaspoon curry powder
1 tablespoon chopped chives
1 tablespoon lemon juice
salt

1. In a heavy skillet over medium high heat, melt the butter and sauté the mushrooms until tender—not more than 1 or 2 minutes. With a slotted spoon transfer the mushrooms to a bowl. Sauté the red pepper strips in the skillet for 5 minutes. Remove the peppers with a slotted spoon to a separate bowl. Cover and chill both the mushrooms and peppers for at least 2 hours.

2. To remove any congealed butter, put the chilled mushrooms in a strainer or colander and rinse with warm water. Pat dry with paper towels. Mix the remaining ingredients in a large bowl. Stir in the mushrooms.

3. Rinse the red peppers in warm water, drain and pat dry. Put the mushroom mixture in a serving bowl on a large platter and surround it with the red pepper strips.

BAGNA CAUDA

Serves 8 to 10

A hot anchovy sauce for raw vegetables (bagna cauda literally means "warm bath")—unusual ones such as turnip and fennel with red pepper, zucchini, summer squash, broccoli.

4 tablespoons butter
2 cloves garlic, chopped
16 anchovy filets, drained and chopped
2 tablespoons flour
2 cups heavy cream

1. In a heavy 1-quart saucepan, melt the butter over medium heat and sauté the garlic for 2 to 3 minutes. Add the anchovies and cook another minute. Stir in the flour and cook for 2 to 3 minutes more.

2. Lower the heat and add the cream. Stir constantly until the sauce is thickened; then continue to stir the mixture while cooking until it has the consistency of sour cream.

3. Serve either in one communal bowl or individual ones for dipping. Try crusty bread for a change of texture.

BRIE EN CROUTE

Serves 4

A preheated oven and a perfect seal on the pastry ensure the success of this elegant cheese in pastry.

8 ounces Food Processor Puff Pastry (see page 275) or ½ of a 17½-ounce package frozen commercial puff pastry, defrosted
1 8-ounce Brie or Camembert with rind intact

1. Preheat the oven to 400°F. Roll and cut the pastry into 2 rounds, one 8½ inches in diameter, the other 10 inches.

2. Put the cheese on the smaller round, cover it with the large round and seal the edges completely, crimping carefully.

3. Cut the excess pastry into strips and decorate the top. Put the encased cheese on an ungreased baking sheet and bake for 15 to 20 minutes, until the pastry is puffy and brown. To serve, cut into wedges. Serve with mustard and cornichons.

Brie en Croûte is simple and elegant.

CELERI REMOULADE

Serves 6

A classic céleri rémoulade requires the big turniplike celery root, not celery.

3 whole celery roots (celeriac)
1 teaspoon salt
2 teaspoons lemon juice
¼ cup Dijon mustard
3 tablespoons boiling water
⅓ cup olive oil
2 tablespoons red wine vinegar
1 tablespoon grated fresh horseradish
salt
freshly ground black pepper

1. Peel the celery roots and cut into julienne strips. Cover the cut vegetable with cold water in a large bowl. Add 1 teaspoon salt and the lemon juice and let stand for 30 minutes to wilt the celery root.

2. In a small bowl, blender or food processor, beat the mustard with the boiling water and add the oil, a few drops at a time, beating constantly. Gradually beat in the vinegar. Stir in the horseradish, salt and pepper.

3. Drain the celery root strips and dry. Combine them with the dressing in a bowl, cover and chill for at least 2 hours. Serve on lettuce leaves on individual plates.

GUACAMOLE

Serves 6

2 large, very ripe avocados, peeled and seeded
juice of 1 lime
½ cup chopped sweet green chilies
2 tablespoons finely chopped red onion
1 large ripe tomato, peeled, seeded and chopped
2 tablespoons finely chopped fresh coriander
¼ teaspoon crushed dried red peppers

1. Cut the avocados into pieces, put them in a blender, add the lime juice and process at high speed until the mixture is smooth.

2. Pour the mixture into a bowl, stir in the remaining ingredients and season with salt.

3. To keep, cover with plastic wrap, making sure it is in direct contact with the guacamole to prevent the air from turning the avocado mixture dark.

For Antipasto, mix vegetables of contrasting colors.

ANTIPASTO

Nothing could be simpler or more handsome than layered vegetables steeped in garlic, bay leaf and black pepper and preserved in fragrant olive oil. Choose vegetables with contrasting shapes and colors. Raw vegetables should be briefly steamed to a tender-crisp consistency (see page 12). Olives and pimentos can go from cans into your jars. Ours have beans, hot peppers, artichoke hearts, stuffed green olives, pimento, baby ears of corn, black olives, baby whole carrots and green beans.

1. Layer the vegetables in a sterile glass jar to a level 1 inch below the top. Lightly sprinkle each layer with crushed thyme and oregano. Add 2 bay leaves, 4 garlic cloves and 12 to 18 peppercorns. Pour in enough olive oil to completely cover all the vegetables.

2. Slide a knife around the inside of the jar between the food and the glass to release air bubbles. Seal and store in a cool dry place. Check the jar after a few days to be sure the olive oil still covers all the vegetables, adding more if not. Vegetables are ready after 1 week and will keep for several weeks, but they must be covered entirely with oil to prevent spoilage.

3. To serve, drain the vegetables and sprinkle with red wine vinegar, freshly ground pepper and coarse salt.

COCKTAIL PARTY

The following recipes are suitable for a large cocktail (or other) party. Choose a tasty few or try them all, expanding or reducing the ingredients by the number served.

MUSSELS WITH AVOCADO SAUCE

Makes 48

Wine-simmered mussels are bathed in an avocado and herb mayonnaise. Cooked in the morning, the mussels chill in their sauce during the day, becoming more delectable as the flavors marry.

48 mussels (buy a few extra to make up for any sand-filled ones; see page 110)
2 cups dry white wine
1 onion, finely chopped
1 ripe avocado, peeled, pitted and mashed
1 cup Mayonnaise (see page 78)
¼ cup chopped watercress
¼ cup chopped fresh parsley
2 tablespoons chopped chives
salt

1. Scrub the mussels and put them in a large pot. Add the wine and onion. Bring to a boil, then lower the heat, cover and simmer over medium heat until the mussel shells open—about 5 to 6 minutes. Remove the pot from the heat and let the mussels cool in the broth.

2. Mix the avocado with the mayonnaise, herbs and salt to taste.

3. Remove and discard the top half shell from each cooled mussel. Drain the liquid from the bottom half shells, and spoon the sauce over the mussels. Cover loosely with plastic wrap and chill.

MUSHROOMS STUFFED WITH ESCARGOTS

Makes 48

The glorious French escargots are snails raised especially for the table. In this country, they can be found canned. Escargots, smothered in the classic combination of garlic and butter, are here tucked away in fresh mushroom caps for a rich, luscious hors d'oeuvre. The mushrooms can be stuffed in the morning and kept tightly covered in the refrigerator. A quick broiling is all that's required at the last minute.

48 medium-size fresh mushrooms
48 canned *escargots*
1 pound soft butter
2 cloves garlic, chopped
1 teaspoon *fines herbes*
2 tablespoons chopped parsley
2 tablespoons chopped celery leaves
salt
freshly ground black pepper

1. Wipe the mushrooms with a damp cloth and remove the stems. Thoroughly rinse and drain the *escargots* and fill each mushroom cap with one snail.

2. Cream the butter and mix in the garlic, herbs and pepper. Spoon approximately ½ teaspoon of this mixture on top of each stuffed mushroom cap.

3. When ready to serve, arrange the stuffed mushrooms on a baking sheet and cook 6 inches under a preheated broiler for 5 minutes.

Note. For a more traditional version, stuff the snails into snail shells or special serving dishes and cover with the garlic-butter mixture before baking.

SHRIMP AND ARTICHOKE TOAST

Makes 48

These should be put together at the last minute to keep the bread from getting soggy, but all the other steps can be completed in advance.

48 frozen artichoke hearts (3 9-ounce packages)
2 pounds small shrimp
2 loaves French bread
2 cups Sauce Rémoulade (see page 79)
48 pimento strips

1. Prepare the artichoke hearts according to package directions. Drain and chill.

2. Put shrimp in a large pot. Add water to cover. Cook uncovered over high heat until the water starts to boil. Drain the shrimp and plunge them into cold water to cool. Peel and devein the shrimp (see page 108). Refrigerate until ready to assemble.

3. About an hour before serving, slice the French bread into 48 thin slices. Toast the slices under the broiler on both sides, then cool.

4. Spread the toast with sauce remoulade, top with an artichoke heart, several shrimp and a pimento strip.

ENDIVE STUFFED WITH CHEESE

Makes 48

The salted chopped tomatoes are sprinkled on at the last minute or the tomatoes will discolor the cheese.

48 Belgian endive leaves, about 5 heads
2 ripe tomatoes
salt
1 pound Camembert or Brie
½ pound Roquefort or other blue-veined cheese
½ cup finely chopped pecans

1. Separate the endive leaves, wash carefully and chill in cold water for 10 minutes to crisp them.

2. Core and seed the tomatoes, chop into small pieces and season to taste with salt. Chill.

3. Mash the cheeses in a bowl until well blended, then fold in the pecans.

4. Drain and dry the leaves. Fill each with the cheese and nut mixture.

5. Sprinkle each stuffed leaf with chopped tomatoes.

NEW POTATOES STUFFED WITH CAVIAR

Makes 48

These can be prepared ahead if carefully covered with aluminum foil and refrigerated until an hour before serving.

48 unpeeled new potatoes, the smaller the better
2 cups sour cream
2 tablespoons chopped chives
1½ cups red lumpfish caviar

1. In a large kettle or saucepan, bring to a boil enough salted water to cover potatoes. Add the potatoes and let the water return to a boil. Lower the heat to medium and boil the potatoes until they are tender but still firm—about 15 to 20 minutes depending upon their size. Drain the potatoes and plunge them into cold water to stop the cooking. When they're cool, cut a thin slice from the bottom of each so they won't roll around when served.

2. Use a small spoon or a melon baller to scoop out a cavity in each potato.

3. Mix the sour cream and chives together and spoon a little into each potato, then add a dollop of caviar. Sprinkle on a few extra chives if you like and chill.

GRILLED SWEETBREADS WITH BACON

Makes 48

Smoothly textured and delicately flavored, sweetbreads are much more interesting than meatballs as a hot hors d'oeuvre.

2 pairs sweetbreads
1 teaspoon salt
dry sherry
2 pounds lean sliced bacon

1. Put the sweetbreads in a saucepan, cover with water, add salt and bring to a boil. Lower the heat, cover and simmer over medium heat until the sweetbreads are firm—about 25 to 30 minutes. Drain and cool.

2. Remove the membrane and stringy tissue from the sweetbreads and cut into 48 small pieces. Put the pieces in a bowl and cover with sherry. Refrigerate at least 1 hour—even better, overnight.

3. Drain the pieces and wrap each in a strip of bacon. Secure with a wooden toothpick (plastic will melt).

4. Put the rolls on a rack in a broiling pan (with sides to catch the grease) and cook 6 inches from the source of heat in a preheated broiler until brown on one side—about 3 to 4 minutes. Turn and broil until brown on the other side, another 2 or 3 minutes. Drain on paper towel and serve hot.

FRESH FIGS WITH PROSCIUTTO

Makes 48

1 8-ounce package Neufchâtel or 8 ounces Petit Suisse
½ pound chèvre (such as Chèvrotin or Montrachet)
48 small fresh figs
48 thin slices prosciutto (about 1 pound)

1. Mash the cheeses together in a bowl until well blended. Shape into 48 small balls.

2. Stem the figs and, starting at the top, slice lengthwise into quarters, but don't cut all the way through. The quarters should hold together at the bottom.

3. Stuff each fig with a ball of cheese, wrap a slice of prosciutto around the base, and secure with a toothpick.

Note. Prosciutto can also be wrapped around wedges of cantaloupe, honeydew or Crenshaw melon or around sesame seed breadsticks.

PATES AND TERRINES

As basic as meat loaf to the New American Cuisine, pâté abounds in as many personal styles as its prosaic relative. Experimentation is high—as it should be with a dish whose origins were the humble necessity of using leftovers. Made-at-home pâtés and terrines are enormously satisfying: all that grinding and mixing yields results to be proud of and enjoyed for days and days. (Refrigerated, it keeps for at least 10 days.)

VEAL, HAM AND PORK TERRINE

Serves 16 to 18

A fine-textured pâté striped with ham and veal and studded with truffles. The fresh pork fat—fatback or trimmings from fresh ham or pork loin are best—gives the terrine a smooth consistency.

¾ pound fresh pork fat, thinly sliced
2 pounds lean pork, ground four or five times
2 eggs
2 cloves garlic, mashed
2 teaspoons salt
½ teaspoon freshly ground black pepper
1 teaspoon dried thyme
1 teaspoon dried marjoram
1 ⅞-ounce can truffles, finely chopped, with liquid (optional)
1 pound smoked ham, sliced ¼-inch thick
1 pound veal scallopini

1. Preheat the oven to 350°F. Line the bottom and sides of a 2-quart loaf pan or terrine mold with pork fat, saving enough to cover the top.

2. In a large bowl mix the pork, eggs, garlic, salt, pepper, herbs and truffles with their juice. Pack ⅓ of this mixture into the fat-lined pan.

3. Top with an even layer of the ham and pack in the second ⅓ of the pork mixture. Top with an even layer of the veal and fill the pan with the remaining pork mixture.

4. Cut the remaining pork fat into strips and put them in a crisscross pattern across the top of the terrine.

5. Set the loaf pan in a shallow roasting pan to catch any drippings and bake the terrine for 1 hour, or until the juices run clear.

6. Cool the baked terrine on a rack, draining off the excess fat. Chill for at least 4 hours to let the meat set before cutting in thin slices. Serve with crusty bread and cornichons.

Veal, Ham and Pork Terrine is smooth, almost creamy, while the Country Pâté is more crumbly.

DUCK LIVER MOUSSE WITH ENDIVE

Serves 6 to 8

Substitute chicken livers if you're inclined, but duck livers have a stronger, gamier flavor.

1½ cups unsalted butter
1 pound duck livers
¼ cup Calvados or apple brandy
1 cup shelled unsalted walnuts
salt
freshly ground white pepper
2 cups whole green beans, washed and trimmed
2 heads Belgian endive, washed and separated

1. In a heavy skillet melt ½ cup of the butter over medium heat and gently sauté the livers until they are lightly browned outside and still pink inside—about 7 minutes. Remove the pan from the heat and let the livers cool.

2. Put the livers, pan drippings, remaining butter, Calvados and walnuts in a blender or food processor and process until the mixture is finely chopped. Add the salt and pepper. Chill until firm—at least 4 hours.

3. Steam or blanch the green beans for 2 to 3 minutes. Rinse them in cold water to stop the cooking and chill.

4. When ready to serve, put a mound of mousse in the center of each plate, arrange the endive leaves in a spoke pattern around the mousse and put a green bean in each spoke.

COUNTRY PATE

Serves 14 to 16

1½ pounds pork liver, sinews removed, finely chopped or ground
1 pound lean ground pork
1 pound fresh pork cut into ½-inch pieces
⅓ cup Calvados or Cognac
½ pound smoked ham, cut into ½-inch cubes
1 teaspoon salt
½ teaspoon freshly ground black pepper
1 onion, chopped
2 garlic cloves, minced
4 shallots, chopped
⅓ cup flour
3 eggs
1 pound sliced bacon

1. Preheat the oven to 350°F. In a large bowl, with your hands, mix all the ingredients except the bacon.

2. Line a 2-quart baking pan or terrine mold—sides and bottom—with bacon, saving 4 or 5 slices for the top. Press the meat mixture firmly into the pan and cover the top with bacon.

3. Put the loaf pan in a roasting pan to catch any drippings. Bake for 1½ hours, or until the juices from the loaf run clear and not pink.

4. Cool the cooked terrine thoroughly on a rack. Drain off any excess fat. Chill completely—at least 4 hours in the refrigerator—to let the meat set before slicing. Serve with Dijon mustard and cornichons.

MEZZE

Many of our favorite first courses derive from the Middle Eastern superfeast of first courses, the *mezze*—the ultimate antipasto, a glorious groaning board of tempting tastes designed to charm and unite the diners in mellow and ritualistic good-fellowship.

Forty or more choices are not unusual, ranging from simple raw fruit—melon, papaya or mango—or vegetables—zucchini, green pepper or tomatoes—to elaborate pastry, all eaten with the fingers or with pita bread.

TARAMASALATA

Makes 2 cups

A thick caviarlike spread to be scooped up with pita bread or raw cucumbers.

4 ounces tarama (carp roe)
⅓ cup lemon juice
¼ cup chopped scallions
2 slices firm-type white bread, crusts removed
1 cup olive oil
salt
freshly ground black pepper
2 tablespoons chopped parsley

1. In a blender or food processor, combine the tarama, lemon juice, scallions and bread and process for a few seconds.

2. With the motor running, gradually add the oil, 1 tablespoon at a time. Scrape into a bowl and season to taste with salt, more lemon and pepper. Chill for several hours. Before serving sprinkle with chopped parsley.

CUCUMBER AND YOGURT SALAD

Makes about 2 cups

3 cucumbers, peeled and sliced
½ teaspoon salt
1 cup plain yogurt
1 clove garlic, mashed
2 tablespoons chopped fresh mint leaves
salt

1. Sprinkle the cucumber slices with ½ teaspoon salt and let stand in a colander for 1 hour to release excess water.

2. Put cucumbers in a bowl with the remaining ingredients and add salt to taste. Let stand in the refrigerator for at least 1 hour.

BABA GHANOUSH
Eggplant Purée

Makes about 2 cups

A mellow mix of smoky roasted eggplant, somewhere between a thick sauce and a composed salad.

1 medium eggplant (about 1 pound)
¼ cup fresh lemon juice
3 tablespoons tahini (sesame seed paste)
1 clove garlic, chopped
3 tablespoons chopped parsley
1 tablespoon olive oil
¼ cup chopped onion
salt
dash of cumin
tomato wedges
fresh mint sprigs

1. Prick the eggplant with a fork 4 or 5 times, then impale the eggplant on a long-handled fork and hold it over a gas flame until the skin is charred all over. If you're using an electric stove, prick the eggplant and broil about 4 inches from the heat, turning frequently.

2. When the eggplant is cool, peel it and chop it into chunks. Purée the eggplant in a blender or food processor with the lemon juice, tahini, garlic, parsley, olive oil and onion until smooth. Season with salt to taste.

3. Mound the mixture on a plate, and sprinkle the top with cumin. Garnish with the tomato wedges and mint.

HUMMUS

Makes about 3 cups

A highly seasoned chickpea purée mixed with sesame seed tahini.

1 1-pound, 4-ounce can chickpeas, drained
½ cup tahini (sesame seed paste)
½ cup lemon juice
2 cloves garlic
salt
paprika

1. Reserve some chickpeas for a garnish and put all the ingredients except salt and paprika in a blender or food processor and purée. Season to taste with salt and chill.

2. Garnish with reserved chickpeas and paprika. Serve with pita bread.

EGGPLANT CAVIAR

Serves 6 to 8

1 large eggplant
2 cloves garlic, chopped
1 large onion, chopped
4 ripe tomatoes, peeled, seeded and chopped
1 green pepper, chopped
½ cup olive oil
2 tablespoons red wine vinegar
1½ teaspoons chopped fresh or ½ teaspoon dried oregano
1½ teaspoons chopped fresh or ½ teaspoon dried basil
1½ teaspoons chopped fresh or ½ teaspoon dried thyme
salt
freshly ground black pepper

1. Slice a large oval from one side of the eggplant. Cut out the inside of the eggplant, leaving a shell ½-inch thick. Reserve the shell.

2. Roughly chop the eggplant. In a large skillet, mix the eggplant, garlic, onion, tomatoes, pepper and oil. Stir over high heat until the vegetables are wilted, about 5 to 6 minutes. Lower the heat and add the remaining ingredients except salt and pepper. Simmer uncovered, stirring occasionally, for 25 to 30 minutes, or until the vegetables are tender and the mixture is thick.

3. When the mixture has cooled, put it in a blender and process at low speed until it is coarsely chopped. Season with salt and pepper and chill. Just before serving, spoon the eggplant caviar into the reserved eggplant shell.

Clockwise from top center: **Avocado slices, Dolmathes, Hummus, olives, Phyllo Turnovers with Three Stuffings, pita bread, feta, Kibbeh, Cucumber and Yogurt Salad and Taramasalata.** *Center:* **Baba Ghanoush with sliced tomatoes and White Bean Salad**

PHYLLO TECHNIQUES. To prepare phyllo dough, lay it flat and cut it lengthwise into 4-inch-wide strips. Stack the strips and cover them with a damp (not wet) cloth.

Take a layer of dough, leaving the stack covered so the dough will not dry out, and brush it with melted butter, using a very soft pastry brush.

Put a second layer of dough on the first and gently butter it. Make as many sets (2 layers of dough for each little pie) as you need to wrap the filling.

Fold in the edges (about ½ inch) of the buttered stack of dough layers and put a heaping tablespoon of filling about 2 inches from one end to make square pies.

Fold over the tail and butter it before making another turn. To vary shapes, try rolling a little less filling into a log or folding the dough back and forth diagonally into triangles.

However you shape the dough, butter each surface before folding it over again. Make at least 2 folds in each pie as you shape it into whatever form you choose.

PHYLLO TURNOVERS

Makes 36

Phyllo dough takes time, patience and agility to make it at home. Fortunately, it's available frozen. Let frozen phyllo dough thaw completely in its wrapping overnight in the refrigerator. Once you begin to use phyllo, work quickly.

½ pound phyllo dough
1 cup melted butter
1 recipe meat, mushroom or cheese filling

1. Make the phyllo turnovers according to the photographs, using the fillings of your choice. Create a different shape for each filling so you can tell them apart.

2. Put the folded turnovers in a single layer in a shallow baking pan or on a cookie sheet that has been lined with foil, then buttered. Chill for at least 1 hour.

3. Bake the chilled turnovers in a preheated 375°F oven until they are brown and crisp—about 15 to 20 minutes.

MUSHROOM FILLING

¼ cup olive oil
2 pounds fresh mushrooms, finely chopped
½ cup chopped fresh parsley
½ cup freshly grated Parmesan
salt

1. Heat the oil in a skillet over medium high heat. Sauté the mushrooms until they wilt. Stir in the parsley and cook until the liquid evaporates, about 10 to 15 minutes.

2. Remove the pan from the heat and stir in the cheese. Salt to taste and cool.

CHEESE FILLING

1½ cups (12 ounces) feta cheese, finely crumbled
2 cups cottage cheese
¼ cup chopped fresh mint or 1 tablespoon dried mint
freshly ground black pepper

1. Mix all the ingredients thoroughly in a bowl.

MEAT FILLING

2 tablespoons olive oil
1 medium onion, chopped
1 pound ground chuck or lamb
½ teaspoon ground allspice
¼ cup pine nuts
⅓ cup Beef Stock (see page 57)
salt
freshly ground black pepper

1. In a skillet, heat the oil and sauté the onion until lightly browned. Add the meat and cook until brown and crumbly. Drain off excess fat by tilting the pan and removing with a spoon or baster.

2. Add the remaining ingredients to the pan and bring to a boil, lower the heat, cover and simmer for 10 minutes. Let cool.

DOLMATHES
Grape Leaves Stuffed with Pilaf

Serves 6

2 cloves garlic, chopped
2 large onions, chopped
½ cup olive oil
2 tomatoes, cored and chopped
1½ cups uncooked brown rice
5¼ cups Chicken Stock (see page 58)
½ cup pine nuts
⅛ cup currants
¼ cup chopped fresh mint or 1 tablespoon dried mint
½ teaspoon ground allspice
½ teaspoon cinnamon
salt
freshly ground black pepper
1 1-pound jar vine or grape leaves
¼ cup lemon juice

1. In a skillet, sauté the garlic and onions in ¼ cup oil until lightly browned. Add the tomatoes and rice and sauté for another 5 minutes. Stir in 3½ cups chicken stock, nuts, currants and seasonings and bring to a boil. Lower the heat and simmer, covered, until the rice is tender and the liquid absorbed—about 30 to 35 minutes. Cool.

2. Wash the leaves in cold water and drain them. Fill and roll them.

3. Mix the remaining oil with the lemon juice and remaining chicken stock. Pour over the dolmathes. Bake at 350°F for 40 to 45 minutes.

DOLMATHES TECHNIQUES. Wash and drain leaves. Lay out each leaf, shiny side down.

Put a heaping teaspoon of filling on the leaf, near the stem, and shape into an oval.

Gently fold the leaves from the stem end. Use any torn leaves to line the baking dish.

When the filling is completely enclosed, carefully fold in the sides.

Finish rolling.

Fill baking dish with packets, seam side down. Moisten with oil, lemon juice and stock mixture.

KIBBEH

Serves 6 to 8

Ground lamb, bulghur wheat and minced onion shaped into mini-sausages, served raw or cooked.

1 cup fine bulghur wheat (available in health-food stores)
1 pound boneless lean lamb (leg or shoulder) ground 4 or 5 times
1 large onion, minced
salt
freshly ground black pepper
Spanish onion rings
lettuce

1. Soak the bulghur in enough water to cover for 1 hour and drain thoroughly.

2. If you're grinding the meat yourself, do it right before making the kibbeh.

3. Mix all the ingredients well and shape into 2-inch logs. Chill for at least 1 hour and serve cold with raw Spanish onion rings on a bed of lettuce.

4. If you prefer your kibbeh cooked, sauté the kibbeh logs over medium heat in 2 tablespoons olive oil until they are browned all over—about 5 to 6 minutes.

WHITE BEAN SALAD

Serves 6

1 pound dried Great Northern beans
¾ teaspoon salt
1 cup olive oil
½ cup lemon juice
3 hard-boiled eggs, chopped
½ cup Greek olives, pitted
2 tomatoes cut into ½-inch-thick slices
salt
freshly ground black pepper
crumbled egg yolk for garnish

1. In a large pot, cover the beans with water, making sure the water level is about 2 inches above the beans. Add the salt and simmer over medium heat for about 2 hours. Add more water if necessary. Drain the beans.

2. In a bowl, mix the olive oil and lemon juice. Beat in the eggs and olives. Fold the beans and the tomato slices into the olive oil mixture. Add salt and pepper to taste. Chill.

3. Sprinkle with crumbled yolk and serve.

TEMPURA

Sixteenth-century Portuguese traders introduced the European notion of deep-fat frying to the Japanese. After four hundred years of refinement, Japanese tempura is probably the most delicate batter-fried food in the world. Because of its lightness and texture, tempura makes a superb hors d'oeuvre—more makes a main course. Almost any meat or fish and most vegetables work for tempura cooking. The secret to the lacy coating: keep the batter chilled—some cooks keep the bowl on shaved ice—and keep the oil hot.

Serves 6

eggplant, sliced ¼-inch thick
fresh mushrooms, or dried black mushrooms reconstituted in hot water for 10 minutes
broccoli flowerets
onion, sliced in ½-inch rings
green beans, blanched for 5 minutes
sweet potato strips or thin slices
carrot strips, tied with pieces of scallion
green or red peppers, seeded and sliced
zucchini, sliced diagonally
chicken breasts, boned, skinned and cut in strips
sea bass, skinned, filleted and cut in 1-inch pieces
scallops, whole or sliced
shrimp, shelled and deveined (see page 108)

DIPPING SAUCE

1 cup reconstituted dashi (a dried fish stock available at Oriental grocery stores) or 1 cup Chicken Stock (see page 58)
2 teaspoons Japanese soy sauce
1 teaspoon sugar
1 tablespoon grated daikon (Japanese white radish) or 1 tablespoon grated icicle radish
1 tablespoon peeled and grated fresh ginger

**The fresh ingredients at
left are coated in a light batter,
then quickly deep-fried for delicate results.**

THE BATTER

½ cup unsifted all-purpose flour
½ cup cornstarch
1 teaspoon salt
1 egg, beaten
⅔ cup water
4 ice cubes
vegetable oil for frying

1. Clean and slice or cut all the ingredients to be cooked and arrange on a platter.

2. Mix the dipping sauce ingredients and put a small bowl of the mixture by each place at the table.

3. Mix the batter by combining the dry ingredients, then add the beaten egg and water. Stir until the batter is blended but still lumpy. Add the ice cubes and stir until the batter is quite cold. Discard the unmelted ice cubes.

4. Heat vegetable oil to the depth of 3 inches in a deep-fryer. When the oil reaches 360°F, use tongs to dunk the food, piece by piece, first in the cold batter and then immediately into the hot oil. The change in temperature will make the coating explode. Deep-fat frying is very quick—nothing should have to cook more than 2 or 3 minutes or less for more delicate foods. Don't crowd the frying pan—it lowers the temperature of the oil and prevents the food from cooking properly.

5. Drain the cooked food briefly. Tempura cookers have a draining rim around the edge of the pan. You can improvise your own with a cake rack over a plate. Serve the tempura on a large platter with sauce nearby for dipping.

6. Between batches of tempura cooking, skim the loose batter particles from the oil to keep them from burning and flavoring the oil.

CAVIAR

Back in the late 1800s, sturgeon were so abundant in U.S. waterways that caviar was given away in saloons, like pretzels. Today these fish (from which most of the elegant little eggs are taken) are mostly found in Russian and Iranian waters. The scarcity has raised our estimations of caviar—and upped the price.

Mistakenly, we usually reserve caviar for champagne-only occasions. But it does make the ordinary special. The process that turns plain fish eggs into caviar is rather simple. The roe is first sieved to remove membranes—the most expensive is sieved by hand. The biggest difference in caviar price is between fresh and vacuum-packed. If the caviar is fresh, a little salt is added. (The word *malassol* on a label means it's been only lightly salted.) If the caviar will be vacuum-packed, more salt is added, and then it's pasteurized.

Caviar is judged and ranked according to the size and condition of the eggs, which fish it comes from and whether it's fresh. The country of origin doesn't matter so much anymore. Iran, now the major world supplier, offers caviars as good as those from the Soviet Union. And fresh Oregon and Washington roe is making America proud.

At the top of the line (and pricing) you'll find fresh, smooth, shiny eggs from beluga sturgeon. Smaller, vacuum-packed, broken or pressed eggs from sturgeon or salmon are at the bottom of the scale, but still quite good. Here are the specifics.

Beluga. A large type of sturgeon that can weigh up to a ton. The eggs, like the fish, are the largest of all caviars and range in color from black to slate gray. The lightest gray eggs are touted as the best, but there's no reason to pay extra for them. In a blind tasting, you probably couldn't tell the difference. The size of the egg, however, does count: large eggs have more fat, which adds to the taste.

Sevruga. From—you guessed it—the sevruga sturgeon, a much smaller fish, weighing only about 50 pounds. The eggs are a little sweeter, milder, smaller and darker than the beluga.

Osetra. A medium-size sturgeon, hard to find but becoming more popular. This type of caviar usually sells for half the price of beluga.

Pressed or broken caviar. The two best buys in caviar. Eggs that are too soft to survive traveling and packaging are deliberately crushed into a thick paste. Many people prefer this pressed caviar because it's usually a little sweeter than unpressed caviar of the same name. Broken caviar is made from sturgeon or salmon eggs that were buried at the bottom of the barrel or crushed during transport. The taste is still good, and the cost is less than that of beluga or sevruga.

Red caviar. The roe from salmon. Its relatively low

Caviar is traditionally served with chopped egg, onion, toast and lemon wedges.

price reflects fashion, not taste. Years ago, roe from many kinds of fish was popular. But as black sturgeon caviar became rare and more costly, it gained status. The availability of red salmon caviar caused its price to go down.

Lumpfish and whitefish caviar. The roe of these two fish is the most plentiful and the least expensive. Although they're naturally closer in color to the salmon caviar, they're dyed black for cachet. Again, prevailing fashion knocked down the price.

You can tell a lot about caviar by just looking at it. The eggs should be firm and smooth and glossy. Stay away from milky-looking eggs.

It's best to buy caviar close to the time you want to eat it. The younger the caviar (whether fresh or vacuum-packed) the better. May, June, October and November are the best months for buying fresh caviar, since that's when the major catches are made. Fresh caviar should be eaten within a month—sooner is even better. Although it won't necessarily spoil after that time, the flavor becomes stronger every day.

Vacuum-packed caviar can be kept up to a year and still be okay, even though it's best eaten within six months. Keep opened caviar refrigerated in the cold meat drawer (between 28°F and 36°F is ideal) and eat it within a month. For both fresh and vacuum-packed, ask your dealer how long the caviar's been sitting on the shelf. Vacuum-packed caviars are produced by Romanoff, Pure-pak, Iron Gate and M. Chernoff and found in many supermarkets.

Stocks and Soups

The making of stocks and the place they occupy as a cornerstone of good cooking is, like the sauces they influence, surrounded by far too much mystique. The frustration with stocks comes only when you don't have any on hand for a recipe that you want to make *right now.* The only thing that stands between you and a munificent stock of stocks is time, not skill.

The French call stocks *fonds de cuisine,* the foundations of cooking. Stock adds flavor to soups, sauces, stews and braised foods and fills your kitchen with comforting aromas, long-simmering promises of warmth to come.

From two stocks, white and brown, come the backbone of most homemade soups. Add a quick fish stock and you've covered all the bases. By starting with a full, fresh-flavored stock, you'll be one step ahead of the game, and soup making should be less than a half hour's pleasure. And just like the stock they came from, these soups freeze well.

Once you start making your own stocks and soups, chances are some of your kitchen habits will change. You'll begin hoarding carcasses and bones, mushroom stems and stray scraps of meat and fish you once threw away. Just wrap any likely candidate well and freeze until you've accumulated enough for the stockpot. Some say frugality is a bonus in itself, but the real reward will be on the table.

Stocks

THE ESSENTIALS

Since stockmaking is a time-consuming procedure, it makes sense to freeze it in recipe-sized portions, either as is or reduced as a demi-glace (see page 58). Begin with a big stockpot, preferably 12-quart or more, made from a heavy material that spreads heat evenly. You'll need a skimmer for lifting off scum and fat and a chinois-type strainer that sits sturdily over another pot or bowl. You'll be pouring from a heavy stockpot, and the last thing you need is a strainer that tips.

There are three basic stocks. Brown stock is made from beef and veal; white stock is made from veal and chicken; fish stock is made from lean whitefish and shellfish. Pork scraps and bones tend to be too sweet for good stock; ham and lamb are too strong. Not that you should discard other bones—ham bones are ideal for cooking greens or split peas, and lamb scraps are *de rigueur* in Scotch broth.

Bones for brown stock are roasted in the oven for both color and flavor. Bones for white stock—chicken, veal and fish—are not. Veal bones (especially calves' feet) are rich in natural gelatin, which is essential in stocks that will be used for jellied soups such as consommé and in aspic. However, commercial gelatin can be added to clear stocks for aspic.

The vegetables used in stock—carrots, onions, celery and leeks—go under the name of "aromatic vegetables." Not only do they give good flavor, they don't overwhelm the meat or fish essence. Aromatics enhance the meat—and the aroma. Starchy vegetables, like potatoes, cloud stocks, and members of the cabbage family tend to assert themselves too strongly.

Stocks are simmered over very low heat, never boiled. And for good reason: boiling incorporates the fat and scum that should be skimmed off the top during cooking to keep the stock clear. Skimming, in fact, is done throughout the cooking with a skimmer (a truly handy tool) or a slotted spoon. Simmering stock should be only partially covered, to allow the steam to escape.

When it's time to cool the stock, it should be done as quickly as possible and *never* covered: it could sour. The final degreasing is done when the stock has finished cooking and is removed from the heat. The fat then rises to the top and can be spooned off easily. Final hard-to-trap bits of fat can be soaked up with paper towels. Chilling the stock causes the fat to form a hard layer on the top, which is easier to remove and which also ensures a totally fat-free stock, a necessity when making consommé. When the stock is completely cool, degreased and ready for storage, airtight containers keep it fresh. Stock can be kept in the refrigerator for up to a week. It will last even longer (up to 3 weeks) if it is brought to a boil every 3 or 4 days. Frozen stock will keep for up to 3 months.

Clarifying stock isn't difficult. Start with fat-free stock (and utensils). For 8 cups of stock, use 3 egg whites. In a large bowl, using a wire whisk, beat 2 cups of cold, strained stock with the egg whites until all is well blended. In a large saucepan, bring the remaining 6 cups of stock to a simmer over medium heat, then slowly pour the hot stock over the stock–egg white mixture in the bowl, beating constantly. Return this mixture to the saucepan and bring it to a simmer, stirring steadily with the whisk to distribute the egg whites evenly throughout. As soon as the stock reaches a simmer, lower the heat as much as possible and stop stirring. Let the mixture barely simmer for 15 minutes, then turn off the heat and let it settle for 10 more minutes. Skim off as much scum from the top as possible. Line a strainer or colander with a clean dish towel or several thicknesses of cheesecloth. Fit it over a deep bowl and pour the stock through the strainer into the bowl. It should be sparkling and clear, ready to be seasoned and served as consommé or chilled for aspic.

WHITE STOCK

Makes about 3 quarts

White stock is used for cream soups and velouté-type sauces. A veal and chicken bone base is most traditional and versatile. Use 2 pounds of bones per quart of stock and a 2 to 1 ratio of bones to meat. Use veal shanks or knuckle bones and have your butcher cut them into 1½- to 2-inch pieces, or slice them yourself with a meat saw. There should be some meat on the bones for flavor; if not, just buy a little extra shank meat. If you don't have a chicken carcass, necks and wings will work fine.

4 pounds veal and chicken bones
2 pounds veal and chicken meat
5 quarts water
2 onions, quartered
2 leeks, trimmed
2 carrots, cut into large chunks
2 stalks celery, trimmed and cut into large chunks
bouquet garni of 6 sprigs parsley, 4 sprigs fresh or 1
    teaspoon crushed dried thyme, 1 bay leaf, 2 whole
    cloves

1. Put all ingredients in a 12-quart stockpot. Cover with the water and add the vegetables and bouquet garni.

2. Bring the mixture just to a boil over high heat. Lower the heat and skim off the accumulated foamy scum. Keep skimming until no scum forms. (It may take a bit of doing

STOCK MAKING. Use a large stockpot since stock can be frozen.

A long simmer is the key to good stock. Skim off foam for clear stock.

Strain the stock using a chinois or colander lined with cheesecloth,

this first round, so don't be discouraged; veal creates more scum than most meats.)

3. Cover the pot and let it simmer very gently for 3 hours. Skim the top from time to time.

4. Strain the stock into a bowl through a cheesecloth-lined colander and let it cool uncovered. If you want to use it the same day, wait 10 minutes, then skim off the visible fat with a spoon and degrease the top of the broth with paper towel. Otherwise, let it cool, then refrigerate the stock and lift off the congealed fat, a much easier method of defatting.

5. Good stock will be full-bodied and rich; taste to be sure. If you want a more concentrated flavor, return it to a clean pot and bring it to a boil over high heat. Lower the heat to medium and let the stock boil uncovered to evaporate some of its water and concentrate the flavor. Taste every 15 minutes until it's perfect.

BEEF OR BROWN STOCK

Makes 4 quarts

Brown stock takes a little more preparation than other stocks, but it also is the most versatile. It's the magic ingredient of so many soups and a battery of sauces. While canned chicken broth and clam juice can be made into passable substitutes for white stock (see page 56), there is nothing packaged that comes anywhere near a carefully produced brown stock. The photographs will demystify the steps in making a fine brown stock.

5 pounds veal shanks with meat
3 pounds beef bones with meat
¼ cup butter
1 pound carrots, chopped
4 onions, coarsely chopped
2 leeks, sliced in half lengthwise
2 cups dry white wine
5 quarts water

bouquet garni of 1 bay leaf, 8 sprigs parsley, 3 sprigs fresh or ½ teaspoon crushed dried thyme, 3 sprigs fresh or ½ teaspoon crushed dried tarragon, 3 sprigs celery leaves

1. The bones should all be cracked or cut into 2-inch pieces. The more bone area exposed, the more flavor and gelatin released during the browning and the cooking. Your butcher can do this for you or you can saw the bones yourself with a special fine-toothed meat saw.

2. Preheat the oven to 400°F. Put the bones in a shallow roasting pan in a single layer and roast them for 1 hour, until very brown. Turn the bones midway through the roasting so they will brown evenly.

3. While the bones are roasting, heat the butter over medium heat in a heavy 12-quart stockpot or kettle. Add the carrots, onions and leeks and sauté until they are golden brown—10 to 15 minutes.

4. Add the browned bones to the vegetables in the stockpot. Pour a cup of boiling water into the roasting pan and scrape up all the browned particles on the bottom. Add this liquid to the stockpot along with the wine, the rest of the water and the bouquet garni.

5. Bring the stock just to a boil over high heat, then lower the heat and start skimming the foamy scum that rises to the top. Remove and discard all the scum that appears; it will be considerable this first round, because of the veal.

6. Cover the stockpot and let it simmer very gently for 10 hours, skimming the top from time to time. If simmering is done overnight, the stock can be cooled uncovered (so it doesn't sour) and untended during the day in a cool place. Strain the stock through a chinois or a colander lined with several thicknesses of cheesecloth.

7. Cool the stock uncovered, skimming off as much fat as possible. If you have time, refrigerate it until the fat congeals and remove hardened layer of fat.

(continued)

8. If you want a concentrated stock, return the stock to a clean pot, then bring it to a boil. Taste every 15 minutes until the flavor is rich and strong.

9. To make a real demi-glace—the classic concentrated meat base for Espagnole Sauce (see page 75) and the more recently used concentrate of the Nouvelle Cuisine—just boil the stock gently for 2 to 3 hours, or until it is reduced to about 3 cups. It will be syrupy in consistency when hot, jellied when chilled. This worth-its-weight-in-gold concentrate can be used in small quantities—a half teaspoon in a recipe for 4—for additional soup and sauce flavor. Dissolved in hot water (use ¾ cup with 1 quart water), this concentrate makes brown stock once again, in the mode (but light-years ahead in flavor) of commercial meat extracts or bouillon cubes. Demi-glace keeps much longer under refrigeration than plain stock, and can also be frozen in ice cube trays for easy access.

CHICKEN STOCK OR SOUP

Makes 6 servings soup, 2 quarts stock

1 stewing chicken, cut up
4 carrots, cut into 1-inch pieces
4 celery stalks with leaves, cut into 1-inch pieces
1 onion, chopped
3 quarts water
bouquet garni of 4 sprigs parsley, 4 sprigs thyme, 2 sprigs sage

1. In a large stockpot, combine all the ingredients. Bring to a boil and skim the foam. Keep skimming as the foam rises.

2. Cover the pot and simmer for 1½ to 2 hours, or until the chicken is tender.

3. If using as a soup, remove the chicken pieces and skin and bone them. Cut the chicken into 1-inch chunks and return it to the soup. Skim the excess fat, remove the bouquet garni and season with salt and pepper.

4. If using as a stock, strain the stock into a bowl through a colander lined with several layers of cheesecloth. Let the stock stand, and as fat collects on the top, skim it off. If you have time, chill the stock and spoon off the hardened fat.

5. If you would like a more concentrated stock, put the stock in a clean pot and boil until the rich taste you want is achieved.

FISH STOCK

Makes 1 quart

Fish stock is used in fish soups, in sauces for fish and for poaching fish. Leaner white-meat fish are recommended because they are not overwhelmingly oily and make a mild, well-balanced stock. And uncooked leftover shellfish scraps such as lobster and crayfish shells add a delicate flavor, as does dry white wine. Fish stock does not require long cooking like meat stocks.

2 pounds lean fish, heads, bones and trimmings, fresh and/or frozen (halibut, whiting and flounder are good choices)
1 small onion, sliced
1 stalk celery, chopped
½ bay leaf
1 teaspoon lemon juice
1 cup dry white wine (optional)
1 quart water

1. Combine the ingredients in a 4-quart saucepan and bring to a simmer over medium heat. Skim off the foam that rises to the top, lower the heat and let simmer uncovered for 30 minutes.

2. Strain through a chinois, a fine sieve, a cheesecloth-lined colander or a dish towel.

EMERGENCY STOCKS

Canned beef and chicken broths and bottled clam juice are good emergency staples for making quick soups or stews. They're not nearly as flavorful as homemade stocks, but they can be helped with a little doctoring. For fast first-aid, use this technique for each stock: simmer it uncovered for 30 minutes with the added seasonings, then strain and use as you would any other stock.

Beef stock. To 2 cups canned beef broth add 2 tablespoons each chopped onion and carrot, 1 tablespoon minced celery, ½ cup dry wine (red or white) and a bouquet garni of 2 parsley sprigs, 1 sprig fresh or ⅛ teaspoon dried thyme and ⅓ bay leaf. A teaspoon of tomato paste is optional.

Chicken stock. To 2 cups of canned chicken broth, add 2 tablespoons each chopped onions and carrot, ⅓ cup dry white wine and a bouquet garni of 2 parsley sprigs, 1 sprig fresh or ⅛ teaspoon dried thyme, 1 sprig celery leaves and ⅓ bay leaf.

Fish stock. To each cup bottled clam juice add ½ cup water and ¼ cup dry white wine, 1 small sliced onion and 2 peppercorns. Simmer for 10 minutes.

ASPIC

Aspic makes the most simple food special. Here are some general types.

Beef. To the basic Brown Stock (see page 57) add 1 large veal knuckle, cracked into pieces, and cook as usual. Strain, chill and remove the fat after chilling. Clarify the stock, cool and then chill until syrupy. Cover and chill until needed, then melt over low heat to use.

Chicken. To the basic Chicken Stock (see page 58) add 1 pound cracked chicken wings and cook as usual. Remove the fat and clarify.

Fish. To the basic Fish Stock (see page 58) add 2 to 3 fish heads or tails and cook as usual. Strain. To clarify stock for aspic, see page 56.

Coating with aspic. Chill the aspic until syrupy. The food that is to be coated with the aspic should be well chilled also. Wipe the food to remove any surface fat that would keep the aspic from clinging. Put the food on a rack set over a shallow pan and spoon some of the syrupy aspic over the food, then chill. Repeat this step until a layer is formed that glazes the food. The drippings in the pan can be remelted over low heat and used again. Chill. If decorations are to be placed on the food, they should be arranged after the first spooning of the aspic.

Molding aspic. Pour the syrupy aspic into the mold. Set the mold on a bed of ice and rotate until the aspic evenly coats the interior of the pan. Add another layer until it is about ¼-inch deep. Fill the mold with the desired mixture (equal parts aspic mixed with finely chopped solids such as meat, fish or vegetables). Top with more clear aspic, then chill until the mold is firm. To unmold, dip the mold into lukewarm water for a few seconds, tap to loosen and invert onto a platter. Additional aspic can be poured into a small pan to a depth of 1 inch. Chill until firm and then cut into cubes or triangles or chop and spoon around foods for sparkling color.

Emergency aspic. Add 1 envelope unflavored gelatin to 1½ cups clarified stock. Stir over low heat until the gelatin is dissolved. Chill until syrupy and use as directed.

Soups

CREAM OF ANY VEGETABLE SOUP

Serves 4

All it takes is good chicken stock base, cream, herbs and almost any fresh seasonal vegetable to make a subtle cream soup. A blender or food processor makes it especially easy, but a food mill does a fine job, too.

2 cups chopped broccoli (or other vegetable)
1 cup chopped onion or leeks (optional)
1 tablespoon chopped parsley and/or other herbs
4 cups Chicken Stock (see page 58)
1 cup heavy cream or Béchamel Sauce (see page 70)
salt
freshly ground black pepper

1. Put the vegetables, parsley and stock in a saucepan and bring to a boil over high heat. Lower the heat and simmer, partially covered, for 10 to 15 minutes, or until the vegetables are tender.

2. In a blender, food mill or food processor purée the soup until it is as fine as you like.

3. Return the purée to the saucepan and stir in the cream or béchamel sauce. (To serve cold, chill for at least 2 hours, then add the cream.) Keep stirring over medium heat until the soup is heated through. Taste for seasoning and add salt and pepper as needed.

4. Serve hot in warm bowls with grated Parmesan, chopped fresh parsley or chives sprinkled on top. For cold soup, check the seasoning—cooling dulls flavors somewhat and you will need more salt, pepper and herbs. Serve in chilled bowls with chopped fresh parsley or chives.

Note. Substitute any of the following vegetables for a different flavor. Use 2 cups chopped raw vegetables, choosing from the following: peeled, seeded tomatoes; watercress, stems and leaves; trimmed mushrooms; zucchini; celery; cauliflower; sorrel leaves.

Leeks. Omit the onion, use 3 cups leeks and 1 teaspoon chopped fresh tarragon.

Onions. Use 3 cups.

Potatoes. Use 2 cups diced onion, 5 cups chicken stock, 2 teaspoons fresh dill and sour cream instead of heavy cream.

Other herbs can be used instead of parsley.

Tomatoes. Use 1 tablespoon chopped fresh basil.

Watercress. Use 2 teaspoons chopped fresh dill.

Mushrooms. Use 2 teaspoons chopped fresh savory.

Zucchini. Use 2 teaspoons chopped fresh oregano.

Celery. Use 1 teaspoon chopped fresh sage.

Cauliflower. Use a dash of nutmeg instead of herbs.

Sorrel. Use 1 teaspoon chopped fresh marjoram.

ONION SOUP

Serves 6

This proud combination of humble ingredients remains a timeless classic.

¼ cup butter
4 large onions, thinly sliced
4 cups Brown Stock (see page 57)
½ cup dry wine (red or white)
salt
freshly ground black pepper
2 tablespoons butter
6 slices French or Italian bread cut to fit inside the soup
   bowls
¾ cup grated Gruyère

1. In a large heavy saucepan, melt the ¼ cup butter over medium heat. After it foams, sauté the onions until tender and richly golden, about 10 to 15 minutes.

2. Add the stock and wine, and bring to a boil. Lower the heat and simmer covered for 20 to 25 minutes. Season with salt and pepper.

3. In a heavy skillet, melt the 2 tablespoons butter over medium heat and brown the bread slices on both sides.

4. Fill 6 heat-proof soup bowls with soup. Add to each a slice of sautéed bread and sprinkle on the Gruyère. Put the bowls under the broiler and broil for a few minutes, until the cheese is melted. Serve immediately.

SOUPE SOUBISE

Serves 6

Soubise, an onion purée, can be used as a garnish, sauce or soup base.

⅓ cup butter
6 large red onions, thinly sliced
4 cups Chicken Stock (see page 58)
1 cup brandy
2 cups heavy cream
salt
freshly ground black pepper
chopped chives

1. In a large heavy saucepan, heat the butter over medium heat and sauté the onions until golden brown, 15 to 20 minutes.

2. Add the stock and brandy and bring to a boil. Lower the

heat, cover the pan and simmer for 20 to 25 minutes, or until the onions are tender.

3. Purée this mixture in a blender or food processor and return it to the saucepan. Stir in the cream and heat the soup until it just begins to bubble around the edges—boiling will curdle the cream. Season with salt and pepper to taste and serve with chopped chives sprinkled on top.

VEGETABLE SOUP

Serves 6 to 8

Vegetable soup is the all-American favorite winter supper for good reason: its mouthwatering array of vegetables and a solid beef base.

10 cups Brown Stock (see page 57)
2 onions or leeks, chopped
4 stalks celery, including leaves, chopped
½ cup chopped fresh parsley
2 parsnips, peeled and cut into ½-inch-thick pieces
6 carrots, cut into 1-inch slices
6 tomatoes, peeled, seeded and chopped
3 cups shredded green cabbage
1 cup 1-inch pieces green beans
1 cup whole-kernel corn
2 cups ½-inch pieces peeled potatoes
salt
freshly ground black pepper

1. In a large heavy stockpot (at least 6-quart capacity) combine all the ingredients except salt and pepper and simmer for 25 to 30 minutes, or until the vegetables are tender.

2. Season with salt and pepper. Serve in warmed soup bowls.

Minestrone. Omit the parsnips. Add 2 zucchini, cut into 1-inch-thick slices; 2 slices uncooked bacon, chopped; 1 clove garlic, chopped; 1 tablespoon chopped fresh basil. After the vegetables are cooked, add 1 cup each cooked cannellini beans and small tube or quill-shaped pasta. Stir in ½ cup grated Parmesan. Serve hot, sprinkled with additional Parmesan.

Vegetable Beef Soup. Add 1½ cups ½-inch chunks of cooked beef to the soup after the vegetables are cooked.

Vegetable Rice or Barley Soup. Omit the potatoes and add 1 cup cooked rice (see page 205) or fine barley to the soup after the vegetables are cooked.

Vegetable Soup has endless variations.

FRESH TOMATO SOUP

Serves 6

¼ cup butter
1 small onion, chopped
1 carrot, chopped
1 cup chopped celery, stalks and leaves
¼ cup flour
1 bay leaf
1 tablespoon chopped fresh or 1 teaspoon dried basil
2 sprigs fresh or ½ teaspoon dried oregano
3 cups peeled, seeded and chopped tomatoes
4 cups Chicken Stock (see page 58)
salt
freshly ground black pepper

1. In a 2-quart saucepan, heat the butter and sauté the onion, carrot and celery for 5 minutes. Stir in the flour, bay leaf, herbs, tomatoes and stock. Cover and simmer for 30 minutes, stirring occasionally.

2. Press the soup through a sieve or food mill. Season with salt and pepper.

SUMMER SQUASH SOUP

Serves 4

Take your choice: a creamy puréed soup without cream or a light vegetable soup with bright pieces of yellow squash, green pepper and red tomato.

1 small onion, chopped
1 clove garlic, minced
2 large yellow squash, sliced
2 tomatoes, peeled, seeded and chopped
½ cup chopped green pepper
2 cups Chicken Stock (see page 58)
1½ teaspoons chopped fresh or ½ teaspoon dried oregano
1½ teaspoons chopped fresh or ½ teaspoon dried basil
1½ teaspoons chopped fresh or ½ teaspoon dried thyme
salt
freshly ground black pepper

1. In a large heavy saucepan bring all the ingredients except salt and pepper to a boil over high heat, then lower the heat, cover and simmer for 15 to 20 minutes, or until the vegetables are tender.

2. Season with salt and pepper and serve hot as is or puréed in a blender or food processor. This soup is also excellent cold, especially as a purée. Serve with croutons.

WINTER SQUASH SOUP

Serves 6

This spicy, warming soup for cold weather can be made with pumpkin instead of squash.

4 cups peeled and cubed butternut squash
⅛ teaspoon ground allspice
⅛ teaspoon ground cinnamon
4 cups Chicken Stock (see page 58)
salt
2 tablespoons butter
2 leeks, sliced

1. In a large heavy saucepan, bring the squash, spices and stock to a boil over high heat. Lower the heat, cover and simmer for 30 minutes, or until the squash is tender. Purée in a processor or blender. Salt to taste.

2. In a clean saucepan, melt the butter over medium heat. When it is hot, sauté the leeks until they are golden, about 6 to 8 minutes. Stir in the squash purée and heat for several minutes. If the soup is too thick, thin it with additional stock. Serve hot with a spoonful of sour cream and chopped parsley.

BLACK BEAN SOUP

Serves 4

2 cups dried black beans, rinsed
½ cup chopped onion
1 cup chopped celery with leaves
½ cup chopped carrots
2 pounds tomatoes, seeded and chopped, or 2 16-ounce cans Italian plum tomatoes
4 cups (approximately) Chicken Stock (see page 58)
1 bay leaf
salt
freshly ground black pepper
⅓ cup dry sherry

1. In a large heavy saucepan, combine the beans, onion, celery, carrots and tomatoes. Add enough stock to cover the beans by 1 inch. Bring to a boil over high heat, lower the heat and simmer, covered or uncovered, for 1 hour. Keep an eye on the stock level and replace evaporated stock.

2. Add the bay leaf, season with salt and pepper to taste and simmer for another hour. Again, add stock as needed to keep the beans covered. Remove the bay leaf.

3. Press the bean mixture through a food mill into a bowl, or purée in a blender or food processor. Return the puréed soup to the saucepan, season again with salt and pepper and add sherry. Bring to a simmer.

4. If you want a thinner soup, add more stock. Garnish with slices of lemon. To serve the soup cold, let it cool to room temperature, then chill in the refrigerator.

HAM AND LENTIL SOUP

Serves 6

Even a bare ham bone will do for flavor, but a chunk of meat and bone gives this soup real soul.

10 cups Chicken Stock or Brown Stock (see page 58 or 57)
2 large onions, chopped
1 carrot, chopped
1½ cups minced celery
about 2 pounds shank end of smoked ham
1½ cups dried lentils
2 tablespoons tarragon vinegar
salt
freshly ground black pepper

1. In a large saucepan, combine the stock, onions, carrot, celery and ham. Cover and simmer for 1 hour. Remove the piece of ham.

2. Add the lentils, cover and simmer until tender, about 40 to 45 minutes. Skin and bone the ham, then cut the meat into chunks. Add the ham and the vinegar to the soup and heat. Season to taste with salt and pepper.

MISO
Soybean Soup

Serves 4

Soybean paste accounts for the flavor and substance of this basic Japanese soup.

4 cups dashi (see Step 1)
½ cup white soybean paste (shiro miso)
1 egg
1 tablespoon water
1 teaspoon oil
2 scallions

1. Measure the powdered dashi according to package directions to make 4 cups broth, add boiling water and stir until the powder is completely dissolved.

2. Stir in the soybean paste.

3. In a small bowl, beat the egg with 1 tablespoon water. In a small skillet, heat the oil over medium heat. Pour in the egg and let it cook until brown on the bottom and firm on top. Remove this omelet from the pan and let cool.

4. Slice the scallion diagonally to make oval slices. Roll up the omelet and cut crosswise into ¼-inch slices. Reheat the soup and divide it into four bowls. Garnish each bowl with scallion slices and egg strips.

Note. Substitute red soybean paste (aka miso) for white in the basic recipe and use steamed baby clams instead of the egg.

HOT AND SOUR PRAWN SOUP

Serves 4

4 dried Chinese black mushrooms
1 teaspoon Oriental sesame oil
4 ounces ground lean pork
1 scallion, chopped
4 cups Chicken Stock (see page 58)
8 large raw shrimp, shelled and deveined (see page 108)
1 tablespoon dry sherry
2 tablespoons white wine vinegar
1 teaspoon Japanese soy sauce
¼ teaspoon Tabasco sauce
2 bean curd cakes (tofu), cut into ½-inch cubes
2 tablespoons cornstarch
1 egg, well beaten
salt
freshly ground black pepper

1. Soak the mushrooms in 1½ cups cold water for 1 hour. Drain and reserve 1 cup of the liquid. Remove the stems and cut the caps into ¼-inch strips.

2. In a saucepan, heat the sesame oil and stir-fry the pork until brown and crumbly. Add the mushrooms and scallion and stir-fry another 2 minutes.

3. Add the stock and simmer, covered, 10 minutes. Stir in the shrimp, sherry, vinegar, soy sauce, Tabasco sauce and bean curd.

4. In a small bowl, mix the cornstarch and the reserved mushroom liquid. Stir this mixture into the soup and continue stirring until the soup is thickened.

5. Slowly pour in the egg in a thin stream, stirring gently. Season with salt and pepper. Add more vinegar and Tabasco sauce if you wish.

SHRIMP AND CRAB GUMBO

Serves 4 to 6

About the only thing sacred in this traditional Cajun soup is the way the roux is made: if it's not browned long enough, the gumbo lacks flavor and color; too high heat and not enough stirring and the roux may burn. Beyond that, there are no rules, just guidelines. Add the vegetables in any proportion you like. Almost any meat, poultry or seafood (or any combination) will do.

1 pound blue-shell crabs, cooked and shelled (see page 106)
¾ cup flour
¾ cup vegetable oil
2 cups chopped onion
¾ cup chopped green pepper
½ cup sliced scallion
½ cup finely chopped parsley
1 clove garlic, crushed
2 cups coarsely chopped tomato
2 pounds andouille or other smoked sausage, sliced ½-inch thick
2 pounds raw shrimp, shelled and deveined (see page 108)
2 pounds fresh okra, sliced ½-inch thick
2½ quarts water
2 bay leaves, crushed
1 tablespoon chopped fresh or 1½ teaspoons dried thyme
¼ teaspoon cayenne pepper
salt
freshly ground black pepper

1. Cook the crabs by dropping them into a large pot of boiling water and cooking until they turn red—about 8 to 10 minutes. Drain and rinse with cold water. Discard the legs and the outer shell. Break off the large claws and break the bodies in half.

2. Make a brown roux by combining the flour and oil in a heavy 7-quart casserole or kettle (don't use cast iron, which would discolor the okra) and mixing until well blended. Cook over medium heat, *stirring constantly,* for at least 30 minutes, until it turns a rich dark brown. During the first 10 minutes of cooking, the mixture will bubble and foam, but this will subside. Since the browning happens quickly during the last five minutes, you may have to lower the heat.

3. Add onion, green pepper, scallion, parsley and garlic to

Shrimp and Crab Gumbo uses varying amounts of vegetables and shellfish—the seasonings are flexible.

A rich dark brown roux starts the gumbo.

the roux and cook over medium heat, stirring constantly, for 10 minutes.

4. Stir in the tomato, sausage, 1 pound of the raw shrimp, crab pieces, okra, 2 quarts of water and the remaining seasonings, except the salt and pepper. Bring to a boil, lower the heat and simmer, covered, for 1 hour, stirring occasionally.

5. Stir in the remaining water and remove the pot from the heat. Let it stand at room temperature for at least 1 hour to blend the flavors. Salt and pepper to taste.

6. When ready to serve, bring the pot back to a boil and stir in the remaining shrimp. Reduce the heat and let simmer, covered, for 15 minutes. Serve over boiled long-grain white rice (see page 205) in deep soup bowls.

Note. Vegetables may be added in any amount. You can also use oysters, chicken, duck, ham, sausage, turkey, pork or game. Brown roux can be made ahead and kept covered in the refrigerator for as long as two weeks. Reheat slowly over medium heat before beginning the gumbo.

OYSTER STEW

Serves 6

4 cups half-and-half or 2 cups milk and 2 cups light cream
1 quart shucked oysters, fresh or canned, with their juice (see page 110)
¼ cup butter
½ teaspoon Worcestershire sauce
salt
freshly ground black pepper

1. In a large heavy saucepan heat the half-and-half over low heat just until it starts to bubble around the edges.

2. Add the oysters and let simmer over low heat until the mixture starts to boil. Don't let it boil, and stir in the remaining ingredients except salt and pepper. Stir until the butter melts. Season to taste with salt and pepper.

SAN FRANCISCO CIOPPINO

Serves 4 to 6

Pronounced cho-pee-no, *and made famous at Fisherman's Wharf.*

¼ cup olive oil
1 large onion, chopped
1 green pepper, seeded and chopped
2 cloves garlic, chopped
¼ pound mushrooms, sliced
1 bay leaf
4 cups Fish Stock (see page 58)
1 cup dry red wine
1 pound raw shrimp, shelled and deveined (see page 108)
2 frozen rock lobster tails, cut into 1-inch slices
16 mussels, scrubbed and debearded (see page 110)
16 littleneck clams, scrubbed
1 2-pound sea bass, cleaned, scaled and cut into 1-inch slices
salt
freshly ground black pepper

1. In a large, heavy, nonaluminum kettle or Dutch oven, heat the oil over medium heat. When it is hot, sauté the onion, green pepper and garlic until golden—about 5 minutes. Add the mushrooms and sauté for 1 minute. Add the bay leaf, stock and wine and bring to a boil over high heat.

2. Lower the heat and add the shellfish and fish. Cover and simmer for 5 to 10 minutes, or until the seafood is cooked. Season to taste with salt and pepper. Remove the bay leaf before serving.

SEAFOOD CHOWDER

Serves 6

6 large white boiling potatoes (baking potatoes break up), peeled and cut into ¾-inch cubes
3 large onions, chopped
6 cups milk
1½ teaspoons chopped fresh or ½ teaspoon dried thyme
1 bay leaf
2 pounds fish filets, fresh or frozen, cut into 1½-inch cubes
1 pound raw shrimp, shelled and deveined (see page 108)
salt
freshly ground black pepper

1. In a large saucepan bring the potatoes, onions, milk and herbs to a simmer over medium heat. Lower the heat and simmer gently for 15 to 20 minutes, or until the potatoes are tender.

2. Add the fish and shrimp and simmer another 5 minutes, or until the shrimp are pink and the fish is tender but not overcooked. Season with salt and pepper. Remove the bay leaf before serving with large chowder crackers.

COLD CUCUMBER SOUP

Serves 4

2 cucumbers, peeled and cut into chunks
1 tablespoon fresh lemon juice
1 cup White Stock (see page 56)
1 cup heavy cream
2 tablespoons sliced scallions
1 tablespoon chopped fresh chives
salt
freshly ground black pepper

1. Put all the ingredients except the pepper and 1 teaspoon of the chives in a blender or food processor and process until they are well blended. A little texture is desirable, so don't overdo the blending.

2. Chill the soup until ready to serve. Sprinkle the remaining chives on top and let everyone add their own freshly ground pepper.

Avocado Bisque. Omit the cucumber and substitute 1 large ripe avocado, peeled and seeded. Add the juice of 1 lime.

Avocado and Cucumber Soup. Use only 1 cucumber and add 1 small ripe avocado, peeled and seeded. Add ¼ cup diced sweet green chilies.

BORSCHT
Beet Soup

Serves 2

Our Russian grandfathers ate it hot with a boiled potato or with mounds of sour cream to balance the sweet-sour taste. We love it just the same way. Double or triple the ingredients if you want more soup.

Cold Cucumber Soup with fresh chopped chives

½ pound fresh beef brisket
1 beef marrowbone, 2-inch piece
2½ cups water
3 beets, peeled and shredded
1 small onion, chopped
¼ teaspoon minced garlic
1 tablespoon firmly packed brown sugar
1 tablespoon fresh lemon juice
salt
freshly ground black pepper

1. Put the beef, marrowbone and water in a pot and bring to a boil. Skim the foam and continue skimming for the first 5 minutes.

2. Add the beets, onion and garlic. Cover and simmer gently for 1 hour, or until the beef is tender. Skim the excess fat, then remove the bone and beef.

3. Stir in the brown sugar and lemon juice. Taste and add more of either, depending upon your taste. Season with salt and pepper.

4. Serve the soup hot with a boiled potato or with sour cream or serve chilled with sour cream or plain yogurt. Serve the beef separately with horseradish.

GAZPACHO

Serves 6

This cold, summery Spanish soup can be a meal in itself.

2 tablespoons olive oil
1 clove garlic, minced
4 slices French or Italian bread, cut into ½-inch cubes
1 cup tomato juice
1 tablespoon red wine vinegar
3 tablespoons olive oil
1 clove garlic
1 onion, quartered
4 tomatoes, peeled, seeded and quartered
1 cucumber, peeled and cut into chunks
1 green pepper, seeded and quartered
1 teaspoon chopped parsley
salt
freshly ground black pepper

1. To make croutons, heat the oil in a heavy skillet over medium heat and sauté the minced garlic for 1 or 2 minutes, then sauté the bread cubes until brown on all sides. Drain on paper towel.

2. Combine the remaining ingredients except salt and pepper in a blender or food processor, in batches if necessary, and process until they are well blended and evenly chopped. The finished soup should be thick with tiny pieces of vegetable. Carefully mix the batches in a bowl. Chill the soup for at least 1 hour.

3. Season with salt and pepper. Serve very cold, garnished with croutons and, if you wish, additional raw vegetables —use ½ cup each of the following chopped vegetables: peeled cucumbers, green pepper, scallions or onions.

COLD LENTIL SOUP

Serves 4

1 cup cooked lentils
1 clove garlic
¼ cup olive oil
2 tablespoons cider vinegar
2 tablespoons water
4 cups plain yogurt
1 cucumber, peeled, seeded and chopped
2 tablespoons chopped fresh or 2 teaspoons dried dill
salt
freshly ground black pepper

1. In salted boiling water, cook the beans, uncovered, in water that rises 1 inch above the level of the beans. Boil the beans for 25 to 30 minutes, depending upon the size of the bean, until the liquid is almost absorbed. Check the water level from time to time, adding water to maintain the level.

2. In a blender or food processor, purée the lentils and their cooking liquid, garlic, oil, vinegar and water. Pour into a bowl and stir in the yogurt, cucumber and dill.

3. Chill until ready to serve. Season to taste with salt and pepper. If the soup is too thick, thin it with Chicken Stock (see page 58).

Sauces

French sauces date back to Roman times, although those that we can relate to today (the Romans and their offspring created some fairly esoteric concoctions) come from the saucepans and cookbook of La Varenne, chef to Henri IV of France in the 1600s. The great pastry chef Carême confirmed this list in *Le Cuisinier Parisien* in 1825. But perhaps the greatest—and most recent—authority on the classic sauces was Auguste Escoffier, who ruled the world of food from the kitchens of London's Carlton Hotel from 1889 to 1921. And so, incredibly, the venerable French *grande cuisine* sauces were not graven in stone (in their current proportions) until the twentieth century. Recently, innovative Nouvelle Cuisine chefs have created starchless, enriched sauces. But to shake any foundation (even stone), it's a good idea to know what you're shaking—especially since classic sauces are still basic to much of the New American Cuisine.

THE ESSENTIALS

There are basically five *sauces mères* (mother sauces) to be mastered: white, brown, and those based on egg, butter or oil. Most sauces in American and European cooking are variations of these. There are exceptions like tomato, which is all vegetable, and *bolognese,* which includes meat. They are included in the pasta sauces (see page 185).

No sauce is impossible, and many are simple, but white and brown sauces take cooking time, and egg sauces require a quick study of egg chemistry. Butter and vinaigrette dressings are very easy to make.

WHITE SAUCES

White sauces, those pale, creamy cloaks most often seen gracing fish, poultry, pasta and eggs, are of two types: béchamels and veloutés. Béchamels are based on milk or cream; veloutés are a bit more complex because of their white stock base.

Both sauces are bound and thickened with a roux, usually a mixture of equal amounts of flour and butter. The initial cooking of the roux is the most important step in making either white sauce. It must be cooked slowly and gently in a heavy saucepan for several minutes to eliminate the raw, pasty taste of uncooked flour and to prepare the flour for its thickening action. But since it's a white sauce, the roux shouldn't brown.

In early white sauce days, cooks thought it necessary to cook the sauce for hours over low heat to overcome this raw flour taste and to concentrate the flavor of the liquid. Now we know that careful cooking of the roux eliminates the flour problem, and the liquid and seasonings used can be flavorful enough so lengthy concentration isn't necessary. The amount of flour used determines the thickness of the sauce. For 1 cup of liquid, use 1 tablespoon each of butter and flour for a thin sauce for soups and light sauces, 2 tablespoons each for a medium sauce (the most common denominator), 3 to 4 tablespoons each for a thick sauce for a gratin or a soufflé base.

The addition of liquid to the roux is really the only tricky step in white sauce making. And wielding a quick whisk is the surest method for eliminating any potential lumps from the sauce. There are two approaches: you can heat the liquid separately and, with the roux off the heat, vigorously beat in all the liquid at once. Or you can gradually add the liquid in a steady stream to the roux over low heat, stirring with a whisk or wooden spoon.

Both béchamel and velouté are *sauces mères* and so provide the perfect medium for more complexly seasoned sauces. In fact, neither is often used by itself, since even a simple addition of cheese or wine changes the character of these delicate bases for the better.

BÉCHAMEL SAUCE

Makes about 2 cups

Named for Louis de Béchamel, steward at the court of Louis XIV, the creamy béchamel was originally a much more complicated sauce, rather like what we now call a velouté. The Italian version, Salsa Besciamella, appears on page 186.

¼ cup butter
¼ cup flour
3 cups milk or half-and-half, heated just to a boil
salt
freshly ground white pepper

1. In a heavy saucepan, melt the butter over medium heat. Stir in the flour with a wire whisk or wooden spoon and cook over very low heat until the flour is pale gold, not brown, about 2 or 3 minutes.

2. Remove the saucepan from the heat and add the hot milk all at once. Beat vigorously with a wire whisk until the roux and liquid are blended.

3. Bring the sauce to a simmer over medium heat, stirring constantly. Lower the heat and let the sauce cook uncovered for 30 to 40 minutes, or until it is reduced by ⅓. Stir occasionally. Season with salt and pepper to taste.

SAUCE CREME OR SAUCE SUPREME
Cream Sauce

Makes about 2½ cups

Classically, a cream sauce is a béchamel enriched with heavy cream and a bit of lemon juice for balance. Adding these two liquids makes the béchamel richer, smoother and more flavorful, more of a complex sauce. Cream sauces are bland, yet substantial enough to work well on pasta, vegetables, fish, eggs or chicken and in gratinéed dishes.

2 cups Béchamel Sauce
½ cup heavy cream
1 tablespoon lemon juice

1. Bring the béchamel to a simmer over medium heat. Beat in the cream with a wire whisk, little by little, keeping the sauce at a simmer.

2. Stir in the lemon juice and check the seasoning. You may need to add salt and pepper.

***From top to bottom:* Espagnole, Béchamel, Sauce aux Champignons and Béarnaise**

MORNAY SAUCE

Makes about 2½ cups

A step beyond the béchamel, mornay is perhaps an even more popular rendition (especially for foods destined to be glazed under the broiler). Serve on veal, chicken, fish, eggs and vegetables.

2 egg yolks
¼ cup heavy cream
2 cups hot Béchamel Sauce (see page 70)
⅓ cup grated Gruyère or Parmesan

1. In a large mixing bowl beat the egg yolks with the cream. Slowly beat in ½ cup of the hot béchamel, 1 tablespoon at a time. Slowly beat this mixture into the rest of the béchamel in a steady stream. Stir the sauce over low heat until hot; do not boil.

2. Remove the pan from the heat and beat in the cheese until it is melted and well blended.

Sautéed Veal with Mornay Sauce (see page 158)

NANTUA SAUCE

Makes about 2⅔ cups

The namesake city for this sauce is Nantes, known as the crayfish capital of France. Nantua's mild béchamel base is traditionally flavored and garnished with crayfish, a scrawny but delectable freshwater crustacean. Butter and heavy cream further enrich this already sinful sauce.

3 tablespoons butter
¼ cup water
shells from 1 1½-pound lobster or 1½-pound crayfish, finely crushed with a hammer
2 cups Béchamel Sauce (see page 70)
½ cup heavy cream

1. In a saucepan bring the butter, water and shells to a boil over high heat. Lower the heat and simmer, uncovered, for 15 minutes. Strain the broth into a bowl, pressing the shells to extract all their juices. Chill the broth until the butter congeals.

Nantua Sauce over eggs baked in tomatoes

2. Bring the béchamel to a simmer over low heat. Stir in the congealed butter from the fish broth (saving the broth for another use). Beat in the cream and bring the sauce back to a simmer before serving.

VELOUTE SAUCE

Makes about 2 cups

Velouter translates as "to make like velvet," and velvety it is. Originally called a sauce blanche *(white sauce) or a* béchamel grasse *(béchamel made with veal stock), the white-stock-based velouté is at the bottom of many cream soups.*

Rarely served as is, but with a bit of wine, pepper and mushrooms, velouté becomes a complementary sauce for fish filets stuffed with lobster. Adding herbs such as thyme, bay leaf, sage, oregano or basil leads to a vast repertoire of sauces for seafood and enhances the flavor possibilities of all velouté-based sauces.

¼ cup butter
¼ cup flour
3 cups White Stock (see page 56), heated
salt
freshly ground white pepper

1. In a heavy saucepan, melt the butter over medium heat. Stir in the flour with a wire whisk or wooden spoon and cook over very low heat until the flour is pale gold (not browned)—about 2 or 3 minutes.

2. Remove the saucepan from the heat and add the hot stock all at once. Beat with a wire whisk until the roux and liquid are blended.

3. Bring the sauce to a simmer over medium heat, stirring constantly. Lower the heat and let the sauce cook uncovered for 40 to 45 minutes, or until it is reduced by ⅓, to 2 cups. Stir occasionally. Season with salt and pepper.

SAUCE AUX CHAMPIGNONS
Mushroom Sauce

Makes about 2½ cups

A not-too-thick mushroom-flavored sauce that is lightened with dry white wine and extra black pepper, this velouté variation is delicious on fish, poultry or veal.

2 cups Velouté Sauce
⅓ cup dry white wine
2 black peppercorns, crushed with a rolling pin
6 mushrooms, chopped

1. In a heavy saucepan, bring the velouté to a simmer over medium heat. Stir in the wine, peppercorns and mushrooms and continue to simmer over medium heat for 2 minutes.

2. Lower the heat and cook until the sauce is thick, about 10 minutes. Strain out the peppercorns and mushrooms.

SAUCE AURORE

Makes about 2 cups

Usually, aurore is a velouté with tomato purée added—but only a sedate few tablespoons for flavor. But some cooks add tomato to a béchamel and call it a sauce aurore, while others add paprika to either white sauce.

2 cups Velouté Sauce
3 tablespoons tomato purée

1. Bring the velouté to a boil over medium heat, stir in the tomato purée, then lower the heat and simmer for 5 minutes.

Stuffed Fish Filets with Velouté Sauce (see page 99)

RAVIGOTE SAUCE

Makes about 2 cups

Ravigoter *means "revive or refresh," and this warm velouté with white wine, shallots, white wine vinegar and herbs is definitely an invigorating culinary experience. There is also vinaigrette-based ravigote, served cold or at room temperature on seafood salad or mussels. The hot sauce is traditionally found on sweetbreads and brains, and is an excellent accompaniment to poultry, such as game hens.*

⅓ cup dry white wine
2 shallots, minced
⅓ cup white wine vinegar
¾ teaspoon fresh or ¼ teaspoon dried tarragon, crushed
¾ teaspoon fresh or ¼ teaspoon dried chervil, crushed
1 teaspoon chopped fresh parsley
1 teaspoon chopped chives
2 cups Velouté Sauce (see page 73)

1. In a small nonaluminum saucepan, combine the wine, shallots, vinegar and herbs. Bring to a boil over high heat, lower the heat to medium and continue to boil until the mixture has been reduced to about 2 tablespoons. Watch carefully, as this happens amazingly fast.

2. Bring the velouté to a boil over medium heat. Stir in the wine-vinegar mixture and blend well.

SAUCE PARISIENNE

Makes about 2¼ cups

2 egg yolks
⅓ cup heavy cream
2 cups Velouté Sauce (see page 73)

1. In a large bowl, beat the egg yolks and cream together. Gradually beat in the hot velouté 1 tablespoon at a time.

2. Return the sauce to a heavy saucepan and simmer until thick. Do not boil.

Roasted Game Hens with Ravigote Sauce (see page 132)

Spinach Timbale (see page 230) with Sauce Parisienne

BROWN SAUCES

Since the heyday of haute cuisine, the making of excellent brown sauces has been simplified into two steps. First, a basic brown stock is made from veal and beef bones (see page 57). Using this stock as the liquid, an espagnole sauce is made with a carefully browned roux as a thickener and a few aromatic vegetables and herbs for additional flavor. The sauce is concentrated with an hour's cooking and then serves as the essential ingredient in a vast family of brown sauces.

A brown or espagnole sauce uses a brown roux instead of a light one. Aromatic vegetables are first sautéed in butter before the flour is added. This is then cooked over low heat until the flour is golden brown, not golden pale. Do watch the pan because if the flour is burned, both its exquisite flavor and its ability to thicken the sauce are lost.

ESPAGNOLE SAUCE
Basic Brown Sauce

Makes about 2 cups

¼ cup butter
1 clove garlic, minced
1 medium onion, chopped
1 carrot, chopped
¼ cup flour
3 cups Brown Stock (see page 57), brought to a boil
½ cup tomato purée
1½ teaspoons fresh or ½ teaspoon dried thyme
½ bay leaf
1 teaspoon chopped fresh parsley (3 sprigs)
salt
freshly ground black pepper

1. In a large heavy saucepan, melt the butter over medium heat and sauté the garlic, onion and carrot until golden—about 5 minutes.

2. Stir in the flour, lower the heat and cook until it is a golden brown, nutty color—about 8 to 10 minutes. Keep stirring with a wire whisk.

3. When the flour is browned, take the pan off the heat and add the boiling stock all at once (or beat it in gradually over low heat). Beat with a wire whisk until the roux and liquid are blended. Beat in the tomato purée and add the herbs.

4. Bring the sauce to a simmer over medium heat, lower the heat and simmer, partially covered, for 45 minutes to 1 hour, or until the sauce has reduced by ⅓, to 2 cups.

5. Strain the sauce and season with salt and pepper.

Tournedos with Bordelaise Sauce (see page 154)

BORDELAISE SAUCE

Makes about 2¼ cups

1 marrowbone, 6 inches long
1 tablespoon butter
2 shallots, minced
½ cup dry red wine
2 cups Espagnole Sauce

1. Put the marrowbone in a small saucepan with enough water to cover and bring to a boil over high heat. Lower the heat and simmer until the marrow is poached and can be pressed easily out of the bone—about 10 minutes. Remove the marrow and push it through a strainer.

2. In a heavy saucepan, melt the butter over medium heat and sauté the shallots and marrow until golden—about 5 minutes. Add wine and boil until reduced to ¼ cup.

3. Stir in the espagnole sauce and simmer before serving.

SAUCE MADERE

Makes about 2½ cups

This is one of the simplest (albeit most seductive) versions of a brown sauce; the only addition to the espagnole is Madeira wine. A classic with ham, it also goes well with veal, chicken, pork or beef.

½ cup Madeira wine
2 cups Espagnole Sauce (see page 75)

1. Simmer the ingredients together for 10 minutes.

SAUCE ROBERT

Makes about 2⅓ cups

Its name suggests a modern-day creation, but sauce Robert has its roots in the early seventeenth century and the appetites of one Robert Vinot. This most venerable brown sauce was even then often served with pork or game, such as venison and goose. There exists a bottled sauce Robert, but it is, not surprisingly, a far cry from the stockpot-to-saucepan variety.

1 tablespoon butter
1 small onion, minced
¼ cup dry white wine
¼ teaspoon sugar
1½ teaspoons Dijon mustard
2 cups Espagnole Sauce (see page 75)

1. In a heavy saucepan, melt the butter over medium heat and sauté the onion until golden. Add the wine and let simmer over medium heat until it is reduced to 2 tablespoons.

2. Stir in the sugar, mustard and espagnole sauce and bring to a simmer before serving.

SAUCE CHASSEUR
Hunter's Sauce

Makes about 3 cups

Brown sauces are certainly not limited to dark meats and game, though that may be the stereotype. Most likely, chasseur was first created for game on the hunter's table (the translation of chasseur is "hunter"), but the sauce is often paired with chicken. The white wine, butter, mushrooms, shallot and tarragon make it a fairly light but still hearty sauce that is equally good with chicken livers, omelets and veal.

½ cup dry white wine or dry vermouth
1 teaspoon chopped fresh or ¼ teaspoon dried tarragon, crushed
2 tablespoons butter
1 shallot, minced
½ pound mushrooms, sliced
2 ripe tomatoes, peeled, seeded and chopped (optional)
2 cups Espagnole Sauce (see page 75)

1. In a small nonaluminum saucepan, combine the wine and tarragon and bring to a boil over high heat. Lower the heat slightly and let boil until the mixture is reduced to 2 tablespoons.

2. In a large heavy saucepan, melt the butter over medium heat and sauté the shallot and mushrooms for 1 or 2 minutes, or until they are wilted. Add the tomatoes and sauté for 5 minutes.

3. Stir in the espagnole sauce and the tarragon-wine mixture and bring the sauce to a simmer over medium heat before serving.

Asparagus and Ham on Puff Pastry with Sauce Madère (see page 173)

EGG SAUCES

Egg sauces have one major advantage over brown and many white sauces: they are almost instant, and have no need of a slowly cooked stock base. To say they are rich is enormous understatement: "luscious," "enticingly thick" and "smooth as silk" are weak descriptions.

A paragraph's apprenticeship in egg chemistry will eliminate the chances of a curdled egg sauce career. First, egg yolks must be warm to absorb or emulsify fats or oils, which is what forms an egg-based sauce. But at too high a heat, the yolk will instantly curdle (or cook into tiny hard bits). Second, a single egg yolk can absorb about 3 ounces of fat; after that point is reached, it simply quits. Therefore, in the making of a warm egg sauce like hollandaise, the egg yolks will do their job as long as they are slowly warmed (but not overheated); this is accomplished by beating in only small amounts of warm butter at a time. In making mayonnaise, don't expect success with cold egg yolks or too much oil. It's that simple.

Both warm and cold egg sauces can be made in a blender or food processor, but if you're finely honing your culinary skills, it's good to learn the by-hand methods.

HOLLANDAISE SAUCE

Makes about 1¼ cups

Hollandaise is also known as Holland or Dutch sauce, which indicates its origins. This thick, rich egg yolk and butter sauce is exceptional by itself and a perfect vehicle for other flavorings, from whipped cream to capers.

3 egg yolks
1 tablespoon water
1 tablespoon lemon juice
½ pound softened butter
salt

1. In the top of a double boiler set over hot (not boiling) water, beat the egg yolks with a wire whisk until they begin to thicken—about 1 minute. Beat in the water and lemon juice.

2. Whisk in 1 tablespoon of butter and keep beating until it is incorporated and the sauce is thick. Continue beating in the butter, 1 tablespoon at a time until it is all incorporated. (If the butter melts too quickly or there is any suggestion of curdling, remove the pan from the heat and beat the mixture over cold water to cool it. Lower the range heat even further.) Season with salt. The finished sauce will not be hot, only warm.

3. If the sauce does curdle, remove it from the heat. Beat a teaspoon of lemon juice or a warm egg yolk with a tablespoon of the sauce in a separate warm bowl. Then beat in the rest of the sauce, ½ tablespoon at a time. If a finished hollandaise should start to separate, beat in a tablespoon of cold water.

4. A handmade hollandaise cannot be held much more than an hour, so plan to serve it soon. To hold it for an hour, place it in a bowl of barely warm, not hot, water

BEARNAISE SAUCE

Makes about 1⅓ cups

3 sprigs fresh or ¼ teaspoon dried tarragon
3 sprigs fresh or ¼ teaspoon dried chervil
1 shallot, minced
4 peppercorns
¼ cup dry white wine
¼ cup white wine vinegar
1¼ cups Hollandaise Sauce
salt
½ pound softened butter

(continued)

Hollandaise on steamed broccoli

Béarnaise on grilled sirloin steak

1. In a small nonaluminum saucepan, combine the herbs, shallot, peppercorns, wine and vinegar. Bring to a boil over high heat, reduce the heat slightly and let boil until reduced to about 1 tablespoon liquid. Remove the peppercorns.

2. Stir in hollandaise and reheat.

3. Serve at once or hold briefly over tepid water.

BLENDER OR FOOD PROCESSOR HOLLANDAISE OR BEARNAISE

Makes ¾ cup

The main difference between machine-made and hand-made hollandaise or béarnaise is that machine beating somehow emulsifies the sauce more efficiently and the egg yolks cannot hold as much butter without getting too thick.

3 egg yolks
2 tablespoons lemon juice (or reduced wine-vinegar mixture for béarnaise)

¼ teaspoon salt
¼ pound butter, melted

1. Put the egg yolks, lemon juice and salt in the container of the machine. Process for 2 or 3 seconds.

2. With the blades still going, slowly pour in the melted butter in a thin, steady stream.

3. To increase the amount, beat in additional melted butter—up to ½ cup—by hand, 1 teaspoon at a time.

MAYONNAISE

Makes 1½ cups

One of the greatest advantages of making your own mayonnaise—either by hand or machine—is that you can use whatever oil or seasoning suits you best. Some people prefer olive oil, others like a milder peanut oil; some prefer lemon juice, others like wine vinegar.

Homemade mayonnaise must be refrigerated and will keep, carefully covered, for about a week. Remember that all homemade mayonnaise starts with room-temperature eggs and oil.

2 egg yolks
½ teaspoon salt
1 teaspoon dry or Dijon mustard
1 tablespoon lemon juice or wine vinegar
1½ cups olive or peanut oil

1. Rinse a bowl with hot water to warm it and beat the egg yolks with a wire whisk until thick—about 1 minute. Beat in salt, mustard and lemon juice.

2. Begin adding the oil, literally drop by drop, making sure each is absorbed before you add the next. As the mayonnaise begins to thicken, it will become lighter in color—it has begun to emulsify. At this point, you can add the oil in slightly larger quantities, but you must still beat each addition thoroughly before adding the next. Keep beating until all the oil has been added. If the mayonnaise is too thick for your taste, thin it with a little lemon juice or vinegar. (This enhances the flavor, as well.)

3. If you add the oil too fast, the mayonnaise will separate. If it should, beat a fresh, warm egg yolk in another warmed bowl for 1 minute. Beat in a few drops of oil, then a teaspoon of the separated mayonnaise. As the new sauce emulsifies, add the separated sauce in larger and larger spoonfuls until it has all been incorporated. Another method is to beat 1 teaspoon prepared mustard in a warm bowl with a tablespoon of the separated sauce, then add the rest of the separated sauce bit by bit.

BLENDER OR FOOD PROCESSOR MAYONNAISE

Makes 1½ cups

Nothing is quicker or easier than making your own mayonnaise in a blender or food processor. Machine beating thickens mayonnaise more than hand beating, so the whole egg is used to compensate. Just be sure that the egg and oil are at room temperature.

1 whole egg
1 tablespoon lemon juice or wine vinegar
½ teaspoon salt
1 teaspoon dry or Dijon mustard
1½ cups oil

1. Put the egg, lemon juice, salt and mustard in the blender. Process for 4 to 5 seconds.

2. With the blade still going, slowly add the oil in a slow, steady stream.

Green Mayonnaise. Blanch 8 to 10 spinach leaves, ¼ cup watercress leaves, ¼ cup parsley leaves, 3 sprigs fresh tarragon, 3 sprigs fresh chervil and 2 scallions in boiling water for 2 minutes. (Blanching is necessary to keep the greens from turning sour in the sauce.) Drain and pat dry. Add the herbs to the blender or food processor with the egg and seasonings and proceed.

Sauce Rémoulade. Fold 1 tablespoon chopped dill pickle, 1 teaspoon anchovy paste, 2 tablespoons chopped capers and 1 tablespoon chopped fresh parsley into 1½ cups mayonnaise and blend well.

BUTTER SAUCES

Butter sauces are very simple, most involving nothing more than creaming butter with seasonings before adding to a hot dish where it melts and releases all the good flavor. *Beurre blanc,* Nouvelle Cuisine's hallmark sauce, was born in the kitchens of French housewives in Anjou, where it accompanied fresh river fish; it is seasoned with a hot reduction of vinegar and shallots. *Beurre noir,* a barely browned butter, uses only butter, parsley and lemon juice.

CLARIFIED BUTTER

½ cup butter

1. Melt the butter over low heat. Remove from heat and let the milk solids settle to the bottom. Skim the foam from the top and strain the clear yellow liquid through cheesecloth or a fine strainer into a container.

Fresh Shrimp with Chive Butter (see page 106)

CHIVE BUTTER

Makes ⅔ cup

Beurre composé (compound butter) is simply butter with seasonings like fresh herbs blended in. Either the butter is melted, then processed in a blender with the additions, or ingredients are mixed by hand. The butter can then be refrigerated or frozen and used a bit at a time to enrich a sauce or soup. Beurre composé also serves well as a simple sauce on any food from seafood to steak. Variations are garlic (ail), anchovy (anchois) and shallot (bercy).

½ cup softened butter
juice of ½ lemon
1 tablespoon chopped fresh chives
salt
freshly ground black pepper

1. In a small bowl, cream the butter, lemon juice and chives with a wooden spoon until soft and fluffy. Season with salt and pepper.

Salmon Steak with Beurre Blanc (see page 99)

BEURRE BLANC
White Butter

Makes about ¾ cup

¾ cup white wine vinegar
2 shallots, minced
½ cup softened butter
1 tablespoon chopped fresh parsley

1. In a small nonaluminum pan, bring the vinegar and shallots to a boil over high heat. Allow the mixture to boil until it has been reduced to 1½ tablespoons.

2. Remove the pan from the heat for a few minutes, then beat in 2 tablespoons butter. As soon as it is creamed, add the rest of the butter, 1 tablespoon at a time, until it is all blended. Mix in the parsley. If the mixture is too liquid, chill it a few minutes and mix again.

BEURRE NOIR OR BEURRE NOISETTE
Brown Butter

Makes about ½ cup

Brown butter has a wonderfully nutty taste that is a nice change on fish, chicken and eggs.

½ cup Clarified Butter (see page 79)
1 tablespoon chopped fresh parsley
1 teaspoon lemon juice

1. In a small heavy saucepan, heat the butter over medium heat until it turns a golden brown. Watch carefully that it doesn't burn.

2. Stir in the parsley and lemon juice and serve hot.

VINAIGRETTES

Vinaigrette dressings are based on oil and vinegar and are most often found on cold salads and as marinades for meat. They are very simple sauces and so depend heavily on fine-quality oil and vinegar for their success. Any number of seasonings can be added in a multiple of combinations, which accounts for their versatility.

VINAIGRETTE DRESSING

Makes ½ cup

This is the simplest salad dressing, but nothing compares to it when the vinegar and oil are first-rate. All other vinaigrettes are variations of this one.

2 tablespoons wine vinegar
6 tablespoons olive oil or vegetable oil
½ teaspoon salt
¼ teaspoon freshly ground black pepper

1. Beat the ingredients together in a small bowl until the salt is dissolved and the other ingredients are well blended, or shake vigorously in a jar with a tight lid.

Mustard Vinaigrette. Add ¼ teaspoon dry or 1 teaspoon Dijon mustard to the basic dressing.

Herbed Vinaigrette. Add 1 to 2 tablespoons chopped fresh herbs—chives, parsley, tarragon, basil, chervil, marjoram or dill—or 1 teaspoon dried herbs to the basic mixture.

Garlic Vinaigrette. Crush a clove of garlic and add it to the mixture. Remove the garlic before serving.

Eggs

If we had to choose one food that epitomizes the New American Cuisine, we'd be hard put—fish, poultry, pasta all come immediately to mind. But in fact, because of their extraordinary versatility, eggs are one of the strongest contenders. All by itself, one egg is a microcosm of the world's cuisine and of the way we eat today: fresh, light and fast. Poached in the morning, as a frittata at lunch, masked in a hollandaise at dinner, eggs can play a leading role at one meal and have an equally graceful part in the next. As an omelet or a meringue they become a class act. The repertoire is infinite, but all is based on variations on a theme (or technique). And that's why we love them.

An almost perfect food, eggs provide protein and most of the essential vitamins and minerals—excluding C, iron, phosphorus, zinc, copper and magnesium—all in a perfectly designed 80-calorie package. The only debatable drawback is the high cholesterol count of the egg yolk—about 260 milligrams each.

This chapter deals with baked, boiled, fried, whipped and poached eggs as they revel in sauces and seasonings. They're whipped into magical ingredients for omelets, soufflés, custards, frittatas and meringues. And, as if that weren't enough, eggs thicken sauces, tenderize batters and doughs, clarify stocks and glaze baked goods.

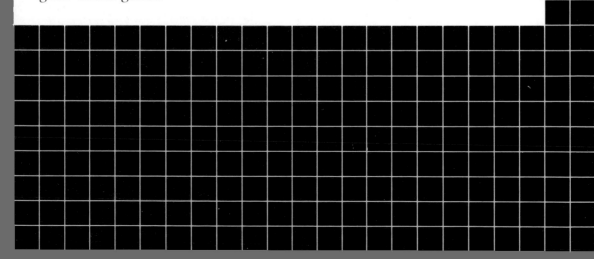

THE ESSENTIALS

The eggs we normally buy are, of course, hen's eggs, graded, sized and dated to U.S. Department of Agriculture standards, and labeled with an extravagance only bored poultry breeders could employ—the grades go from AA to C, but most supermarkets stock only AA and A grades, and for practical purposes, that's all anyone needs. Sizes are based on weight per dozen—30 ounces for jumbo, 27 for extra-large, 24 for large, 18 for medium. Most cookbooks, including this one, base their recipes on the standard large egg (in poultry parlance), which averages 2 ounces, or ¼ cup. (If you find yourself with a different size, beat another egg to make up the volume or remove some beaten egg to reduce the volume.) Somewhere on the box, an expiration date is stamped stating the date after which the eggs should not be sold. Eggs keep well under refrigeration, but their nutritional value declines after 5 weeks of storage. It is true that fresh eggs do taste better and should be used in recipes where eggs are the main ingredient. Your best bet for finding the freshest eggs is a busy store with a turnover heavy enough to ensure daily deliveries.

Venerable eggs do have their advantages. They are superior for hard-boiling because they peel more easily, and older egg whites whip into greater volume than fresher ones. Contrary to myth, there is almost no flavor or nutritional difference between white and brown eggs. Old eggs, incidentally, don't die, they just float away, which is a wonderful indication of freshness. Put dubious eggs in a bowl of water; those that rise to the top are not long for this world.

All these recipes are geared to produce the perfect egg, but not everyone loves a perfect egg. Adjust cooking times to suit your tastes—from soft and runny all the way to hard and crumbly.

Eggs keep best in the refrigerator, but they behave best in recipes at room temperature—65°F to 70°F. Recipes always assume room-temperature eggs. It's a good trick to get them out a half hour ahead; in a pinch, soak them in hot tap water for a few minutes before using.

SOFT-BOILED EGGS

The aristocrat of many a breakfast table is the perfect soft-boiled egg, the white softly set and the yolk runny. Its top is sheared off with a knife and the egg is spooned out of its shell, held steady by the oval egg cup.

1. Lower the large egg into enough boiling water to cover it completely. Immediately turn down the heat and let it simmer gently for 3 minutes. Cook a jumbo egg 4 minutes.

2. Put the cooked egg in cold water briefly to stop the cooking and cool it enough for handling.

Note. Not everybody has a room-temperature egg first thing in the morning. Prick the bottom of a cold egg with a needle to keep it from cracking and simmer 5 minutes.

EGGS MOLLET

Sometimes called coddled eggs, these eggs have a white firm enough to handle, but a still-soft yolk. They can be used interchangeably with poached eggs in recipes. Really fresh eggs should be poached—they don't peel well when boiled—and older eggs (4 or 5 days) should be coddled because their whites are no longer thick and don't adhere to the yolks in poaching.

1. Lower eggs into enough boiling water to cover, turn down the heat and simmer gently for 5 to 6 minutes. Plunge into cold water to stop the cooking. Crack the eggshells gently all around and peel carefully, leaving the eggs whole.

Hard-Boiled Eggs with (*clockwise*) Mayonnaise Vinaigrette, Guacamole (see page 42), Sour Cream and Caviar and à la Russe.

HARD-BOILED EGGS

Hard-boiled eggs should have a firm white and a firm yolk. Too often the yolks are rubbery—edged in green, no less—from cooking at too high a heat. Eggs to be hard boiled should be at least 4 or 5 days old or they will be impossible to peel neatly.

1. Gently lower eggs into enough boiling water to cover, turn down the heat and simmer very gently for 10 to 12 minutes. Cover with cold water immediately to help separate the skin from the egg and make peeling easier.

2. Crack the eggshell all over with the back of a spoon and start shelling at the wide end, where the air space is located.

3. Put shelled eggs in cold water and chill thoroughly before cutting or slicing.

EGGS A LA RUSSE

Serves 4

An elegant first course that is easy to put together, eggs à la russe owes it lineage more to the French than to the Russians. It is simply hard-boiled eggs in a vigorous "Russian" dressing.

4 hard-boiled eggs, peeled
4 crisp lettuce leaves
1 cup sour cream
½ cup Mayonnaise (see page 78)
2 tablespoons ketchup
2 teaspoons anchovy paste
2 tablespoons chopped fresh parsley
2 tablespoons chopped sweet pickle
2 teaspoons lemon juice

1. Cut the eggs in half lengthwise and put 2 halves on a lettuce leaf on each of 4 small serving plates.

2. In a bowl, combine the remaining ingredients and stir until well blended.

3. Spoon the sauce over the eggs and serve.

Eggs with Mayonnaise Vinaigrette. In a small bowl, mix ½ cup Mayonnaise (see page 78), ⅓ cup olive oil, ¼ cup red wine vinegar, 1 teaspoon salt, ¼ teaspoon freshly ground black pepper and 1 teaspoon sugar until well blended. Chill and stir again before serving.

Eggs with Sour Cream and Caviar. Mix ½ cup sour cream, ½ cup yogurt and 1 tablespoon chopped chives in a bowl. Add a spoonful of red caviar before serving.

Eggs in Burgundy (see page 84)

POACHED EGGS

The egg without its shell simmers gently in water for a tender egg white surrounding a still-soft yolk. It is a brunch standby served with slices of fried ham or Canadian bacon on toasted and buttered English muffins and covered with Hollandaise (see page 77) as eggs Benedict.

1. To poach a single egg, use a cold egg from the refrigerator and break it carefully into a cup. Bring a small saucepan of water and either ½ teaspoon salt or 1 teaspoon white vinegar to a simmer. (If you want the white to cover the yolk, make sure the water is at least 2 inches deep; use 1 inch of water if you want the yolk to show—it will sit above the cooking white.)

2. Stir the simmering water rapidly to make a whirlpool in the center of the pan. This will wrap the white around the yolk. Slip the egg into the whirlpool and simmer for 3 or 4 minutes, or until the white is firm and the yolk still soft. Remove the cooked egg with a slotted spoon and let it drain for a minute before serving.

Note. To make poached eggs in quantity, use a large skillet of simmering salted or vinegared water. Slip each egg carefully into the water, spacing them apart. Remove from heat and add just enough cold water to stop cooking. Remove eggs with a slotted spoon. If you're using the eggs in a recipe that calls for them chilled, cool in cold water. Old eggs do not poach well—their whites tend to float free of the yolks in thin, watery wisps—so use them for eggs mollet.

EGGS BENEDICT

Serves 4

1 tablespoon butter
4 slices cooked ham
2 English muffins, split
4 poached eggs
1½ cups Hollandaise Sauce (see page 77)

1. In a skillet, heat the butter and sauté the ham slices until lightly browned and hot, about 5 minutes.

2. Toast the English muffin halves and put them on serving plates. Top each with a slice of ham and a poached egg. Spoon the sauce over the egg. If you wish, sprinkle with chopped chives or paprika.

EGGS PORTUGAISE

Serves 4

Eggs and rice have met under many guises; a tomato-enriched brown sauce brings them together here.

2 tablespoons butter
1 shallot, minced
½ cup dry red wine
2 tomatoes, peeled, seeded and chopped
½ cup Espagnole Sauce (see page 75)
salt
2 cups cooked rice
2 tablespoons butter
4 poached eggs

1. In a saucepan, melt the butter and sauté the shallot for 5 minutes. Add the wine and boil until almost dry. Add the tomatoes and espagnole and simmer for 10 minutes. Season with salt.

2. Mix the hot rice with the butter. Make a bed of rice on serving plates. Top with eggs and spoon on the sauce. Serve at once, sprinkled with chopped parsley if you wish.

POACHED EGG WITH ASPARAGUS

Serves 2

4 thin diagonal slices of French bread
butter
6 paper-thin slices of prosciutto
12 spears of hot steamed asparagus
2 poached eggs
salt
freshly ground black pepper
⅔ cup grated Gruyère

1. Sauté the bread in butter until golden brown on both sides. Put on a heat-proof serving plate.

2. Add the prosciutto, then the asparagus, egg, salt and pepper to taste and the Gruyère. Broil until the cheese is slightly melted.

EGGS IN BURGUNDY

Makes 4

Sunny islands in a maroon sea, eggs simmered in Burgundy, mellowed with chicken broth and seasoned with parsley and sautéed onions, will inspire you to poach Burgundian as often as you fry American. And the technique is simplicity itself: use only a small amount of liquid so the yolks remain above the liquid level (that way, they stay yellow).

⅓ cup red Burgundy wine
⅓ cup Chicken Stock (see page 58)
2 tablespoons chopped fresh parsley
2 slices bacon, chopped
1 tablespoon minced onion
4 eggs
salt
freshly ground black pepper

1. In a small bowl, mix the wine, stock and parsley, and set aside. In a heavy 9-inch skillet, fry the bacon over medium high heat until crisp. Pour off all but 1 tablespoon fat. Lower the heat to medium and sauté the onion for 2 to 3 minutes.

2. Add the wine mixture to the skillet and bring to a boil, lower the heat and simmer for 1 minute. Crack each egg into a cup and then slip it into the simmering liquid. Poach for 3 to 4 minutes, season with salt and pepper and serve in shallow bowls with some of the poaching liquid spooned over the top, or over a slice of toasted French bread.

EGGS IN ASPIC

Makes 4

Simmered, delicately flavored with fresh herbs, this French classic still relies on the humble poached egg. The sparkling aspic and soft-centered egg make an impressive presentation for a light summer lunch or first course.

4 poached eggs
2 envelopes unflavored gelatin
3 cups well-seasoned clarified Chicken or Beef Stock
   (see pages 58 and 57)
⅓ cup lemon juice
fresh dill, watercress or tarragon sprigs

1. Cool poached eggs in cold water and drain but do not dry them.

2. In a saucepan, soften the gelatin in ½ cup of the broth. Stir over medium heat until the gelatin is dissolved. Remove the saucepan from heat and stir in remaining broth and lemon juice. Chill until the aspic is syrupy and the consistency of unbeaten egg whites, about 30 to 40 minutes.

3. Spoon a ¼-inch layer of aspic into each of 4 individual molds or 6-ounce custard cups. Put sprigs of fresh dill, watercress or tarragon on top of the aspic layer. Chill until almost firm, about 15 minutes. Keep the remaining aspic at room temperature.

4. Trim any ragged edges from the poached eggs with a sharp knife. To keep the yolks from breaking, put them carefully, yolk side down, on the firm aspic in the molds. Fill the molds with the remaining aspic, completely covering the eggs and chill until firm—at least 4 to 5 hours. Put the remaining gelatin mixture in a shallow pan to chill until firm. It can be diced and used as a garnish.

5. To serve, dip the molds in lukewarm water for several seconds, tap them to loosen the aspic and invert onto individual plates. Garnish with fresh dill, watercress or tarragon sprigs and the aspic cubes. For a dressing try homemade Mayonnaise (see page 78) or a mixture of equal amounts of mayonnaise and sour cream.

BAKED EGGS

Baking, or shirring, as it is sometimes called, is an interesting change of pace from boiled or poached.

1. Preheat the oven to 350°F. Butter a small casserole or ramekin for each serving, slide in 1 or 2 eggs and sprinkle them with salt and pepper.

2. Bake 10 to 15 minutes, or until the whites are firm but the yolks are still runny.

Baked Eggs with Cream. Spoon 1½ tablespoons of heavy cream per egg over the eggs before baking.

Baked Eggs with Tomatoes and Cream. Line buttered ramekins with thin slices of tomato. Add the eggs, salt, pepper and cream.

Baked Eggs with Cheese. Line buttered ramekins with slices of hard cheese—Jarlsberg, Gruyère, muenster or Cheddar—then add eggs, salt and pepper. Can be baked with or without cream.

Baked Eggs with Chicken Livers. Sauté 2 chicken livers per serving over medium heat in 2 teaspoons of butter until browned—about 5 minutes. Line buttered baking dishes with the livers and drippings from the skillet, add the eggs, salt and pepper.

Baked Eggs Florentine. Line buttered baking dishes with well-drained, cooked chopped spinach. Add eggs, salt and pepper. Spoon ¼ cup Mornay Sauce (see page 72) over each egg and bake.

Baked Eggs with Tomatoes and Cream

Eggs in Brown Butter with Artichokes

Scrambled Eggs with Smoked Salmon in Brioche

FRIED EGGS

Sunny side up or over easy, few can deny that the aroma of eggs, bacon and coffee is among the more sublime morning moments. Yet more than a few of us are afraid of hard eggs. The secret is to cook slowly—high heat makes the protein in eggs tough.

1. Melt enough fat—butter or bacon grease—over medium high heat to cover the bottom of a heavy skillet thinly and evenly. When the fat is sizzling, add the eggs carefully so the yolk doesn't break.

2. Lower the heat and fry slowly until the white is firm and the yolk still soft. Serve at once for sunny side up. If you want them over easy, gently turn with a spatula and cook 30 seconds more on the other side.

Note. For foolproof fried eggs, use a nonstick skillet, preparing them with fat as above.

Oeufs au Beurre Noisette (Eggs in brown butter). Prepare fried eggs as above and put on thin slices of French bread that have been sautéed in butter. Add an additional 1½ teaspoons butter for each egg to the skillet and cook over medium heat until the butter browns. It will happen quickly, so watch carefully. Remove from the heat immediately and spoon over the eggs.

Oeufs au Beurre Noisette et Artichauts (Eggs in brown butter with artichokes). Follow the instructions above, but before spooning the browned butter over the eggs, use it to sauté sliced (frozen and defrosted, fresh parboiled or canned) artichoke hearts for 1 or 2 minutes. Deglaze the skillet with 1½ teaspoons lemon juice for each egg. Lift out the artichoke hearts with a slotted spoon and arrange them beside the toast and eggs. Pour the brown butter and lemon juice mixture over the eggs and serve.

Oriental Eggs. Prepare fried eggs and put them on a warm plate. For each egg stir 1 teaspoon soy sauce and 1 teaspoon brown sugar into the drippings in the skillet. Add 1 tablespoon sliced scallion per egg and sauté for 1 minute. Spoon scallion mixture over eggs.

Mexican Eggs. Prepare fried eggs and put on whole tortillas that have been fried in shallow oil until crisp. Sprinkle with chopped sweet green chilies, chopped tomatoes and shredded Monterey jack.

SCRAMBLED EGGS

Serves 1

There's a great controversy that rages over how to scramble eggs: high heat or low, water or milk, cream or sour cream, even wooden spoon or spatula. Whatever works is fine. Just keep the heat low—scrambled eggs can get tough, too—so the eggs don't overcook. Creamy, moist eggs are preferred by connoisseurs.

2 eggs
2 tablespoons cream, milk or water
¼ teaspoon salt
freshly ground black pepper
2 tablespoons butter

1. In a bowl, beat the eggs with the liquid and seasonings.

2. Melt the butter in a small, heavy skillet over medium heat. Add the egg mixture and cook slowly over low heat, stirring gently. Stir until the mixture is firm but still moist—the eggs continue to cook off the heat. Serve at once.

Scrambled Eggs with Smoked Salmon in Brioche. Slice the top off a large warmed brioche and hollow it out. Add ¼ cup slivered smoked salmon and 1 tablespoon fresh chopped dill to the egg mixture before scrambling. Fill the brioche shell with the scrambled eggs and salmon and serve the buttered brioche top on the side.

Scrambled Eggs with Mushrooms and Peppers. Sauté ½ cup sliced fresh mushrooms and 2 tablespoons minced green pepper in the 2 tablespoons butter for 2 to 3 minutes. Add the egg mixture and scramble.

Scrambled Eggs au Poivre. Stir 2 tablespoons soft cheese (such as Pepper Boursin or Alouette) with black pepper into the beaten egg mixture before scrambling.

OMELET

Serves 1

Delicious by itself, a French omelet is also an ever-ready envelope for whatever filling you crave or have on hand, from caviar and sour cream to leftover meat, fish or bits of cheese. Individual omelets take from ¼ to ½ cup filling, but there are no hard and fast rules. Larger omelets are made the same way as individual ones; just double or triple all the ingredients.

There's more mystique to the perfect omelet pan than there should be. The main requirement is a good, heavy skillet with sloping sides that spreads the heat evenly. It must be well seasoned or have a nonstick lining. Use the right size skillet for the number of eggs being cooked. Individual 2- or 3-egg omelets should be cooked in a pan 7 to 8 inches across the top; omelets of 4 to 5 eggs should be cooked in a 9- to 10-inch pan. Omelets made with more than 5 eggs can be cooked in larger pans, but they are usually not rolled but are cut into wedges, like a frittata.

3 eggs
¼ teaspoon salt
freshly ground black pepper
2 tablespoons butter

1. In a bowl, beat the eggs and seasonings until just blended.

2. Heat the butter over medium high heat in a heavy 8-inch skillet until it sizzles; be careful not to let it brown.

3. Add the egg mixture and tilt the pan to make sure it spreads evenly across the whole surface. Let it cook a few moments to set the edges, then lift the edges gently with a spatula or fork to let the uncooked egg run underneath. Repeat in several places until the center of the omelet is firm but still moist, no more than 2 or 3 minutes.

4. If you want to add filling, do it now. Put it in a strip down the middle of the omelet.

5. Fold ⅓ of the omelet toward the middle (over the filling). Fold over the opposite ⅓ of the omelet, making a slim roll. Tilting the pan toward a warm serving plate, slide the omelet out.

Sour Cream and Watercress Omelet. Fill the omelet with ¼ cup sour cream mixed with ¼ cup chopped watercress.

Omelet with *Fines Herbes*. Add 2 tablespoons mixed chopped fresh herbs (or 2 teaspoons mixed dried herbs) to the beaten egg mixture. Use combinations of chives, parsley, tarragon, basil, chervil and celery leaves.

Vegetable Omelet. Sauté ¼ cup chopped onion and ½ teaspoon minced garlic in butter over medium heat for 3 to 4 minutes, or until golden. Add ½ cup peeled and diced eggplant, green pepper or zucchini and 1 small tomato, seeded and diced. Sauté an additional 5 minutes or until thick. Season with salt and freshly ground black pepper and use as filling.

Gruyère Omelet. Sprinkle ½ cup shredded Gruyère (or other hard cheese) over the finished omelet, or use as filling.

Omelet *(above)* **and Puffed Omelet** *(below)*

PUFFED OMELET

Serves 1

With a julienne vegetable filling (pea pods, carrots, zucchini and tomato) this omelet fits into the whole-meal category. You can also make a lavish version with creamed crab and artichokes inside; one with raspberry jam and rum can supply a sweet finish to a meal.

3 eggs, separated
1 tablespoon milk
¼ teaspoon salt
2 tablespoons butter

1. Preheat the broiler. In a large bowl, beat the egg yolks with the milk and salt until smooth. In a separate bowl, beat the egg whites until they form peaks. Gently fold the beaten whites into the yolk mixture.

2. In a heavy 8-inch overproof skillet, heat the butter over medium heat until it sizzles. Be careful not to let it brown. Pour in the omelet mixture and spread evenly across the pan with a spatula. Let it cook undisturbed until the bottom is lightly browned. Lift the edges with a spatula to check the bottom.

3. Put the skillet 8 inches from the heat in the broiler and brown the top lightly—about 3 to 4 minutes.

4. Remove the skillet from the broiler and spoon a filling over half the omelet. Gently fold over the other half with a spatula, covering the filling. Slide the omelet onto a warm plate and serve at once.

Julienne of Vegetables Omelet. Julienne 6 snow peas, ¼ cup zucchini and ¼ cup carrot. Seed and dice a small tomato. Melt 1 tablespoon butter in a small heavy skillet over medium heat and sauté the vegetables for 5 minutes.

Creamed Crab and Artichoke Heart Omelet. Heat ½ cup cooked crab or lobster meat and 4 cooked artichoke hearts in ½ cup medium white sauce seasoned with 1 tablespoon sherry until it simmers.

Raspberry and Rum Omelet. In a small saucepan, melt 2 tablespoons raspberry jam with 1 tablespoon dark rum. Add ½ cup fresh or frozen (drained) raspberries. Fills 1 omelet, and serves 2 for dessert.

Apple and Calvados Omelet. Peel, core and slice 1 small apple. Sauté the slices in 1 tablespoon butter over medium heat for 5 minutes, or until tender. Sprinkle with 2 teaspoons sugar and 2 tablespoons Calvados or other apple brandy. Stir gently and cook another minute. Fills 1 omelet and serves 2 for dessert.

FRITTATA

Serves 4

A frittata is simply a flat, thick Italian omelet. The filling is mixed with the eggs, and the resulting batter is slowly cooked in a skillet like a giant pancake. Some cooks even flip the frittata to cook the other side, but a less risky method is to run it under the broiler. It's just as good at room temperature as hot. Colorful and hearty fillings work best: mushroom and bacon, potatoes and ham, sausage and peppers or zucchini and onion.

6 eggs
½ teaspoon salt
freshly ground black pepper
½ cup grated Gruyère
1 tablespoon olive oil
1 tablespoon butter

1. Beat the eggs with the seasonings. Stir in the grated cheese.

Mushroom and Bacon Frittata

2. Preheat the broiler. In a heavy, ovenproof 10-inch skillet, heat the oil and melt the butter over a medium heat. Add the egg mixture and lower the heat. Cook undisturbed until the bottom is golden brown when edge is lifted.

3. Put the skillet 6 inches under the source of heat in the broiler for 30 seconds, or until the top of the frittata is golden brown. Cut into wedges.

Mushroom and Bacon Frittata. Fry or broil 4 slices of bacon until crisp. Drain and crumble. Add bacon, 1 cup sliced fresh mushrooms, 2 tablespoons chopped fresh parsley and 2 tablespoons minced scallions to the beaten eggs.

Potato and Ham Frittata. Boil 2 small potatoes; peel and slice. Fold potato slices and ½ cup diced smoked ham into beaten eggs.

Sausage and Pepper Frittata. Use 4 ounces hot or sweet Italian sausage. Slash the sausage casing and remove the meat. Fry over medium heat until brown and crumbly. Drain off excess fat and cool sausage slightly. Stir the sausage and ⅓ cup minced green pepper into the beaten eggs.

Zucchini and Onion Frittata. Saute 1 cup diced zucchini and 1 diced onion in 1 tablespoon olive oil over medium heat for 5 minutes. Stir into beaten eggs.

VEGETABLE CUSTARD

Serves 4 to 6

Most of us think of custards as dessert. But, like all egg-based dishes, they take equally well to the less sweet things in life—vegetables, for instance, arranged in layers for lots of visual and taste interest. And it only looks complicated. The layered vegetables are simply drenched with a mixture of egg, Parmesan and milk. As with any custard, the key to its creamy texture is baking it in a mold which sits in a pan containing an inch of water.

¼ pound fresh green beans, cut into small pieces
1 small cauliflower, cut into pieces
8 medium asparagus spears, cut into 2-inch pieces
4 large leeks (white part only), quartered lengthwise
1 tablespoon butter
2 tablespoons dry bread crumbs
1 cup grated Parmesan
4 eggs
1 cup half-and-half
1 teaspoon salt
¼ teaspoon freshly ground black pepper

Vegetable Custard is simpler than it looks. Vegetables alternate in contrasting layers for visual interest.

1. Preheat the oven to 350°F. In a large pot, bring at least 2 quarts of salted water to a rapid boil over high heat. Parboil each vegetable in turn for 2 minutes, remove from the pot and plunge into cold water to stop the cooking. Drain and chop.

2. Butter a 2-quart charlotte mold or other deep oven-proof bowl of similar size. Dust the mold with bread crumbs.

3. Layer the vegetables into the mold, alternating colors: green asparagus, white leeks, green beans, white cauliflower. Sprinkle ⅓ cup grated cheese over each of the first three layers.

4. In a bowl, beat the eggs, half-and-half, salt and pepper. Slowly pour this mixture over the vegetable-cheese layers, allowing it to soak through the layers and fill the mold.

5. Put the mold in a shallow baking pan with 1 inch of hot water. Bake 1 hour—replacing water as it evaporates—or until the center of the custard is firm. Let stand 10 minutes. Loosen the sides of the custard with a long knife and invert onto a serving platter.

CHEESE SOUFFLE

Serves 4

Soufflés used to be the sole province of restaurants and professional chefs. Unfortunately, they've also become a catchword for fancy cooking. The truth is, a soufflé is no harder to produce than a cake; it takes only a gentle hand to blend in the egg whites. A white sauce enriched with egg yolks and stiffly beaten egg whites are the only ingredients essential to any main-course soufflé.

Cheeses, vegetables, seafood, meat and herbs in any combination can be folded into the basics to change the flavor. There is only one golden rule: diners wait for soufflés because soufflés cannot wait for diners. Soufflés proceed in quick, majestic fashion from the oven to the table, because as they cool they fall—and therein lies their evil reputation.

4 tablespoons butter
1 cup plus 1 tablespoon grated sharp Cheddar or
   Gruyère, or ½ cup each grated Gruyère and Parmesan
3 tablespoons flour
1 cup hot milk
½ teaspoon salt
¼ teaspoon cayenne pepper
4 egg yolks at room temperature
5 egg whites at room temperature
⅛ teaspoon cream of tartar

1. Preheat the oven to 400°F. Grease the bottom and sides of a 1½-quart soufflé dish or charlotte mold with 1 tablespoon of the butter, then sprinkle in 1 tablespoon of grated cheese you are using for the soufflé. This will ensure a crisp, brown crust.

2. In a heavy 2-quart saucepan, make a Béchamel Sauce with the remaining 3 tablespoons of butter and the flour, milk, salt and pepper (see page 70). Take the pan off the heat and beat in the egg yolks, one at a time, with a wire whisk. Stir in the remaining cup of cheese.

3. Beat the egg whites until foamy, then add the cream of tartar to stabilize the stiffened whites. Continue to beat until peaks form. The whites should be glossy, not dry.

4. Lighten the warm béchamel-cheese sauce by stirring in a large dollop of beaten egg white. Add the remaining egg white to the bowl and gently fold in with a rubber spatula. Cut through the center of the mixture with the spatula and draw it toward the edge of the bowl. Lift sauce from below up against the side of the bowl and over to the center. Cut down again and repeat. Turn the bowl as you continue this folding motion, until the cheese sauce is barely mixed with the egg whites. Unincorporated white will still show.

5. Pour this mixture into the prepared soufflé dish and put it on the bottom shelf of the oven. Turn the heat down to 375°F and bake for 25 to 30 minutes. For a French-style soufflé, the outside should be brown and crisp with the center still creamy. For a soufflé cooked evenly throughout, bake at 325°F for 45 minutes. Serve at once.

Note. To make an 8-cup or 2-quart soufflé for 6 people, use 4½ tablespoons each butter and flour, ¾ teaspoon salt, ¼ teaspoon cayenne pepper and 1½ cups milk for the béchamel; 6 egg yolks and 7 or 8 egg whites beaten with ¼ teaspoon cream of tartar; 1½ cups cheese. Bake for 35 to 40 minutes.

If you don't have a soufflé dish large enough, you can add capacity to a 1- or 1½-quart soufflé dish by tying a buttered aluminum foil or parchment collar around the outside edge to extend the dish 2 inches in height and hold the expanding soufflé. (This trick makes a soufflé look professional, too.)

Broccoli and Cheese Soufflé. To serve 4, add ½ cup grated cheese and ½ cup minced cooked broccoli. To serve 6, add ¾ cup grated cheese and ¾ cup chopped cooked broccoli.

Broccoli and Cheese Soufflé

Spinach and Onion Soufflé. To serve 4, sauté 1 small minced onion in 1 tablespoon butter for 5 minutes. Add ½ cup chopped, squeezed dry spinach. Fold into the sauce. To serve 6, use 1 large onion and ¾ cup spinach and 1 tablespoon butter.

Chicken and Mushroom Soufflé. To serve 4, sauté 4 large chopped mushrooms in 1 tablespoon butter. Stir in ½ cup minced cooked chicken and fold into sauce. To serve 6, use 6 large mushrooms, 1 tablespoon butter and ¾ cup chicken.

Salmon Soufflé. To serve 4, add 1 small minced onion sautéed in 1 tablespoon butter and ½ cup flaked cooked salmon and 1 tablespoon chopped fresh dill. To serve 6, use 1 medium onion, 1 tablespoon butter, ¾ cup salmon, and 1 tablespoon chopped dill.

VANILLA SOUFFLE

Serves 6 to 9

A sweet soufflé is a glorious, lighter and airier version of the main course. Beaten egg whites give the texture to these soufflés as well, but its basic sauce is a cooked mixture of milk, sugar and starch rather than a flour-thickened béchamel.

6 tablespoons butter
6 tablespoons all-purpose flour
¼ teaspoon salt
1 cup milk
5 egg yolks
½ cup sugar
2 teaspoons vanilla extract
5 egg whites
¼ teaspoon cream of tartar

1. Preheat the oven to 350°F. In a saucepan, melt the butter and stir in the flour. Then stir in the salt and milk and continue stirring over medium heat until the sauce thickens.

2. In a large bowl, beat the egg yolks until thick. Gradually beat in the sugar, 1 tablespoon at a time, until thick. Fold the egg yolks into the milk mixture, then fold in the vanilla.

3. Beat the egg whites until foamy. Then add cream of tartar and beat until stiff but not dry. Fold ¼ of the egg whites into the custard, then fold in the remaining egg whites. Pour this mixture into a 2-quart soufflé dish.

4. Put the dish in a pan with 1 inch of hot water. Bake for 1 hour, or until the soufflé is puffed and brown. Serve at once.

Chocolate Soufflé. Add 3 ounces (3 squares) chopped semisweet chocolate to the hot milk mixture, stirring until the chocolate is melted.

Lemon Soufflé. Add grated rind of 2 lemons to egg yolks beaten with sugar.

Grand Marnier Soufflé. Omit ¼ cup of the milk. When the custard is removed from the heat, fold in ¼ cup Grand Marnier and grated rind of 1 orange.

Apple Calvados Soufflé. Omit ¼ cup of the milk. When the custard is removed from the heat, fold in ¼ cup Calvados. Fold in 1 apple, peeled, cored, shredded and well drained.

HOT MOCHA SOUFFLE

Serves 6

1 tablespoon butter
⅓ cup plus 1 tablespoon granulated sugar
2 tablespoons cornstarch
1 cup milk
1 tablespoon instant coffee
3 ounces semisweet chocolate, grated (or 3 ounces chocolate bits)
1 teaspoon vanilla extract
5 egg yolks
6 egg whites
¼ teaspoon cream of tartar

1. Preheat the oven to 400°F. Grease the bottom and sides of a 2-quart soufflé dish or charlotte mold with the butter. Dust with 1 tablespoon sugar.

2. Mix the cornstarch, remaining sugar and milk in a heavy saucepan and stir constantly over medium heat until the sauce simmers and thickens. Add the coffee, chocolate and vanilla extract and stir until the sauce is smooth. Remove from the heat.

3. In a large bowl, beat the egg yolks with a whisk until pale and thick. Gradually beat in the chocolate mixture. Cool until lukewarm.

4. Beat the egg whites in the large bowl of an electric mixer or by hand in a copper bowl with a whisk. As soon as they become foamy, add the cream of tartar. Beat until the egg whites form soft peaks and adhere to a lifted beater or whisk.

5. Lighten the coffee-chocolate mixture by stirring in a scoop of the beaten egg whites. Add the remaining egg whites to the bowl and gently fold them into the coffee-chocolate sauce until just barely mixed. Streaks of white will still show.

6. Pour this mixture into the prepared soufflé dish. Put on the bottom shelf of the oven, reduce the heat to 375°F and bake for 40 to 45 minutes, or until slightly firm to the touch. Serve immediately. To gild the lily, serve with fresh whipped cream or Crème Anglaise (see page 247).

Seafood

We're eating seafood today as never before, learning from Europeans and Orientals, who have always prized their fish above all else, and insisted on its absolute freshness. New restaurants serving only seafood are opening their doors every day, and seafood markets can hardly keep up with the demand. Improved technology and shipping allow us to sample fresh Channel turbot or Louisiana crayfish in season.

Fish cakes are definitely "out"—unless you're enjoying a freshly made cod cake on a Boston pier. What we look for now are whole fish, sparkling firm from the sea, lusty black lobsters, delicate mountain trout glimmering with a thousand rainbows. Fresh and simply prepared, with a few herbs, lemon and butter—what could better cap a summer's day? Perhaps a generously stocked fish stew on a cold winter's evening or bit of gravlax for breakfast. The beauty of fish lies in its versatility. The very gentleness and range of its flavors beg for innumerable preparations, as today's restaurant and home cooks are glad to demonstrate.

So boil, broil, stew, grill, marinate, poach, sauté or bake; and try whatever seafood looks freshest. You've a whole new repetoire to choose from.

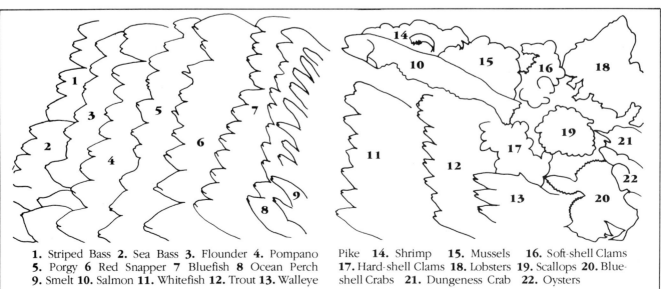

1. Striped Bass **2.** Sea Bass **3.** Flounder **4.** Pompano **5.** Porgy **6** Red Snapper **7** Bluefish **8** Ocean Perch **9.** Smelt **10.** Salmon **11.** Whitefish **12.** Trout **13.** Walleye Pike **14.** Shrimp **15.** Mussels **16.** Soft-shell Clams **17.** Hard-shell Clams **18.** Lobsters **19.** Scallops **20.** Blue-shell Crabs **21.** Dungeness Crab **22.** Oysters

THE ESSENTIALS

The bounty of the sea, lakes and streams brings with it the clean, refreshing scents of its natural waters. Sea-salty or mountain-lake lean, each fish shows off its freshness with firm clear eyes, shiny bright skin, tight scales and red gills. A good fish market feels alive with this freshness and has none of the telltale fishy smell of many-days-old catch. Fish that feels soft or looks dull is showing its age.

Buying fish is a world unto itself. It hasn't changed much since the days when fishwives plied their baskets along banks of the Seine and in sleepy little fishing villages. They may have sold their fish whole, but fish-mongers today offer a great array of cuts, depending upon the type and size of the fish as well as personal inclination.

Fresh fish is sold whole, drawn (gutted but with the scales and fins still intact), dressed (gutted with the scales and fins removed) or split (gutted with the scales and fins removed and cut into halves with the backbone removed). Larger fish are cut into steaks, and many smaller fish are skinned and boned and sold as filets. Filets are the easiest to cook and to eat, but they have less flavor than fish cooked bones and all.

Certain kinds of shellfish are sold live, like lobsters, soft-shell crabs, clams, mussels and oysters. In fact, these should always be bought live or frozen, since the fresh meat deteriorates quickly. Scallops and shrimp are not sold live and can be given the usual freshness check for firmness and good, clean smell. Live crabs are shipped nationwide in season. You can often find their cleaned, shelled, sweet meat packed in refrigerated tins, which should also be used quickly. Frozen crab meat is an excellent alternative, too.

No doubt, the fresher the fish, the better it tastes. So store it for only a day, in the coldest part of the refrigerator; if you must keep it longer, wrap it securely and freeze it. Wrap fresh fish loosely so the air can circulate around it. Defrost frozen fish slowly in the refrigerator and use immediately. Never buy frozen fish that shows any sign of having been defrosted and refrozen; check for ice crystals.

Because of its great delicacy, it's important not to overcook fish. Too much cooking is guaranteed to dry it out or toughen. Err on the side of undercooking and you will be pleasantly surprised at the improvement in taste and texture.

It is hard to give a formula for how much fish serves how many people. In general, count on about 1 pound of whole fish per person, a half pound of fish steak per person and one-third to one-half pound of fish filets per person. Shellfish is even more difficult to estimate; it depends on the rest of the meal—one half dozen oysters is a good hors d'oeuvre, one quart of mussels or clams serves as a main course.

SALTWATER FISH

1. Striped bass. A lean, juicy and delicate fish with firm white flesh.

2. Sea bass. A member of the grouper family, sea bass is very similar to striped bass in texture and flavor. Filets, steaks and whole fish are sold.

3. Flounder. One of the most versatile fish, flounder is usually sold in filets, which can be cooked by any quick method because they are so tender. American soles are varieties of flounder; dab, gray sole, lemon sole and fluke are all similar flat, delicious fish. The famous Dover sole of the English Channel is a different fish used in the same ways. Flounder is the most popular frozen fish.

4. Pompano. A fatty fish with a rich but mild flavor, pompano come from the South Atlantic and Gulf of Mexico. It forms a wonderful crust when broiled, and in its native New Orleans it is cooked *en papillote* (in paper) with wine, vegetables and herbs.

5. Porgies. These tiny Atlantic fish are also known as scup. Usually sold whole, they are at their flakiest when rolled in cornmeal and pan-fried.

6. Red snapper. A beautiful fish from the Gulf of Mexico with white, creamy flesh, red snapper is an all-time favorite. Red snappers are sold whole or as steaks or filets for baking, frying, poaching or grilling.

7. Bluefish. A sport fisherman's delight, bluefish put up a good fight all along the Atlantic coast. Their rich, dark meat has a delicate but distinctive flavor that is at its best baked or broiled.

8. Ocean perch. A good portion of the frozen fish filets consumed in this country go under the generic name of ocean perch. Red perch, sea perch and redfish all are ocean perch and have bland, somewhat coarse white meat that takes well to seasonings and sauces.

9. Smelt. A relative of salmon, these tiny, silvery fish migrate upstream to spawn in great masses. They are very tasty, but oily, and are usually dipped in flour or crumbs and fried whole. Some cooks bone them, but many think the bones are tender enough to eat.

FRESHWATER FISH

10. Salmon. A cold-water fish that spends part of its life at sea, salmon is considered one of the finest eating fish in the world. It has firm, oily flesh that ranges from light pink to dark red, depending on the species. Try whole fresh salmon poached in a court bouillon or salmon steaks broiled with butter.

11. Whitefish. Herring-like freshwater fish from cold northern lakes, whitefish have fatty but firm white flesh. They are sold whole or in filets and are prepared like trout. Smoked whitefish is very popular, and whitefish roe is made into caviar.

12. Trout. There are many varieties of small freshwater trout—rainbow, mountain, Dolly Vardens, speckled and brook—each a single delicate serving whether sautéed, broiled, baked, poached or grilled.

13. Walleye pike. Pike is a popular freshwater game fish with a lean, firm white flesh that takes well to baking and braising. Fish quenelles are often made of pike.

SHELLFISH

14. Shrimp. These popular clawless crustaceans range from small (300 to a pound) to 5-inch giants. All turn pink when cooked and tough when overcooked. Larger shrimp are called prawns in Europe. Scampi, which taste like large shrimp, are actually saltwater crayfish with tiny claws.

15. Mussels. Cousins to clams, mussels have shiny blue-black shells and sweet, tender meat. They should be bought live with the shells tightly closed. Once derogatorily termed "the poor man's oyster," they are now one of the New Cuisine's favorites, steamed in white wine.

16. Soft-shell clams. Also called "steamers." These New England tidal-flat clams bury themselves in the sand and use their long, characteristic "necks" as siphons to gather food. They are tender enough to eat raw, but are most often steamed. The long razor clams of the West Coast are also soft-shell clams.

17. Hard-shell clams. The cherrystone clams in the picture are medium-size hard-shell clams, which live in deeper water than soft-shell clams and have shorter necks and rounder shells. Littleneck clams are smaller versions of the same species; quahogs are larger. Hard-shell clams should be bought live and tightly closed. Small ones are eaten raw or steamed. Larger ones are used for chowder.

18. Lobster. To many cooks, lobster is the greatest delicacy the sea has to offer. It is also the largest crustacean, with the most usable meat. Its relative, the rock lobster, is smaller and without claws. The best lobster weighs 1 to 2 pounds and is cooked live by boiling, steaming or broiling.

19. Scallops. Named for their lovely fluted shells, scallops live in bays or inlets and at sea. The tiny bay scallops are sweeter, and sea scallops are brinier. Oddly, we eat only the muscle that holds the two shells together and not the rest of the meat. In France, all the meat, including the "coral" is used.

20. Blue-shell crab. An East Coast native, the blue-shell crab makes a meal an occasion, since it's a lot of work to eat it. In late spring and early summer, caught between molts, it becomes the delicate soft-shell crab that is sautéed in butter and eaten whole.

21. Dungeness crab. A crab from the West Coast, it is larger and meatier than its eastern relative. A third U.S. variety is the fabulous king crab from the north Pacific.

22. Oysters. Cultivated in commercial beds since Roman times, oysters come in many varieties with subtly different tastes. Many feel there is no point in eating them any way but raw with a squirt of lemon. Also found in stews lately, they're lightly poached as a first course.

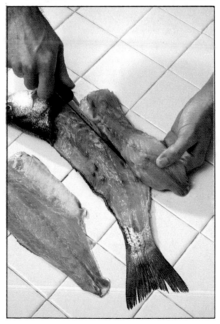 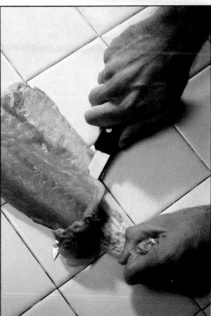

DRESSING AND FILLETING A FISH. Working from tail to head, scrape off the scales on both sides with a long, sharp knife or fish scaler. Slice off the fins.

Make a gash along the bottom edge from the anal opening to the head. Cut the entrails at the throat and discard them. Rinse the fish.

At the tail end, cut through the flesh to the backbone. Keeping the knife as close to the bone as possible, slice away the top side of the fish, pulling the meat off in a single piece.

Repeat on the other side. Pick out any remaining bones. You now have two filets to cook and a skeleton, head and tails for fish stock.

To skin the filets, lay them skin side down. Start at the tail and carefully scrape the flesh from the skin.

Cut a deep pocket in a dressed fish, slicing almost to the top fin.

Mix the stuffing and fill the fish, but be careful not to overstuff.

Insert metal skewers through both sides of the fish. Lace and tie off.

BAKED STUFFED FISH

Serves 3

Small fish such as trout or flounder can be served individually. Larger red snapper, pompano, bluefish, mackerel or sea bass will serve about as many people as the pounds they weigh. This recipe is for a 3-pound red snapper; the amount of stuffing can be used for 3 small fish or increased proportionately for larger fish. Fish should be baked in a preheated 425° F oven; the rule of thumb is about 8 to 10 minutes per pound. This will vary with the thickness of the fish, so start checking the tenderness and color (it will loose its translucency) of the flesh nearest the backbone very early on.

1 whole red snapper (about 3 pounds), dressed
salt
freshly ground black pepper
¼ cup butter
6 scallions, sliced
8 mushrooms, sliced
1 clove garlic, minced
½ cup chopped celery
¼ cup chopped parsley
2 tablespoons chopped fresh or 2 teaspoons dried dill
1½ cups fresh bread crumbs
2 eggs
½ cup Fish Stock (see page 58) or Chicken Stock (see page 58)
1 cup flaked cooked crab meat
juice of 1 lemon
¼ cup butter, melted

1. Preheat the oven to 425°F. Wash the fish and pat dry. Enlarge the pocket of the body cavity with a sharp knife. Sprinkle inside and out with salt and pepper.

2. In a small heavy skillet, melt the ¼ cup butter over medium heat. Add the vegetables and sauté until golden —about 5 minutes. Let the mixture cool. In a large bowl, combine the sautéed vegetables with the herbs, bread crumbs, eggs, fish stock and crabmeat and mix until well blended.

3. Stuff the fish and close the opening with skewers and thread. Mix the lemon juice and melted butter. Brush one side with lemon butter and lay the fish, buttered side down, on a foil-lined shallow baking pan. Brush the top side of the fish with the remaining lemon butter.

4. Put in the middle of the oven and bake for 25 to 30 minutes before you test the flesh nearest the backbone with a fork. If it is opaque and separates easily from the bone, it is done.

5. To transfer the fish to a separate serving platter, lift it gently by the foil lining of the pan. Remove the skewers and thread. Trim the excess foil from the edges.

WHOLE SMALL BAKED FISH

Serves 4

Often simple is best, and that's never truer than with fine, fresh baby fish like trout, whitefish or the tender little cods known as scrod.

4 small whole fish (¾ to 1½ pounds each), dressed
salt
freshly ground black pepper
¼ cup melted butter

1. Preheat the oven to 425°F. Salt and pepper the trout and put in a buttered shallow baking dish. Brush with melted butter and bake for 8 to 10 minutes before checking for doneness by probing the flesh near the backbone. If it is white and easy to separate from the bone, the fish is ready.

2. Serve the fish hot with wedges of lemon or with sauce (see below).

Baked Fish with Sauce Aurore. Prepare Sauce Aurore (see page 73) using fish stock. Simmer 5 minutes. Coat the hot fish with the sauce and garnish with sliced raw mushrooms and sprigs of dill.

Herbed Baked Fish. Add sprigs of fresh herbs—parsley, marjoram, thyme, dill and/or tarragon—to the cavity of the fish before baking and add 1 tablespoon chopped fresh herb leaves to the melted butter for basting.

STUFFED FILETS WITH MUSHROOM AND WINE VELOUTE SAUCE

Serves 4

4 fish filets (flounder, red snapper, haddock or other lean whitefish)
salt
freshly ground black pepper
2 cups chopped cooked lobster or crab meat
¼ cup melted butter
2 cups Sauce aux Champignons (see page 73)

1. Butter a shallow baking dish and preheat the oven to 350°F. Sprinkle the filets on both sides with salt and pepper. Spoon a quarter of the lobster or crab meat on one end of each, and roll the filet up around the filling. Put the rolls, seam side down, in the baking dish and brush generously with melted butter.

2. Bake for 20 to 25 minutes, or until the fish is white. While the fish bakes, make the sauce aux champignons.

3. To serve, arrange the rolled filets on a platter. Spoon the sauce over them.

BROILED FISH STEAKS

Serves 4

Fish steaks—thick crosscuts of larger fish like salmon, swordfish, red snapper, halibut and even tuna—are available fresh and frozen. They are broiled just like beefsteaks, but take less time and have none of the excess fat. The ideal thickness for grilling is about 1 inch; when

Baked Fish with Sauce Aurore

they are any thicker, the outside dries out and the inside isn't cooked; when they are thinner, they dry out too rapidly.

4 fish steaks, about ½ pound each and 1-inch thick
salt
freshly ground black pepper
¼ cup melted butter
juice of ½ lemon

1. Preheat the broiler. Sprinkle the steaks with salt and pepper. Mix the butter with the lemon juice and brush on both sides of the steaks. Put the steaks on a greased shallow broiling pan.

2. Broil 4 inches from the heat for 5 minutes. Turn the steaks over, brush with the butter mixture and broil another 4 or 5 minutes or until the flesh is no longer translucent. If you're grilling the fish outdoors, use the same technique.

Salmon Steak with Beurre Blanc. Broil salmon steaks and serve with Beurre Blanc (see page 80).

POACHED SALMON WITH GREEN SAUCE

Serves 4 to 6

Cooking a whole large fish is a dramatic event; it seems to mark a special occasion. The basic technique for poaching fish remains the same, no matter what the variety or size. The guidelines are simple: poach 6 to 8 minutes per pound, and never let the stock boil, just simmer.

1 4- to 5-pound whole salmon, dressed
1 lemon, sliced
1 large onion, sliced
1 tablespoon whole pickling spice
about 2 cups dry white wine
1 recipe Green Sauce (see page 39)
2 tablespoons Pernod

1. You can poach on top of the stove or in the oven. If using the oven, preheat to 325° F. Wash the fish under cold water and pat dry. Put the fish on a double layer of cheesecloth large enough to wrap around it comfortably and leave ends for lifting. Put the lemon and onion slices across the top of the fish and sprinkle it with the pickling spice. Wrap up the cheesecloth, then, using the ends as handles, pick up the fish and put it in a fish poacher or a foil-lined baking pan.

2. Add enough wine to half cover the salmon. Cover the pan or seal the foil (making a loose but airtight package) and poach in the oven for 25 to 30 minutes, or until the fish feels firm to the touch. On top of the stove, simmer it, covered, over low heat for 20 to 25 minutes. While the fish cooks, make the green sauce and spike it with the Pernod.

3. To serve hot, lift the salmon by the cheesecloth tabs to a warm platter and unwrap. Serve from the meat on top of the skeleton first, then remove the backbone and ribs in a single piece, starting at the tail. Serve the sauce from a separate bowl.

4. To serve cold, let the fish cool, uncovered, in the poaching liquid. Lift by the cheesecloth tabs and put the salmon on a serving board or platter. Unwrap the top of the fish and carefully peel away the skin on the exposed side and scrape off the layer of dark meat. Using the cheesecloth, turn the fish over. Discard the cheesecloth and peel and scrape the second side. Cover the fish with a damp cloth and chill for at least 2 hours. Garnish with slices of lime and cucumber and sprigs of fresh dill. Serve with the sauce.

FISH A LA MEUNIERE
Fish Sautéed in Butter

Serves 2

Fresh small fish or filets need nothing more complicated than a brief sautéing in butter and oil and a sprinkling of lemon juice, salt, pepper and parsley. Classic in its simplicity, this may be one of the original French comfort foods.

¼ cup flour
¼ teaspoon salt
freshly ground black pepper
2 small fish or large fish filets
2 tablespoons butter
1 tablespoon oil
1 tablespoon lemon juice
1 tablespoon chopped fresh parsley

1. Combine the flour, salt and pepper in a shallow pan. Dredge the fish in the mixture and shake off the excess. This coating will produce a good crisp brown edge.

Poached Salmon with Green Sauce

2. In a heavy skillet large enough to hold the fish comfortably without overlapping, heat the butter and oil over medium heat. Add the fish and sauté until golden brown—about 1 or 2 minutes per side for filets, 4 or 5 minutes for small whole fish or until the fish is no longer translucent.

3. Remove the fish to a warm platter. Add the lemon juice and parsley to the pan and scrape up the browned particles. Drizzle this sauce over the fish and serve at once.

Fish with Almonds. Omit the lemon juice and sauté ½ cup slivered almonds in the pan juices for a minute, then pour over the fish.

GRILLED FISH WITH HERBS

Serves 4

Something about fish grilled with herbs conjures up visions of south of France summers. You, too, can marinate any small fish in white wine, lemon juice, olive oil and herbs and grill them to the same effect. A wire grill basket that holds fish securely while they are turned is a great help.

12 small whole fish (butterfish, whiting, smelts or baby bluefish), dressed
salt
freshly ground black pepper
¼ cup dry white wine
2 tablespoons lemon juice
¾ cup olive oil
1 clove garlic, chopped
⅓ cup fresh herb leaves (chives, thyme and parsley)
1 bay leaf
12 branches fresh rosemary
6 stalks fennel, cut into 1-inch pieces

1. Sprinkle the fish with salt and pepper and put in a shallow dish. In a small bowl whisk together the wine, lemon juice and oil. Stir in the garlic and herb leaves, bay leaf, and ½ teaspoon salt and pour over the fish. Let the fish marinate 1 hour at room temperature. Turn them often.

2. Meanwhile, prepare the charcoal fire and light it. When the coals are gray, drain the fish and stuff each with a sprig of rosemary and some fennel stalk. Put the fish in a grill basket or on an oiled grill 6 inches from the fire and cook 5 to 6 minutes on each side.

Grilled Fish Wrapped in Dried Fennel. Larger fish that must cook longer need some protection from the hot coals as they cook. Marinate a 4- to 5-pound red snapper, striped bass, whitefish or small salmon as you would the smaller fish. Substitute dried fennel stalks for the fresh fennel. Drain the fish and stuff with rosemary branches. Line the grill basket with a thin layer of dried fennel stalks, put the fish across them, then cover the fish with more stalks and close the basket. Cook 6 inches from the fire, 10 to 15 minutes per side, depending on the thickness of the fish. The dried fennel will burn, giving an aromatic flavor to the fish.

POACHED TROUT

Serves 4

Poach any fish or filets in court bouillon, a quick stock based on water and vegetables, sometimes wine. It adds flavor to a number of different sauces.

4 trout, dressed
salt
1 onion, sliced
1 lemon, sliced
1 bay leaf
6 peppercorns
½ cup dry white wine
1 cup Fish Stock (see page 58) or Chicken Stock (see page 58)

1. Preheat the oven to 350° F. Sprinkle the trout with salt and place them side by side in a shallow baking pan (or a skillet for stove-top poaching). Add the onion, lemon, bay leaf, peppercorns, wine and stock. Cover the pan tightly with foil. Bake in the middle of the oven for 10 to 15 minutes, or until tender (or barely simmer on top of the stove for the same amount of time).

2. Serve the fish warm with lemon or lime wedges.

Poached Trout with Velouté Sauce. Make a Velouté Sauce for the fish using ¼ cup butter, ¼ cup flour and 1½ cups of the poaching liquid (see page 73).

Poached Trout with Ravigote Sauce (see page 74).

Cold Poached Trout with Watercress-Lime Sauce. Let the poached trout cool in its liquid, uncovered. Strip off the skin and put the trout on a serving platter. Cover the fish and chill. Make a Velouté Sauce with ¼ cup butter, ¼ cup flour, 2 tablespoons lime juice and 1½ cups poaching liquid (see page 73). Take off the heat and stir in ½ cup sour cream. Put the sauce in a bowl, cover and chill. When ready to serve, stir 1 cup coarsely chopped watercress leaves into the sauce. Completely cover the cold fish with the sauce and garnish with lime slices.

PAUPIETTES OF LEMON SOLE

Serves 4

A paupiette is a filet that is wrapped around a filling. Lemon sole is stuffed with lobster mousse, then glazed with champagne sauce.

4 lemon sole filets, 8 ounces each
juice of 1 lemon
8 ounces pike filets
2 1-pound lobsters
1 egg white
1 teaspoon fresh lemon juice
1½ cups heavy cream
salt
pinch white pepper

¼ cup Clarified Butter (see page 79)
1 medium onion, sliced
6 shallots, sliced
1 clove garlic, mashed
2 carrots, sliced
3 celery stalks, sliced
⅓ cup Cognac
⅓ cup Madeira
4 ripe tomatoes, peeled, seeded and chopped
⅓ cup chopped fresh parsley
2 bay leaves
1½ teaspoons chopped fresh or ½ teaspoon dried thyme
1 tablespoon chopped fresh or 1 teaspoon dried tarragon
salt
freshly ground black pepper
2 tablespoons tomato paste
dash Tabasco sauce
2 cups dry white wine
1 cup heavy cream

1 cup Fish Stock (made with champagne instead of water; see page 58)
½ cup Hollandaise Sauce (see page 77)
½ cup whipped cream

fruits for garnish: kiwi, grapes, nectarine, strawberries, orange, cherries

1. Split the filets lengthwise, cutting not quite all the way through and open out. Flatten and brush them with lemon juice.

2. In a blender or food processor, combine the pike, meat from the two lobster tails (uncooked), egg white, lemon juice and cream. Blend until smooth and pasty. Stir in ½ teaspoon salt and a pinch of white pepper. Chill.

3. Prepare the sauce by heating the butter in a large

skillet. Add the onion, shallots, garlic, carrots and celery and sauté over high heat until soft, about 3 minutes. Reserve any coral and roe from the lobster. Remove all the claw meat, chop and set aside.

4. Crush all the shells, add them to the skillet, then add the Cognac and set aflame. Add the Madeira, tomatoes, parsley, bay leaves, thyme, tarragon, salt and pepper to taste, tomato paste, Tabasco sauce and 1 cup of wine. Simmer for 5 minutes, mashing the shells to extract the juice. Simmer another 15 minutes, then add the remaining wine. Cover and simmer for another 30 minutes. Pour the mixture into a sieve and press firmly to extract juices.

5. In a saucepan, add the lobster claws, roe and coral to the sauce and simmer until the sauce is reduced to ¾ cup. Stir in the cream and simmer until 1 cup remains. Simmer 10 more minutes. Chill. Beat this sauce into the lobster mousse, then spread it evenly on the fish filets and roll them up, starting at the pointed end of the filet. Refrigerate for 1 hour to set the mousse.

6. Put the rolled filets on a rack above boiling water and steam until the fish turns white, about 8 to 10 minutes. Let the fish drain well, then slice the rolls crosswise into ½-inch-thick slices. Arrange the slices in a circle on a heat-proof plate.

7. To prepare the glaze, mix the fish stock with the hollandaise sauce and whipped cream. Spoon the glaze over the sliced fish. Put the plates under the broiler and broil until the glaze melts and bubbles, about 5 to 6 minutes. Fill the center of the fish circle with fruit.

FISH POACHED IN MACON WINE

Serves 4

¼ pound fat bacon, cut into chunks
1 large onion, sliced
3 cloves garlic, chopped
1 2- to 2½-pound pike, cut into 2-inch pieces
1 2- to 2½-pound perch, cut into 2-inch pieces
2 2-pound eels, skinned and cut into 2-inch pieces
bouquet garni of several sprigs of thyme and tarragon
¼ teaspoon salt
white Mâcon or other dry white wine to cover
1 egg yolk
⅓ cup heavy cream
⅓ cup softened butter
2 tablespoons flour

1. In a skillet, fry the bacon until crisp, then add the onion and garlic and sauté for 5 minutes. Add the fish pieces, bouquet garni, salt to taste and enough wine to cover the fish. Cover the skillet, bring to a boil, then reduce the heat and simmer until the fish is cooked, about 10 minutes.

2. Remove the bouquet garni. Remove the fish pieces and let them cool. Meanwhile, thicken the broth. In a small bowl, combine the egg yolk with the cream and beat until well blended. Add this mixture to the hot broth. Next, mix the butter and flour and add to the broth, stirring over low heat until slightly thickened. Taste the thickened broth and add salt to taste.

3. Remove the bones from the cooled fish and return the fish to the simmering sauce. Let the fish heat through, then serve on thinly sliced, toasted French bread that has been rubbed with garlic.

DRUNKEN FISH

Serves 2

peanut oil for frying
2 egg whites
½ teaspoon cornstarch
8 ounces fish filets (cod, haddock or halibut), cut into 2-inch pieces
1 cup small pieces mook yee (dried tree fungus), presoaked in cold water
4 teaspoons cornstarch
1 cup pork broth (see below)
1 cup shao hsing (rice wine) or dry sherry
salt
4 teaspoons sugar

1. In a large skillet, heat the oil to 350° F over medium high heat (use a candy or deep-frying thermometer to check the temperature). In a small bowl, beat the egg white with ½ teaspoon cornstarch until foamy. Coat the pieces of fish with the egg mixture and drop them into the hot oil. Fry the fish until cooked but not brown, about 2 to 3 minutes. Drain on paper towel, then put the fish on a platter and add the mook yee around the fish as a garnish.

2. In a small saucepan, combine the remaining ingredients and cook over medium heat, stirring constantly, until sauce bubbles and thickens. Spoon sauce over the fish.

PORK BROTH

Makes about 3 cups

1 pound pork bones
½ pound meaty pork trimmings
salt
1 onion, chopped
2 teaspoons chopped fresh ginger

1. In a large saucepan, heat 1 quart of water and add the pork bones, pork trimmings, salt to taste, onion and ginger root. Cover and simmer for 1 hour, skimming the foam that rises to the top.

2. Strain the broth through cheesecloth, then cover and refrigerate. The pork broth will keep in the refrigerator for 1 week (remove any hardened fat as it forms) and in the freezer for 1 month or more.

Leftover fresh salmon is ideal for Cold Salmon Mousse.

COLD SALMON MOUSSE

Makes 1½-quart mold

2 cups cooked and flaked salmon
2 scallions, chopped
¼ cup chopped fresh or 1 tablespoon dried dill
¼ cup lemon juice
2½ cups Chicken Stock (see page 58)
2 cups sour cream
2 envelopes unflavored gelatin

1. Oil a 1½-quart mold. In a blender or food processor, combine the salmon, scallions, dill, lemon juice and 2 cups of the chicken stock and purée until very smooth. Pour this mixture into a large bowl and stir in the sour cream.

2. In a small saucepan, combine the gelatin and the remaining cold chicken stock to soften. Stir over low heat until the gelatin is completely dissolved. Add the gelatin-stock mixture to the salmon and sour cream and blend thoroughly. Pour evenly into the mold and chill until the mousse is set—about 2 hours.

3. To unmold, dip the mold briefly in warm water to loosen the mousse. Top the mold with a platter and invert.

SEAFOOD DILL SALAD

Serves 2

Scandinavians have a passion for fish salads and for dill as well.

½ pound bay scallops
4 ounces flounder filet
1 tablespoon oil
½ cup chopped celery
1 tomato, cored, seeded and chopped
2 scallions, sliced
2 tablespoons chopped fresh or 2 teaspoons dried dill
¼ cup olive oil
2 tablespoons lemon or lime juice
1 teaspoon sugar
freshly ground black pepper
⅛ teaspoon curry powder
salt

1. Preheat the broiler. Oil a shallow baking dish and put the scallops and flounder in it in a single layer. Brush the seafood with oil and broil for 4 or 5 minutes, or until white and tender but not overcooked. (You need not turn the seafood.)

2. Let the seafood cool. Break the flounder into bite-size pieces. In a bowl, combine the seafood, vegetables and dill. Beat the remaining ingredients together, seasoning to taste with salt and pepper, and pour over the salad.

3. Gently toss the salad with the dressing and arrange it on a bed of lettuce on a serving plate. Chill and serve cold.

SEVICHE

Serves 6

Seviche is a smooth cold (but hotly spiced) salad that is marinated in lime juice, which "cooks" the raw fish, changing it from translucent to opaque.

1½ pounds firm whitefish filets (such as red snapper, pompano, haddock or scallops)
fresh lime juice to cover, about 1 cup
1 tomato, cored, seeded and chopped
¼ cup sliced scallions
½ cup sweet green chilies, fresh or canned and drained, chopped
2 tablespoons chopped fresh coriander leaves or parsley
⅓ cup olive oil
salt
freshly ground black pepper

1. Cut the filets into ½-inch-wide strips and put the strips in a shallow glass or earthenware dish. Cover the fish with lime juice. Chill, covered, for 6 hours, or until the fish is white and tender.

2. Gently stir in the remaining ingredients and keep the seviche cold until ready to serve.

BOILED LOBSTER

Serves 2

3 quarts boiling water
1 tablespoon salt
2 live lobsters, 1½ to 2 pounds each (small ones are more tender)
½ cup or more melted or Clarified Butter (see page 79)

1. Bring the water to a rapid boil in a 6-quart pot. Add the salt. Grab the lobsters behind their heads and plunge them into the water. Cover and let simmer for 5 minutes for the first pound of each lobster and 3 minutes per pound thereafter.

2. Take the lobsters out of the water. Serve with the hot butter, nutcrackers and plenty of napkins.

LOBSTER SALAD

Serves 4

1½ cups cooked lobster meat
½ pound fresh mushrooms, sliced
1 pint fresh raspberries
6 tablespoons olive oil
2 tablespoons sherry wine vinegar
2 tablespoons Dijon mustard
1 tablespoon chopped fresh or 1 teaspoon crushed dried tarragon
2 tablespoons sour cream
salt
freshly ground black pepper
4 kiwi fruit

1. Chill the lobster meat, mushrooms and raspberries. Beat the oil, vinegar, mustard, herbs and sour cream together with a whisk. Season to taste with salt and pepper.

2. When ready to serve, peel and slice the kiwi and arrange the lobster meat, mushrooms and fruit on individual plates. Spoon the dressing over all.

SHELLING A LOBSTER. Lay the lobster on its back. With a heavy knife, split it down the middle without going through the back.

Arch the tail toward the back and break it off. Either push the tail meat out or use scissors to cut through the undershell and lift out the meat.

Crack the claws in the center with a nutcracker and the meat will come out easily.

CANTONESE LOBSTER

Serves 2

2 1½-pound lobsters
flour
1 cup peanut oil
2 cloves garlic, chopped
4 ounces ground raw pork
1 teaspoon yellow bean sauce
½ cup Pork Broth (see page 103)
1 teaspoon sugar
1 teaspoon peeled chopped fresh ginger root
2 scallions, sliced
salt

1. With a cleaver, chop the raw lobsters into large chunks (see page 105), leaving the claws whole. Roll the chunks, shells and all, in flour. In a large skillet, heat the oil over medium high heat, then sauté until the shells are red and the meat is white, about 8 to 10 minutes.

2. Remove the pieces of lobster and drain on paper towel. Drain off all the peanut oil except 2 tablespoons. Sauté the garlic and pork in the oil until the pork is brown, about 8 to 10 minutes. Stir in the bean sauce, broth, salt, sugar and ginger, then add the lobster pieces and continue to cook for 5 minutes. Stir in the scallions and serve immediately.

CRAB AND SHRIMP BOIL

Serves 6

Fresh from the market, these compatible crustaceans are boiled with a combination of spices and herbs called "crab boil" or "shrimp boil." They're then presented, shell and all, with melted butter and crusty bread—and the fun begins.

6 quarts water
1 lemon, sliced
¼ cup whole pickling spice
1 tablespoon salt
2 bay leaves
12 live blue-shell crabs
3 pounds jumbo shrimp
1 pound butter, melted
3 lemons, cut into wedges

1. Bring the water to a rolling boil over high heat in an 8-quart pot. Add the sliced lemon and seasonings and boil 2 minutes. Drop in the crabs and shrimp; when the water returns to a full boil, drain the shellfish and rinse with cold water.

2. Serve at once with melted butter and lemon wedges. Have plenty of picks, sharp knives and mallets on hand.

SHELLING A CRAB. Pull off the apron covering the crab's belly. Discard the gills, intestinal vein and stomach. Reserve the green liver (tomalley) and orange roe.

Use a pick or sharp knife to dig out the crab meat found on either side of the body under the gills.

Gently crack the claws with a mallet and pull or suck out the meat.

PEKING CRAB AND VEGETABLES

Serves 4

A subtle rainbow of pink crab, pale and dark green vegetables and white sauce makes this Peking entrée.

2 pounds Alaskan king crab legs, cut into 6-inch lengths
1 bunch broccoli tops
1 head Chinese cabbage (siu choy), coarsely chopped
4 teaspoons cornstarch
1½ cups Pork Broth (see page 103)
¼ teaspoon sugar
salt

1. Broil the crab legs for 5 to 6 minutes each side. (If using frozen crab legs, do not thaw first.) Steam the broccoli and the cabbage separately (see page 12) until tender but still crisp. Arrange the crab, broccoli and cabbage in an attractive pattern on a large platter, then prepare the sauce.

2. In a saucepan, combine the cornstarch, broth, sugar and salt and cook over medium heat, stirring constantly until the sauce thickens slightly. Spoon the sauce evenly over the vegetables and crab and serve.

FRESH SHRIMP WITH CHIVE BUTTER

Serves 4

½ teaspoon salt
1 stalk celery with leaves, chopped
1 bay leaf
3 whole peppercorns
1 pound raw shrimp in the shell
1 recipe Chive Butter (page 79)

1. Bring 2 cups of water to a rolling boil in a big pot. Add the salt, celery, bay leaf and peppercorns and let boil for 2 minutes.

2. Drop in the shrimp. As soon as the water returns to a full boil, remove from heat. Drain, shell and devein (see page 108) while warm. Keep the shrimp warm on a platter.

3. Top with chive butter. If shrimp have cooled, run platter under the broiler and broil 2 to 3 minutes, or until hot again.

Traditional Cajun Shrimp Etoufée combines shellfish, seasonings and fish stock.

SHRIMP ETOUFFEE

Serves 4

Shrimp Cajun style. Etouffée means "smothered."

¼ cup flour
½ cup butter
1 cup chopped onion
½ cup chopped green pepper
½ cup chopped celery, including leaves
3 cloves garlic, finely minced
1 pound raw shrimp, shelled and deveined (see page 108)
¼ teaspoon cayenne pepper
1 tablespoon lemon juice
½ cup thinly sliced scallions

2 tablespoons minced parsley
1 cup water or Fish Stock (see page 58)
salt
freshly ground black pepper

1. Make a brown roux by combining the flour and butter in a 5-quart saucepan. Cook the roux over medium heat, *stirring constantly,* until it turns golden, about 15 to 20 minutes.

2. Add the onion, green pepper, celery and garlic and sauté for 20 minutes.

3. Add the remaining ingredients. Bring to a boil, lower the heat and simmer for 10 to 12 minutes, or until the shrimp are tender, stirring occasionally. Season with salt and pepper. Serve over long-grain rice (see page 205).

CREVETTES EN FOLIE
"Extravagant" Shrimp

Serves 2

10 bay prawns or jumbo shrimp
2 cups water
1 cup dry white wine
2 cloves garlic, peeled
2 shallots, peeled
1 clove
1 bouquet garni of 1 sprig thyme, 1 bay leaf, 1 sprig parsley and a 2-inch strip of orange rind
3 carrots
½ fennel bulb
1 celery heart
2 medium leeks, washed
pinch saffron
¼ teaspoon cinnamon
¼ teaspoon sugar
pinch cayenne pepper
salt
freshly ground black pepper

4 fresh mint leaves
1 teaspoon peeled, minced fresh ginger
3-inch strip orange peel, slivered
3 drops orange juice
1 tablespoon minced parsley
2 tablespoons minced onion

1. If the prawns have heads, cut them off and reserve. Shell and devein the prawns. Make a court bouillon by combining the water, wine, garlic, shallots, clove and bouquet garni in a large saucepan and bring the mixture to a boil.

2. Chop all the vegetables into large pieces and put them in the bouillon in the order listed, timed so the carrots cook about 15 or 20 minutes, the fennel about 10 to 12 minutes, the celery and leeks 7 to 10 minutes. They should all be cooked but firm. Season with saffron, cinnamon, sugar, cayenne, salt and pepper to taste.

3. Put the vegetables and a bit of the bouillon in individual soup bowls and keep warm. If there were prawn heads, simmer them in the bouillon for 5 minutes. Remove the heads and discard. Simmer the prawns for 3 minutes, or until pink.

4. Add the prawn in a star pattern to the soup bowls, garnish with mint, ginger, orange peel, juice, parsley and onion. Serve immediately—speed is essential. The broth can be used for sauces.

HOT SHRIMP MOUSSE
WITH SAUCE AURORE

Serves 4

Delicate pink mousse was once not a possibility in the home kitchen; sieving it by hand took hours. Now, with a blender or food processor, its lightness is close to instant.

SHELLING SHRIMP. Hold shrimp by the tail and peel off the outer covering. Discard the shells or add them to the cooking water.

DEVEINING SHRIMP. Slit the back of the shrimp with the point of a sharp knife. Discard the black intestinal vein.

1 pound filet of sole, well chilled (cold fish will produce a better purée in the machine)
¼ pound peeled raw baby shrimp, well chilled
½ teaspoon salt
pinch of freshly ground black pepper
⅛ teaspoon freshly ground nutmeg
3 eggs
2 cups heavy cream
1 recipe Sauce Aurore (see page 73)

1. Preheat the oven to 325°F. Grease 4 individual 1-cup baking dishes or custard cups. Process the sole filets in the blender or food processor until coarsely chopped. Add the shrimp and process until both are finely chopped, then blend in the seasoning and eggs for a few seconds. With the motor still running, slowly add the cream in a steady stream until it is completely incorporated.

2. Pour this mixture into the baking dishes and put them in a pan with enough hot water to come halfway up the sides of the baking dishes. Bake in the middle of the oven for 15 to 20 minutes, or until firm.

3. While the mousse bakes, make the sauce. Unmold and serve warm with sauce.

SHRIMP WITH COCONUT MILK AND PEAS

Serves 4 to 6

A succulent Indian way with shrimp.

2 pounds raw shrimp, shelled and deveined (see page 108)
2 tablespoons cider vinegar
1 teaspoon salt
2 cups grated fresh coconut
½ cup coriander seeds
2½ cups warm water
¼ cup corn oil
2 tablespoons grated fresh ginger root
2 cloves garlic, chopped
1 small onion, chopped
2 teaspoons turmeric
1 teaspoon ground cumin
½ teaspoon ground black mustard seeds
½ teaspoon ground white mustard seeds
1 cup fresh peas or 1 10-ounce package frozen peas, thawed
2 tablespoons chopped fresh coriander

1. In a large bowl, marinate the shrimp in vinegar and salt for at least 1 hour. In a blender or food processor, finely chop the coconut and coriander seeds with 1 cup warm water. Add the remaining water, then strain the liquid through cheesecloth into a bowl, squeezing out all the moisture, and reserve the liquid.

2. In a large skillet, heat the oil and sauté the ginger, garlic and onion for 5 minutes. Stir in the shrimp with its marinade and sauté until the shrimp are pink, about 3 minutes. Add the coconut liquid, turmeric, cumin and mustard seeds and simmer for 15 minutes to let the flavors meld, stirring occasionally.

3. Add the peas and salt to taste. Simmer 5 minutes more. Serve with chopped coriander sprinkled on top.

MUSSELS WITH RAVIGOTE SAUCE

Serves 2

A hot Ravigote Sauce appears on page 74. This cold mustard dressing of the same name is a natural for cold shellfish.

¾ cup dry white wine
1 bay leaf
4 whole cloves
18 mussels, scrubbed and debearded (see page 110)
2 tablespoons red wine vinegar
5 tablespoons olive oil
2 tablespoons minced onion
1 tablespoon Dijon mustard
1 hard-boiled egg, sieved
1 tablespoon fresh chopped or ½ teaspoon dried chervil
1 tablespoon chopped parsley
salt
freshly ground black pepper

1. In a heavy saucepan or skillet, bring the wine, bay leaf and cloves to a boil. Reduce the heat, add the mussels, cover and simmer for 8 to 10 minutes, or until the shells open. Drain and remove the top shell of each mussel, leaving the mollusks in their bottom shells. Arrange on a platter, cover and chill.

2. Make the dressing by combining the remaining ingredients in a bowl and beating with a whisk until thick. Cover the mussels with the sauce and keep chilled until ready to serve.

Crab Meat and Artichoke Ravigote. Arrange crab meat on cooked cold artichoke bottoms and cover with cold ravigote sauce for a first course.

PREPARING MUSSELS. Discard any broken or heavy mussels—they're probably filled with sand. Scrub them well and remove the beard by pulling firmly.

When serving mussels out of the shell, you might want to pull off the brown border and discard it.

PREPARING CLAMS. Scrub hard-shell clams well and soak in water for 30 minutes to get rid of the sand. Insert a stiff-bladed knife near the hinge, twist and the shell will open. Cut the muscle by running the knife around the edge.

PREPARING OYSTERS. Hold an oyster in a cloth towel to protect your hands. Insert a rounded oyster knife ½ inch from the hinge. Twist the shell open and cut the muscle.

SAFFRON MUSSELS

Serves 1

Steamed mussels cook in a flash and yield plenty of savory broth to soak up with crusty bread.

1 quart mussels
1 cup dry white wine
2 shallots, chopped
⅛ teaspoon saffron threads
¼ cup chopped parsley
½ lemon

1. Remove the beards and scrub the mussel shells well with a stiff brush and rinse. Discard any open or cracked ones.

2. In a deep saucepan, combine the wine, shallots, saffron and parsley and bring to a boil over high heat. Reduce the heat, add the mussels, cover and simmer until the shells open—8 to 10 minutes. Discard any that haven't opened.

3. Serve the mussels in a shallow soup bowl with their broth, the lemon half (to squeeze over them) and French bread.

OYSTERS OR CLAMS ON THE HALF SHELL

Serves 1

To many shellfish lovers, raw "on the half shell" is the only proper way to eat cherrystone and other small hard-shell clams.

6 to 12 live oysters or clams, scrubbed, soaked and
   chilled
2 cups crushed ice
¼ lemon
freshly ground black pepper

1. Scrub the shells clean under running water. For clams especially, a 30-minute soaking in salt water helps dislodge sand from inside the shell. Keep the cleaned mollusks well chilled until you are ready to shuck them and eat.

2. Open the shells just before eating, as shown on page 110 for oysters and page 110 for clams. Open the shells over a bowl to catch the juices. Discard the flatter half of the oyster shell, and either half of the clam shell.

3. Make a bed of crushed ice in a shallow bowl and put the half shells with the raw oysters or clams on the ice so that they are held level. Strain the juice from the bowl through cheesecloth and pour the juice over the oysters or clams.

4. Season each raw oyster or clam with a few drops of lemon juice and black pepper. Then, eat the oysters or clams and drink the briny juice from the shell.

GRILLED SCALLOPS

Serves 4

Marinated in fresh ginger and soy sauce, the scallop's sweet taste is well balanced by the smoky charcoal flavor.

2 pounds sea scallops
salt
freshly ground black pepper
½ cup peanut oil
1 clove garlic, chopped
3 tablespoons slivered fresh ginger
¼ cup Japanese soy sauce
¼ cup dry sherry
juice of 1 lemon
4 scallions, sliced

1. Put the scallops in a shallow dish and sprinkle lightly with salt and pepper. Mix the remaining ingredients in a bowl and pour over the scallops. Marinate for 1 hour at room temperature or longer in the refrigerator.

2. Meanwhile, prepare the charcoal fire and light it. Drain the scallops and divide them evenly among four long skewers or put them in a grill basket. Grill 6 inches from the heat over gray coals for 5 to 6 minutes on each side.

Note. The scallops can also be broiled indoors. Try using 1-inch chunks of firm-fleshed fish such as cod, haddock or halibut.

SCALLOP AND VEGETABLE SALAD

Serves 4

A study in green and white, this refreshing summer salad is a study in textures as well: creamy avocado, tender scallops, and crisp vegetables.

1 pound sea scallops
approximately ¼ cup lime juice
salt
4 scallions, sliced
¾ cup olive oil
¼ cup red wine vinegar
2 tablespoons drained capers
1 clove garlic, minced
1 tablespoon chopped fresh or 1 teaspoon dried dill
2 ripe avocados
arugula leaves
2 cups small cauliflower pieces
1 small zucchini, sliced
¼ pound green beans, cut into long slivers
1 pound fresh green peas, shelled

1. Put the scallops in a small skillet and cover with lime juice. Add salt to taste and scallions and simmer, uncovered, for 5 minutes, or until the scallops are white. Drain and chill.

2. While the fish chills, beat the olive oil, vinegar, capers, garlic, and dill together in a small bowl. Add salt to taste and let stand at room temperature.

3. Cut the avocados in half and remove the pits. Rub the raw surfaces with lime juice to keep them from turning brown. Fill the cavity of each avocado half with cold scallops. Make a bed of arugula leaves on a platter and arrange the filled avocados and raw vegetables on top. Beat the vinaigrette again, pour it evenly over the salad and serve.

SUSHI AND SASHIMI

Japan's contribution to our love of seafood has been the incredibly popular sushi and sashimi; shops selling the fresh, raw fish morsels have cropped up on every other corner in Los Angeles, and Japanese restaurants have proliferated in all major U.S. cities. And now we want to bring it home.

Sashimi are the simple raw fish filets, served as is, with rice alongside. Sushi is slightly more complex: the fish is served on top of small mounds of vinegared rice with a touch of *wasabi* (green horseradish) or rolled inside a seaweed *(nori)* wrapper with the rice and *wasabi.* Both are served with tiny bowls of soy sauce and pink pickled ginger slices.

Sushi and sashimi combinations are endless: fluke, squid, tuna, salmon, shrimp, lobster, crab, caviar, eel can be dressed with herbs or vegetables. The shape of the rolls varies, too. Cylinders and cones are the most common.

To undertake sushi or sashimi at home, you need a sharp eye and a sharp knife. Raw fish, even more than cooked fish, must be very fresh, so go to a trusted fish market. Keep the fish refrigerated or packed in ice.

To cut raw fish for sushi or sashimi, use your sharpest knife and resharpen it as you go along. Filets sliced against the grain have the best texture. With a little practice, you'll be able to make paper-thin slices or tiny strips. The Japanese cut the fish in many ways: thin, flat slices, strips, cubes, rectangles and even shreds.

Japanese rice, available at Oriental markets, is similar to our unconverted long-grain white rice. The Japanese steam their rice and prefer it a little sticky so it can be eaten with chopsticks.

VINEGARED RICE FOR SUSHI

Enough for approximately 36 sushi

3 cups uncooked long-grain rice
3½ cups cold water
1 cup *su* (rice wine vinegar)
½ cup sugar
1 teaspoon salt

1. Put the raw rice in a colander and rinse it under cold running water until the water is clear. This will remove the powdery starch. Drain the rice and put it in a heavy 3-quart saucepan. Add the cold water and let stand undisturbed for 1 hour to soften the grains slightly. Bring the water to a boil, turn down the heat, cover tightly and simmer for 20 minutes. Turn off the heat and let the rice stand, covered, for 5 minutes.

2. While the rice is cooking, put the *su,* sugar and salt in a saucepan and heat to a boil.

3. Spread the cooked rice out in a shallow roasting or baking pan and slowly start stirring in the vinegar mixture, fanning the rice with a piece of cardboard or hand fan at the same time. By simultaneously cooling the rice and mixing it with vinegar mixture you coat the grains and make them shiny and lustrous; letting the rice simply soak up the vinegar makes it dull and lumpy. When the rice is thoroughly coated with the vinegar mixture, it's ready for making sushi.

PRESSED SUSHI

1. Line an 8-inch-square pan with plastic wrap. Spoon in a ¾-inch layer of vinegared rice. Make a paste of dried *wasabi* and water. Brush on a layer of *wasabi,* then cover with thin slices of mackerel, sole, flounder, salmon or whatever caught your eye at the market. Cover with plastic wrap and a piece of cardboard cut to fit the pan. Weigh down the cardboard with canned goods or weights and chill. When ready to serve, discard the top plastic wrap and use the bottom layer of plastic wrap to remove the sushi from the pan. Cut the block of sushi into rectangles ¾ inch by 1½ inches.

SHAPED SUSHI

1. Shape the vinegared rice into ovals about 1½ inches long and ¾ inch wide with moistened fingers. Make a paste of dried *wasabi* and water and brush it over the top of each rice oval. Cover with thinly sliced sashimi filets (flounder, salmon, sea bass, red snapper, scallops and tuna are good choices) or shelled, deveined raw shrimp that's been butterflied to lie flat, strips of raw squid, octopus or crab.

ROLLED SUSHI

1. Start with a sheet of *nori* (dried seaweed) laid near the edge of a bamboo sushi mat or a small towel. Spread a ½-inch layer of vinegared rice on top. Make a fairly even row of caviar, thin omelet, small slices of fresh or pickled vegetables or a slice of raw fish down the center (lengthwise), or combine them for a mosaic effect. Season with *wasabi.* Use the mat or towel to roll up the seaweed combo very tightly. It may take two attempts to keep it tight. Wrap the roll in plastic wrap and chill. When you're ready to serve, cut the roll into 1-inch slices.

Clockwise from left: **Shad roe, frogs' legs, squid, eels, octopus and snails**

SQUID

Squid (calamari) are very popular and common among Mediterranean gourmets, and are becoming so with us. They come fresh or frozen and taste like very firm shrimp. Fresh squid can be simmered in salted water for 15 to 20 minutes to tenderize the meat before proceeding with recipes.

Cooked squid is easier to dismantle and skin. Remove the head just below the eyes. (Rub the skin off the tentacles for a succulent mouthful in recipes.) Take out the ink sac intact if possible. Pull the long, bonelike, plastic-looking, transparent shell out of the center of the body. Finally, rub off the dark skin and the floppy finlike flaps. The remaining oval core of meat, which is the part of squid used in recipes, is sliced crosswise into thin rings or stuffed.

Poached squid can be served cold in a vinaigrette dressing (see Octopus Vinaigrette, page 114) or cooked further with seasonings.

BROILED SQUID

Serves 2

1 cup uncooked squid rings
2 tablespoons melted butter
1 teaspoon chopped fresh or ¼ teaspoon crushed dried rosemary
¼ teaspoon salt
freshly ground black pepper

1. Put the squid rings in a shallow broiling pan. Brush the squid with melted butter and sprinkle the top with the rosemary, salt and pepper.

2. Broil 2 to 3 inches from the heat source just long enough to brown the squid—2 or 3 minutes. Serve hot with lemon wedges.

SQUID WITH LINGUINE AND PEAS

Serves 6

½ cup olive oil
2 cloves garlic, chopped
1½ pounds uncooked squid, trimmed and sliced
4 cups chopped tomatoes
1 tablespoon chopped parsley
½ teaspoon dried marjoram
freshly ground black pepper
salt
½ cup dry white wine
2 cups fresh or frozen peas
1 pound linguine, cooked and drained
¼ cup freshly grated Parmesan

1. In a large heavy saucepan, heat the oil over medium heat and sauté the garlic for 2 minutes. Add the squid, tomatoes and seasonings and sauté another 2 minutes. Stir in the wine and peas, bring to a boil, reduce the heat and simmer, covered, for 8 to 10 minutes. Season with salt and pepper.

2. Toss the linguine with the hot sauce on a warm platter. Sprinkle with Parmesan and serve at once.

OCTOPUS

Much prized in Japan and increasingly appreciated in the United States, the menacing octopus yields very sweet, slightly chewy meat. It takes several hours of simmering to tenderize even a baby octopus, so keep your purchase less than 3½ pounds. Stores that sell them usually remove the ink sac and clean the octopus.

Simmer the octopus, covered in salted water, for 2 to 3 hours, or until the tentacle meat can easily be pierced with the point of a knife. Drain and cool. Break off the tentacles and remove the black skin and suction cups that cover them. They will peel off effortlessly if they have been cooked enough. The tentacle meat is now ready to use.

OCTOPUS VINAIGRETTE

Serves 2 to 4

1 cup cooked and slivered octopus meat
1 tablespoon lemon juice
3 tablespoons olive oil
1 clove garlic, minced
1 tablespoon chopped parsley
salt
freshly ground black pepper
chicory or romaine leaves

1. Mix all the ingredients except the lettuce in a small bowl. Chill and serve the salad on lettuce-lined plates.

FRIED OCTOPUS WITH PESTO

Serves 6

tentacle meat from a cooked 3- to 3½-pound octopus
2 eggs, beaten
1½ cups fine dry bread crumbs
¾ teaspoon chopped fresh or ¼ teaspoon dried oregano
½ teaspoon chopped fresh or ½ teaspoon dried basil
1 tablespoon grated Parmesan
corn oil to fill a skillet to a depth of 1 inch
½ recipe Pesto (see page 187)

Fried Octopus with Pesto

1. Cut the octopus meat into bite-size pieces. Dip each piece into the beaten eggs and then into the bread crumbs that have been mixed with the herbs and cheese.

2. Heat the oil to 375°F and add the octopus. Fry until golden brown on both sides, about 5 minutes.

3. Drain the fried octopus on paper towel and serve with pesto.

EEL

Eels are sold fresh (sometimes still wiggling) or smoked. These slippery creatures have a tender, mild white meat which can be skinned and broiled with herbs or melted butter in minutes.

Smoked eel, skinned and flaked, makes a wonderful cold salad mixed with vegetables and a mayonnaise and sour cream dressing.

JELLIED EEL MOLD

Makes 1 quart

An unusual and beautiful cold summer dish.

1 fresh eel (2 pounds), skinned and cut into 2-inch
    pieces
1 cup Chicken Stock (see page 58)
½ cup dry white wine
1 envelope unflavored gelatin
¼ cup cold water
½ cup sliced celery and leaves
1 cooked carrot, cut into thin slices
1 dill pickle, sliced
2 tablespoons chopped parsley

1. Cover the eel with salted water in a saucepan and simmer, covered, for 15 to 20 minutes, or until tender. Drain and cool. Remove the meat from the bones and dice it.

2. In a large bowl, mix the eel, stock and wine. In a small saucepan, stir the gelatin into the cold water to soften. Then stir over low heat until the gelatin is completely dissolved. Add to the stock and wine and mix thoroughly. Cover the bowl and refrigerate until the gelatin mixture is syrupy—about 30 minutes to 1 hour.

3. Oil a 1-quart mold. Fold the celery, carrot, pickle and parsley into the partially jelled aspic and pour the mixture into the mold.

4. Chill until set—at least 2 hours. To unmold, dip the mold into warm water for a few seconds, tap to loosen and invert the salad onto a platter.

SHAD ROE

Early spring marks the time the shad start upstream to spawn, and that amounts to Christmas for shad roe fanatics. Enclosed in their natural membrane, these much-prized fish eggs are usually sold in pairs enough for two servings. When cooked they taste like mild caviar.

The simplest and most classic way to prepare shad roe is to carefully cut the pairs apart and sauté them in butter over medium heat for 10 to 15 minutes, then season with salt, pepper, parsley and lemon. Overcooking dries out the roe and kills their delicate flavor.

POACHED SHAD ROE WITH WINE SAUCE

Serves 4

Simmered in wine and pickling spice, shad roe is then sauced with a simple cream and mushroom combination.

2 pairs shad roe
½ to ¾ cup dry white wine
1 bay leaf
6 peppercorns
2 whole cloves
¼ cup butter
¼ pound fresh mushrooms, sliced
¼ cup flour
1 cup heavy cream
⅓ cup chopped parsley
salt
freshly ground black pepper

1. Cut the shad roe in two and put them in a heavy skillet. (Don't use aluminum or cast iron.) Cover the roe with wine and add the bay leaf, peppercorns and cloves. Bring to a simmer over medium heat, lower the heat, cover tightly, and continue simmering for 10 to 15 minutes, or until the roe feel firm to the touch.

2. Drain off the poaching liquid, saving ½ cup for the sauce, and keep the roe warm. In a heavy saucepan, melt the butter over medium heat and sauté the mushrooms for 1 or 2 minutes. Stir in the flour and cook another 1 or 2 minutes. Stir in the poaching liquid, cream and parsley and continue cooking until the sauce is smooth and beginning to thicken—about 5 minutes. Season with salt and pepper.

3. Put the roe on warm plates and spoon the sauce over them. Crisp slices of garlic bread are a good accompaniment.

SNAILS

Earthy but fine, *escargots* are the very essence of Burgundy (along with the wine, of course), especially when drenched in a classic snail butter with parsley and garlic. They are available fresh, still in their shells, or canned without their shells. The lovely shells can be washed and reused, or fresh shells can be purchased to go with canned snails. This is important because the traditional way to prepare snails is packed back in their home with butter and herbs.

ESCARGOTS DE BOURGOGNE
Snails in Butter and Garlic

Serves 4

A rich and redolent first course, escargots *should be served with French bread to capture the remarkable juices.*

1 tablespoon butter
2 small carrots, minced
6 shallots, minced
1 leek, minced
2 cloves garlic, minced
½ cup dry red wine
24 canned snails, drained, with 24 shells
¼ cup softened butter
¼ cup chopped parsley
2 cloves garlic, minced

1. In a heavy saucepan, melt the butter over medium heat. When it is hot, add the carrots, shallots, leek and garlic and sauté 5 minutes.

2. Add the wine and snails and bring to a boil over high heat. Reduce the heat and simmer, covered, for 10 minutes. Remove the snails with a slotted spoon and set aside to cool. Boil the liquid until the vegetable mixture is almost dry.

3. Cream the butter with the parsley and garlic.

4. Assemble the snails by putting first a tiny dollop of the vegetable mixture, then a cooked snail in each shell. Seal the hole in each shell with some of the creamed butter mixture. If the snails sit for a while before cooking, the flavor will be all the better (refrigerate them if more than an hour).

5. When ready to eat, preheat the oven to 400°F. Arrange the snails on special snail dishes, with an indentation for each shell, or put them in a shallow baking dish. Bake for 10 minutes, or until very hot. Serve with shell holders, if you have them, and seafood forks.

FROGS' LEGS

In a blind taste test, you'd think you were eating especially mild and tender chicken. Special varieties of frogs are raised for the table, and only their hind legs are considered edible. A delicacy, frogs' legs are available fresh, frozen and canned.

Four pairs make a serving. Many say they are at their best dusted with flour, salt and pepper and sautéed in butter and oil over medium high heat for 5 minutes.

FROGS' LEGS WRAPPED IN BACON

Serves 4

Frogs' legs have very little fat, so wrapping them in bacon keeps them basted during broiling. Lemon juice and herbs balance the richness of the bacon.

16 pairs frogs' legs (about 4 pounds)
2 tablespoons lemon juice
freshly ground black pepper
1 tablespoon chopped parsley
½ teaspoon dried crushed or 1½ teaspoons chopped fresh tarragon
½ teaspoon dried crushed or 1½ teaspoons chopped fresh chervil
16 slices bacon

1. Preheat the broiler. Sprinkle the frogs' legs with lemon juice, pepper and herbs. Wrap each pair in a slice of bacon, secured with a wooden toothpick. Put the wrapped frogs' legs on a shallow broiling pan.

2. Broil 4 inches from the heat for 5 or 6 minutes per side, or until the bacon is crisp. Serve hot.

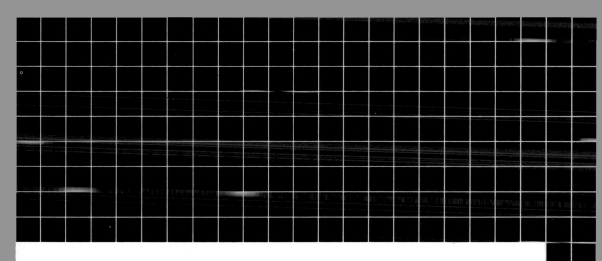

Poultry

It's no wonder that we've rediscovered poultry. Chefs have long acknowledged its versatility; as Brillat-Savarin wrote in the nineteenth century, "Poultry is for the cook what canvas is to the painter."

From the pearl-white flesh of a tiny game hen to the rich dark meat of a gamy duck, the tastes satisfy our need for both the light and the rich: something that brings out the best of sweetly frail marjoram or stands up to a port wine sauce.

With its built-in options of into-the-sauté-pan-and-onto-the-plate, boned chicken breasts have replaced deep-fried chicken as an American classic, and rosy pink duck breasts with mango are giving duck à l'orange a good chase. Some things can never be improved on, however: roast turkey remains a year-round classic, and rightfully so, with the newly popular option of freshly killed birds. Even Cornish game hens are available fresh.

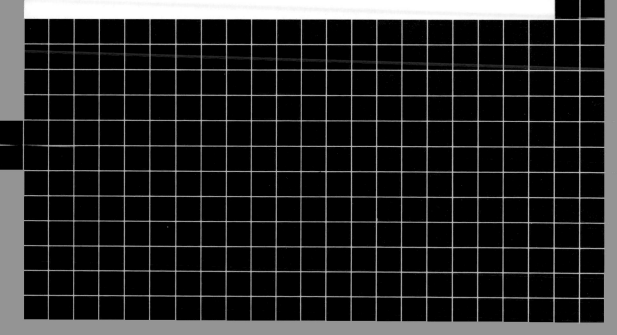

Chicken

THE ESSENTIALS

The only thing more variable than the ways to cook chicken are the names for marketing different ages and weights of essentially the same bird. The names most used for the different chicken sizes are listed below.

Broiler. Almost interchangeable with fryers and often labeled "broiler-fryer," these are 1½- to 3-pound chickens that are 7 to 8 weeks old. Broilers are frequently sold split in half. They can be cut up for sautéing or frying as well as broiling, and whole ones can be roasted.

Fryer. Really the same as broilers, but a fryer can weigh as much as 4 pounds and is sold whole, quartered or cut into pieces. Fryers are certainly tender enough to broil. The French word *poulet* refers to a broiler-fryer-size chicken.

Pullet. A term used more in butcher shops than supermarkets, pullet refers to small (4- to 5-pound) roasting or stewing chickens. They make excellent chicken soup.

Roaster. These are larger chickens that weigh between 5 and 7 pounds. Slaughtered at 3 to 5 months, they are usually sold whole. They are best when roasted and carved.

Stewing chicken. These older birds—a year or more—weigh from 6 to 7 pounds. They are too tough to roast, but poaching or braising makes them tender and brings out their rich flavor, which is superior to that of younger birds. These are the best chickens for soup. They are often referred to as fowl.

Capon. A large and meaty emasculated rooster, the capon is the tastiest roasting chicken. A 6- to 9-pound bird raised in 4 to 5 months is just as tender as a fryer. A layer of fat just under the skin makes capons naturally self-basting and very succulent.

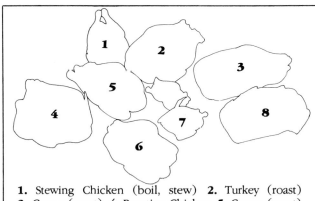

1. Stewing Chicken (boil, stew) **2.** Turkey (roast) **3.** Goose (roast) **4.** Roasting Chicken **5.** Capon (roast) **6.** Broiler-fryer **7.** Game Hens (roast, broil) **8.** Duck (roast)

The best-tasting chickens are fresh-killed young birds that are farm-raised. The exercise and varied diet (with no hormones) enhance their flavor. However, unless you raise your own, these are a rare luxury these days.

Commercial chickens today are mass-produced in carefully controlled environments to ensure the heaviest weight from the least food in the shortest amount of time. These are, for the most part, the only chickens in our markets. Even kosher chickens and the chickens sold in most live-poultry stores are mass-produced. When very fresh, the young birds are plump and tender, but not very flavorful. The older birds have more taste.

Freshness, not brand name, is the key to the best mass-produced chickens. The U.S. Agriculture Department says that 7 days is the shelf life of fresh chicken when it is properly stored (refrigerated). You can buy from a fresh poultry market, a trusted butcher or supermarket that has a high turnover.

Good fresh chicken will have no odor. The skin will be smooth and there will be no discoloration. Color of the skin, however, simply indicates what the chicken was fed. A yellow skin means the feed was corn; white skin means it was wheat and barley. Pale yellow indicates a hybrid-corn feed. Preferences tend to be regional and ethnic. Areas with strong Northern European populations prefer white-skinned chickens; Italian and Spanish communities think yellow-skinned chickens look healthier. Southerners and Midwesterners are accustomed to pale yellow skin.

Since freshness is so important, chickens should not be

kept in the refrigerator more than a day or two. If you are not using the chicken right away, freeze it in an airtight wrap and maintain it at 0° F. Remove the giblets, which deteriorate faster, and freeze them separately. Chicken can be frozen for up to 6 months; the giblets only 3 months.

To keep a chicken in the refrigerator, remove the giblets and excess fat and wash the bird under cold water. Pat dry and wrap loosely in wax paper or butcher's paper. (The airtight environment of the supermarket wrapping makes a breeding ground for bacteria.) Rubbing the chicken with lemon juice will help keep it fresh in the refrigerator. Store the giblets separately.

There are probably more recipes for chicken than for any other meat. Happily though, if you master the basic techniques of several cooking methods, all the recipes you come across will be simple variations on a theme.

BASIC ROAST CHICKEN

Serves approximately 1 person per pound

Roast chicken is good either hot or cold, seasoned simply with salt and pepper, with lemon or herbs or with more esoteric Oriental spices. It needs scarcely more attention than putting it in the oven.

1 5- to 9-pound roasting chicken
salt
black pepper
½ cup melted butter

1. Preheat the oven to 425° F. Wash the chicken under cold water and dry. (Use the giblets for stock.) Sprinkle the chicken inside and out with salt and pepper, truss by tying the wing tips to the body and the leg bones together with string, and lay it on its side on the rack of a shallow roasting pan. Brush the top with butter.

2. Roast the chicken for 15 minutes, basting once or twice with butter. Turn it over onto the other side, brush the top with butter and let it roast another 15 minutes, basting once or twice with butter. For the third and final roasting period, put the bird breast side up. Baste with the pan juices and let it cook until done—count on 15 to 20 minutes per pound altogether for an unstuffed bird that was at room temperature at the start. Test by pricking the meaty part of the leg; if the juices run clear rather than pink, it is done. On a large bird, a meat thermometer in the thigh should register 180° F.

3. Let the roast stand for 15 minutes to settle before you cut the trussing strings and carve (see page 135). To make a sauce, pour off the fat and deglaze the pan with chicken stock or dry white wine.

Basic Roast Chicken is simple and delicious.

Herb Chicken. Fill the cavity of the bird with several sprigs of fresh herbs or ½ teaspoon dried herbs and add 1 teaspoon chopped fresh or ½ teaspoon dried tarragon to the basting butter. Substitute basil, rosemary, oregano, sage, dill or any other herb and 2 garlic cloves, if you like.

Lemon Chicken. Cut a lemon in quarters and rub the chicken inside and out with it before salting and peppering. Put the lemon quarters, several sprigs of parsley and 2 cloves of garlic in the cavity before roasting. You can also toss in a quartered onion and several more cloves of garlic.

POULE AU POT
Poached Chicken

Serves 6

A poached stewing hen provides 2 courses for lunch or dinner. First the broth is served; then the chicken and vegetables are presented with a horseradish sauce.

To make poached chicken with a younger bird, use chicken stock for the liquid to intensify the flavor. The cooking time will be less—about an hour.

Because it is so flavorful, poached stewing chicken, cooled, skinned and boned, makes the best cooked chicken for other recipes.

1 stewing hen, about 6 pounds
2 carrots, sliced
2 leeks, tied together
3 cloves garlic, crushed
1 onion, sliced
1 stalk celery, with leaves, sliced
salt
10 peppercorns
bouquet garni of 3 sprigs of fresh parsley, 3 sprigs fresh or ½ teaspoon dried thyme and 1 bay leaf
6 carrots, cut into 2-inch lengths
6 leeks, halved lengthwise
2 cups sour cream
2 or more (to taste) tablespoons prepared white horseradish

1. Wash the chicken under cold water. The giblets can be used in the poaching liquid. Put the chicken, the first set of vegetables, 1 teaspoon salt, the peppercorns and the bouquet garni in a large, deep stewpot or stockpot. Add water to cover the chicken.

2. Bring the water to a boil and skim the surface. Reduce the heat so that the liquid barely simmers, partially cover the pot and let cook for 1½ hours.

3. Add the remaining carrots and leeks and let simmer

another 30 minutes. Check the chicken to see if it is ready by piercing the thigh; if the juices run clear and yellow, it is done. If not, keep checking every 10 minutes.

4. While the chicken is cooking, make the horseradish sauce by mixing the sour cream and horseradish. Salt to taste. Let it sit, covered, in the refrigerator for 30 minutes.

5. When the chicken is tender, remove it with carrots and leeks and arrange on a platter. Use the broth for soup, removing the bouquet garni and the peppercorns; salt to taste and sprinkle with fresh chopped parsley. Carve the chicken and serve with the sauce.

BASIC BROILED CHICKEN

Serves 4

Split small chickens (2-pound range) in half for 2 people; quarter larger ones to serve 4 people. Since these birds are tender but not overly flavorful, it is important to season them as they cook and to baste often. Marinating the chickens improves flavor, too.

2 2-pound broiling chickens
salt
freshly ground black pepper
¼ cup butter
1 clove garlic, minced
1 tablespoon lemon juice

1. Preheat the broiler. Split or quarter the chicken, wash under cold water and dry. Sprinkle both sides lightly with salt and pepper.

2. In a small saucepan, melt the butter and add the garlic and lemon juice. Brush this mixture over the chicken and put the chicken bone side up on the rack of a broiler pan.

3. Broil the chicken at least 6 inches from the source of heat for 15 to 20 minutes on each side, basting often. The chicken is done when the thigh juices run clear.

Herbed Chicken. Add 1 tablespoon fresh chopped or 1 teaspoon dried herbs— tarragon, basil, marjoram, oregano, parsley and/or dill—to the butter.

Marinated Chicken. Make a marinade of ⅓ cup olive oil, ⅔ cup dry white wine, 2 tablespoons chopped onion, 1 crushed garlic clove, 1 teaspoon crushed dried rosemary, salt and freshly ground black pepper. Put the chicken in a shallow pan and coat it with the marinade. Let sit at least 1 hour at room temperature, or longer in the refrigerator, turning occasionally. Drain the chicken before putting on the broiler pan; baste with the marinade every 5 minutes while broiling.

CUTTING UP POULTRY. To split into halves, turn the chicken back side up. With a sharp knife, cut through both sides of the backbone and remove it.

Open out the chicken, inside facing up. Cut through both sides of the breastbone and pull it out.

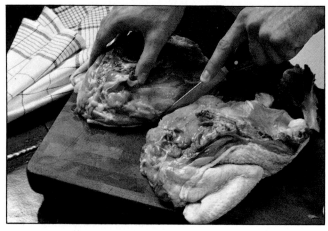

Cut the chicken into halves where the breastbone was removed.

To cut into quarters, locate the hip joint. Skin side up, fold the leg against the breast and cut along the fold line.

To remove the wing from the breast, locate the ball and socket joint. Cut through the joint until the wing and breast are separated.

To cut into eighths, find the slight indentation at the top of the joint. With the leg skin side up, cut at the indentation.

CHICKEN SAUTE WITH HERBS AND WHITE WINE

Serves 4

Chicken sauté has replaced deep-fried chicken in many of today's kitchens. By deglazing the pan after the bird is cooked, you can create hundreds of simple sauce variations. Two tricks will make sautés almost foolproof. The first is to use a heavy frying pan that's large enough to hold all the chicken in a single layer without overlapping. If crowded, the chicken will steam, not brown; if too spread out, it will cause the fat to overheat and burn. The second trick is to use butter in combination with oil. Butter alone will burn at the temperatures needed for proper browning. Of course, olive oil, chicken and bacon fat offer their own flavors.

Since this is a master recipe, we will indicate where variations can be made as we describe each step.

1 2½- to 3-pound broiler-fryer chicken, cut up
salt
freshly ground black pepper
1½ tablespoons butter
1½ tablespoons corn oil
1 tablespoon chopped fresh herbs—tarragon, basil, parsley, rosemary, dill, chervil, marjoram—or ½ teaspoon dried herbs, crumbled
½ cup dry white wine

1. Wash the chicken and dry it with paper towel. Sprinkle each piece lightly with salt and pepper.

2. In a large heavy skillet, heat the butter and oil over medium high heat; it should just coat the bottom of the pan. Add the chicken pieces, skin side down, and sauté, turning frequently, until they are golden brown. This should take about 10 minutes.

3. Lower the heat and sprinkle the chicken with the herb or herbs of your choice. (Aromatic vegetables like shallots, onions, carrots and garlic can be added here.) Cover the pan and cook for 35 to 40 minutes. Test the pieces for doneness by pressing them with a finger or cutting into the dark meat to make sure all traces of pinkness are gone. If they are springy, they are done. Remove the cooked breast pieces and keep them warm, re-cover the pan and cook the rest of the chicken (thighs and drumsticks) for an additional 10 minutes or more.

4. When the pieces are done, remove them from the pan and keep warm. Pour off the fat, but be careful not to discard the meat juices in the pan, which are full of flavor.

5. Deglaze the pan by pouring in the wine and, while it simmers over medium high heat, scraping up the browned particles in the pan with a wooden spoon. (Other liquids that can be used for deglazing include stock, aromatic fruit juice, vinegar, tomato juice and/or vegetable cooking liquid.) Let the sauce simmer a few minutes to concentrate the flavor.

6. Pour the sauce over the chicken and serve. Or enrich it with ⅓ cup heavy cream, stirring over medium high heat until it thickens slightly.

Vegetable Chicken Sauté. Add 1 small onion, 1 carrot and 1 stalk celery, all finely chopped, to the chicken in Step 3. Or add 1 small onion, 2 tomatoes and ¼ pound mushrooms, all finely chopped, at the same point. If you like, the sauce can be puréed in a blender or strained.

Chicken Sauté with Salt Pork, Pancetta or Bacon. Brown 4 slices of bacon or 2 ounces of chopped salt pork or pancetta over medium heat until the bacon is crisp or the pork fat is rendered. (If you use salt pork, omit the salt.) Use the rendered fat instead of butter and oil to brown the chicken. Add 1 teaspoon grated lemon rind with the crumbled bacon or pork.

Chicken Sauté with Mushrooms. Add ¼ pound sliced mushrooms to the chicken in Step 3. Finish the sauce with the heavy cream (see Step 6 above).

CHICKEN PROVENCALE

Serves 4

1 3- to 3½-pound chicken, cut into eighths
salt
freshly ground black pepper
¼ cup olive oil
2 green peppers, seeded and cut into strips
2 onions, thinly sliced
2 cloves garlic, minced
2 carrots, shredded
2 tomatoes, peeled, seeded and chopped
1 cup dry white wine
1½ teaspoons chopped fresh or ½ teaspoon dried rosemary
1½ teaspoons chopped fresh or ½ teaspoon dried thyme
1½ teaspoons chopped fresh or ½ teaspoon dried basil

1. Wash the chicken and pat dry. Season with salt and pepper.

2. Heat the olive oil and brown the chicken pieces on all sides in a large skillet or Dutch oven.

3. Add the remaining ingredients, cover and simmer until the chicken is tender, about 35 to 40 minutes. Skim the excess fat. Serve with steamed new potatoes and parsley.

Chicken Sauté with Herbs and White Wine (see page 123) is the basis for endless variations.

COQ AU VIN

Serves 6

An old classic, still it's perhaps the best way to braise or stew a chicken: brown it in bacon fat (or salt pork) with aromatic vegetables, then simmer with wine and herbs. In this version the flavor is intensified with a flaming of Cognac.

½ cup diced slab bacon or salt pork
1 5- to 6-pound stewing hen, cut into pieces, or 2 2½- to
    3-pound frying chickens
freshly ground black pepper
6 shallots, chopped
1 clove garlic, minced
4 carrots, cut into 2-inch lengths
¼ cup Cognac
2 cups dry red wine
bouquet garni of 1 bay leaf, 3 sprigs of fresh parsley,
    3 sprigs fresh or ½ teaspoon dried thyme and
    2 sprigs fresh or ¼ teaspoon dried rosemary
2 tablespoons butter
18 pearl onions
18 small mushrooms or ½ pound mushrooms, sliced

1. In a large heavy skillet or Dutch oven, fry the bacon pieces over medium heat until crisp. Remove them with a slotted spoon and drain on paper towel.

2. Wash the chicken pieces under cold water and pat dry. Sprinkle lightly with pepper (the bacon drippings provide enough salt). Brown the chicken in the drippings over medium high heat on both sides. Remove the chicken to a platter while you sauté the shallots, garlic and carrots over medium heat for 5 minutes.

3. Return the chicken to the pan and let it heat through. Remove from heat. Add the Cognac, and gently heat. Don't overheat or the alcohol will boil off. Turn off the heat. Light the Cognac with a match and pour it, flaming, over the chicken while you shake the pan to spread it out. Keep shaking the pan until the flames are extinguished.

4. Add the wine and bouquet garni (tied with string or in cheesecloth) to the pan. Bring to a boil over high heat, lower the heat and simmer, tightly covered, for approximately 1 hour for a stewing hen, 45 minutes for a younger bird, or until the chicken is tender.

5. While the chicken is simmering, melt the butter in a heavy skillet over very low heat and sauté the onions, covered, very slowly. Shake the pan frequently, so they cook evenly. It should take 25 to 30 minutes for the onions to be tender but not browned. Remove them with a slotted spoon. Turn up the heat and sauté the mushrooms in the onion butter for 1 or 2 minutes.

6. When the chicken is tender, skim the fat from the top of the liquid, remove the bouquet garni and add the onions and mushrooms. Let the liquid simmer another 5 minutes to heat them through. Salt if necessary and serve garnished with the bacon pieces.

CHICKEN WITH CREAM AND CALVADOS

Serves 4

When the apple trees in the Normandy fields open their first blossoms, locals begin thinking about "Poulet Vallé d'Auge" with its heavy cream and the local apple brandy or Calvados.

1 2½- to 3-pound frying or broiling chicken, cut into
    eighths
salt
freshly ground black pepper
2 tablespoons butter
1 tablespoon corn oil
¼ cup Calvados or applejack
½ cup Chicken Stock (see page 58)
2 egg yolks
½ cup heavy cream
1 tablespoon chopped fresh parsley

1. Wash the chicken under cold water and pat dry. Sprinkle lightly with salt and pepper. Brown the chicken in the butter and oil as you would in any sauté.

2. When the chicken pieces are browned, remove the pan from the burner. Heat the Calvados gently in a small saucepan (if you overheat it and evaporate the alcohol, it won't ignite). Remove from the heat, and light it with a match, taking care to hold it at arm's length. As soon as the flame has diminished, pour the flaming Calvados over the chicken pieces, shaking the pan constantly to spread the Calvados about and eventually put out the flames.

3. Return the pan to low heat, cover it and let the chicken cook until tender. Start checking in 25 or 30 minutes. When the chicken is done, remove the pieces to a warm platter while you make the sauce.

4. Skim off the fat in the pan, add the stock and then bring it to a simmer over medium heat, scraping up all the brown particles.

5. In a small bowl, beat the egg yolks briefly with the cream. Slowly add the hot pan juices, a tablespoon at a time, to the egg-cream mixture, beating all the while with a wire whisk. Keep the heat very low and the sauce won't curdle.

6. Return the sauce to the pan and cook over very low heat, stirring constantly, until it thickens enough to coat a spoon—about 5 to 6 minutes. Don't let the sauce boil.

7. Serve the chicken completely coated with the sauce and sprinkled with parsley.

Coq au Vin is an enduring classic.

Chicken with Cream and Calvados

CHICKEN WITH OLIVES

Serves 6

2 2- to 3-pound frying chickens, cut into eighths
salt
freshly ground black pepper
paprika
⅓ cup olive oil
1 large onion, chopped
2 green peppers, seeded and slivered
2 red peppers, seeded and slivered
2 cloves garlic, minced
2 pounds Italian plum tomatoes, peeled, seeded and
   chopped
1½ cups Chicken Stock (see page 58)
1 bay leaf
½ teaspoon saffron threads
1½ teaspoons chopped fresh or ½ teaspoon dried thyme
1½ teaspoons chopped fresh or ½ teaspoon dried basil
1½ teaspoons chopped fresh or ½ teaspoon dried oregano
½ teaspoon ground cumin
12 pitted green olives
12 pitted black olives
½ cup dry red wine

1. Sprinkle the chicken pieces lightly with salt, pepper and paprika. In a large skillet or Dutch oven, heat the oil and brown the chicken pieces on all sides. Remove the chicken and set aside.

2. Add the onion, peppers and garlic to the drippings and sauté for 5 minutes. Add the tomatoes, stock and remaining ingredients. Bring to a boil, lower the heat and simmer for 5 minutes.

3. Add the chicken pieces, cover and simmer until the chicken is tender, about 35 to 40 minutes. Season to taste with salt and pepper. Serve hot with Steamed Rice (see page 203).

CHICKEN BIRYANI

Serves 4 to 6

Fragrant musty spices and yogurt provide a powerful marinade, then sauce for the chicken, which is layered with rice and saffron for this Indian specialty whose preparation is a sensual experience.

6 onions
4 cloves garlic
1 piece peeled fresh ginger, 1 inch by 2 inches
10 cloves
20 peppercorns
1 tablespoon cardamom seeds, removed from pods
¼ teaspoon ground cinnamon
1 teaspoon ground coriander
1 teaspoon white poppy seeds
¼ teaspoon ground mace
1 tablespoon salt
½ cup plain yogurt
3 tablespoons lemon juice
2 teaspoons saffron threads
2 tablespoons milk
½ cup vegetable oil
2 bay leaves
4 black cardamoms in pods
1 2- to 2½-pound chicken, cut up
2 cups raw long-grain rice
1 teaspoon salt

1. In a blender or food processor, chop 3 of the onions. Add the garlic, ginger, cloves, peppercorns, cardamom seeds, cinnamon, coriander, poppy seeds, mace, 1 tablespoon salt, yogurt and lemon juice and process until finely chopped.

2. In a small bowl, soak the saffron in milk. In a large frypan, heat the oil and sauté the remaining onions, thinly sliced, with the bay leaves and black cardamoms until the onions are tender and lightly browned. Stir ⅔ of the sautéed onions into the yogurt mixture.

3. In a large bowl, marinate the chicken in the yogurt mixture for 2 hours. Then, in a large saucepan, simmer the chicken in the marinade for 15 minutes and salt to taste.

4. Preheat the oven to 350° F. Remove the chicken and simmer the marinade, stirring occasionally, until it is a thick paste. Put the chicken in a 5-quart baking dish and spoon the thickened marinade over it.

5. Put the rice and 1 teaspoon salt in a saucepan with boiling water to cover and simmer for 5 minutes. Drain and spoon the rice over the chicken. Top with the remaining sautéed onions and spoon the saffron and milk evenly over the rice. Cover the casserole and bake until the chicken is tender, about 40 to 45 minutes. Sprinkle with slivered almonds and golden raisins and serve.

CHICKEN STEW WITH COUSCOUS

Serves 6 to 8

¼ cup butter
2 tablespoons olive oil
2 3-pound chickens, quartered
2 cups chopped onions

2 cloves garlic, chopped
8 large tomatoes, cored, seeded and diced
⅓ cup tomato paste
1 cinnamon stick
2 navel oranges, peeled and chopped
salt
freshly ground black pepper
2 cups couscous
1 teaspoon salt
½ cup water
½ cup white raisins
⅓ cup pine nuts

1. In a large stockpot, heat the butter and oil over medium high heat. Brown the chicken pieces on all sides, lower the heat and add the onion, garlic, tomatoes, tomato paste, cinnamon stick and oranges. Season with salt and pepper. Cover and cook until the mixture simmers.

2. In a large bowl, mix the couscous and the salt. Add water, a little at a time, until the couscous is all crumbly and damp—hands make the best mixers. Add the raisins and pine nuts to the couscous.

3. Put the couscous in a colander, put the colander in the stockpot over the chicken and cover.

4. Lower the heat so the chicken stew simmers gently and cook until the chicken is tender, about 1 hour, stirring the couscous with a fork from time to time to keep the grains separate. Skim the excess fat from the stew and season to taste with salt and pepper. Serve the stew on a bed of couscous.

SOUTHERN FRIED CHICKEN

Serves 4 to 6

Fresh from the skillet makes a world of difference in America's all-time favorite.

2 2- to 2½-pound chickens, cut into eighths
1 cup unsifted all-purpose flour
2 teaspoons salt
¼ teaspoon white pepper
½ teaspoon ground celery seed
1 teaspoon paprika
1 cup corn oil
1 cup lard

1. Wash the chicken and pat dry. In a small bowl, mix the flour, salt, pepper, celery seed and paprika. Coat the chicken in the flour mixture, shaking off the excess.

2. Using 2 large skillets, heat oil and lard until just

smoking. Add the chicken pieces, skin side down, and fry until brown. Turn and brown the other side.

3. Partially cover the skillet and cook for 35 to 40 minutes, turning the chicken pieces from time to time. Cook until the juices in the chicken run clear with no trace of pink. Drain the pieces on paper towel. Serve hot with cream gravy, or cold.

CREAM GRAVY

Makes 2½ cups

¼ cup cooking fat from fried chicken
¼ cup seasoned flour from fried chicken
2 cups half-and-half

1. Drain off all except ¼ cup of fat from one of the skillets. Stir in the seasoned flour used to coat the chicken and cook for 1 to 2 minutes. Gradually stir in the half-and-half. Stir over medium heat until the sauce bubbles and thickens. Season to taste with salt and pepper.

HERB BATTER FRIED CHICKEN

Serves 4 to 6

Batter makes a thicker and crunchier coating than flour and the herbs and lemon rind give it piquant flavor.

2 2- to 2½-pound chickens, cut up
salt
freshly ground black pepper
2 eggs
½ cup milk
1 cup unsifted all-purpose flour
1 teaspoon baking powder
1 teaspoon salt
1 teaspoon chopped fresh or ½ teaspoon dried thyme
1 teaspoon chopped fresh or ½ teaspoon dried sage
1 teaspoon chopped fresh or ½ teaspoon dried marjoram
1 teaspoon grated lemon rind
deep vegetable shortening or oil heated to 350° F

1. Wash the chicken and pat dry. Sprinkle each piece lightly with salt and pepper.

2. In a bowl, combine the remaining ingredients except the fat and beat until smooth and well blended.

3. Coat each piece of chicken with the batter and drop into the heated fat and fry for 30 to 35 minutes, or until golden brown. Drain on paper towel.

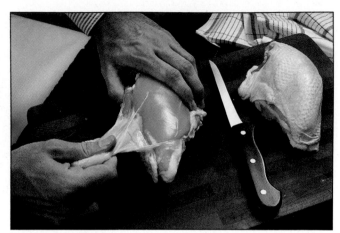

SKINNING AND BONING A CHICKEN BREAST. To remove the breastbone, lay the breast skin side down and with a sharp knife slit the membrane covering the bone. Fold back the breast halves to expose the breastbone and pull it free. Remove wishbones and cut breast into halves.

Using your fingers, gently pry away the thin, flat yellow cartilage attached to the narrow end of the breast meat. Pull the skin from the chicken breast.

To remove the collarbones at the top of the chicken breast, locate them with your fingers and cut away the meat and tendons.

Continue pulling off the meat until it is completely detached from the ribs. Follow the same procedure for the other breast half.

COLD CHICKEN CUTLETS WITH HERB MAYONNAISE

Serves 4

An elegant, but simple alternative for summer suppers or cool picnics.

2 whole chicken breasts, boned and skinned
salt
freshly ground black pepper
1 egg, well beaten
1½ cups dry bread crumbs
⅓ cup corn oil
½ cup Mayonnaise (see page 78)
¼ cup milk
1 tablespoon chopped onion

2 tablespoons finely chopped pitted black olives
¼ cup finely chopped parsley
1½ teaspoons chopped or ½ teaspoon dried tarragon
1 lemon, sliced

1. With a mallet or a cleaver, pound the chicken breasts until they are paper-thin. Sprinkle lightly with salt and pepper. Coat the chicken with the beaten egg, then cover with bread crumbs, pressing firmly to make sure the crumbs adhere. Put in a single layer on waxed paper and let dry for about 20 minutes.

2. In a large frying pan, heat the oil and brown the chicken on both sides. Drain on paper towel and chill.

3. In a small bowl, mix the rest of the ingredients except the lemon, blend well and season with salt. Serve the cutlets topped with lemon slices and the sauce.

SUPREMES AU CHASSEUR
Sautéed Chicken Breasts with Hunter's Sauce

Serves 4

Suprêmes are the French term for chicken breasts.

4 chicken breasts, skinned, boned and halved
salt
freshly ground black pepper
¼ cup butter
Sauce Chasseur (see page 76)—omit the butter

1. Sprinkle the breasts lightly with salt and pepper. In a heavy skillet, melt the butter and, when it is hot, sauté the chicken breasts over medium heat until they are brown and feel springy to the touch—about 10 to 12 mintues.

2. Remove the breasts and keep warm on a platter. Proceed with the sauce chasseur in the same pan.

3. To serve, spoon the sauce over the warm chicken.

STIR-FRY GREEN CHICKEN

Serves 4

¼ cup peanut oil
1 clove garlic, chopped
1½ pounds chicken breasts, skinned and boned
4 scallions, cut into 1-inch pieces
1 red bell pepper, seeded and cut into 1-inch chunks
1 bunch broccoli, stemmed and cut into ½-inch-thick slices
4 ounces pea pods
2 tomatoes, cut into wedges
¼ cup soy sauce
1 cup Chicken Stock (see page 58)
1 tablespoon cornstarch
2 tablespoons chopped fresh coriander

1. In a large skillet or wok, heat the oil over high heat and sauté the garlic for 2 minutes.

2. Cut chicken into 1-inch pieces and add to the pan. Stir-fry for 5 to 6 minutes, or until cooked.

3. Add the scallions, pepper, broccoli and pea pods. Stir-fry for 4 to 5 minutes, or until the vegetables are tender but still crisp, then add the tomatoes.

4. In a small bowl, mix the soy sauce, stock and corn-starch. Stir this mixture into the skillet and continue stirring until it thickens. Salt to taste. Sprinkle with coriander and serve with rice.

Suprêmes au Chasseur garnished with raspberries

SAUTEED CHICKEN BREASTS WITH GINGER SAUCE

Serves 4

Ginger and cream are an East-meets-West combination, testimony to the Oriental influence in our food. Don't be afraid to eliminate the cream and sauté your choice of vegetables alongside.

4 chicken breasts, skinned, boned and halved
⅛ teaspoon salt
freshly ground black pepper
flour
2 tablespoons butter
2 tablespoons oil
2 shallots, minced
2 scallions, thinly sliced
1 tablespoon peeled, minced fresh ginger
½ cup heavy cream

the chicken, let it cool, then skin and bone it and cut it into small chunks.

2. Add the rice to the chicken broth and simmer until all the liquid is absorbed and the rice is almost tender, about 20 minutes. Stir in the chicken, tomatoes, curry, cinnamon, nuts, mint and cream. Season to taste with salt and pepper.

3. Preheat the oven to 350°F. Line a 3-quart shallow, oval baking pan with 8 sheets of phyllo dough, brushing each sheet with melted butter (see page 50). Fill the baking pan with the rice mixture, then cover with 8 sheets of phyllo dough, brushing each with melted butter. Trim the edges of dough with a sharp knife. To decorate top, use a sharp knife to cut slashes like diamonds about ⅛-inch deep in the dough.

4. For decoration, brush 3 sheets of dough with melted butter, fold in half to make 6 layers. Using a cookie cutter, cut 6 chickens (or other shapes) out of the layered dough; arrange them on top of the pie. Cut strips from the remaining dough to put around the edges. Brush again with melted butter.

5. Bake for 1 hour, or until puffed and brown. Serve hot with bowls of pine nuts, yellow raisins, orange sections and chopped mint.

Rock Cornish Game Hens

THE ESSENTIALS

These are the tiniest of chickens—1 to 2 pounds. Smaller hens make individual servings; the larger ones might make 2. They are tender enough for roasting whole, or broiling split in half.

While their flavor is milder than that of squab or game birds, Rock Cornish game hens are good substitutes for other small birds in many recipes. They are frequently treated as if they were game and roasted or glazed with tart fruit flavors.

ROAST GAME HENS WITH MUSTARD GLAZE

Serves 2

A brown, crisp roasted bird glazed with mustard is a beautifully turned-out little package.

2 1½-pound Cornish game hens, giblets removed
salt
2 tablespoons melted butter

1 tablespoon Dijon mustard
¼ cup walnut oil
¼ cup tarragon vinegar
1 teaspoon crushed green peppercorns

1. Preheat the oven to 400°F. Wash the game hens and pat dry. Sprinkle inside and out with salt and put on a rack in a shallow roasting pan. Brush with half of the melted butter and roast in the middle of the oven for 30 minutes.

2. In a small bowl, combine the mustard, walnut oil, vinegar and peppercorns. When the birds have roasted 30 minutes, brush them with the glaze. After an additional 15 minutes, brush them again.

3. The birds should be done after 1 hour in the oven. Test by moving the leg up and down; it if moves easily, they are done. Or pierce the fleshy part of the thigh with a fork; juices should be clear.

4. Remove the birds to a warm serving platter or to plates. Mix the remaining glaze and ¼ cup water with the pan juices and bring to a boil on top of the stove, scraping to loosen all particles. Pour juices over the hens.

Roast Game Hens with Ravigote Sauce. Omit the glaze and baste the hens with melted butter during cooking. Serve with Ravigote Sauce (see page 74) and ripe fresh figs.

BROILED SPLIT GAME HENS

Serves 4

Whether they are broiled or grilled over charcoal, a ginger, Madeira and fruit glaze adds beauty and flavor to these small birds.

4 game hens
salt
freshly ground black pepper
¼ cup ginger marmalade
½ cup Madeira wine
6 ounces pineapple juice
2 tablespoons red wine vinegar

1. Split the game hens in half. Wash them under cold water and dry. (Save the giblets for stock.) Sprinkle both sides with salt and pepper and put in a shallow pan.

2. In a small saucepan, melt the marmalade over low heat. Remove the pan from the heat and stir in the remaining ingredients. Pour this marinade over the game hens and let sit for an hour.

3. Preheat the oven broiler or prepare the charcoal fire. Remove the game hens from the marinade and let them drain, reserving the liquid for basting.

4. If you're using an oven broiler, put the hens on a broiling pan skin side down. Cook at least 6 inches from the heat for 15 minutes then brush with the marinade. Turn, cook an additional 10 to 15 minutes, or until the birds are tender and the legs move easily, then brush with the marinade and broil another 5 minutes.

5. Over charcoal, cook the birds 8 inches from the heat, skin side down, for 15 minutes. Turn and cook on the other side for 10 to 15 minutes. As game hens are turned, brush them with marinade.

6. In a small saucepan, bring the remaining marinade to a simmer over medium heat and let it cook 5 minutes, or until slightly thickened. Serve the hens on a warm platter, glazed with the hot marinade. Garnish with fresh sliced kiwis and strawberries.

CRANBERRY STUFFED GAME HENS

Serves 4

Cranberries are an underused natural resource. Combined with pecans, they make a fitting stuffing for any bird.

3 cups bread cubes
salt
dash white pepper
¾ teaspoon chopped fresh or ¼ teaspoon dried thyme,
   marjoram and sage
4 game hens, fresh or frozen and thawed
freshly ground black pepper
¼ pound bacon, chopped
1 medium onion, chopped
¼ cup chopped celery
½ cup cranberries, fresh or frozen
⅓ cup chopped pecans
1 6-ounce can frozen orange juice concentrate, thawed
¾ cup water
1 teaspoon aromatic bitters

1. To prepare the stuffing, toast the bread cubes in a 300°F oven for 30 minutes, or until hard and brown. In a small bowl, toss the cubes with ¼ teaspoon salt, pepper and herbs. Set aside.

2. Preheat the oven to 400°F. Wash the hens under cold water and pat dry. Sprinkle the birds inside and out with salt and pepper.

Broiled Split Game Hens garnished with fresh strawberries and kiwi

3. In a heavy skillet over medium high heat, fry the bacon until crisp. Remove and drain on paper towel. Lower the heat to medium and sauté the onion and celery in the bacon fat for 5 minutes. Remove the skillet from the heat and stir in the cranberries, nuts and bread cube mixture.

4. In a small bowl mix the orange juice, water and bitters. Pour ½ of this mixture into the cranberry stuffing and reserve the rest for basting the birds.

5. Stir the stuffing until it is well blended and all the liquid is absorbed. Fill each bird and sew or skewer the openings and tie the legs together.

6. Put the stuffed birds on the rack of a shallow roasting pan. Roast in the middle of the oven for 1 hour, or until the birds are tender, basting with orange juice mixture every 15 minutes.

7. Remove the birds to a warm platter and serve with the pan juices spooned over them.

Basic Roast Turkey, basted with butter, has a crisp golden skin and tender meat.

Turkey

THE ESSENTIALS

No longer just a holiday bird, turkey is available year-round. And for good reason: one roasted turkey makes plenty of good—and different—meals. A classic of the New American Cuisine, stuffed and roasted turkey and all the Thanksgiving trimmings can be found on page 312. But an unstuffed bird provides meat for salads, sandwiches and curry and even the carcass can be used as a base for soup (see page 136).

Commercially raised whole turkeys are bred to have more and firmer white breast meat than their wild counterparts. Most are sold frozen, but many markets regularly offer fresh-killed turkeys or will special-order them. Buy fresh turkeys when possible: they're juicier and more flavorful. If you can get a wild turkey from your butcher, do. It won't be as pretty or tender, but the taste will more than compensate.

Turkeys range in size from 5 to 30 pounds. The smaller, younger ones can be broiled or braised, but roasting is still the most popular method. Larger turkeys have proportionately more meat. A 10-pound turkey serves 6 to 8 people; a 20-pound turkey serves 16 or more. Many frozen whole turkeys are labeled "self-basting," which means that fat has been injected under the skin to keep the meat

moist during cooking. Better to do your own basting with your own choice of fat.

Turkey growers are not behind the times—they're now selling turkey parts. Lovers of dark meat can buy legs and thighs to roast alone. Turkey breasts are very meaty, and they can often be used in recipes calling for veal.

Like any poultry, fresh turkey must be very fresh and kept carefully refrigerated. Frozen turkey should show no signs of previous defrosting or freezer burn.

Turkey must be defrosted before you cook it or you will have trouble timing it. Almost all the directions on turkey packaging call for overcooking, which dries out the breast meat. A turkey is done when the leg moves easily, the juices run clear, and a meat thermometer inserted in the flesh of the thigh (but not touching the bone) registers 170° to 175°F.

BASIC ROAST TURKEY

Serves approximately 1 person per pound

There are several schools of thought on roasting turkeys. The high-heat method, which starts the bird breast up at 425°F and, after 30 minutes, lowers it to 350°F, ensures a well-browned, very crisp skin and takes less time. The slow-roasting method keeps the bird at a constant 325°F throughout its cooking time, which might be as much as an hour or more longer. Your choice.

An unstuffed bird should be trussed, to keep the extremities from overcooking and to hold it together during turning.

1 12- to 14-pound whole turkey
salt
freshly ground black pepper
3 sprigs parsley
1 large onion, quarterd
1 stalk celery with leaves, cut in half
1 small carrot, cut in half
½ cup melted butter

1. Preheat the oven to 325°F. Wash the turkey under cold water and pat dry. Sprinkle inside and out with salt and pepper. Put the vegetables in the cavity and truss.

2. Put the turkey on its side on the rack of a shallow roasting pan. Brush the top with butter and put in the oven. Let it roast 1 hour. Baste with butter if it is not self-basting. Turn the turkey over and roast on the other side for 30 minutes, basting with the pan juices. Finally, put the turkey breast side up, baste with pan juices and let it roast an additional 30 minutes before you start testing for doneness. If at any point the bird looks as though it is getting too brown, cover with aluminum foil. Baste often during the final cooking period.

3. Let the turkey rest 20 minutes before carving it. For a simple sauce, pour off the fat in the roasting pan, then deglaze the pan with White Stock (see page 56) or stock made with the giblets while the turkey cooked.

4. To serve the turkey cold, let it cool completely before carving and serve it at room temperature or chilled with homemade Mayonnaise (see page 78).

CARVING A TURKEY. Steady the turkey with a carving fork and cut the skin between the breast and thigh. Push the thigh outward with the side of the knife. Slice down through the hip joint, separating leg from the turkey.

Find the joint between the thigh and the drumstick and slice through. Holding the thigh steady, cut slices of dark meat from the thigh and drumstick.

To remove the wing, slice through the breast and the shoulder joint. A piece of breast meat will be attached.

To slice the breast, hold the turkey steady and slice down diagonally through the meat.

TURKEY CURRY

Serves 4

Turkey Tetrazzini may be the clichéd vision for leftover turkey; but we prefer a good strong yogurt-based curry.

¼ cup butter
1 onion, chopped
1 tart apple, peeled, cored and chopped
1 clove garlic, minced
⅓ cup raisins
⅓ cup slivered almonds
⅓ cup flour
1 tablespoon curry powder
2 cups yogurt
3 cups diced cooked turkey
salt
freshly ground black pepper

1. In a heavy 2- to 3-quart saucepan, melt the butter over medium heat. When it is hot, sauté the onion, apple and garlic for 5 minutes. Add the raisins and almonds and sauté 1 minute. Stir in the flour and curry powder and cook for 1 or 2 minutes to reduce the rawness of the flour and release the flavor of the curry spices.

2. Stir in the yogurt and whisk until the sauce is blended. Simmer to thicken. Stir in the turkey, season with salt and pepper and cook over low heat until the turkey is heated through.

3. Serve with rice and chutney.

TURKEY STOCK OR SOUP

For a full-bodied soup add barley, rice and more vegetables.

1 turkey carcass
4 stalks celery with leaves, cut into 1-inch pieces
2 carrots, cut into 1-inch pieces
1 onion, sliced
6 peppercorns
1 bay leaf
4 whole cloves
3 quarts water
1 bouquet garni of 2 sprigs each parsley and thyme, tied together

1. Use the bones left from a roast turkey and crack them with a cleaver or hammer. Put them in a large kettle and add any skin or neck pieces and the remaining ingredients.

2. Bring to a boil and skim off the foam that rises to the top. Cover and simmer for 2 hours. Remove the bones, peppercorns, cloves and bouquet garni.

3. To serve as soup, skim excess fat from the top and salt to taste. To use as stock, strain the liquid through a colander lined with several layers of cheesecloth. Skim the excess fat or, if you have time, chill and spoon off the hardened fat.

Duck

THE ESSENTIALS

In 1873 a clipper ship captain returned to Long Island from China with nine white ducks. Their many progeny are the commercial Long Island or White Peking ducks raised for American tables. These ducks are fatty, but new duck farms are breeding leaner birds; watch for them.

Rich and succulent, duck breasts have gained new popularity. Their strong versatile flavor comes through even in cold salads. Using the breast meat separately eliminates the problem that arises when a duck is cooked whole: the breast is overdone, the rest is very underdone. Duck should be served pink.

Technically speaking, a duck is a bird that is more than 10 weeks old and weighs upward of 5 pounds. The 4- to 5-pound birds that are most available are 7- to 8-week-old ducklings.

Most duck is sold frozen. Look for the smooth skin and even coloring of fresh birds and check for signs of previous freezing and defrosting, which affects both flavor and tenderness. Avoid birds with any pink ice around the meat.

ROAST DUCKLING

Serves 4

A different duck à l'orange—the orange is inside the bird and a currant glaze coats the outside.

1 4-pound duckling
salt
freshly ground black pepper
1 navel orange, cut into wedges
juice and grated rind of 1 orange
1 cup currant jelly
1 tablespoon Dijon mustard

1. Wash the duckling and dry with paper towel. Sprinkle inside and out with salt and pepper.

2. Put orange wedges in the body cavity, tie the legs

Vietnamese Duckling, stuffed with oranges, onions, garlic and peppers, is first marinated, then grilled.

together and turn the wings under. Put the duckling on a rack in a shallow, foil-lined roasting pan. Prick the duckling all over with the tines of a fork to allow the fat to escape. Roast the duckling in a 350°F oven until the leg moves up and down easily, about 2 hours.

3. In a saucepan, mix the remaining ingredients and heat until bubbly and smooth. About 20 minutes before the duckling is done, spoon some of the glaze over the duckling and roast for 10 minutes. Repeat. After the second glazing and roasting, remove the duckling to a large platter and spoon the remaining glaze over the duckling. Let meat sit for 10 to 15 minutes to allow juices to settle and then serve with Wild Rice (see page 207).

BROILED DUCKLING

Serves 4

Broiled duckling is so straightforward we scarcely think to try it, but broiling keeps the flesh moist while making the skin crisp.

1 4-pound duckling
salt
freshly ground black pepper
2 teaspoons fresh or 1 teaspoon dried sage
2 teaspoons fresh or 1 teaspoon dried rosemary

1. Quarter the duckling and trim off all excess fat and skin. Wash the pieces, pat dry and sprinkle lightly with salt and pepper, then rub with sage and rosemary. Prick the skin all over with the tines of a fork.

2. Put the duckling pieces skin side down on a broiler pan and broil 6 inches away from the heat for 25 minutes. Turn and broil for another 20 minutes.

VIETNAMESE DUCKLING

Serves 4

Duck takes well to charcoal cooking. Because a lot of fat is released, use a drip pan—make one out of a double thickness of heavy-duty aluminum foil or use an old loaf pan. It should be long and narrow to fit your grill. Put it in front of the coals if your rotisserie spit moves away from you, behind the coals if the spit rotates toward you.

2 4-pound ducklings, fresh or frozen and thawed
salt
freshly ground black pepper
2 navel oranges, each cut into 6 wedges
2 onions, quartered
2 cloves garlic
2 4-ounce cans sweet green chilies, drained
1 cup water
1 cup cider vinegar
2 teaspoons turmeric
2 tablespoons chopped fresh ginger

1. Wash the ducklings under cold water and pat dry. Sprinkle inside and out with salt and pepper. For rotisserie or oven cooking, leave the ducks whole and fill the body cavities with orange sections and onion wedges; put the ducks in a shallow pan.

2. In a blender or food processor, process the remaining ingredients until you have a coarse purée for a marinade.

Pour this marinade over the ducklings and let sit at room temperature for 2 hours, turning occasionally.

3. Light the charcoal fire or preheat the broiler. For the rotisserie, spear the ducks firmly on the rod and cook over gray coals for 2 hours, or until brown and crisp. Baste with the marinade every 15 minutes.

4. In a conventional oven, put the ducks on a rack in a roasting pan. Prick the skin all over with a fork to release the fat during cooking. Roast at 350°F for 2 hours, basting with the marinade every 15 minutes. Roast until the skin is crisp and brown and the meat is tender.

5. With either method, the wings and legs may brown too quickly and be in danger of burning. If this happens, simply cover them with foil.

6. Serve the ducklings hot.

DUCKLING BREAST WITH MANGOES

Serves 4

Mangoes and brandy balance the dense savory duckling breasts.

4 small ducklings
salt
freshly ground black pepper
¼ cup corn oil or rendered duckling fat
2 mangoes, peeled and sliced
¼ cup brandy

1. Cut up the ducklings as you would a chicken (see page 122). Skin and bone the breasts.

2. Make duck stock by putting the skin and bones (including the backbones and necks) and the giblets in a large saucepan. Save the legs for another use. Cover with water and bring to a boil over high heat. Lower the heat and simmer, covered, for 1 hour to make stock.

3. Sprinkle the breasts lightly with salt and pepper. In a large saucepan, heat the oil and sauté the breasts until brown on both sides but still pink inside.

4. Measure out 1 cup of the duck stock. Combine it in a saucepan with the mango slices. Bring to a boil, lower the heat and simmer uncovered until the sauce thickens slightly—about 5 to 6 minutes. Stir in the brandy and bring the sauce back to a boil for 1 minute.

5. To serve, arrange the breasts on a warm platter and spoon the sauce over them. Garnish with additional mango slices, if you like.

ROAST WILD DUCK

Serves 2

Any type of wild duck works well—mallards, pintails, wood ducks, teals, canvasbacks, redheads.

2 wild ducks, dressed, about 2 pounds each
salt
dash freshly ground black pepper
7 tablespoons all-purpose flour
2 tablespoons butter
2 cups water
1 small cooking apple, quartered
1 potato, cut into chunks
1 onion, quartered

1. Sprinkle inside cavities of the ducks with salt and pepper. Coat the birds in 3 tablespoons of flour.

2. In a 6-quart Dutch oven, melt the butter and brown the birds well on all sides. Remove the ducks to a platter. Add the remaining flour to the pan drippings and cook, stirring constantly, until the flour is brown. Remove the pan from the heat and let it cool a little.

3. Add the water, salt and pepper, return the pot to the heat and stir until the sauce is thickened.

4. In a bowl, mix the apple, potato and onion. Fill the duck cavities with this stuffing and skewer the ducks closed. Put the ducks in the Dutch oven in the sauce, cover, bake and baste in a 325°F oven for 2 to 2½ hours, or until the duck is tender and the juices run clear.

Goose

THE ESSENTIALS

There is something comforting about goose, particularly when it's roasted with an Apple and Sausage Stuffing (see page 315). But the New Cuisine has taken this Old World classic under its wing, teaming it with fennel and Calvados.

Most goose in the United States is slaughtered at 4 to 6 months and weighs from 6 to 14 pounds, which makes it tender enough to roast. Older birds must be braised. Since most of our goose is sold frozen, it is important that it has not been defrosted at any point in its distribution. Check for smooth skin and no blemishes. Any signs of icing under the wrapper indicate defrosting and refreezing, which affects both flavor and tenderness.

ROAST GOOSE WITH FENNEL AND CALVADOS

Serves 6 to 8

This regional roast goose from Normandy combines strong fennel and even stronger Calvados with the goose liver and pork. Tart apples poached in Calvados and white wine go alongside.

1 12- to 14-pound goose
salt
freshly ground black pepper
1 tablespoon butter
2 onions, chopped
1 cup chopped fresh fennel
4 tart cooking apples, peeled, cored and chopped
½ pound lean ground pork
½ cup chopped slab bacon
2 eggs, beaten
1 goose liver, chopped
¼ teaspoon ground allspice
½ teaspoon salt
pinch freshly ground black pepper
½ cup Calvados or apple brandy

WINE-POACHED APPLES

6 to 8 tart cooking apples, peeled and left whole
⅓ cup Calvados or apple brandy
3 cups dry white wine
½ cup sugar

1. Remove the giblets, wash the goose under cold water and pat dry. Using a trussing needle or other sharp-pointed tool, prick the skin of the goose all over the top, making sure not to prick the meat underneath. This is important since it allows excess fat (not the meat's juices) to escape and baste the birds. Rub the goose inside and out with salt and pepper.

2. In a heavy skillet, melt the butter over medium heat and sauté the onions, fennel and apples for 5 minutes. Remove from the heat and let cool.

3. In a large bowl combine the pork, bacon, eggs, liver and seasonings. Add the apple-onion mixture and blend well.

4. Preheat the oven to 350°F. Fill the goose with the stuffing mixture and truss with a skewer or needle and thread. Put the goose on a rack in a large roasting pan. Cook in the lower half of the oven for 2½ to 3 hours, or until tender. The leg will move up and down easily when the bird is done. During roasting, baste the goose every 30 minutes with Calvados and spoon out extra fat accumulated in the pan. Let rest at least 20 minutes before carving.

5. To poach the apples, combine them with the Calvados, wine and sugar in a heavy saucepan. Bring the liquid to a boil, reduce the heat and simmer, uncovered, for 10 to 15 minutes, or until the apples are tender. Serve the apples hot around the roast.

Squab

THE ESSENTIALS

Squabs are found in the very best restaurants in town, but few of the diners realize that they're just domestic pigeons raised for the table. Their taste is mild and sweet, and they are tender enough to be split and broiled or to be roasted, just as Rock Cornish hens.

The smallest birds you are likely to find in your market, squabs usually weigh between ¾ pound and 1½ pounds and constitute a single serving, or at most 2 servings.

Most frequently available frozen, squab should be carefully checked for signs of previous defrosting and smooth, evenly colored skin.

Recipes for squabs and Rock Cornish hens are really interchangeable, although their different flavors change the final results.

BROILED SQUAB WITH RASPBERRY VINEGAR SAUCE

Serves 4

When raspberry and blueberry and other yet more lyrical vinegars started appearing on our shelves, we were delighted with their untold possibilities. Raspberry vinegar sauce is a new classic, and the sweet-tartness of raspberries gives this dish a distinctive and fresh flavor that melds perfectly with the mild gaminess of squab.

4 squabs
salt
freshly ground black pepper
1 cup raspberry vinegar
¼ cup minced shallots
2 cups White Stock (see page 56)
2 tablespoons heavy cream
¼ cup butter
1 cup fresh raspberries

1. Split the squabs just as you would chicken (see page 122). Sprinkle with salt and pepper. Put skin side down on a broiling pan and cook 6 inches from the heat for 6 to 8 minutes. Turn and cook an additional 6 to 8 minutes. The birds should be crisp and brown on the outside, still pink inside. Keep them warm while you make the sauce.

2. In a small, heavy, nonaluminum saucepan, bring the vinegar and shallots to a boil over high heat. Lower the heat slightly and let the mixture boil down until approximately ½ cup remains.

3. Add the stock and boil the mixture down to about 1 cup liquid. Remove the pan from the heat and beat in the cream and butter.

4. Put the squabs on warm serving plates and spoon sauce over each. Garnish with fresh raspberries and serve at once.

SQUAB SALAD

Serves 4

A cold version of broiled squab. The meat takes nicely to sherry vinegar and bitter greens and walnuts.

2 squabs
salt
freshly ground black pepper
2 cups (bite-size pieces) endive or watercress
2 cups (bite-size pieces) arugula or escarole
⅓ cup chopped walnuts
½ cup sherry vinegar
¼ cup chopped shallots
½ cup Chicken Stock (see page 58)
¼ cup heavy cream

1. Split the squabs, season with salt and pepper and broil (see page 122). Let cool. Remove the meat from the bones and cut it into slivers.

2. Arrange the greens on 4 individual plates. Put the squab meat on top of the greens and sprinkle with the walnuts. Chill.

3. In a small, heavy, nonaluminum saucepan, bring the vinegar and shallots to a boil over high heat. Lower the heat slightly and let the mixture boil down to 2 tablespoons. Remove from the heat and stir in the stock and cream. Season to taste with salt and pepper. Chill the dressing for at least 1 hour.

4. When ready to serve, spoon the dressing over the squab and greens.

Game

The New American Cuisine seeks the constant stimulation of new tastes, once-strange combinations, unexplored marriages of ingredients. It's not surprising that game should hold such rich new culinary magic—we weren't brought up on it—so there are whole new frontiers of preparation and tasting to explore.

Like many other New Cuisine foods, most game is seasonal, and the sharp, brisk days of fall stimulate our appetites for these intense and rich meats. Some game, such as rabbit and quail, is raised commercially and can be found year-round. All are available frozen to answer your call of the wild.

THE ESSENTIALS

The most important thing to remember about game is that animals in the wild get a great deal more exercise than the poultry and fatted calves raised for market. This means the meat is dry, with a lot more sinew than fat, and needs a lot of care in the preparation to keep it moist. For example, game birds are often prepared wrapped in bacon or salt pork.

Most fresh-killed game—small birds like quail are an exception—must be hung in a cool, dry, airy place for several days to several weeks while natural enzymes go to work tenderizing the meat and developing the characteristically gamy flavor of wild meat. Game meat bought from a butcher will certainly have had this tenderizing treatment. Do check the age of the game when killed. Younger birds, rabbits and deer are tenderer and can be cooked by quicker methods than more venerable ones.

PHEASANT WITH CHARTREUSE

Serves 2

Pheasant is a medium-size bird that usually serves 2 people. Guinea hen and partridge can be cooked in the same ways with chartreuse, a spicy liqueur made of balm, hyssop, angelica leaves, cinnamon, mace and saffron, and a potent flavoring for the rich meat.

1 pheasant (about 2 pounds), fresh or frozen and thawed
salt
2 teaspoons crushed green peppercorns
¼ cup melted butter
⅓ cup green chartreuse
2 tablespoons currant jelly
grated rind of ½ lemon

1. Preheat the oven to 350°F. Wash the pheasant under cold water and dry. Sprinkle inside and out with salt and peppercorns. Put the bird breast side up on the rack of a shallow roasting pan and coat heavily with melted butter.

2. After roasting for 15 minutes, baste again with butter. In a small bowl, mix the chartreuse, currant jelly, lemon rind and remaining butter to make a glaze. When the bird has roasted 30 minutes, baste with the glaze. At 45 minutes, baste with glaze again and check for doneness by moving a leg up and down. If it moves easily, the bird is ready to serve. If not, continue roasting another 10 to 15 minutes.

3. When the bird is done, mix any remaining glaze with the pan juices and spoon over the pheasant. Fresh figs and pomegranates make a pretty and appropriate accompaniment.

PHEASANT STEW

Serves 4

Chestnuts and mushrooms give this stew an earthy, fresh-from-the forest flavor. Pancetta (salt cured Italian bacon) and a wealth of vegetables enrich it.

2 2- to 2½-pound pheasants, quartered
salt
freshly ground black pepper
2 teaspoons crushed Herbes de Provence (or use ½ teaspoon each dried or 1 teaspoon fresh rosemary, thyme, basil and tarragon)
16 thin slices of pancetta or prosciutto
¼ cup butter
¼ cup corn oil
1 carrot, chopped
1 onion, chopped
1 cup chopped fresh fennel
½ cup chopped parsley
1½ cups dry white wine
1½ cups Chicken Stock (see page 58)
1 pound small cèpes or cultivated mushrooms
1 pound chestnuts, peeled and cooked (see page 314)

1. Lightly sprinkle the pheasant pieces with salt and pepper. (The pancetta is very salty, so use a light hand.) Rub the pieces with the herbs, then wrap them in pancetta and tie in place with string.

2. In a Dutch oven, heat the butter and oil and brown the pheasant pieces on all sides. Add the carrot, onion, fennel, parsley, wine and stock. Cover and gently simmer until the pheasant pieces are tender, about 1 to 1½ hours. Put the pheasant on a warm platter and take off the string.

3. Add the mushrooms and chestnuts and simmer for 10 minutes. Season with salt and pepper, then skim the excess fat from the top of the pan juices. Spoon pan juices over the pheasant.

4. If desired, mix 2 tablespoons butter with 2 tablespoons flour into a paste (*beurre manié*). Drop this paste into the pan juices and stir over medium heat until slightly thickened. Serve with tiny new potatoes and Brussels sprouts.

ROAST MALLARD DUCK

Serves 4

Wild duck has a superb flavor that is well worth struggling to get at; it makes a festive meal with wild rice, sautéed chestnuts and a strong red wine. A young duck needn't be

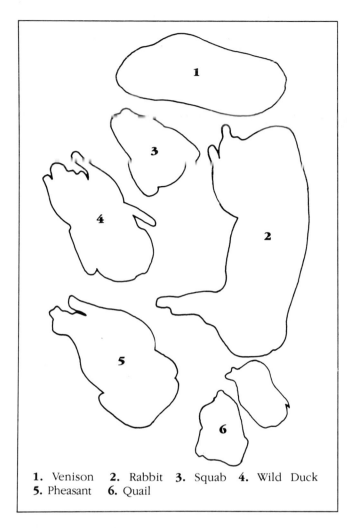

1. Venison 2. Rabbit 3. Squab 4. Wild Duck
5. Pheasant 6. Quail

marinated (a flexible breast bone is a clue to immaturity), but it improves with an hour or so of soaking in red wine with an onion stuck with cloves. Like any game, ducks need continual basting during roasting, or they should be covered with bacon or thin slices of salt pork. Wild duck fanciers come in two schools: those who like their meat rare and those who like it well done. For rare duck, roast at 450° F for 18 to 20 minutes. One duck will serve 2 people.

2 3- to 3½-pound mallard ducks
salt
freshly ground black pepper
2 cloves garlic, halved
1 lemon, sliced
1 onion, quartered
6 slices bacon

1. Preheat the oven to 350°F. Wash the ducks under cold water and pat dry. (Save the giblets for stock.) Rub inside and out with salt, pepper and the cut sides of the garlic cloves. Divide the garlic, lemon and onion between the 2 birds, putting half in each duck's body cavity.

2. Put the duck, breast side up, on the rack of a roasting pan. Truss, then drape 3 slices of bacon across the top of each. Roast for 45 minutes to 1 hour, or until the legs move easily.

3. For an *au jus* sauce, pour the fat from the roasting pan into a saucepan. Add 1 cup dry red wine to the pan and simmer, scraping all brown particles loose. Spoon sauce over duck and garnish with orange segments.

ROAST QUAIL

Serves 4

Tiny quail are an exquisite delicacy when served pink and moist inside, crisp and brown outside, with a brandy and wine sauce. The technique: sauté the birds in butter first, then roast briefly.

8 quail
salt
freshly ground black pepper
⅓ cup butter
¼ cup brandy
2 shallots, chopped
½ cup dry white wine
¼ cup butter

1. Preheat the oven to 400°F. Wash the quail under cold water and pat dry. Salt and pepper inside and out. In a large, heavy skillet melt the butter over medium heat. When it is hot, brown the quail evenly on all sides.

2. Put the browned birds, breast side up, on the rack of a shallow roasting pan. Baste with the skillet juices and roast for 10 to 15 minutes.

3. Remove the birds to a platter and keep warm. Deglaze the pan on top of the range with brandy, scraping with a wooden spoon to get up all the brown particles. Add the shallots and wine and let boil until the liquid is reduced by half. Off the heat, stir in the butter a tablespoon at a time, season with salt and pepper and spoon this sauce over the quail. Serve at once.

QUAIL ON TOAST WITH PATE

Serves 2

Braised quail flavored with pâté and truffles, shallots, tarragon and cream, served on toast spread with yet more pâté, is a royal feast.

4 quail, fresh or frozen and thawed
salt
freshly ground black pepper
3 tablespoons butter
3 shallots, chopped
½ cup dry white wine
1 teaspoon chopped fresh parsley
1 teapoon chopped fresh or ½ teaspoon crushed dried tarragon
1 2¾-ounce can good goose liver pâté
½ cup heavy cream
2 slices firm white bread, crusts removed

1. Wash the quail under cold water and pat dry. Sprinkle inside and out with salt and pepper.

2. In a large heavy saucepan or Dutch oven, melt the butter over medium heat. When it is hot, add the birds and brown slowly on all sides. Add the shallots and sauté for 1 or 2 minutes.

3. Add the wine and herbs. Bring to a boil, reduce the heat and simmer, tightly covered, for 20 to 30 minutes, or until the quail are tender.

4. Remove the quail and keep warm. Add half the pâté to the pan juices and stir until well blended. Stir in the cream and let it simmer over medium heat until the sauce begins to thicken—about 5 minutes.

5. Toast the bread and spread with the remaining pâté. Cut each piece in 2 diagonally and put on a serving platter. Top each piece with a quail and spoon the sauce over the birds.

SAUTEED QUAIL

Serves 6

12 8- to 10-ounce quail
salt
freshly ground black pepper
⅓ cup butter
2 tablespoons oil
1 teaspoon chopped fresh or 1 teaspoon crumbled dried rosemary
juice of 1 lemon
¼ cup finely chopped parsley
2 tablespoons chopped chives

1. Lightly sprinkle the quail inside and out with salt and pepper. In a large skillet, heat the butter and oil and brown the quail on all sides.

2. Add the rosemary and lemon juice, cover and simmer gently until the quail are tender, about 30 to 35 minutes. Put the quail on a serving platter.

3. Add parsley and chives to the pan juices and boil for 1 minute. Pour the pan juices over the quail.

BRAISED PARTRIDGE

Serves 2

Braising small birds like partridges or pheasants with cabbage or sauerkraut is a northern European custom and a savory way to tenderize older game.

4 small or 2 large partridges (about 3 pounds)
salt
freshly ground black pepper
4 slices bacon
¼ cup butter

2 cups sauerkraut
1 tart apple, cored and chopped
½ cup dry red wine
½ cup orange juice

1. Wash the birds under cold water and pat dry. (Save the giblets for stock.) Sprinkle inside and out with salt and pepper.

2. In a heavy 2-quart Dutch oven, fry the bacon over medium heat until crisp. Remove the bacon and drain on paper towel. Add the butter to the bacon fat and brown the birds on all sides over medium heat.

3. When the birds are brown, add the sauerkraut, apple, wine and juice. Bring the liquid to a boil, reduce the heat and simmer, covered, for 1 hour, or until the birds are tender. Check occasionally to make sure there is enough liquid. Add wine if necessary during cooking.

4. To serve, put the birds on a platter surrounded by the sauerkraut. Crumble the bacon pieces over the top.

RABBIT STEW

Serves 4 to 6

Unless there is a hunter in your family, the rabbit you buy is a commercially raised animal that tastes very much like a dry, mature stewing chicken and can be cooked like one. This is a traditional German braised rabbit stew.

1 4- to 5-pound rabbit, cut up
½ cup red wine vinegar
½ teaspoon salt
about ½ cup flour
freshly ground black pepper
¼ cup butter
¼ cup oil
1 onion, chopped
3 cloves garlic, chopped
½ pound mushrooms, sliced
1 cup tomato juice
½ cup dry white wine
1 tablespoon chopped fresh or 1 teaspoon crushed dried rosemary
1 tablespoon chopped fresh or 1 teaspoon crushed dried basil
1 tablespoon sugar
1 tablespoon whole pickling spice, tied in cheesecloth
3 tomatoes, peeled, seeded and chopped

1. Put the rabbit pieces in a large bowl and add the vinegar and salt. Add enough water to just cover the pieces. Let soak overnight in the refrigerator.

2. Wash the rabbit under cold water and pat dry. Roll the pieces in the flour mixed with salt and pepper. (Or shake in a paper bag.)

3. In a large heavy skillet or Dutch oven, heat the butter and oil over medium high heat. When the fat is hot, sauté the rabbit pieces until brown on all sides.

4. Add all the remaining ingredients except the tomatoes. Bring to a boil, reduce the heat and simmer, covered, for 15 minutes, or until the meat is tender. Add the tomatoes and simmer another 5 minutes, or until the tomatoes are soft.

5. Remove the cheesecloth bag. Serve the rabbit on a bed of hot noodles, covered with sauce.

CAJUN RABBIT

Serves 4

½ cup white wine vinegar
¼ cup olive oil
¼ cup dry red wine
½ cup finely chopped onion
1 bay leaf, crushed
¼ teaspoon black pepper
dash allspice
½ teaspoon salt
1 small clove garlic, chopped
2 pounds rabbit, cut up
flour for coating
½ cup vegetable oil
½ cup flour
2 cups chopped onion
1 cup chopped green pepper
1 teaspoon minced garlic
1 teaspoon salt
¼ teaspoon red pepper flakes
½ teaspoon cayenne
½ teaspoon black pepper
2 cups water
2 8-ounce cans tomato paste
juice of ½ lemon
¼ cup minced parsley
¼ teaspoon thyme
½ cup dry red wine
1 tablespoon chopped chives

1. In a large bowl, combine the first nine ingredients. Marinate the rabbit pieces in the refrigerator for at least 3 hours, turning occasionally. Drain and discard the marinade. *(continued)*

Cajun Rabbit

2. Coat each piece with flour, shaking to remove excess. In a large skillet, heat the oil and brown the rabbit on all sides. Remove the rabbit and set aside. Stir the ½ cup flour into the pan juices and cook until golden brown. Then stir in the onion and green pepper and sauté for 8 minutes. Stir in the remaining ingredients and simmer for 5 minutes.

3. Add the rabbit pieces, cover and simmer, stirring occasionally, until the rabbit is tender, about 1 hour and 20 minutes. Salt to taste and serve over rice (see page 205.)

RABBIT IN RED WINE

Serves 6

Close your eyes and you'll think you're eating coq au vin—but better.

1 3- to 3½-pound rabbit, cut into 6 pieces
salt
freshly ground black pepper
½ cup flour
6 slices bacon, chopped
2 onions, chopped
1 cup chopped celery leaves
bouquet garni of 1 bay leaf, 3 sprigs thyme, 3 sprigs
   rosemary, 3 sprigs savory or chervil, tied together
1 cup Brown Stock (see page 57)
1½ cups dry red wine
18 small onions
18 button mushrooms

1. Wash the rabbit and pat dry. Sprinkle the pieces lightly with salt and pepper. Coat the pieces with flour, shaking off the excess.

2. In a large skillet or Dutch oven, fry the bacon until brown and crisp. Add the rabbit and brown the pieces on all sides.

3. Add the onions, celery leaves, bouquet garni, stock and wine. Cover and simmer gently until the rabbit is tender, about 1 to 1½ hours.

4. Add the onions and mushrooms, cover and simmer until the vegetables are tender, another 15 to 20 minutes. Season with salt and pepper and remove the bouquet garni. Serve with noodles.

5. The pan juices may be thickened with 2 tablespoons butter and 2 tablespoons flour mixed to a paste. Add this paste to the stew and simmer until thick.

ROAST VENISON

Serves 6 to 8

Roast venison, like venison steak, needs tenderizing. One trick is to marinate the meat overnight in buttermilk, which will soften tough sinews. When roasting, use a meat thermometer. rare meat registers 130 degrees; medium 140 degrees. In general, venison requires about 30 minutes of roasting time per pound at 350° F.

1 4- to 5-pound boneless roast of venison (either leg cut
   or loin cut)
buttermilk to cover
salt
freshly ground black pepper
1 clove garlic, mashed
1 onion, sliced thin
5 or 6 slices bacon or sheets of thin-sliced salt pork
2 cups water

¼ cup cider vinegar
1 cup tomato juice
2 tablespoons sugar
2 cups sliced celery and celery leaves

1. In a large bowl, cover the venison with buttermilk. Refrigerate overnight, or at least 2 hours.

2. Preheat the oven to 350°F. Drain the meat and wipe dry, Rub with salt, pepper and garlic. Set on the rack of a roasting pan and put the onion slices, then the bacon strips on top of the roast. Insert the meat thermometer into the center of the thickest part of the venison.

3. Roast approximately 30 minutes per pound. Let the finished roast sit 15 minutes before carving.

4. When the roast is done, skim the excess fat from the pan juices. Add the remaining ingredients to the pan juices in a saucepan and bring to a boil, scraping loose all the brown particles. Spoon the pan juices over the sliced venison.

SAUTEED VENISON STEAKS

Serves 6

6 8- to 10-ounce slices leg of venison, ½-inch thick
salt
freshly ground black pepper
1 teaspoon ground sage
1½ cups dry red wine
1 teaspoon crushed juniper berries
flour
¼ cup butter
¼ cup corn oil

1. Sprinkle the venison lightly with salt and pepper. Dust with sage.

2. Put the venison into a shallow glass or earthenware bowl, add the wine and juniper berries and marinate at room temperature for 2 hours, or refrigerate overnight. Reserve 1 cup of the marinade.

3. Drain the venison and dry with paper towels. Coat the slices with flour and shake off the excess. In a large skillet, heat the butter and oil and brown the venison slices on both sides. Cover the skillet and sauté the slices until brown outside and slightly pink inside, about 15 to 20 minutes (longer cooking makes the venison tough). Remove the slices to a serving platter.

4. Add the reserved marinade to the skillet and bring to a boil, scraping loose all the brown particles. Pour over the venison. Serve with wild rice and asparagus.

Meat

Not so long ago, there was a great furor about meat—and, like most great furors, it soon died down. Americans altered their eating habits slightly—for the better, we think. As rich red meats became more expensive, and their health-related aspects were questioned, we began treating them more like precious jewels: a commodity to be savored, but in smaller and higher-quality portions. A filet mignon might be enjoyed, but an herbed veal stew laden with vegetables is to be savored.

We've returned to tried and true basic cooking techniques to bring out the best in some cuts; others need a new turn. Nothing beats broiled flank steak, but round steak requires braising; pork chops, too, benefit from a moist-heat method, and delicate veal scallopine need nothing more than a quick sautéing. Meat cookery no longer tries to disguise its subject; it only seeks to enhance its best qualities.

So the trend toward light and true has affected our attitudes toward meat; it's all part of the integrity of the New American Cuisine.

All meat needs tender care; it is very perishable. No matter whether it's beef, lamb or pork, chopped meat should either be eaten the day of purchase or frozen for future use. Roasts and larger cuts keep in the refrigerator up to 4 days. Wrap all meat loosely so air circulates around it and store it in the coldest part of the refrigerator. Cool cooked meats before refrigerating, and wrap loosely also.

In general, count on ¼ pound of lean, boneless meat per serving, ½ pound of fat-trimmed steak, chops or roasts and 1 pound of bony cuts such as spareribs or breast of veal.

Throughout the chapter, we show you cuts of beef, veal, lamb, pork, smoked pork products and innards as you will find them at your supermarket or butcher, and the proper methods for cooking each cut.

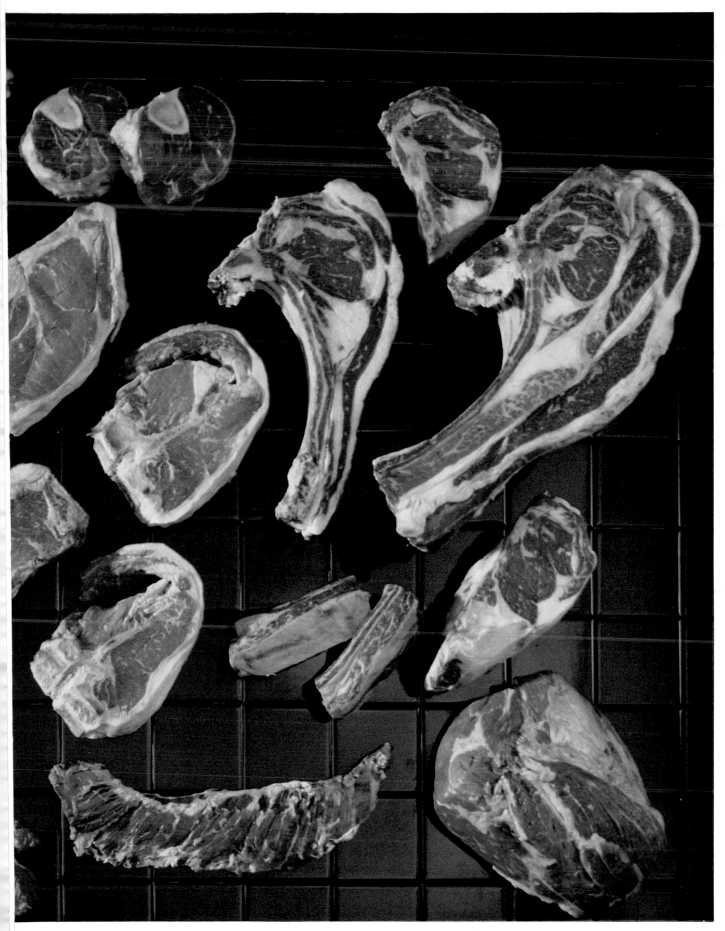

1. Heat the oil in a wok or heavy skillet over high heat. Add garlic and beef and stir-fry—keep stirring the food around—until the beef is brown on both sides, about 5 to 6 minutes.

2. Push the beef to the edges of the pan and add the scallions, snow peas and mushrooms. Stir-fry for 3 to 5 minutes, or until the peas are bright green and tender-crisp.

3. Mix the stock, cornstarch and soy sauce until well blended. Add them to the wok with the tomato and stir until the broth is hot and slightly thickened, about 3 to 4 minutes. Serve at once over Steamed Rice (see page 205) or vermicelli.

BRAISED SHORT RIBS WITH HORSERADISH SAUCE

Serves 4

4 pounds beef short ribs
salt
freshly ground black pepper
2 tablespoons butter
2 onions, sliced
2 carrots, sliced
1 cup chopped celery and leaves
2 tablespoons flour
2 cups peeled, seeded and chopped tomatoes
1 cup Chicken Stock (see page 58)
¼ cup prepared horseradish

1. Preheat the oven to 400°F. Sprinkle the ribs lightly with salt and pepper and put in a shallow baking pan. Roast for 30 minutes, or until the ribs are brown; this will render a lot of the fat. Pour off the fat.

2. In a heavy skillet or Dutch oven, melt the butter over medium heat. When it is hot, add the vegetables and sauté 5 minutes, or until the onions are golden. Stir in the flour and cook another 2 minutes. Add chopped tomatoes and stock and stir until bubbly.

3. Add the browned ribs. Bring to a boil over high heat, reduce the heat and simmer, tightly covered, for 1½ hours, or until the ribs are tender. Add chicken stock from time to time to prevent sticking and to keep up the level of the liquid.

4. Stir the horseradish into the sauce and simmer 5 minutes. Serve the ribs with boiled new potatoes, buttered and sprinkled with parsley.

Veal

THE ESSENTIALS

The best veal is milk fed and under 6 weeks old, but tender veal 12 weeks old is found more easily. Its flesh is a pale pink (not pale red, which is called calves' meat by some), its fat a delicate ivory color. Veal has little, if any, fat or marbling; calves are too young to have developed much. Be careful not to overcook veal; it is an exceptionally delicate and intrinsically tender meat, but will lose both of those virtues if subjected to too long or too high heat. Roasts should be larded, or wrapped in fat; braising also keeps lean cuts succulent. And sautéing is a very fast method for scallopini.

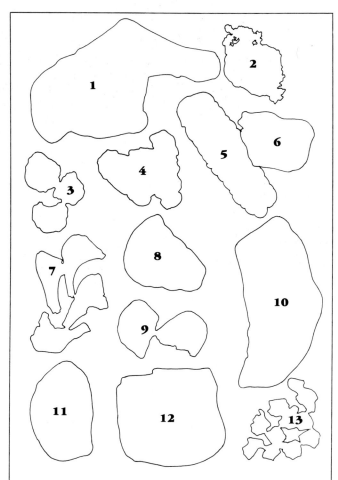

1. Shoulder (braise, roast) 2. Ground Veal (braise, pan-fry, roast) 3. Shank (braise) 4. Scallops (braise, pan-fry) 5. Boneless Shoulder Roast (braise, roast) 6. Rib Roast (roast) 7. Rib Chops (braise, pan-fry) 8. Boneless Leg Roast (braise, roast) 9. Loin Chops (braise, pan-fry) 10. Breast of Veal (braise, roast) 11. Leg Steak (braise, pan-fry) 12. Blade Roast (braise, roast) 13. Stew (braise)

VEAL SCALLOPINI IN WINE

Serves 4

Scallopini is any thin, lean meat, but veal is most prized for its tender light flavor, now more than ever.

8 veal scallopini, pounded to ¼-inch thick
salt
freshly ground black pepper
flour
2 tablespoons butter
2 tablespoons oil
½ cup mushrooms, sliced (optional)
1 tablespoon lemon juice
½ cup dry white wine
1 tablespoon chopped parsley

1. Sprinkle the veal lightly with salt and pepper and dredge lightly in flour, shaking off excess.

2. Heat the butter and oil in a large heavy skillet over high heat. When the fat is hot, sauté the veal quickly—a minute or so on each side—and put on a warm platter. If necessary, cook the veal in separate batches to avoid crowding the pan.

3. When all the veal has been browned, sauté the mushrooms for 1 minute in the pan. Deglaze the pan with the lemon juice and wine, scraping up all the browned particles as the liquid boils.

4. To serve, spoon the pan juices over the veal and sprinkle the top with chopped parsley.

Sautéed Veal with Mornay Sauce. Sauté the veal as described above through Step 2. Serve with Mornay Sauce (see page 72) and garnish with tiny spiced apples.

PAILLARD OF VEAL WITH SAGE AND PROSCIUTTO

Serves 4

Paillards are large, thin slices from the leg.

1½ pounds veal scallopini, ¼-inch thick
salt
freshly ground black pepper
flour
¼ cup vegetable oil
½ cup dry white wine
2 tablespoons butter
1½ teaspoons chopped fresh or 1 teaspoon dried sage
4 thin slices prosciutto

1. Sprinkle the veal slightly with salt and pepper. Dredge in flour, shaking off any excess. In a large, heavy skillet, heat the oil over high heat. When the oil is very hot, brown the veal quickly—1 minute or so a side—and put on a warm platter. Cook the veal in batches to avoid crowding the pan.

2. When the veal is browned, drain the oil from the pan. Deglaze the pan with the white wine, scraping up all the browned bits as the wine boils. Stir in the butter and sage.

3. Cover each slice of veal with a slice of prosciutto and the pan juices and serve immediately.

OSSO BUCO MILANESE
Braised Veal Shanks

Serves 4

The only reason to eat Osso Buco, many say, is for the rich marrow found in the center of each shank bone. Hind shanks have more meat than front ones, but the amount of marrow—an unknown until you start eating—is the true test of quality. Serve with Risotto Milanese (see page 208).

8 3-inch-long slices veal shank
salt
freshly ground black pepper
flour
¼ cup butter
¼ cup oil
1 carrot, minced
1 onion, chopped
1 stalk celery, chopped
1 clove garlic, minced
¾ cup dry white wine
1½ pounds Italian plum tomatoes, peeled and chopped
1½ cups Chicken Stock (see page 58)
1 teaspoon chopped fresh or ½ teaspoon dried sage
1 teaspoon chopped fresh or ½ teaspoon dried rosemary
1 tablespoon chopped parsley

GREMOLATA

2 cloves garlic, minced
2 teaspoons grated lemon rind
¼ cup chopped parsley
4 anchovy filets, minced (optional)

1. Sprinkle the veal shanks lightly with salt and pepper. Dredge the pieces in flour. In a large heavy skillet, Dutch oven or roasting pan (the veal should fit in a single layer), heat the butter and oil over medium heat. When it is hot, sauté the veal until it is browned on all sides. Remove the

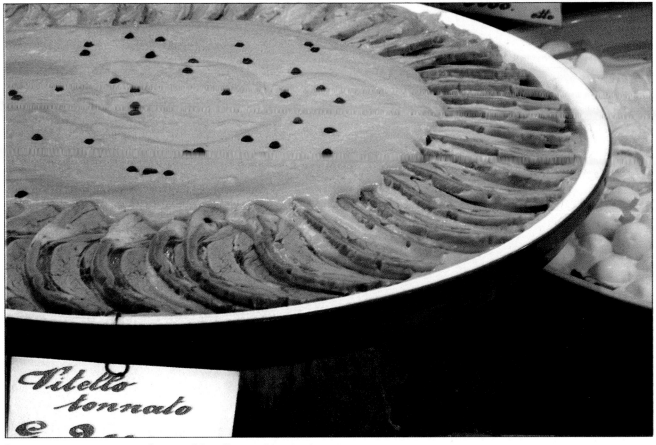

A creamy tuna sauce and very thin slices of braised veal are combined in Vitello Tonnato.

veal to a platter, reduce the heat to medium and add the vegetables and 1 clove garlic to the pan. Sauté until golden—about 5 minutes.

2. Return the veal to the pan. Add the wine and bring it to a boil for 1 minute. Add the tomatoes, stock, sage and rosemary and 1 tablespoon parsley and bring to a boil. Reduce the heat and simmer, tightly covered, for 1 to 1½ hours, or until the veal is tender.

3. Mix a *gremolata* by combining the 2 cloves garlic, lemon rind, ¼ cup parsley and anchovy filets. Serve the *gremolata* sprinkled over the veal shanks.

VITELLO TONNATO
Roast Veal with Tuna Sauce

Serves 4 to 6

3 pounds boneless leg of veal
salt
freshly ground black pepper
1 7½-ounce can water-packed tuna, drained
1 2-ounce can flat anchovy filets, drained and chopped
2 cloves garlic, chopped
2 carrots, shredded
1 cup dry white wine
½ cup white wine vinegar
½ cup Brown Stock (see page 57)
⅓ cup olive oil
2 hard-boiled egg yolks, sieved
3 tablespoons capers
lemon wedges
capers for garnish

1. Season the veal with salt and pepper.

2. In a heavy pot or Dutch oven over medium heat, mix the tuna, anchovies, garlic, carrots, wine, vinegar and stock. Then add the veal and simmer, covered, turning it occasionally, for 1 to 1½ hours, until the veal is tender but slightly firm.

3. Let the veal cool in the broth. Remove the veal, slice it paper-thin and overlap the slices on a large serving platter.

4. In a blender, process the pan juices, oil, egg yolks and capers until smooth. Pour this sauce over the veal and refrigerate for several hours. Serve cold with lemon wedges, sprinkled with additional capers.

SAUTEED VEAL CHOPS

Serves 4

2 tablespoons butter
4 rib or loin veal chops, 1 inch thick
salt
freshly ground white pepper
½ cup marsala wine

1. In a skillet, heat the butter. Sprinkle the chops with salt and pepper. Brown the veal chops slowly on both sides for 20 to 30 minutes. Put the chops on serving plates.

2. Add the wine to the skillet and bring to a boil, scraping loose all the brown particles. Lower the heat and simmer for 5 minutes. Spoon the juices over the veal chops.

Veal Chops with Vegetable Sauce. Mix 3 tablespoons flour with 1½ cups Chicken Stock (see page 58) and stir into the pan juices until the sauce thickens. Add ½ cup each cooked baby carrots, baby whole onions and 1-inch celery pieces, 1 teaspoon each chopped fresh or ¼ teaspoon each dried chervil and summer savory. Simmer 5 minutes and spoon sauce over chops.

Veal Chops with Cream Sauce. Stir 1 recipe Salsa Besciamella (see page 186) into the pan juices, adding 2 tablespoons each finely chopped parsley and celery leaves. Simmer 5 minutes then spoon over the chops.

STUFFED BREAST OF VEAL

Serves 6

1 4- to 5-pound piece boned breast of veal
salt
freshly ground white pepper
1½ teaspoons fresh chopped or ½ teaspoon dried thyme
1 cup fresh whole-wheat bread crumbs
1 cup chopped cooked green beans or carrots
1 cup squeezed dry chopped fresh or frozen spinach
1 tablespoon grated onion
¼ cup butter
2 cups Chicken Stock (see page 58)

1. Pound the veal until it is a flat sheet about ½-inch thick. Sprinkle the veal with salt, pepper and thyme.

2. In a bowl, mix bread, beans, spinach and onion with salt and pepper to taste. Spread the mixture down the center of the length of veal.

3. Preheat the oven to 400°F. Roll the veal lengthwise, tying with string every 1½ inches. Put the veal, seam side

Sautéed Veal Chops

down, into a baking pan. Spread the veal with butter.

4. Roast the veal for 30 to 40 minutes or until brown. Remove from the oven and add the stock to the pan. Cover the pan with foil, lower the heat to 350°F and roast, covered, for another 1 to 1½ hours or until the veal is easily pierced with a fork. Cool for 20 minutes before cutting into ¼ inch thick slices.

5. Pour the pan juices into a saucepan and boil for 5 minutes. Spoon the juices over the veal.

VEAL SHOULDER ROAST

Serves 6 to 8

1 4- to 5-pound boneless veal shoulder roast
3 sprigs each fresh oregano, thyme and sage
6 ounces thinly sliced pancetta or bacon
freshly ground black pepper

1. Preheat the oven to 350°F. Put the veal roast into a shallow roasting pan. Lay the herbs on the roast and cover with pancetta or bacon. Tie in place if necessary. Sprinkle the roast heavily with pepper. Salt is not necessary since the pancetta and bacon are already salty.

2. Roast for 2 to 2½ hours or until the meat thermometer registers 170°F for well done. Remove the roast from the oven and let it stand for 20 minutes to allow the juices to settle. Remove the pancetta or bacon and the herbs, then cut the veal into thin slices. The veal can be served with Sauce Espagnole (see page 75).

BRAISED VEAL ROAST

Serves 6 to 8

1 4- to 5-pound boneless veal loin roast
salt
freshly ground white pepper
¼ cup butter
2 leeks, trimmed and sliced
1 clove garlic, chopped
½ cup tomato juice
½ cup dry red wine

1. Sprinkle the roast with salt and pepper. In a Dutch oven, heat the butter and brown the veal on all sides. Add the leeks and garlic and sauté for another 5 minutes.

2. Add the tomato juice and wine, cover tightly, and simmer over low heat for 1 to 1½ hours or until the veal is tender. Add more wine if necessary to keep the veal from sticking. Let the veal stand for 20 minutes and then cut into slices and serve with the pan juices.

Tomatoes and wine add piquancy to Veal Marengo.

VEAL MARENGO

Serves 4

2 pounds boneless veal, cut into 1-inch cubes
salt
freshly ground black pepper
2 tablespoons olive oil
2 cloves garlic, chopped
1 cup chopped onion
6 tomatoes, peeled, seeded and chopped, or 1 can
(1 pound, 12 ounces) tomatoes, drained and chopped
½ cup dry white wine
1 cup Brown Stock (see page 57)
12 pearl onions, peeled
12 mushrooms, halved
½ cup chopped parsley

1. Sprinkle the veal lightly with salt and pepper. In a heavy skillet or Dutch oven, heat the oil over medium high heat. When it is hot, brown the veal on all sides, cooking in batches to keep from crowding the pan.

2. When the veal is browned, remove it and reduce the heat to medium and sauté the garlic and chopped onion for 5 minutes. Return the veal to the pan, add the tomatoes, wine and stock and bring the liquid to a boil. Reduce the heat, cover the pan and simmer for 45 minutes to 1 hour, or until the veal is tender but still firm.

3. Add the pearl onions, mushrooms and parsley and simmer an additional 15 minutes. Serve with rice or noodles.

Lamb

THE ESSENTIALS

The finest lamb, imported from New Zealand or Australia, is still called "spring lamb," despite its year-round availability. It is younger, with a leg that weighs from 4 to 7 pounds; its meat (like that of any lamb under a year) is quite pink, with pink bones as well, and white, pearly fat. Saddle and rack of lamb are cuts often savored for special occasions, but whether you prefer a traditional leg or tiny, tender chops, be sure to cook them medium to medium-rare so as not to destroy the flavor.

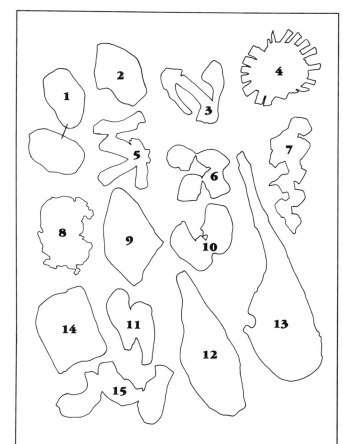

1. Leg Steaks (roast) **2.** Rack (roast) **3.** Rib Chops (broil, pan-broil, pan-fry, roast) **4.** Crown Roast (roast) **5.** Riblets (braise) **6.** Loin Chops (broil, pan-broil, pan-fry) **7.** Stew (braise) **8.** Ground Lamb (broil, pan-broil, pan-fry) **9.** Breast of Lamb (braise, roast) **10.** Sirloin Chops (broil, pan-fry) **11.** Shanks (braise) **12.** Frenched Leg (roast) **13.** Untrimmed Leg (roast) **14.** Square-cut Shoulder (roast) **15.** Shoulder Arm Chops—Round-bone (braise, broil, pan-fry, pan-broil)

LAMB STEW

Serves 10 to 12

Honest and straightforward, lamb stew gets its character from long, slow cooking.

5 pounds boneless lamb, cut into 1-inch pieces
salt
freshly ground black pepper
flour
½ cup butter
3 quarts water
4 tomatoes, peeled, seeded and diced
¼ cup chopped fresh parsley
1 pound pearl onions, peeled
12 carrots, cut into 1-inch lengths
4 white turnips, diced
24 new potatoes, peeled and halved
4 cups fresh shelled peas or 2 10-ounce packages frozen peas

1. Sprinkle the lamb lightly with salt and pepper and dredge it in flour. In a heavy 5- or 6-quart pot or Dutch oven, melt the butter over medium heat. When it is hot, brown the lamb pieces in batches, so the pan isn't crowded. Remove the browned lamb and set aside.

2. When all the lamb has been well browned, return it to the pot. Add the water, tomatoes and parsley. Bring to a boil, reduce the heat and slowly simmer the meat, tightly covered, for 1 to 1½ hours, or until almost tender.

3. Add the onions, carrots, turnips and potatoes and simmer, covered, for another 30 minutes, or until the vegetables are tender. Add the peas and simmer for another 5 minutes. Check the seasoning and add salt and pepper if you think they are needed.

LAMB KORMA
Lamb Stew

Serves 4

The Indian version of lamb stew, with a medley of aromatic seasonings.

¼ cup raw cashews
3 dried hot chilies
1 1-inch piece peeled ginger
1 2-inch cinnamon stick, broken into small pieces
2 cloves garlic
2 tablespoons white poppy seeds
1 tablespoon coriander seeds

1 teaspoon cumin seeds
½ cup water
½ cup Brown Stock (see page 57) or water
⅓ cup Clarified Butter (see page 79)
1 cup chopped onion
2 teaspoons salt
½ teaspoon saffron threads, soaked in 1 tablespoon boiling water
½ cup plain yogurt
2 pounds lean, boneless leg or shoulder of lamb, cut into 1-inch chunks
2 tablespoons chopped fresh or 2 teaspoons dried coriander
1 tablespoon fresh lemon juice
lemon slices
mint leaves

1. In a blender, grind together the cashews, chilies, ginger, cinnamon stick, garlic, poppy seeds, coriander, cumin and water. Add the stock to the spice mixture and mix well.

2. In a large skillet, heat the butter and sauté the chopped onion for 5 minutes, or until golden brown. Add the salt, saffron and its liquid, spice mixture and yogurt. Mix well.

3. When the butter-spice mixture is heated through, add the lamb and simmer the stew, covered, for 1 hour, or until the lamb is tender. Just before serving, mix in the coriander and lemon juice and salt to taste. Garnish with lemon slices and mint leaves.

SADDLE OF LAMB WITH PINK PEPPERCORNS

Serves 4

Nouvelle Cuisine has brought us the rosy luxury of pink peppercorns. Milder than black, they make a pretty marriage with pink lamb, raspberries and tiny vegetables.

1 6- to 7-pound leg of lamb or saddle of lamb, boned, with bones reserved
4 cups water
1 onion, chopped
1 large carrot, chopped
1 cup chopped parsley
½ cup butter
salt
freshly ground black pepper
½ cup red currant jelly
2 tablespoons pink peppercorns
2 zucchini, sliced and steamed
4 baby carrots, steamed
raspberries

1. Roast the lamb bones in a 425°F oven until brown, about 1 hour. Put the bones in a large saucepan, add water, the onion, carrot and parsley and boil down to 1 cup of liquid. Strain the liquid and reheat to boiling. Remove the liquid from the heat and beat in the butter, 1 tablespoon at a time. Season with salt and pepper and keep warm.

2. In a small saucepan, melt the currant jelly. Sprinkle the lamb with salt and pepper and brush with some of the melted jelly. Put it on a broiling pan with a rack and broil 6 inches from the source of heat, brushing with jelly from time to time, until the lamb is brown and crusty outside and rare inside, about 15 to 20 minutes on each side.

3. Cut the lamb into slices and top with the sauce. Sprinkle with pink peppercorns and garnish with the vegetables and raspberries.

STUFFED LAMB RIBLETS

Serves 4

Lamb riblets come from the lower part of the ribs—a flavor-laden, but less meaty, rack of lamb.

2 racks of lamb riblets
1 clove garlic, cut in half
salt
freshly ground black pepper
1½ teaspoons chopped fresh or ½ teaspoon dried
    rosemary
6 slices firm whole-wheat bread, cubed
2 tablespoons melted butter
1 onion, chopped
1 cup cooked, squeezed-dry and chopped fresh spinach
    or 1 10-ounce package frozen chopped spinach,
    thawed and squeezed dry
juice of 1 lemon
½ teaspoon *fines herbes*
½ teaspoon crushed fennel seed
1 egg, beaten
juice of 2 lemons
⅓ cup currant or mint jelly

1. Preheat oven to 350°F. Rub the lamb with the cut garlic and sprinkle with salt, pepper and rosemary.

2. To make the stuffing, combine the bread, butter, onion, spinach, juice of 1 lemon, *fines herbes,* fennel and egg in a large bowl and mix until well blended.

CARVING A LEG OF LAMB. To slice a roast leg of lamb, hold the narrow end firmly and slice down and away with a very sharp knife.

3. Put 1 rack of ribs, bone side up, on a working surface. Spread the stuffing evenly over the lamb. Cover with the second rack of ribs, bone side down. Tie the sections together with string and put them on the rack of a shallow roasting pan. Roast for 1 hour.

4. In a small saucepan, heat the lemon juice and jelly until the jelly melts. Mix well and spoon over the ribs. Let the ribs cook another 30 minutes, basting with the glaze every 10 minutes.

5. To serve, cut and discard the string and slice between the rib bones.

CROWN ROASTS OF LAMB

Serves 12

Each crown roast is made from 2 racks of lamb—attached rib chops—trimmed and tied together.

2 crown roasts of lamb, each made with 2 racks of 6 lamb ribs
salt
1 tablespoon fresh chopped or 1 teaspoon dried crumbled rosemary
1 tablespoon fresh chopped or 1 teaspoon dried crumbled thyme
freshly ground black pepper
lamb trimmings from the roast, ground

1 1-pound loaf firm white bread, crumbled
½ cup melted butter
1½ cups orange juice
2 tart cooking apples, peeled, cored and diced
1 cup chopped dried apricots
½ teaspoon ground nutmeg

4 large potatoes, boiled, peeled and mashed
⅓ cup melted butter
1 large onion, chopped
1 bunch broccoli, flowerets only
½ cup grated Parmesan
½ cup milk

1. Preheat the oven to 350°F. Season the crown roast with salt, rosemary, thyme and pepper. In a heavy skillet, sauté the ground lamb trimmings over medium heat until brown and crumbly. Discard the excess fat.

2. To make the fruit stuffing, combine ½ of the cooked lamb trimmings in a large bowl with the bread crumbs, butter, orange juice, apples, apricots and nutmeg.

3. For the vegetable stuffing, mix the remaining ingredients and the other half of the cooked lamb trimmings in a separate bowl.

4. Put each crown roast in a shallow roasting pan. Pack the center of one with fruit stuffing and the other with vegetable stuffing. Cover the stuffings with aluminum foil. Place the pans in the preheated oven and roast for 1½ hours. The roasts should be brown and crisp outside, but the meat still pink inside. Cook the lamb for 2 hours if you like your lamb well done.

5. When the roasts are done, remove from the oven and let them sit in their roasting pans for at least 15 minutes to make carving easier. Carefully lift the roasts to warm serving platters. To carve, slice between the ribs.

HERB GARLIC LAMB CHOPS

Serves 4

8 rib or loin lamb chops
1 clove garlic, mashed
salt
2 tablespoons butter
½ cup dry white wine
1 teaspoon chopped fresh or ¼ teaspoon dried rosemary
2 teaspoons chopped fresh or ½ teaspoon dried mint

1. Rub the chops with garlic and then sprinkle with salt. In a skillet, heat the butter and brown the chops quickly over medium heat, on both sides. The chops should be crusty outside and pink inside.

2. Remove the chops to serving plates and add wine and herbs to the pan drippings. Bring to a boil on top of the stove and simmer for 5 minutes, scraping loose all the brown particles. Spoon the pan juices over the chops and serve.

Sesame Lamb Chops. Use 1 tablespoon Oriental sesame oil or chili oil instead of butter and prepare the chops as above. Deglaze the pan with sake or white wine. Use 1 tablespoon minced scallions and 1 teaspoon grated fresh ginger instead of herbs.

BUTTERFLIED LEG OF LAMB

Serves 8

1 5-pound leg of lamb
1 cup Garlic Vinaigrette Dressing (see page 80)
1 tablespoon chopped fresh or 1 teaspoon dried rosemary

1. To butterfly a leg of lamb, take the leg and slash it lengthwise on its underside (the less fatty side). Carefully cut around the bone and remove it. At this point the meat will open out into a rough butterfly shape.

2. Gently pound the lamb to an approximate thickness of 1 inch. Half cover the meat with the garlic vinaigrette dressing and marinate for 2 hours at room temperature or overnight in the refrigerator—longer will not improve the flavor. Grill or broil the lamb 6 inches from the source of heat for 15 to 20 minutes per side for pink meat.

Note. To stuff a boned leg of lamb, use one of the stuffing recipes from the crown roasts of lamb. Spread the stuffing down the center of the butterflied lamb and roll the lamb around the stuffing. Tie with twine at 1½-inch intervals and roast at 350°F for 1 to 1½ hours.

Lamb shanks are tenderized in red wine and orange juice and then grilled.

GRILLED LAMB SHANKS

Serves 4

4 small young lamb shanks
salt
freshly ground black pepper
1 clove garlic, chopped
1 medium onion, grated
1 green pepper, minced
½ cup olive oil
⅓ cup red wine
1 6-ounce can frozen concentrated orange juice

1. Salt and pepper the lamb shanks. In a saucepan, cover the lamb with water and gently simmer the meat until it is almost tender, about 1 hour. Remove the lamb and cool.

2. Put the lamb shanks in a shallow dish and marinate for 2 hours with the remaining ingredients. Drain.

3. Grill the lamb 8 inches above hot coals for 20 to 30 minutes, turning the shanks every 5 minutes.

Note. Serve the shanks with Green Rice (see page 206) and grilled eggplant, prepared by dipping eggplant slices into the remaining marinade and grilling them on a foil-lined rack for 5 minutes on each side, brushing with marinade several times.

Pork

THE ESSENTIALS

Good pork has a pink to white color, with very white fat. Shoulder and leg meats will be somewhat darker and have a coarser texture, since they are the most used muscles. Nutritionists recommend that pork be cooked to an internal temperature of 160°F to eliminate the possibility of trichinosis, but it is important, nevertheless, not to overcook it or the meat will toughen and dry out. The juices of cooked pork will be clear, not pink. Surprisingly, pork loin is not a fatty cut of meat and often needs wrapping in a layer of fat when roasted for extra succulence. Braising keeps chops tender since they have no marbling like beef.

We refer to cured pork as ham, which also once meant a pork leg. Cured ham (either in brine or dry, by salt) can be smoked as well. Prosciutto, Virginia and Smithfield hams are dry cured; so called country-style hams have been dry cured, then smoked and aged—often up to a year. Dry cured hams should be kept in a dry, cool place, not refrigerated. They are quite rich and should be served in very thin slices. Much of the ham we buy in supermarkets has been cured in brine and has water added (up to 10 percent) and needs refrigeration. Like any meat, ham with the bone has the most flavor; canned hams have the least flavor.

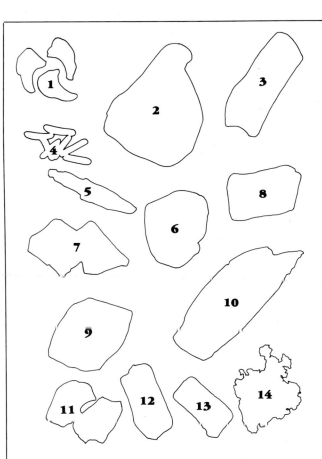

1. Rib Chops (braise, broil, pan-broil, pan-fry) **2.** Fresh Ham (roast) **3.** Rib Roast (roast) **4.** Breakfast Sausages (braise, pan-fry, roast) **5.** Pork Tenderloin (roast, braise) **6.** Blade Roast (roast) **7.** Country Ribs (bake, grill) **8.** Picnic Shoulder (roast) **9.** Square-cut Shoulder (roast) **10.** Spareribs (roast, broil, braise) **11.** Blade Chops (braise, broil, pan-broil, pan-fry) **12.** Center Loin Roast (roast) **13.** Salt Pork (used as seasoning) **14.** Ground Pork (broil, pan-broil, pan-fry, roast)

JIMMY'S BARBECUED SPARERIBS

Serves 4

The sauce is best on ribs, but it gives panache to chicken, too.

4 ripe tomatoes, peeled, seeded and chopped
2 large onions, finely chopped
1 clove garlic, minced
1 tart apple, cored, peeled and chopped
1 teaspoon turmeric
¼ cup butter
¼ cup cider vinegar
2 tablespoons Worcestershire sauce
juice of ½ lemon
1 bay leaf
½ to ¾ teaspoon Tabasco sauce
1½ teaspoons dry mustard
½ teaspoons chili powder
½ teaspoon salt
4 pounds spareribs, sectioned

1. In a large saucepan, combine all the ingredients except spareribs and bring to a boil. Lower the heat and simmer, uncovered, stirring occasionally, until the sauce is thick, about 30 to 35 minutes.

2. Press the sauce through a sieve or food mill.

3. Preheat oven to 450°F. Put spareribs on cookie sheet. Loosely cover them with aluminum foil and roast for 15 minutes. Reduce heat to 350°F and brush ribs liberally with sauce.

4. Continue roasting for 30 minutes. Turn ribs, brush with sauce and roast for an additional 30 minutes.

GERMAN-STYLE PORK BACK RIBS

Serves 4

Sauerkraut apples and caraway seeds are traditionally baked with pork in German kitchens. Back ribs, also called country-style ribs, are meatier than spareribs.

4 pounds pork back ribs
salt
freshly ground black pepper
2 onions, sliced
2 tart apples, peeled, cored and sliced
1 pound sauerkraut
1 cup beer, dry white wine or cider
2 teaspoons caraway seeds

1. Preheat the oven to 400°F. Sprinkle the ribs lightly with salt and pepper and put in a shallow roasting pan. Roast for 30 minutes, or until the ribs are browned and the fat is rendered. Pour off the fat and let cool.

2. Put the ribs in a 2-quart Dutch oven or heavy skillet. Cover with the remaining ingredients and bring to a boil over high heat. Reduce the heat and simmer, tightly covered, for 45 minutes, or until the ribs are tender. Serve the ribs on a bed of sauerkraut, apples and onions.

STUFFED PORK CHOPS

Serves 4

4 rib pork chops, at least 1-inch thick
salt
freshly ground black pepper
1 tablespoon butter
1 small onion, diced
1 celery stalk, diced
1 tablespoon chopped parsley
1½ teaspoons chopped fresh or ½ teaspoon dried thyme
¼ cup fine dry bread crumbs
½ cup white wine
2 cloves garlic, minced
1 cup White Stock (see page 56)

1. Trim the chops of excess fat, chop the fat and reserve. Make pockets in the chops as shown below. Sprinkle the chops inside and out with salt and pepper.

2. In a small heavy skillet, melt the butter over medium heat and sauté the onions and celery for 3 to 4 minutes. Remove from heat and stir in the parsley, thyme and bread crumbs. If the stuffing is too dry, add a teaspoon or so of stock to moisten it.

3. Divide the filling between the four chops, putting some in each pocket. Skewer the pockets closed with wooden toothpicks.

4. In a heavy skillet, large enough to hold all 4 chops in a single uncrowded layer, render reserved pork fat to coat the bottom. Remove the crisp pieces and discard. When the fat is quite hot, sear the stuffed chops over medium heat until browned, about 5 to 6 minutes on each side.

5. Remove the chops and drain any fat from the pan. Deglaze the pan with the wine over medium high heat, letting it reduce by half.

6. Return the chops to the pan. Add the garlic and stock. Bring to a boil, reduce the heat, cover tightly and simmer 15 minutes. Turn the chops and simmer for another 15 minutes or until tender. Serve the chops with the pan juices.

Slit the pork chop horizontally, carefully cutting almost to the bone.

Stuff with filling and then skewer the pockets closed with wooden toothpicks.

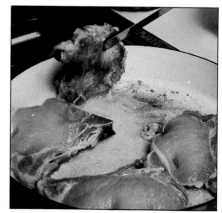

Brown the stuffed chops on both sides, turning them gently before braising.

ROAST PORK LOIN

Loins of pork suitable for roasting come with the rib bones or boneless. Bones add flavor to the meat but boneless makes it easier to carve into thinner slices. Have the butcher remove the chine bone from the bottom of the roast for easier slicing.

1 pork loin, with or without bones
salt
freshly ground black pepper
1 clove garlic, mashed
fresh herbs (optional)

1. For each serving, allow 12 ounces pork with bone or 6 to 8 ounces boneless pork. Trim all but ½ inch of the fat to keep the roast from drying out. Sprinkle with salt and freshly ground pepper. Rub the garlic all over the roast or cut the garlic into slivers and poke them into tiny holes made with the tip of a sharp knife. Holes can also be stuffed with small sprigs of thyme, sage or chervil.

2. Put the pork, fat side up, in a shallow roasting pan and roast at 350°F for about 30 minutes per pound or until a meat thermometer registers 180°F. Cool for 20 minutes, then cut into slices, 1 slice with a rib, 1 without. Serve with Sauce Robert (see page 76).

STIR-FRY PORK WITH ZUCCHINI AND NOODLES

Serves 4

1½ teaspoons salt
½ pound Chinese egg noodles or ½ pound vermicelli
1 teaspoon sesame oil
5 tablespoons plus ½ teaspoon peanut oil
1 teaspoon cornstarch
2 teaspoons soy sauce
2 teaspoons sherry
¾ teaspoon sugar
½ pound lean pork, thinly sliced
2 medium zucchini, cut into ½-inch pieces
1 scallion, sliced
1 clove garlic
1 slice fresh ginger
¾ cup Chicken Stock (see page 58)

1. In a large pot of boiling water with 1 teaspoon of salt added, cook the noodles until tender but still firm. Drain and toss with sesame oil and 1 tablespoon peanut oil. Cover and refrigerate the noodles for 2 hours or overnight.

Roast Pork Loin with Sauce Robert (see page 76)

2. In a blender or food processor, blend the cornstarch, 1 teaspoon soy sauce, sherry, ¼ teaspoon sugar and ½ teaspoon peanut oil. Pour this marinade over the pork slices and set aside.

3. Wash and slice the zucchini and scallion. Mash the garlic and the ginger with the flat of a knife. In a small bowl, mix the remaining sugar, salt and soy sauce and the stock. Set all within easy reach of the frying pan or wok.

4. In a frying pan or wok, heat 2 tablespoons of the peanut oil. When it is very hot, fry the noodles (like a large pancake) over high heat for 2 minutes on each side. Remove the noodles to a large platter and keep warm in a low oven.

5. Put the remaining 2 tablespoons peanut oil into the pan. When it is very hot, add ginger and garlic. Add the pork with the marinade and stir-fry for about 3 minutes. Then add the zucchini and scallion and stir again. Add the stock mixture and cover for about 3 minutes. Spoon over the noodles and serve immediately.

INDONESIAN PORK SATE

Serves 4

Ground peanuts are an important ingredient in Indonesian cooking. Combine peanuts with tomato, onion, lemon and red pepper flakes for an addictive sauce for grilled pork.

2 pounds lean boneless pork, cut into ¾-inch pieces, or long thin strips of pork scallopini
salt
freshly ground black pepper
½ cup soy sauce
4 cloves garlic, chopped
1 small onion, chopped
2 tablespoons oil
1 large onion, chopped
1 cup Fresh Tomato Sauce (see page 186)
2 tablespoons peanut butter

1 to 2 teaspoons red pepper flakes (to taste)
2 tablespoons lemon juice

1. Sprinkle the pork pieces very lightly with salt and pepper and put them in a bowl. Add the soy sauce, garlic and small chopped onion and let the pork marinate at room temperature for 2 hours, turning the meat occasionally.

2. Prepare and light a charcoal fire or preheat your broiler. Drain the pork and spear on skewers. When the coals are gray, grill the pork 8 inches above them for 15 minutes, turning frequently, or broil for the same length of time.

3. Make the sauce over the hottest part of the grill or on top of the range. Heat the oil in a heavy saucepan. When it is hot, brown the remaining onion, sautéing for about 5 minutes. Stir in the remaining ingredients and bring the sauce to a simmer.

4. Serve with the sauce alongside.

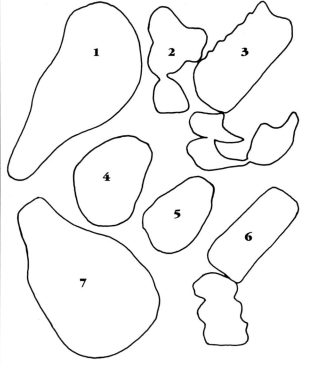

1. Country Ham (roast, bake) **2.** Ham Hocks (braise) **3.** Smoked Pork Loin (roast, bake, pan-fry) **4.** Ham, Shank End (roast, bake) **5.** Ham, Butt End (roast, bake) **6.** Canadian Bacon (broil, pan-fry, bake) **7.** Whole Ham (roast, bake)

BAKED HAM

Serves 12

As good as baked ham is for a large dinner, it's even better thereafter in a pasta sauce or jambon persille, or as a starter for a bean soup. Hams come completely or partially cooked, but it takes 10 minutes per pound to heat a cooked one through. For partially cooked ham, count on 20 minutes per pound and a meat thermometer reading of 160° F. Hams with the bone in have more flavor.

1 small precooked smoked ham (about 8 pounds), bone in
whole cloves
2 tablespoons Dijon mustard
1 cup Madeira wine
1 cup apricot nectar

1. Preheat the oven to 350° F. With a sharp knife, trim the brown skin up to the shank end of the ham exposing the fat underneath. Score the fat in a diamond pattern so that the mustard and glaze can penetrate. Spread the fatty surface with mustard and stud each diamond with a clove. Put the ham on the rack of a shallow roasting pan, mustard side up, and bake, 10 minutes per pound.

2. In a small bowl, mix the wine and nectar. Baste the ham every 15 minutes with this mixture.

3. Let the ham rest 15 minutes before carving. Pour off the fat from the roasting pan into a saucepan. Add 1 cup of liquid (use any remaining basting liquid with water added), then bring to a boil, scraping up all the brown particles. Boil 1 minute and spoon this sauce over each serving.

HAM AND LEEKS AU GRATIN

Serves 4

8 leeks
½ teaspoon salt
3 cups diced cooked ham
¼ cup butter
¼ cup flour
1 cup beer
1 cup heavy cream
2 cups grated Gruyère
freshly ground black pepper

1. Wash the leeks carefully to remove all the sand. Discard the roots; chop the green stems and reserve, put the trimmed leeks in a saucepan and just cover with water.

Add ½ teaspoon salt, bring to a boil, reduce the heat and simmer, covered, for 15 minutes, or until tender.

2. Preheat the oven to 400° F. Butter a shallow baking pan or gratin dish. Drain the leeks and put them in a pan, then arrange the ham on top.

3. In a heavy saucepan, melt the butter over medium heat. When it is hot, sauté the chopped leek greens for 5 minutes. Stir in the flour and let cook for 2 minutes. Gradually add the beer, stirring constantly until it is incorporated. Add the cream in the same way and let the sauce cook until it begins to thicken. Stir in the cheese. When the cheese is melted, season with salt and pepper. Spoon the sauce over the ham and leeks.

4. Bake in the middle of the oven for 30 minutes, or until the top is browned.

ASPARAGUS AND HAM ON PUFF PASTRY WITH SAUCE MADERE

Serves 4

Sauce Madère (see page 76)
½ recipe Food Processor Puff Pastry (see page 275) or
  ½ 17¼-ounce package frozen puff pastry (see Step 2)
8 thin slices ham, approximately 2½ × 4 inches
8 spears asparagus, boiled or steamed tender-crisp

1. Make the sauce and hold in reserve.

2. If using frozen puff pastry, thaw the package for 20 minutes, then unfold and remove 1 sheet. (Use rest of package in another recipe.)

3. Preheat the oven to 400° F. Cut the pastry into 4 5-inch squares. Cut 4 strips, ½-inch wide, from one side of each square, turning the squares into 5 × 3-inch rectangles. Brush the edges of the rectangles, which will be the bottoms of the shells, with water. Press the ½-inch strips in place to form the sides of the shells. Overlap the strips at the corners and trim off any excess dough.

4. Prick the bottoms of the pastry shells with a fork at ½-inch intervals and put the shells on a cookie sheet. Bake in the middle of the oven for 12 to 15 minutes, or until puffed and lightly browned.

5. Roll a slice of ham around each asparagus spear and put in a shallow baking pan. Heat in the oven with the pastry for 5 minutes.

6. Reheat the Sauce Madère. When the pastry shells are baked, top each with 2 ham and asparagus rolls and spoon sauce over the top.

1. Smoked Tongue (bake) **2.** Tripe (braise) **3.** Beef Heart (braise) **4.** Fresh Tongue (braise) **5.** Beef Kidneys (broil, braise) **6.** Lamb Kidneys (broil, braise) **7.** Calves' Liver (broil, pan-fry) **8.** Sweetbreads (broil, braise) **9.** Brains (braise, broil) **10.** Beef Liver (braise, broil)

Innards

THE ESSENTIALS

Organs and glands, much loved by our forefathers, are finding their way into the New American Cuisine. American cookbooks have many recipes for what we so delicately term variety meats; the English call them offal, but perhaps the best word is *innards*.

Sweetbreads, tripe, kidneys, brains, tongue, liver and hearts are all extremely perishable, and some take special care before cooking. Bought fresh, they should be loosely wrapped and stored in the coldest part of the refrigerator for no more than 24 hours. All freeze well.

Brains. Calves' brains are considered the best, but beef, pork and lamb brains are also good. All should be absolutely fresh when purchased. That means a shiny moist surface, a delicate pink color and a plump, full texture. Allow ¼ pound of brains per serving. To prepare, cover with salted water and soak for 2 hours, changing the water several times. Drain and put in a saucepan. Cover with fresh water, add 2 tablespoons vinegar, 1 teaspoon salt, 1 sliced onion and 1 bay leaf. Bring to a boil, reduce the heat and simmer, covered, for 20 minutes. Let cool in the water, then drain and remove the outer membranes carefully with your fingers. Store covered in cold water in the refrigerator until ready to use.

Hearts. Hearts need only to be washed and trimmed of tubules and membranes before they are cooked. They taste rather like mild liver. Beef hearts are the largest (weighing up to 4 pounds) but also the toughest. Count on ½ pound per person.

Kidneys. Veal kidneys are the most prized. They are tender, similar in texture to liver. Figure 4 servings from a pair of beef kidneys; 3 from veal; 1 from pork; and it takes several lamb kidneys to make a portion. The outer membranes and tubules must be removed, and in the larger kidneys, interior fat should be discarded. Beef and pork kidneys should be soaked in cold water with 2 tablespoons of vinegar or lemon juice for an hour before cooking. The milder veal and lamb kidneys need only be rinsed. All kidneys toughen if they are overcooked.

Liver. One of the most common variety meats, calves' liver is certainly considered the most prized liver by many.

Like much offal, it is perishable; cook it within a day of purchase. Fresh liver has a glossy pale brown look to it, so avoid any dull meat. Some butchers remove the outer membrane; if not, pull it off before cooking. Liver toughens when overcooked.

Sweetbreads. These are the thymus glands of a sheep. Very delicate, very perishable and highly regarded by epicures, they should be bought as fresh as possible, or frozen. Allow ¼ pound per serving. Cook sweetbreads in cold water for 30 to 40 minutes, changing the water several times. Put in a saucepan and cover with water. Add 2 tablespoons lemon juice or vinegar and 1 teaspoon salt. Bring to a boil, reduce the heat and simmer, covered, for 15 minutes. Plunge into cold water to cool, then remove the membranes with your fingers and the connecting tubes and fat with a sharp knife.

Tongue. Fresh tongue has a more delicate flavor than pickled or smoked tongue. The smaller lamb and pork tongues are the best, but hard to find. Although beef tongues can be as large as 6 pounds, keep your choice to 3 pounds or less. Good both hot and cold, tongue is a popular delicatessen meat. Tongue is tough and must be simmered for 1½ to 2 hours, depending on the size. Add 1 sliced onion, 1 sliced lemon, 2 bay leaves, 1 teaspoon salt and 6 peppercorns to the cooking water. Drain and cool. Skin and trim off the fat and gristle and the small bones at the root end.

Tripe. Both smooth and honeycomb are part of a cow's stomach. Tripe is usually processed before it is sold, but it is still tough and needs extended cooking to be edible. Once it is tender—you can tell only by taking a bite—it has a lovely and delicate flavor. Soak tripe in cold water for 1 hour. Drain and put in a saucepan with fresh water to cover, 2 teaspoons salt, 6 peppercorns, 1 onion studded with several cloves, 1 bay leaf and several stalks of celery with leaves. Bring the water to a boil, reduce the heat and simmer, covered, for 1 to 5 hours. Test for tenderness periodically after the first hour.

SAUTEED CALVES' LIVER WITH PORT AND JUNIPER SAUCE

Serves 4

Calves' liver is more delicate than beef liver and is a good candidate for a quick sauté. Beef liver is better braised with a lot of onions. Both are highly perishable and should be used within a day of purchase.

¼ cup butter
4 shallots, chopped
2 pounds calves' liver, cut into 4 slices, membranes removed

salt
freshly ground black pepper
flour for dredging
1 cup port wine
6 dried, whole juniper berries, crushed

1. Heat the butter in a large frypan and sauté the shallots over medium heat until translucent.

2. Salt and pepper the liver and coat lightly in flour.

3. Add the liver slices and sauté until the liver is well browned but still pink inside, about 5 minutes on each side.

4. Remove the liver to a warm platter. Add the port wine and juniper berries to the pan juices and boil for 1 minute over high heat to deglaze. Pour the sauce over the liver, and serve.

DANISH STUFFED CALVES' HEARTS

Serves 6

6 cups dried bread cubes
½ teaspoon salt
dash white pepper
1½ teaspoons each chopped fresh or ½ teaspoon each dried thyme, marjoram and sage
3 cups Brown Stock (see page 57)
¼ cup melted butter
6 calves' hearts, washed and trimmed
½ cup dry red wine
3 tablespoons butter
3 tablespoons flour
1 tablespoon red wine vinegar
freshly ground black pepper

1. Bake the bread cubes at 300°F for 30 minutes, until browned. In a large bowl, combine the bread with ½ teaspoon salt, white pepper, herbs, butter and 1 cup of the stock. Mix well. Stuff the hearts and sew or skewer the openings.

2. Preheat the oven to 350°F. Put the stuffed hearts in a shallow baking pan and cover with the remaining stock and wine. Cover tightly with foil and bake for 1½ to 2 hours, or until the hearts are easily pierced with a fork. Remove the hearts to a warm platter and skim the fat from the pan, leaving the liquid. Boil until you have 1½ cups.

3. In a heavy saucepan, melt the butter over medium heat. Stir in the flour and cook 2 minutes. Add 1½ cups of the braising liquid and whisk until the sauce thickens. Season with salt and black pepper. Spoon the sauce over the hearts and serve.

BEEF AND KIDNEY PIE

Serves 6 to 8

Rich, aromatic and traditionally English.

2 tablespoons oil or bacon fat
2 beef kidneys, soaked, trimmed and sliced
2 pounds beef chuck, cut into 1-inch cubes
2 large onions, sliced
3 cups Brown Stock (see page 57)
1 cup dry red wine
1 tablespoon chopped fresh or 1 teaspoon crushed dried
   thyme
salt
freshly ground black pepper
½ pound small mushrooms, left whole
⅓ cup flour mixed with ½ cup cold brown stock
½ recipe Basic Pastry (see page 267)

1. In a large heavy saucepan or Dutch oven, heat the oil over medium heat. When it is hot, add the kidneys and beef and sauté until well browned. Add the onions and sauté for 2 to 3 minutes.

2. Add 2½ cups stock, wine, thyme and salt and pepper to taste. Bring to a boil, reduce the heat, cover and simmer for 1 hour, or until the meats are tender. Stir in the mushrooms and the flour-stock mixture and keep stirring until the sauce begins to thicken slightly. Pour the stew into a round 2-quart baking dish.

3. Preheat the oven to 400°F. On a floured surface, roll the pie crust into a circle at least 2 inches larger than the top of the casserole. Put the pastry over the top of the stew and seal the edges to the sides of the dish. Make several slits in the pastry to let steam escape.

4. Put the baking dish on a shallow pan to catch any drippings and bake for 25 to 30 minutes, or until the pastry is brown and crisp.

CAPELLI D'ANGELO WITH TRUFFLES AND SWEETBREADS
Angel Hair Pasta with Truffles and Sweetbreads

Serves 4

Capelli d'angelo—*angel hair pasta—is as unbelievably fine as the name implies. Sweetbreads and truffles must then be the angel's halo—the perfect finishing touch.*

¼ cup butter
1 pair sweetbreads, soaked, parboiled and trimmed (see
   page 175), cut into small pieces
1 tablespoon finely chopped truffles or mushrooms
1 egg yolk
1 cup heavy cream, whipped until partially thickened
salt
freshly ground black pepper
8 ounces *capelli d'angelo*

1. Boil 4 quarts of water for the pasta.

2. Meanwhile, in a heavy skillet or saucepan, melt the butter over medium heat. When it is hot, add the sweetbreads and sauté for 5 minutes. Add the truffles and sauté 1 minute. Remove the pan from the heat.

3. In a bowl, beat the egg yolk. Gently mix in the cream. Stir the cream and egg yolk into the sweetbread and truffle mixture. Season to taste with salt and pepper. Return the pan to a very low heat and stir the sauce until it heats through and begins to thicken. Don't let it boil.

4. Add 1 teaspoon salt to the now boiling water, then the pasta. Test the pasta after 2 minutes. When it is *al dente,* still "firm to the tooth," drain it and put on a warm platter. Toss gently with the sweetbread and cream sauce and serve immediately.

SWEETBREADS AND KIDNEYS EN BROCHETTE

Serves 4

2 veal kidneys or 4 lamb kidneys, cleaned and trimmed
2 pairs sweetbreads, soaked, parboiled and trimmed
   (see page 175)
salt
freshly ground black pepper
1 pound bacon, cut into 4 ¼-pound slices
1 tablespoon chopped fresh or 1 teaspoon crushed dried
   rosemary
about 1 cup dry sherry

1. Season the veal and lamb kidneys with salt and pepper. Cut veal kidneys into ½-inch-thick slices; halve lamb kidneys lengthwise. Cut the sweetbreads into 1½-inch pieces. You should have 4 pieces of each.

2. Roll up a piece of kidney and a piece of sweetbread in each slice of bacon. Put the rolls seam side down in a shallow dish. Sprinkle with rosemary and pour in enough sherry to half cover the rolls.

3. Let the meat marinate for 30 minutes. Turn the rolls marinate on the other side another 30 minutes.

Bacon-wrapped Sweetbreads and Kidneys en Brochette can be grilled outdoors or broiled indoors.

4. Make a charcoal fire or preheat the oven broiler. Drain the rolls and skewer each so that the bacon is held in place. Alternate kidney and sweetbread pieces.

5. Grill 8 inches from the fire over gray coals, or 6 inches from the heat in the broiler. Turn every 5 minutes until the bacon is crisp and brown—about 15 minutes in all.

SWEETBREADS AND PROSCIUTTO SOUBISE

Serves 4 to 6

⅓ cup butter
4 large yellow onions, chopped
1 cup heavy cream
¼ pound thinly sliced prosciutto or smoked ham, minced
4 sweetbreads, soaked, parboiled and trimmed (see page 175), cut into small pieces
salt
freshly ground black pepper
2 pounds asparagus spears, steamed and kept warm
2 tomatoes, peeled, seeded and chopped

1. In a large heavy saucepan, melt the butter over low heat and add the onions. Let them cook for 30 to 35 minutes over very low heat without browning. The onions should become thick and mushy, like a rough purée.

2. In a blender or food processor, purée the onions and their cooking liquid. Return the purée to the saucepan and stir in the cream, prosciutto, sweetbreads and salt and pepper to taste. Simmer without boiling for 5 minutes.

3. Put the asparagus on a warm platter, cover it with the sweetbread and ham mixture, and top with chopped tomatoes.

BRAINS IN BLACK BUTTER

Serves 6

Browned clarified butter seasoned with capers and lemon is a Frenchman's favorite. No wonder—it's sweet, delicate and quickly prepared.

3 whole calves' brains, simmered and trimmed
½ cup Clarified Butter (see page 79)
3 tablespoons capers
2 tablespoons lemon juice

1. Cut the brains into ½-inch-thick slices. In a heavy frying pan, heat 2 tablespoons of the butter over medium heat. When it is hot, sauté the brains for 1 or 2 minutes and remove them to a warm platter.

2. Add the remaining butter and cook until it turns golden brown. Don't let it burn. Stir in the capers and lemon juice and pour the sauce over the brains.

CREOLE TRIPE

Serves 6 to 8

2 pounds tripe, simmered until tender (see page 175)
2 tablespoons butter
1 green pepper, cored, seeded and chopped
2 large onions, chopped
1 clove garlic, chopped
2 tablespoons flour
2 pounds tomatoes, peeled, seeded and chopped, or 1 29-ounce can tomatoes, chopped
1 6-ounce can tomato paste
1 cup diced smoked ham
1 tablespoon chopped fresh or 1 teaspoon dried thyme
salt
freshly ground black pepper

1. Cut the tripe into small pieces. In a heavy 2- or 3-quart saucepan, melt the butter over medium heat. Add the green pepper, onions and garlic and sauté 5 minutes. Stir in the flour and let it cook 2 minutes.

2. Add the tomatoes, tomato paste and ham and stir until the sauce is well blended and beginning to thicken.

3. Stir in the tripe and thyme and simmer 3 or 4 minutes to heat through. Season with salt and pepper and serve.

SWEET AND SOUR TONGUE

Serves 6

2 pounds smoked beef tongue, boiled and trimmed (see page 175)
2 tablespoons butter
1 large onion, chopped
2 tablespoons flour
1½ cups Brown Stock (see page 57)
⅓ cup cider vinegar
¼ cup firmly packed brown sugar
½ cup raisins
½ large lemon, sliced paper-thin
salt
freshly ground black pepper

1. Cut the tongue into thin slices. In a large heavy skillet, melt the butter over medium heat. When it is hot, add the onion and sauté for 5 minutes. Stir in the flour and cook 2 minutes. Gradually stir in the stock, vinegar, sugar, raisins, and lemon slices and continue cooking until the sauce begins to thicken. Season to taste with salt and pepper.

2. Add the tongue slices and let them simmer until hot, about 3 to 4 minutes. Serve immediately.

Pasta

In the last few years this country has gone pasta mad, leaving behind a history of macaroni and cheese and canned spaghetti with tomato sauce. Pasta makers are no longer gourmet equipment. Pesto sauce, that aromatic blend of basil, garlic and olive oil, is causing a boom in the sale of basil seed. Fresh pasta sections are thriving in shops across the country. The New American Cuisine values its quick preparation, its ready combination with any number of the freshest ingredients and the endless variety of its shapes and textures.

Almost instantly, we discovered the subtlety, versatility and glory of the noodle. We have learned from Italy, where spaghetti, macaroni and myriad forms of noodles go by the ubiquitous name of pasta, that noodles know no bounds. Tiny butterflies or shells of pasta give substance to fragrant broths. White and green noodles tossed with sautéed chunks of ham, fresh mushrooms and bits of onion are coated in heavy cream and sprinkled generously with freshly grated Parmesan cheese. Dressed simply in butter and grated cheese, little hats of pasta are stuffed with chicken livers and parsley. Thin rods of spaghetti nestle with fresh clams in a sauce of white wine and clam broth. The variations of pasta shapes and sauces are endless. The saucing, stuffing and construction of pasta dishes has become as serious and infinitely variable to us as to an Italian cook.

Pasta can be served as first course, followed by chicken or most any meat or seafood or as a light lunch or dinner entrée.

THE ESSENTIALS

Pasta literally means "paste." It's also a generic term for all varieties of what we call spaghetti, macaroni and noodles. Technically speaking, U.S. law defines commercial spaghetti and macaroni as a paste of flour and water; only noodles must be a minimum 5.5 percent egg solids.

Homemade pasta, on the other hand, is generally made of eggs and flour with no water. Eggs make the dough easier to work by hand, and more nutritious. Fashioned in as many sizes and shapes as the commercial variety, homemade pasta can be used in place of commercial pasta. What it's called—spaghetti, noodles or linguine, fettuccine or tagliatelle—depends on the shape it takes and the language you speak.

The Italians have refined pasta into a greater number of sizes and shapes than anyone else, so it follows that we adopt their terminology. Spaghetti, for example, is a shape, and *macaroni* a generic term. And they take their definitions very seriously. Tagliatelle are long, narrow noodles that are a specialty of Bologna. At the chamber of commerce there, a sealed glass case holds a solid-gold noodle 1 millimeter thick and 6 millimeters wide—the standard dimensions for the perfect raw tagliatelle noodle.

While the shapes seem arbitrary, there's a method to their measures and moldings. Meat sauce doesn't stick very well to long, slim shapes, so it is most often served with shells or twisted shapes that will catch bits of sausage or ground beef. Sauces based on olive oil cling to the thinnest noodles.

Once you're accustomed to the feel of the dough at different stages, homemade pasta isn't at all frightening. A simple hand-cranked kneading and cutting machine does the hardest work—making a pliable, elastic dough out of the raw ingredients—and the trickiest—rolling and cutting the dough.

Imported pasta is worth trying, too. Because of its native flour, it has a chewier consistency, and because it expands more in cooking than domestic brands, you can use a little less per serving. There are hundreds of pastas to try—shapes for soups and for sauces, shapes to be stuffed and to be layered or baked.

Another alternative is fresh pasta made daily in specialty shops or Italian groceries. Many varieties of stuffed pasta—ravioli with meat or cheese, tortellini with meat or spinach—are readily available either fresh or frozen.

Pasta is equally good hot or cold and invites a limitless number of sauces, from simple butter and grated cheese

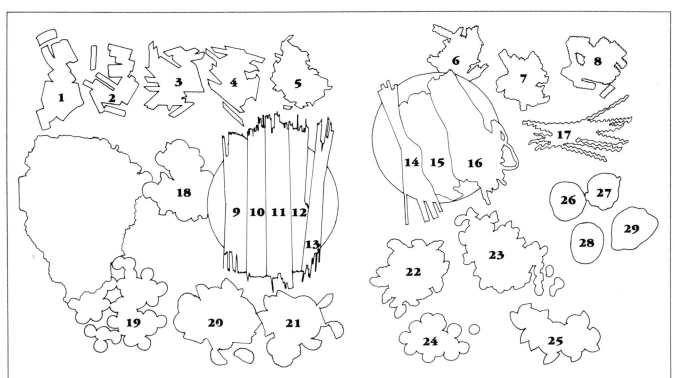

1. Rigatoni **2.** Ziti **3.** Penne Verde (quills) **4.** Penne **5.** Pennette **6.** Fusilli (wheels) **7.** Fusilli Verde **8.** Fusilli (spindles) **9.** Capellini **10.** Linguine Verde **11.** Linguine **12.** Maccheroni alla Chitarra **13.** Spaghettini **14.** Fettuccine **15.** Fettuccine Verde (fresh) **16.** Fettuccine (fresh) **17.** Fusilli Longo

18. Cannaroni Regati **19.** Tortellini **20.** Agnolotti Verde **21.** Agnolotti **22.** Gnocchi **23.** Lumache (snails) **24.** Bottoni (buttons) **25.** Conchiglie (seashells) **26.** Tagliarini **27.** Tagliarini Verde **28.** Capelli d'Angelo (angel hair) **29.** Tagliatelle

A delicate Shrimp and Herb Sauce (see page 188) is perfect with angel hair pasta.

or olive oil and garlic to classic meat and vegetable preparations. The only rule to serving pasta is that it should be firm and slightly chewy—the *al dente* Italians refer to. Always cook pasta quickly in a large pot of rapidly boiling water with a few tablespoons of oil added to prevent sticking. The pot should be big enough to keep boiling when cold macaroni is added. As soon as the water bubbles again after the pasta has been put in, start checking the pasta. Fresh pasta cooks in less than 1 minute; dried pasta takes longer; check package directions and start tasting several minutes before the pasta is supposed to be done.

Parmesan, the glory coat of any pasta dish, should ideally be freshly grated over each plate. More and more, we're seeing a chunk of Parmesan and a grater right on the table. Pre-grated cheese rapidly dries out and loses flavor. A well-wrapped chunk of Parmesan will keep in the refrigerator for several months.

HOMEMADE PASTA

Purists claim that using any kind of machine for pasta making is not only a sacrilege but a compromise of flavor and texture. We simply don't agree. A good hand-cranked machine is sturdy, easy to operate and clean, not to mention a real convenience. It helps knead the dough to a proper elasticity, then rolls it quite thin for cutting. The cutting rollers for both thin noodles and wide noodles are great timesavers. Cutting the pasta dough by hand—either running a pizza-type slicer over the rolled-out dough or rolling up the dough and slicing it like a jellyroll—works fine, but these methods take patience and more than a little dexterity.

There are electric machines on the market, but with the hand-cranked machine you are always in control: you have flexibility in the thickness of your noodles and you have a choice of two widths for long noodles and a wide sheet for lasagne layers or for cutting squares to wrap as cannelloni. With a bit of practice, you can make your own Ravioli (see page 192) and other stuffed pastas.

This recipe makes 4 generous servings of pasta to be sauced and eaten as the main course of a meal. But don't let that stop you. Pasta can be made in any size batch. The rule of thumb is ¾ cup flour to every egg, and 1 egg for every serving. It's understandable if you get carried away. If you find that you've made too much, let the pasta dry completely on a flat surface, gather it gently (it's fragile) and store it loosely covered in a dry place. It will keep up to a month.

Makes 1¼ pounds—4 servings

3 cups unsifted all-purpose flour
salt
4 eggs
1 tablespoon oil (optional)

1. On a flat smooth surface, mix the flour and 1 teaspoon salt. Scoop the flour into a mound with a rubber spatula or a pastry scraper and dig a well in the middle with your hands. Crack the eggs, 1 at a time, and drop them into the well.

2. Mix the eggs and flour with your hands. Scrape up the edges toward the middle with the spatula or scraper if the mixture spreads out too much. Keep mixing until the dough is stiff and all the flour is incorporated. If it seems too sticky to handle, add a little more flour.

3. Gather the dough into a ball and, using the heel of your hand, knead it by pushing down and away from you as hard as you can. Fold the dough in half, rotate it a quarter turn and repeat the kneading movement. Knead until the

dough is fairly smooth—about 5 minutes. The kneading will be finished in the pasta machine. If you prefer, use a food processor: combine all ingredients and process until a dough ball is formed—no further kneading is required. If the dough is too stiff, add 1 or 2 teaspoons of water. Cut the dough into 4 equal parts and cover 3 with an inverted bowl to keep them from drying out.

4. Set the machine's rollers to their most open position and feed the first quarter of dough through. Just stuff it in with your fingers this first time; as you crank it through, it will take on a nice flat shape. Fold the rolled dough in half lengthwise and crank it through again. Fold it widthwise and repeat. Continue this process until the dough is supple, elastic and smooth. If it is at all sticky, dust it with flour and roll it through again. (Keep in mind that the weather will affect the consistency.)

5. Adjust the rollers a notch closer together and roll the dough through (don't fold it this time). Continue rolling the dough thinner and thinner—notch by notch—until it's the thickness you want. There's no question that an extra pair of hands is helpful at this point to catch the long sheet of dough as it comes out of the rollers and to help guide it into the rollers straight. If you're going it alone, just proceed slowly, making sure the dough doesn't heap into a pile as it leaves the rollers or enter the rollers at a funny angle.

6. Extra hands are helpful for cutting the dough, too. Otherwise, cut the long, thin strip from Step 5 into manageable lengths with scissors, and feed each length through the cutters separately. Lay the cut noodles on a clean counter to dry or hang them over a string. For lasagne. use scissors to cut the long strip of dough into lengths to fit into your lasagne pan.

7. Repeat Steps 4, 5 and 6 with the other quarters of dough.

8. To cook the pasta, bring 4 quarts of water for each pound of raw noodles to a rolling boil. (The water will come to a boil faster if you cover the pot.) Add 1 tablespoon salt. If you're worried about sticking, add 1 tablespoon oil. Put all the pasta into the pot at once so it will cook evenly. Stir with a wooden spoon or fork (it's gentler on the pasta) to be sure it is all underwater and not bunched up. Cover the pot until the water returns to a boil—it shouldn't take much more than 30 seconds. As soon as the water is bubbling again remove the cover and test a piece of pasta. If you can bite it easily, it's ready.

9. Drain the pasta in a colander. Shake the colander a few times to speed draining and put the pasta in a warm serving bowl. Toss gently with butter, oil or sauce, using wooden spoons or salad servers. Serve at once.

MAKING PASTA. With your hands, mix eggs and flour until the dough is stiff.

Using the heel of your hand, knead the dough for 5 minutes.

Roll the dough by hand or with a pasta machine until it is the desired thickness.

10. For cold pasta dishes, rinse the hot pasta in cold water to stop the cooking and cool it. Use the same procedure for pasta that is to be stuffed and baked or for lasagne.

Spinach Pasta. Thaw a 10-ounce package of frozen chopped spinach. Wrap the thawed spinach in a dish towel and squeeze it out over the sink until the spinach is as dry as you can get it. Turn it out on a board or put it in a processor and mince it. Add the spinach to the eggs in Step 1 of the basic recipe, mixing together with your fingers before you start working in the flour. You may need a bit more flour to keep the dough from being sticky, and the kneaded dough may be a little softer than the basic dough. Just make sure the dough handles easily. Dust sticky dough with flour.

Herb Pasta. Add 1 cup of minced fresh herbs—parsley, chives, basil and/or thyme—to the eggs in Step 1. Mix the herbs and eggs by hand, then incorporate the flour.

Tomato Pasta. Add 4 tablespoons of tomato paste to the eggs in Step 1 of the basic recipe. The pasta will not have a tomato flavor but it will have a lovely color.

Whole-Wheat Pasta. Substitute 1½ cups whole-wheat flour for half the white flour in the basic recipe. The dough will be softer than the basic dough. If it's sticky, dust with white flour, not whole-wheat.

PASTA SAUCES

Pasta is not sauced by pasta sauces alone. You can improvise with the classic cooking sauces (see pages 69 to 80). Many of the fresh-flavored sauces given below are simple and can be prepared quickly. If you have a supply of pasta on hand, you can literally put together a meal in minutes. Unless otherwise indicated, the amounts of sauce are for about 1 pound uncooked pasta, which is enough to serve 4.

OIL, GARLIC AND PARSLEY SAUCE

Serves 4

½ cup olive oil
2 cloves garlic, minced
1 cup chopped fresh parsley
salt
freshly ground black pepper

1. In a heavy skillet, heat the oil over medium heat until it is hot but not smoking. Add the garlic and sauté until golden but not brown—about 2 to 3 minutes.

2. In a warm bowl or pan, gently toss the hot, well-drained pasta with the oil and garlic, parsley and salt and pepper to taste and serve immediately.

Fusilli with Fresh Tomato Sauce

MARINARA SAUCE

Serves 4

¼ cup olive oil
2 cloves garlic, minced
1 small onion, chopped
¼ cup chopped fresh parsley
6 large tomatoes, peeled, seeded and chopped, or
   1 1-pound, 14-ounce can Italian plum tomatoes packed
   in tomato purée
salt
freshly ground black pepper

1. In a heavy saucepan, heat the oil over medium heat until it is hot but not smoking. Add the garlic and onions and sauté until golden—about 4 to 5 minutes.

2. Stir in the parsley, tomatoes and salt and pepper to taste and cook, partially covered, over medium heat for another 25 to 30 minutes, or until the sauce is thick. Stir occasionally to prevent sticking.

3. Toss gently with cooked pasta and serve immediately, sprinkled with Parmesan.

FRESH TOMATO SAUCE

Makes about 2 cups

2 tablespoons butter
3 strips bacon, chopped
1 small carrot, finely chopped
1 small onion, finely chopped
⅓ cup chopped celery leaves
1 tablespoon flour
1½ cups Chicken Stock (see page 58)
2 pounds Italian plum or regular tomatoes, chopped
1 clove garlic, mashed
1 teaspoon chopped fresh or ½ teaspoon crumbled dried
   basil
1 teaspoon chopped fresh or ½ teaspoon crumbled dried
   thyme
¼ teaspoon sugar
1 bay leaf
salt
freshly ground black pepper
¼ cup tomato paste (optional)

1. In a large saucepan, melt the butter and fry the bacon until it is wilted but not brown. Add the carrot, onion and celery and sauté for 5 to 6 minutes. Stir in the flour, then the stock, tomatoes, garlic, basil, thyme, sugar and bay leaf. Add ½ teaspoon salt.

2. Cover and simmer, stirring occasionally, until the sauce is thick, about 1 hour. Press the sauce through a sieve or food mill. Season to taste with salt and pepper. The color of the sauce can be improved by stirring in the tomato paste.

3. Refrigerate, covered, until ready to use.

SALSA BESCIAMELLA
Béchamel Sauce

Makes 2 cups

A basic cream sauce often used to top baked or filled pasta, the Italian version of béchamel uses Parmesan and Romano for flavoring.

¼ cup butter
¼ cup flour
2 cups half-and-half
2 eggs (optional)
¼ cup grated Parmesan
¼ cup grated Romano
salt
freshly ground black pepper
dash nutmeg

1. In a heavy saucepan, melt the butter over medium heat. Stir in the flour and let it cook 1 minute. Gradually add the half-and-half, stirring with a wire whisk over medium heat until the mixture comes to a boil and begins to thicken.

2. Lower the heat and continue to cook for 2 or 3 minutes, stirring constantly.

3. If you want to enrich the sauce with eggs, beat them in a separate bowl. Remove the sauce from the heat. A little bit at a time, stir several tablespoons of hot sauce into the bowl of eggs. Then gradually beat the egg-sauce mixture into the saucepan with the whisk. (This procedure keeps the eggs from coagulating in the hot sauce.) When the eggs are safely incorporated, continue with the recipe.

4. Over very low heat, add the cheese, salt and pepper to taste and nutmeg, stirring until the cheese has melted. Remove the sauce from the heat, cover and keep warm until ready to use.

5. Add the sauce to the cooked, drained pasta in a warm serving bowl and toss gently. Sprinkle with additional grated cheese and serve at once.

Linguine with Pesto

SAUCE ALFREDO

Serves 4

Whether or not the Alfredo whose name graces this sauce actually devised it or simply made it famous is not clear. However, he did run a restaurant in Rome where he served fettuccine alla Alfredo with great flourish using gold utensils for the final tossing of sauce and newly made fat noodles.

1 cup heavy cream
½ cup butter, softened
1 cup freshly grated Parmesan
salt
freshly ground black pepper

1. In a heavy saucepan over medium heat, bring the cream and butter to a bare simmer. Remove from the burner, but keep warm.

2. Heat a large serving bowl for tossing the noodles. Pour in the cream-butter mixture; add the cooked, drained noodles, cheese, salt and pepper to taste. Toss gently until the noodles are coated, and serve immediately.

PESTO
Basil Sauce

Serves 4 to 6

Genoa is the homeland for this remarkable basil and garlic sauce, irresistible on any shape of pasta. Purists make it in a marble mortar, but a blender or a food processor works fine. However, there is no substitute for fresh basil.

2 cups fresh basil leaves, loosely packed
2 cloves garlic
¼ cup pine nuts or walnuts
¾ cup olive oil
½ cup freshly grated Parmesan
¼ cup freshly grated Romano
salt
freshly ground black pepper

1. Combine the basil, garlic, nuts and oil in a blender or food processor and purée. Scrape this mixture—every last drop—into a mixing bowl and beat in the cheeses by hand with a wooden spoon.

2. When the pasta is cooked, add a tablespoon of the cooking water to the Pesto to heat it and thin it slightly, season with salt and pepper, then gently toss with the hot pasta and serve immediately.

WHITE CLAM SAUCE

Serves 4

24 raw cherrystone clams
1 tablespoon olive oil
1 clove garlic, minced
1 pound mushrooms, sliced
¼ cup dry white wine
1 teaspoon chopped fresh or ½ teaspoon dry crushed
    oregano
⅓ cup chopped fresh parsley
salt
freshly ground black pepper

1. Clean the clams and put in a covered saucepan over high heat until they open—about 5 minutes. Remove the clams from their shells, rinse off any sand and chop coarsely. Strain the cooking liquid through cheesecloth to remove sand and save for the sauce.

2. In a heavy saucepan, heat the oil over medium heat and sauté the garlic for 2 or 3 minutes, or until golden. Add the mushrooms and sauté an additional minute. Stir in the

Paglia e Fieno—"straw and hay"

wine, clam juice, herbs and salt and pepper to taste. Bring to a boil, lower the heat and simmer, uncovered, for 3 or 4 minutes. Add the clams and heat through. Remove the pan from the heat, but keep warm.

3. Heat a large serving bowl. Add cooked, drained pasta and pour in the clam sauce. Toss gently and serve.

PAGLIA E FIENO
Straw and Hay

Serves 4 to 6

2 eggs
½ cup freshly grated Parmesan
½ cup heavy cream
1 cup chopped prosciutto
8 ounces Homemade Pasta (see page 184)
8 ounces Spinach Pasta (see page 185)
2 cups peas, cooked and kept warm
freshly ground black pepper

1. In a small bowl, beat the eggs with the cheese. In a small saucepan, heat the cream and prosciutto until warm.

2. Heat a large serving bowl. When the pasta is cooked and drained, put it in the bowl. Add the egg and cheese mixture, cream and prosciutto, peas and pepper and toss gently. (Prosciutto is quite salty; taste before adding salt.)

SHRIMP AND HERB SAUCE

Serves 4

8 ounces angel hair pasta
4 tablespoons olive oil
4 tablespoons butter
2 cloves garlic, chopped
1 pound raw shrimp, shelled and deveined (see page 108)
juice of 1 lemon
1 tablespoon chopped fresh or 1 teaspoon dried basil
1 tablespoon chopped fresh or 1 teaspoon dried parsley
1 tablespoon chopped fresh or 1 teaspoon dried
    marjoram
1 tablespoon chopped fresh or 1 teaspoon dried chervil
1 tablespoon chopped fresh or 1 teaspoon dried dill
1 tablespoon chopped fresh watercress
salt
freshly ground black pepper

1. Cook the pasta in boiling salted water until tender but still firm. Drain and rinse with boiling water to keep the pasta from sticking together.

2. In a large skillet, heat the oil and melt the butter. Sauté the garlic and shrimp until the shrimp just turn pink, about 3 to 4 minutes.

3. Stir in the lemon juice and herbs. Gently toss the pasta with the garlic-shrimp mixture until all the strands are coated. Season with salt and pepper and serve at once.

MUSSELS, SHRIMP AND WINE SAUCE

Serves 4

12 mussels, cleaned and debearded (see page 110)
¼ cup butter
1 onion, chopped
1 clove garlic, minced
¼ cup flour
1 cup dry white wine
2 cups heavy cream
24 small shrimp, shelled and deveined (see page 108)
¼ cup chopped fresh parsley
salt
freshly ground black pepper
¼ cup freshly grated Parmesan

1. Put the mussels with ½ cup water in a covered saucepan over high heat until the shells open—it shouldn't take more than a minute or two. Remove the mussels from their shells and reserve in a bowl. Strain the juice from the pan through a fine strainer or cheesecloth and pour over the mussels.

2. In a heavy saucepan, melt the butter over medium heat. When it is hot but not browning, add the onion and garlic and sauté until golden—about 5 minutes. Stir in the flour and let it cook a full minute. Gradually add the wine, stirring all the while, and then the cream. Cook the sauce over low heat until it bubbles and becomes thick, about 5 minutes. Stir in the mussels and their juice, the shrimp, parsley and salt and pepper to taste and let the shellfish heat through—not more than 2 or 3 minutes. (This will cook the shrimp and keep the mussels tender.)

3. Heat a large serving bowl. Combine cooked, drained pasta and the sauce in the bowl and toss gently. Sprinkle with the cheese and serve at once.

ZUCCHINI AND EGGPLANT SAUCE

Serves 4

8 ounces pasta
1 clove garlic, chopped
¼ pound mushrooms, sliced
1 onion, chopped
¼ cup olive oil
2 zucchini, chopped
1 small unpeeled eggplant (about 1 pound), chopped
4 tomatoes, chopped and the juices drained off
1½ teaspoons chopped fresh or ½ teaspoon dried oregano
1½ teaspoons chopped fresh or ½ teaspoon dried summer savory
salt
freshly ground black pepper

1. While making the sauce, cook the pasta in boiling salted water until tender but still firm. Drain and keep warm.

2. In a large skillet over medium high heat, sauté the garlic, mushrooms and onions in oil until the onions are golden, about 5 minutes.

3. Lower the heat, add the zucchini and eggplant. After cooking the vegetables for 6 to 8 minutes, stir in the tomatoes and herbs and cook for another 3 to 4 minutes. Season to taste with salt and pepper. When you're ready to serve, spoon the sauce over the pasta.

PASTA PRIMAVERA

Serves 2

8 ounces linguine
¼ cup butter
¼ cup olive oil
2 shallots, minced
2 cloves garlic, minced
2 small carrots, cut into paper-thin slices
2 large ripe tomatoes, chopped
1 cup tiny broccoli flowerets
8 fresh mushrooms, sliced
12 snow peas, trimmed
1½ teaspoon chopped fresh or ½ teaspoon dried basil
salt
freshly ground black pepper
grated Parmesan

1. Cook the linguine in boiling salt water until tender but still firm. While the linguine is cooking, heat the butter and oil in a skillet and sauté the shallots and garlic for 5 minutes.

2. Add the vegetables and herbs and cook until they are heated through but still crisp, about 5 to 6 minutes.

3. Drain the pasta and put it into a serving bowl. Add the vegetables and toss the mixture gently. Season with salt and pepper to taste and serve with grated cheese.

SAUCE BOLOGNESE

Makes 4 quarts

There are times when nothing will do but a basic homemade tomato sauce with meat, seasoned with the right vegetables and herbs. This recipe is purposely large—the sauce freezes well. Use a shaped pasta to catch every bit of the sauce.

6 slices bacon, chopped
¼ cup chopped prosciutto (about 2 ounces)
4 cloves garlic, chopped
2 large onions, chopped
4 carrots, shredded
1 cup chopped celery
1 pound mushrooms, chopped
2 pounds lean ground chuck
1 pound lean ground veal
1 pound lean ground pork
4 pounds Italian plum tomatoes, peeled, seeded and chopped, or 2 2-pound, 3-ounce cans Italian plum tomatoes
1 cup dry white wine
1 12-ounce can tomato paste
1 cup Chicken Stock (see page 58)
1 tablespoon chopped fresh or 1 teaspoon crushed dried oregano
1 tablespoon chopped fresh or 1 teaspoon crushed dried basil
salt
freshly ground black pepper

1. In a heavy 6-quart pot or Dutch oven, fry the bacon over medium high heat until crisp. Add the prosciutto, garlic, onions, carrots and celery and sauté for 5 minutes. Add the mushrooms and sauté for an additional minute. Remove from heat.

2. In a large heavy skillet, sauté the meat in batches over medium high heat until brown and crumbly. Spoon off excess fat as it accumulates. As the batches of meat are browned, add them to the bacon-vegetable mixture.

3. When all the meat has browned, add the remaining ingredients to the pot. Bring to a boil over high heat, lower the heat and simmer, partially covered, for 1 hour, stirring occasionally, until the sauce is thick.

4. To serve, toss the sauce in a warm serving bowl with cooked, drained pasta. Have freshly grated Parmesan cheese on hand so everyone can add their own. (Count on 1 to 1½ cups sauce per serving of pasta.) Freeze extra sauce in small batches so it can be used as needed.

PUTTANESCA SAUCE

Serves 4 to 6

A sauce as lusty as its name, puttanesca (in the style of a whore) bespeaks all the good seasonings of southern Italy.

⅓ cup olive oil
¼ loaf Italian bread, cut into ½-inch cubes
1 clove garlic, minced
2 large onions, chopped
½ cup chopped red bell pepper
½ cup chopped green bell pepper
¼ cup drained capers
1 cup sliced pitted black olives (Italian or Greek)
1 2-ounce can flat anchovy filets, chopped
freshly ground black pepper

1. In a large heavy skillet, heat the oil over medium high heat until very hot but not smoking. Sauté the bread cubes until brown and crisp on all sides. Remove the browned cubes and drain on paper towel. Lower the heat slightly and sauté the garlic, onions and peppers for 5 minutes, or until the onions are golden and limp. Add the capers, olives and anchovies and stir until heated through. Remove the skillet from the heat, but keep warm.

2. In a large heated serving bowl, combine cooked, drained pasta with the sauce. Season to taste with pepper. Toss gently. Sprinkle with the garlic croutons and serve.

BROCCOLI, ANCHOVY AND CREAM SAUCE

Serves 4 to 6

¼ cup olive oil
1 onion, chopped
1 bunch broccoli, broken into flowerets
6 anchovy filets, chopped
2 egg yolks
1 cup heavy cream
freshly ground black pepper

1. In a heavy skillet, heat the oil over medium heat until it is hot but not smoking. Add the onion and sauté for 5 minutes, or until golden. Add the broccoli and sauté another 5 minutes, or until the broccoli is tender yet crisp. Stir in the anchovies and remove from the heat.

2. In a large heated serving bowl, beat the egg yolks with the cream. Add cooked, drained pasta, the broccoli-anchovy mixture and pepper. (The anchovies make extra salt unnecessary.) Toss gently and serve immediately.

STUFFED PASTAS

Stuffed pastas are heartier than simply sauced flat or round noodles, but they don't have to be heavy. If you make your own dough, you will find the finished pasta much lighter and fresher-tasting than you ever imagined. And, of course, you will have complete control over the stuffing, the seasoning and the saucing. We suggest a stuffing and sauce for each, just to get you started and to explain the techniques for putting it all together. But all can be personalized with your favorite ingredients.

AGNOLOTTI ALLA PUTTANESCA

Serves 6

Agnolotti ("little sheep") are a wonderful shape for herb and spinach pasta and, for many, are easier to put together than ravioli. They can be stuffed with anything you like, from cheese to ground beef, but we have chosen a chicken liver filling to go with the puttanesca sauce.

2 tablespoons butter
1 onion, chopped
1 pound chicken livers
2 hard-boiled eggs, chopped
2 tablespoons heavy cream
salt
freshly ground black pepper
1 recipe Homemade Pasta dough (see page 184)
cornmeal
1 recipe Puttanesca Sauce

1. Make the filling first. In a heavy skillet, melt the butter over medium heat and sauté the onion 5 minutes. Add the chicken livers and sauté until browned on all sides but still slightly pink in the center—about 5 minutes. Remove the skillet from the heat and let the livers cool until you can handle them. Turn the livers out on a board and chop. In a large bowl, mix the chopped livers, onions, eggs, cream, salt and pepper to taste until well blended. Cover and set aside.

2. Make the pasta in the machine and roll out at the thinnest setting. Lay the strips of pasta on a lightly floured surface and cut out 30 rounds, 4 inches across. Use a small bowl or dish as a guide and a sharp knife to cut.

3. Put a spoonful of filling on one side of each pasta round, then moisten the edges with water and fold the round in half over the filling, pressing down the edges to seal them. Sprinkle a flat surface with cornmeal to keep the pasta from sticking and lay the filled agnolotti on the

Agnolotti alla Puttanesca

cornmeal to dry for an hour. Wrap and refrigerate or freeze the agnolotti at this point if you are not ready to cook them.

4. To cook the agnolotti, bring 4 quarts of water to a rolling boil. Add 1 tablespoon salt and gently drop in the filled pastas. Stir carefully with a wooden spoon to keep them separate. When the water returns to a boil, cook for 5 minutes. Lift out the cooked agnolotti with a slotted spoon or strainer and shake gently to drain.

5. Put the cooked agnolotti on a warm serving platter and sauce with hot puttanesca. Toss gently and serve at once.

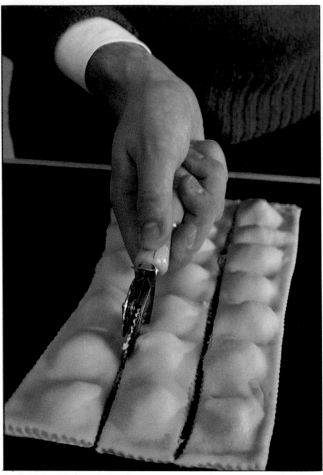

Homemade pasta dough can be used for Ravioli with Spinach Stuffing and Cheese Sauce.

RAVIOLI WITH SPINACH STUFFING AND CHEESE SAUCE

Serves 4

Once you have mastered basic pasta dough, making ravioli is a simple next step. You can vary the stuffing with ground meats, cooked sausage, ricotta cheese and fresh herbs in any combination.

1 cup cooked chopped or 1 10-ounce package frozen
   chopped spinach, thawed and squeezed dry
1 egg
⅓ cup freshly grated Parmesan
¼ cup heavy cream
1 clove garlic, minced
⅛ teaspoon ground nutmeg
salt
freshly ground black pepper
1 recipe Homemade Pasta dough (see page 184)
cornmeal
1 recipe Salsa Besciamella (see page 186)

1. Put the spinach in a towel and squeeze out as much of the liquid as you can. Chop the spinach very fine. In a bowl, beat the egg, then mix in the spinach, Parmesan, cream, garlic, nutmeg and salt and pepper to taste.

2. Take the pasta recipe through the kneading (Step 3). On a lightly floured surface, roll out the dough into a rectangle 14 by 24 inches.

3. On half of the dough, space out tablespoons of stuffing in even rows. Plan on 7 rows of 3 across to give you plenty of room between individual ravioli. (With practice you can make smaller ravioli.) Brush the other half of the dough with water and fold it, wet side down, over the rows of stuffing. With your index finger, carefully press the dough together between each row of stuffing, first in one direction, then in the other, making sure to press the outside edges as well. This will eliminate air bubbles in the seams and seal the ravioli.

4. With a rolling pizza cutter or pastry jagger—the fluted ones make a prettier pattern—cut down the center of the sealed seams to separate the ravioli.

5. Sprinkle a dry surface with cornmeal to prevent sticking and lay the ravioli on it to dry for an hour. When the ravioli are dry, they can be wrapped and refrigerated for several days or frozen for several months, depending on when you want to serve them.

6. To cook the ravioli, bring 4 quarts of water to a rolling boil over high heat. Add 1 tablespoon salt. Gently drop in the ravioli and stir carefully with a wooden spoon to be sure they do not stick to one another. Cook the ravioli for 5 to 6 minutes after the water returns to a boil. Lift out the ravioli with a slotted spoon or strainer and let them drain briefly. Serve immediately on a warm platter, topped with *salsa besciamella* .

VEGETABLE LASAGNE

Makes 8 generous servings

We tend to think of lasagne only as meat-filled. Not true—try vegetables and cheese with spinach noodles instead.

1 pound spinach lasagne noodles
2 tablespoons olive oil
1 cup chopped peeled eggplant
1 cup chopped peeled zucchini
1 cup chopped mushrooms
½ cup chopped onion
2 cloves garlic, chopped
2 cups Fresh Tomato Sauce (see page 186)
1 pound ricotta
1 pound mozzarella, shredded
½ cup grated Parmesan

1. Preheat the oven to 350°F. Cook the noodles in 4 quarts of boiling salted water until they are flexible but still firm, about 10 to 12 minutes. Put the noodles in a single layer on waxed paper.

2. In a frypan, heat the oil and sauté the eggplant, zucchini, mushrooms, onion and garlic for 8 to 10 minutes, or until the vegetables are tender. Stir in the tomato sauce and remove from the heat.

3. Spread a thin layer of sauce on the bottom of a 9×13×2-inch baking pan. Top with a layer of noodles, a layer of sauce, a layer of ricotta and a layer of mozzarella. Continue layering, ending with the noodles and a layer of sauce. Bake until bubbly, about 40 to 45 minutes. Let stand 15 minutes, then cut into serving pieces.

TORTELLINI

Serves 8

Tortellini are little pasta dumplings that can be boiled in water like ravioli and served with sauce, or cooked in soup like conventional dumplings, a favorite way of serving them in their native Bologna.

1 pound ground veal
1 tablespoon olive oil
1 onion, minced
1 clove garlic, minced
1 egg, beaten
1 tablespoon chopped fresh parsley
2 tablespoons grated Parmesan
½ teaspoon salt
freshly ground black pepper
1 recipe Homemade Pasta dough (see page 184)
cornmeal

1. In a heavy oiled skillet, brown the veal until crumbly. Drain off any excess juices in a sieve and put the cooked meat in a large bowl to cool. Heat the olive oil in the skillet and sauté the onion and garlic over medium heat for 5 minutes. Add this to the meat in the bowl.

2. When the meat and onion mixture is cool, add the egg, parsley, cheese, salt and pepper to taste and mix until well blended. This is the filling.

3. Make the pasta in the machine and roll out at the thinnest setting. Put the strips of pasta dough on a lightly floured surface and cut out 2-inch rounds with a biscuit cutter or a sharp knife around a glass.

4. Top each round with a teaspoonful of filling. Moisten the edges of the rounds with water and fold each round in half, pressing the edges together to seal them. To complete the typical tortellini hat shape, moisten the two ends of the half circles and pinch them together.

5. Sprinkle a flat surface with cornmeal to prevent sticking and set the finished tortellini on the cornmeal to dry for an hour. The dried tortellini can be wrapped and refrigerated for a day or two or they can be frozen for months.

6. Cook the tortellini in 4 quarts boiling water with 1 teaspoon salt added for 2 or 3 minutes; drain and serve topped with heated sauce, or added to chicken stock with extra Parmesan on the side.

COLD PASTAS

VEGETABLE PASTA SALAD

Serves 4

8 ounces bow-tie pasta
1 cup raw broccoli tops
1 cup cherry tomato halves
1 cup peeled eggplant cubes, reserve skin for garnish
1 cup heavy cream
2 tablespoons Dijon mustard
2 tablespoons chopped celery leaves
4 teaspoons chopped scallions
salt
freshly ground black pepper

1. Cook the pasta in 2 quarts boiling water with 1 teaspoon salt added until tender but still firm (see page 183). Drain and rinse with cold water, then chill.

2. When the pasta is cold, combine the remaining ingredients in a large bowl, season with salt and pepper and mix well. Chill. When you're ready to serve the pasta, garnish with petals cut from the eggplant skin.

SCALLOP AND SPINACH PASTA SALAD

Serves 4

8 ounces spinach penne
⅔ cup olive oil
1 pound sea scallops, each cut into two round slices
2 zucchini, cut into ¼-inch-thick slices
½ pound spinach, torn into bite-size pieces
2 tomatoes, peeled, seeded and chopped
2 tablespoons chopped fresh or 2 teaspoons dried dill weeds
¾ teaspoon chopped fresh or ¼ teaspoon dried marjoram
¾ teaspoon chopped fresh or ¼ teaspoon dried thyme
1 lemon, cut into paper-thin slices
salt
freshly ground black pepper

1. Cook pasta in 3 quarts boiling water with 2 teaspoons salt added until tender but still firm (see page 183). Drain and rinse with cold water, then chill. In a frypan, heat the oil over medium high heat and sauté the scallops until they turn white, about 2 to 3 minutes. Cool.

2. In a large serving bowl, mix the pasta, scallops and oil drippings and the remaining ingredients. Toss well and season with salt and pepper. Refrigerate until ready to serve.

COLD TOMATO SAUCE

Serves 4

Almost like a salad dressing, this cold, oil-based sauce mixes well with cold, tiny fusilli.

½ cup olive oil
1 clove garlic
½ cup fresh basil leaves, tightly packed
4 tomatoes, peeled, seeded and chopped
salt
freshly ground black pepper

1. Combine the oil, garlic and basil in a blender or food processor and process until the basil and garlic are finely chopped. In a bowl, combine this with the tomatoes, add salt and pepper and stir until blended.

2. Cool cooked pasta under cold running water. Drain well and gently toss with the tomato sauce.

Scallop and Spinach Pasta Salad

Corkscrew noodles and lima beans create Pasta e Fagiola Salad.

Giant rigatoni are perfect for this Tuna Pasta Salad.

PASTA E FAGIOLA SALAD

Serves 4

8 ounces spinach fusilli
1 cup cooked lima beans or cannellini
2 small red peppers, chopped
1 cup cooked chickpeas
¼ cup chopped parsley
½ cup Mayonnaise (see page 78)
½ cup sour cream
¼ cup chopped chives
1½ teaspoons chopped fresh or ½ teaspoon dried savory
salt
freshly ground black pepper

1. Cook the fusilli in boiling salted water (see page 183). Drain and chill. Mix the pasta with the remaining ingredients, seasoning with salt and pepper. Chill.

2. When you're ready to serve, check the seasoning. (Chilling affects flavor.)

TUNA PASTA SALAD

Serves 4

8 ounces giant rigatoni
1 cup cooked artichoke hearts
2 6½-ounce cans tuna, drained
8 scallions, sliced
⅔ cup olive oil
¼ cup lemon juice
2 tablespoons drained capers
1 garlic clove, crushed
salt
freshly ground pepper

1. Cook the rigatoni in boiling salted water until tender but firm (see page 183). Drain, rinse with cold water, drain again and chill.

2. Combine the remaining ingredients with the rigatoni, season with salt and pepper and mix well.

Like fragile dumplings, spaetzle will float to the top of the water when cooked.

SPAETZLE

Not all homemade noodles are Italian, or even cut into uniform shapes. Noodles play an important role in Northern and Eastern European cuisines, too, and one version, made free-form off the bottom of a cake pan, is as versatile as any pasta. Called spaetzle, these little dumplings are used in soups or served by themselves with an assortment of dressings, from butter and poppy seeds to sour cream and herbs. Spaetzle are frequently offered instead of potatoes or rice with stews and roast meats. They are light and delicate and fun to make.

Serves 4

1 cup unsifted all-purpose flour
3 eggs
½ teaspoon salt
freshly ground black pepper
¼ cup milk
⅛ teaspoon nutmeg
1 tablespoon chopped fresh parsley
2 tablespoons butter
poppy seeds or grated Parmesan

1. Set a large pot of water—at least 4 quarts—over a high heat. Add 1 teaspoon salt.

2. In a bowl, combine the flour, eggs, salt, pepper, milk, nutmeg and parsley. Beat with a wire whisk until the batter is well blended and slightly stiff. It should cling to the whisk.

3. When the water in the pot is simmering, you are ready to start the noodles. You will need a smooth, flat, portable surface to work from. An overturned cake pan can be a first-rate spaetzle maker. Pour ¼ cup of batter onto the surface.

4. Holding the cake pan over the simmering water and using a long metal spatula, scrape off a sliver of batter, about ¼-inch wide, and let it fall into the water. It will sink to the bottom of the pot. Continue to scrape off slivers of dough until the first batch of batter is used up. Replenish the batter supply on the cake pan and scrape off another set of noodles. Repeat until all the batter has been used.

5. The noodles will rise to the surface of the water when they have cooked. Butter an ovenproof serving dish. As the noodles that are done float to the surface, lift them out with a slotted spoon. Let them drain a minute over the pan, then put them in the serving dish with a little butter and keep them warm in a low oven (about 150°F). Continue making new noodles and lifting out cooked ones in alternate steps. Butter each new layer of noodles in the serving dish to keep them from sticking.

6. Sprinkle the finished noodles with poppy seeds or grated cheese and serve hot.

ORIENTAL NOODLES

Japanese noodles made of buckwheat or soy flour are a lunchtime staple in soup or topped with vegetables or with Shrimp Tempura (see page 52). Here are four basic types of noodles that are easily found in Oriental food stores.

Ramen instant noodles. Add them to a small amount of boiling water and cook 1 to 2 minutes. No rinsing is needed.

Fine somen noodles. Cook in boiling water for 3 to 4 minutes, drain and serve.

Medium soba noodles. Cook in boiling water for 6 to 7 minutes, drain and serve.

Thin udon noodles. Cook in boiling water for 12 to 15 minutes, drain and serve.

JAPANESE NOODLE SALAD

Serves 4

The combination of soy sauce and noodles may seem odd at first, but it's absolutely addictive when lightened with lemon and tender-crisp vegetables.

8 ounces linguine or medium soba noodles
8 scallions, sliced
2 carrots, coarsely shredded
12 cherry tomatoes
2 medium to large stalks raw broccoli, peeled and thinly sliced

½ cup olive oil
½ cup soy sauce
juice of 1 lemon
1 clove garlic, chopped
½ teaspoon Tabasco sauce
¼ cup toasted sesame seeds

1. In a large bowl, mix cooked and rinsed pasta with the scallions, carrots, tomatoes and broccoli.

2. Beat together the oil, soy sauce, lemon juice, garlic and Tabasco sauce. Pour this dressing over the salad and toss to coat everything. Chill. Just before serving, sprinkle with sesame seeds.

HIYASHI SOMEN

Serves 4

Refreshing, cold somen (buckwheat or soy flour noodles) gives soup an Oriental flavor.

16 ounces somen noodles
1½ cups Chicken Stock (see page 58)
1 tablespoon grated fresh ginger
1 scallion, sliced
2 tablespoons soy sauce

1. In a medium saucepan, cook the noodles in boiling water for 3 to 4 minutes, or until tender but still firm. Drain the noodles and rinse in cold water.

2. Mix the noodles with ice cubes until they are very cold, then drain and divide into 4 serving bowls. Mix the remaining ingredients in a small bowl and spoon this mixture over each serving of noodles. Toss and serve.

THAI CRISP FRIED NOODLES

Serves 4 to 6

3 tablespoons soy sauce
juice of 2 lemons or limes
2 tablespoons rice wine vinegar (su)
4 to 5 tablespoons granulated sugar (white or brown)
3 tablespoons fish sauce (available in Oriental markets)
2 bunches (12 ounces) rice-flour vermicelli
oil for deep-frying
1 large onion, finely chopped
5 cloves garlic, finely chopped
1½-pound pork filet, thinly sliced and cut into 1-inch strips
1 whole chicken breast, boned and thinly sliced and cut into 1-inch strips
3 tablespoons small shrimp, cooked or raw
6 dried Chinese mushrooms, soaked and finely sliced
2 small fresh chilies (serrano or jalapeño), seeded and finely sliced
4 eggs, beaten
½ pound fresh bean sprouts
2 scallions, finely chopped
¼ cup chopped fresh coriander
6 scallions, chopped

1. In a bowl, mix the soy sauce, lemon or lime juice, vinegar, sugar and fish sauce. Set aside.

2. Tear the noodles into small handfuls. In a large wok or skillet, heat the oil and fry each bunch of noodles until they puff up. The oil must be very hot or the noodles will be tough. Turn the noodles and briefly fry them on the other side until crisp and pale gold. Repeat the frying with each bunch and drain them on paper towel. Layer them on paper towel until all the noodles are cooked.

3. Pour off the remaining oil, leaving approximately 6 tablespoons in the wok. Lightly fry the onion and garlic. Add the pork and cook 5 to 6 minutes, then add the chicken and stir-fry for 3 more minutes.

4. Add the shrimp, mushrooms and chilies. Reduce the heat and add the soy sauce mixture. Simmer for 3 minutes. Then make a hole or well in the middle of the ingredients and pour in the beaten eggs. Let the eggs set, then add the bean sprouts and noodles, turning and tossing lightly to coat with the sauce and mix the meats. When everything is heated through, transfer to a serving platter and sprinkle with the coriander and scallions.

Beans, Rice and Grains

They're the heart of all cuisines, the staple foods of more than half the world—and notably ignored by many of the residents of the other half. "Boring" is the first reaction, and so they're served plainly cooked, backstage understudies to main-course meats and vegetables. Wrong, we say. These foods deserve a few leading roles; with a little coaching, they have enough character to stand on their own or play strong supporting roles.

There's enough range in the variety of beans to supply different protein-rich preparations for weeks on end; enough versatility in a single pot of rice to turn it yellow or green or into salad; and enough backup grains (couscous, bulghur wheat and barley) for a few more evenings—before beginning another round of variations on the theme.

After all, the New American Cuisine explores and employs the richness of this land, turning the humdrum into the unusual with a simple change of attitude.

Beans supply an amazing amount of protein; combined with a bit of meat, they satisfy nutritionists' standard protein requirements. As soups, main course, salads and side dishes, they lend an ever-changing (and interchangeable) substance to meals.

Rice is certainly lighter, but full of nutrients too. Long- or short-grained, converted or brown, it is probably the most popular starch on today's menus—not much of a change from centuries ago.

And couscous, bulghur wheat and barley make substantive and unusual additions to the table.

Black Bean

Black-eyed Pea

Chickpea

Beans

THE ESSENTIALS

Most beans by themselves are not highly flavored, so they obligingly take on the tastes of the meats, vegetables and seasonings they are cooked with. For hot dishes, cooking dried beans with seasonings is more effective than doctoring up canned beans.

Beans can play musical chairs; used interchangeably in recipes, particularly if their cooking times are similar.

Dried beans have the great advantage of a long shelf life—up to a year. Most dried beans can be soaked overnight or parboiled for 2 minutes and allowed to stand for an hour to soften before cooking, but since modern drying methods leave more moisture in the bean, they do not require long soaking.

Canned precooked beans are now available in many varieties, particularly in ethnic food markets. They can be used straight out of the can in salads and dips.

The most common beans found in our markets are listed below with their most traditional uses.

Black beans. A staple of Latin American cooking, black beans are used in soup with sherry or rum and are often prepared with rice and cheese. They are tender and almost sweet. They require at least 1½ hours of cooking.

Black-eyed peas. Also called cowpeas, these beans have a distinctive black or yellow eye. In the South they are traditionally cooked with salt pork and ham hocks and eaten on New Year's Day to bring prosperity for the year. At other times stewed with onions and chicken broth, they're good and hearty. They should cook about 1 hour.

Cannellini beans. Large white kidney beans used in Italian cooking, in soups and salads, cannellini or fasiola beans are larger than our navy beans and have a fluffier texture. Available canned as well as dried in Italian markets, they take 1 to 2 hours of cooking.

Chickpeas. A staple both of Mexican and Middle Eastern cooking, chickpeas are also called garbanzo beans. Shaped like small hazelnuts, they have a wrinkled exterior, a nutty flavor and a slightly crunchy texture. They require long cooking—up to 1½ to 2 hours—to become tender, so precooked canned chickpeas are popular and really just as good. Chickpeas are the main ingredient in Middle Eastern Hummus (see page 52).

Fava beans. Available fresh, dried or canned, these broad beans are used in stews and salads and as a side dish on their own. Dried fava beans take about 1½ hours to cook.

Flageolets. Small pale green beans popular in France with roast lamb, these native American haricots have a fresh and delicate flavor. They come precooked in cans or dried. The latter must be cooked about 1 hour.

Kidney beans. Their name comes from their shape, and their colors range from deep maroon to white (see cannellini). Kidney beans have a firm skin and a tender, sweet interior. They require less than 1 hour's cooking. They are much used in Latin American cooking, often with rice, and are popular here with chili.

Lentils. The only dried beans that do not require soaking before they are cooked, lentils come in a variety of colors—green, red, brown, gray, yellow and black. Very important in Indian cooking, lentils make fine soups, salads and mix well in pilafs and sausage or vegetable dishes. Lentils take about 25 to 30 minutes to cook, depending on the size of the beans.

Lima beans. Available fresh, dried and frozen, lima beans are used in casseroles and side dishes. Baby lima beans are used the same way, although they are sweeter and more tender. Also called butter beans because of their texture, these South American natives are grown extensively in Madagascar. Dried baby limas cook in an hour; larger butter or Fordhook limas take longer—1½ hours.

Mung beans. Tiny lentillike beans cultivated in India

Lentil

Kidney Bean

and China, mung beans are known as *moong dal* in India, where they are used in curries. We know them best as the source of bean sprouts. Cook mung beans for 1 to 1½ hours, depending upon the size of the beans.

Navy beans. These small white beans, similar to Great Northern beans, were a major provision of U.S. ships in the nineteenth century—and thus they got their name. They are all the more famous for being the main ingredient of Boston baked beans. They cook in 1 hour.

Pinto beans. Medium-size, longish beans that are speckled with brown when they are dried, pintos turn a magical pink when they are cooked. Used a great deal in Mexican cooking, they come canned or dried and take 1½ hours to cook. Red beans are similar to pintos and are used in the same way.

Split peas. Both green and yellow dried peas are small skinless legumes that combine with ham to make thick, filling soups with a flavor akin to that of fresh garden peas. Split peas cook in less than 1 hour.

BLACK-EYED PEAS WITH HAM

Serves 4

Black-eyed peas and pork have a natural Southern affinity that is never challenged, although, like all regional specialties, it is widely interpreted.

½ cup (about 4 ounces) diced salt pork
1 onion, chopped
1 cup dried black-eyed peas, rinsed and picked over
1 hot red or green pepper, chopped
1 cup diced smoked ham

1. In a large heavy saucepan or Dutch oven, fry the salt pork over medium high heat until crisp. Remove the

cooked pieces with a slotted spoon, drain on paper towel, and save for later.

2. In the rendered pork fat, over medium heat, sauté the onion for 5 minutes. Add the peas, red pepper, ham and enough water to cover the beans by 2 inches.

3. Bring the liquid to a boil, lower the heat and simmer, covered, for 1 to 1½ hours, or until the beans are tender. Check periodically to see if more water is needed to keep the beans from sticking. When the beans are almost tender, uncover and simmer until the liquid is absorbed.

4. Serve hot with the crisp salt pork pieces sprinkled on top. The salt pork makes extra salt unnecessary.

CANNELLINI SALAD WITH TUNA

Serves 4

2 cups drained cooked cannellini beans
2 cups drained cooked chickpeas
1 small onion, chopped
2 7½-ounce cans tuna, drained
¼ cup chopped fresh basil
½ cup chopped Italian parsley
½ cup olive oil
3 tablespoons red wine vinegar
salt
freshly ground black pepper

1. In a large bowl, combine the cannellini, chickpeas and onion. When these are well mixed, add the tuna, basil and parsley.

2. In another bowl, mix the oil and vinegar for the dressing. When you're ready to serve, pour the dressing over the salad, add freshly ground black pepper to taste and toss.

Genuine Italian Seafood Risotto is a simple variation of Risotto Milanese.

RISOTTO MILANESE
Braised Rice with Saffron

Serves 8

The best risotto needs constant stirring and attention to ensure that it is firm and creamy, never mushy or runny. The preparation is simple; variations are endless. Marrow can be sautéed with the onion or dried Italian mushrooms are soaked for 30 minutes and then both mushrooms and liquid stirred into the rice.

6 to 7 cups Chicken Stock (see page 58)
¼ cup butter
1 onion, minced
2 cups uncooked Arborio rice
½ cup dry white wine
⅛ teaspoon saffron threads
¼ cup softened butter
½ cup freshly grated Parmesan

1. In a saucepan, heat the stock and bring to a simmer. Meanwhile, in a heavy 3-quart saucepan or Dutch oven, melt ¼ cup butter over medium heat. Sauté the onion in the butter for 5 minutes, or until tender but not brown.

2. Add the rice and, stirring constantly, cook it until the grains are coated with butter and slightly opaque.

3. Add the wine to the rice and let it boil as you stir the rice. When it is almost completely absorbed, add 2 cups of the simmering stock to the pan and cook, uncovered, until it is almost absorbed. Stir frequently to make sure the rice doesn't stick. Repeat with 2 more cups of stock.

4. In a bowl, crumble the saffron threads, pour 2 cups of the simmering stock over them and steep for several minutes. When the rice has almost absorbed the second addition of stock, add the stock with saffron to the pan and cook until it is absorbed, still stirring.

5. When this last addition has been absorbed, test the rice for tenderness. You may not need more stock. If the rice is still too firm, add only ½ cup stock at a time until the rice is ready.

6. Use a fork to gently stir in the softened butter and cheese. Serve immediately.

Seafood Risotto. Stir in ½ cup whole pitted black olives, ¼ cup diced pimento, ¾ cup cooked, shelled and deveined shrimp and ¾ cup cooked, sliced sea scallops into the Risotto Milanese and serve very hot.

COUNTRY RISOTTO

Serves 4 to 6

½ cup butter
1 onion, sliced
2 red peppers, seeded and cut into strips
1 4-inch-long beef marrowbone
½ cup dry red wine
1 cup diced smoked ham
3 cups uncooked Arborio or long-grain rice
½ teaspoon crumbled saffron thread
1½ quarts Chicken Stock (see page 58)
1½ cups fresh shelled peas or 1 10-ounce package frozen peas, thawed
½ cup chopped parsley
1 cup grated Parmesan

1. In a large frypan over medium heat, melt the butter and sauté the onion and peppers for 5 minutes, or until the onion is golden.

2. Reduce the heat and add the marrow (scooped out of the bone), wine, ham and rice. Cook until the wine has evaporated.

3. Stir in the saffron and half the stock. Cook, uncovered, stirring occasionally, until the stock is absorbed. Add the remaining stock and the peas and continue cooking and stirring until the stock is absorbed and the rice is tender, about 20 to 25 minutes.

4. Salt to taste and serve, sprinkled with parsley and cheese.

Grains

THE ESSENTIALS

Meat-and-potatoes was the old byword for dinner, and no one questioned the potatoes part—it was necessary to have a belly-filling starch, after all. As our technological/import skills sharpened, rice became a viable choice, and beans of all descriptions worked their way into our diets.

But it was the Sixties back-to-the-earth/health-food movement that gave grains new popularity. Kasha, eaten for centuries by the Russians, became a known and liked commodity here. Barley, long used for cereals only, came

back to the table. Bulghur, Turkey's cracked wheat, surfaced in salads as well as kibbeh. And couscous, North Africa's answer to rice, emerged as an integral part of the stew called by its name, desserts or as a simple side dish.

All make a welcome change from the other starches; all are coming into their own in the New American Cuisine.

COUSCOUS PILAF

Serves 6

Couscous is a finely ground wheat, closely related to semolina. It replaces rice as the main starch in North African countries, and is the national dish of Morocco. Here the confusion begins, for the word couscous *refers not only to the grain—which is eaten for breakfast as a cereal and with sugar and sweet currants as a dessert—but also to the entire stew, where the grain is steamed above a fragrant mix of lamb, chicken or beef and vegetables. Steamed, it has a feathery-light consistency; cooked in stock, as a pilaf, it is a bit more dense.*

½ cup butter
2 cups couscous
½ cup pine nuts
½ cup yellow raisins
grated rind and juice of 1 lemon
4 cups Chicken Stock (see page 58)
salt

1. In a large saucepan, combine all the ingredients and simmer over medium heat, stirring constantly, until the mixture reaches the consistency of mashed potatoes. Season with salt.

MILK AND HONEY COUSCOUS

Serves 8

Eaten as breakfast or dessert, this cinnamon-scented apple and almond couscous is a good change from oatmeal.

2 cups couscous
1 quart milk
½ cup honey
1 teaspoon cinnamon
2 apples, peeled, cored and chopped
1 cup slivered toasted almonds

1. In a large saucepan, combine all the ingredients. Stir constantly over medium heat until the mixture thickens. It will have about the same consistency as hot cereal. Serve hot with cream or milk.

KASHA

Serves 4

A nutty brown, granular cereal full of earthy flavor and aroma, it is also known as buckwheat groats. Kasha's stick-to-the-ribs goodness goes best with beef or other hearty foods. It's especially popular in Russia, where it's used in soups, stuffings and as a sweet or as a seasoned preparation unto itself—a staple like polenta or pasta in Italy.

1½ cups coarse kasha
2 egg yolks
1 quart Chicken Stock (see page 58)
½ teaspoon salt
¼ cup butter or gravy
1 large onion, chopped

1. In a skillet, mix the kasha and egg yolks and stir over low heat until the kasha is dry and crumbly.

2. Add the stock and salt, cover and simmer, stirring occasionally, until the liquid is absorbed, about 15 minutes.

3. Meanwhile, melt the butter or heat the gravy in a frypan and sauté the onions until they are golden, about 5 minutes. Add the onions to the kasha.

Kasha and Noodles. After cooking, mix in 2 cups cooked bow-tie noodles.

Kasha and Lentils. After cooking, mix in 1 cup cooked lentils, 1 cup chopped tomatoes and 1 clove chopped garlic.

TABBOULEH WITH ROMAINE LEAVES

Serves 6

Tabbouleh salad is made from bulghur wheat, yet another variation of our most popular grain. It is formed when wheat grains are boiled and dried, then cracked or ground. Popular in Middle Eastern cuisine, it is often combined with ground lamb and pine nuts for kibbeh.

2 cups bulghur wheat
1 bunch scallions, chopped
3 medium tomatoes, cored and chopped
2 cloves crushed garlic
½ cup chopped parsley
¼ cup chopped fresh or 1 tablespoon dried mint
½ cup olive oil
juice of 2 lemons
salt
freshly ground black pepper
romaine lettuce

1. In a large bowl, soak the bulghur in 4 cups water for about 1 hour. Drain well. Add all the ingredients except salt, pepper and the romaine. Mix well and season with salt and pepper to taste. Add more lemon if necessary.

2. Serve on romaine leaves with wedges of lemon.

Barley Salad. Substitute 2 cups cooked barley for bulghur.

Vegetables

It's not that we've become a nation of vegetarians, but our romance with things mostly green and exceedingly fresh gives pause for thought. Linked to our infatuation with things healthy—jogging and sports, less cholesterol and more fiber—recent technology has helped the popularity of freshness. California and Florida have learned they can easily supply more than avocados year-round, and a flood of previously out-of-season produce is flown in daily from nations around the world. But more than likely, the affair started when we discovered, quite simply, how very good and full of flavor vegetables can be—when we tasted the difference between soggy canned green beans and fresh local beans.

We wholeheartedly supported the open-air produce stands that have brightened the corners of many cities and smaller towns. The many-colored mountain of potatoes, mounds of red and green lettuces, stacks of leeks and hills of golden squash have seduced us away from the frozen fast-and-easy. The joyous bounty of the changing seasons—slender spring asparagus, summer pole beans, fall pumpkins and winter white turnips—puts us back in touch with the earth. Since vegetables are the stuff of the New American Cuisine, you'll find other vegetable recipes throughout the book. Please check the Index.

THE ESSENTIALS

Freshness is the key to good produce. Vegetables reach their peak in the ground or on the vine, and start losing taste, texture and nutritional value the moment they are harvested.

Unless you live right where it's grown, you will always be days away from a vegetable's best moment, but it still makes sense to follow the seasons and look for local produce that hasn't had to travel too far, or for some of the root vegetables and winter squashes that have a longer shelf life in deep winter.

Look for crisp, brightly colored vegetables. Never settle for tired old vegetables that have lost their color and texture. You can't revive them.

Greens. An enormously varied category—greens can refer to salad lettuces **(1, 2, 6, 8, 12, 25, 26)**, vegetable

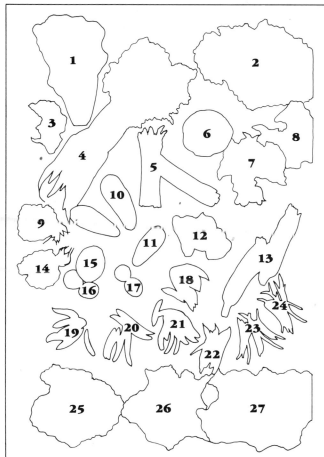

1. Romaine Lettuce **2.** Loose Leaf Lettuce **3.** Spinach **4.** Carrots **5.** Asparagus **6.** Iceberg Lettuce **7.** Radishes **8.** Boston Lettuce **9.** Watercress **10.** Sweet Potatoes **11.** Idaho Potato **12.** Bibb Lettuce **13.** Corn **14.** Arugula **15.** Rutabaga **16.** Turnips **17.** New Potatoes **18.** Snow Peas **19.** Lima Beans **20.** Fava Beans **21.** Peas **22.** Pink Beans **23.** Wax Beans **24.** Green Beans **25.** Red-leaf Lettuce **26.** Chicory **27.** Escarole

tops such as turnips and beets and leafy vegetables like spinach **(3)**, kale **(57)** and mustard greens **(67)**. Buy tender young greens and avoid woody stems and thick, coarse veins—these will be old and bitter. Some salad greens, like arugula **(14)**, watercress **(9)** and escarole **(27)**, take well to a quick poaching, then shredding for soups or sauces. Others (kale, for instance) are puréed and served as a vegetable or used as a base for soup. Some can be sautéed in butter or, more traditionally, slowly cooked with meaty bones.

4. Carrots. A real staple, carrots serve as seasoning, vegetable and garnish. Look for firm, smooth carrots with a bright color. Carrots with green root tops or cracks should be avoided. In the spring, try tender baby carrots. You can stir-fry, steam or boil, glaze with butter and moisten with cream, or purée.

5. Asparagus. The tender young shoots of the asparagus plant are cut from March through May in most parts of the country. Look for firm spears and tight tips. Size does not matter for flavor, but pick uniform spears so they will finish cooking at the same time. Peel the stems of jumbo spears to within 1 inch of the tips; slender spears need little preparation. Boil, steam or stir-fry them, but don't overcook them. Try them coated in butter and sprinkled with lemon juice, covered with hollandaise or vinaigrette dressing or wrapped in ham or puffs of pastry and served with a delicate sauce.

7. Radishes. Bright red radishes are sharp and delicious with sweet butter and dark bread, or simply sliced in salads. Look for crisp, firm, bright radishes, preferably with the greens still attached.

10. Sweet potatoes. Sweet potatoes should be firm, smooth-skinned and blemish-free. Light-colored skins mean a pale, mild flesh, while dark skins mean a darker, sweet flesh. Slice them for tempura, purée for a pie and, of course, bake them.

Potatoes. Tender new potatoes **(17)** are available from January to September; the other varieties are sold year-round. Look for firm specimens with no sprouting eyes, black spots or greenish tinge. New potatoes, long white potatoes and red and white round potatoes are moist and best for boiling, steaming and frying. Russet and Idaho potatoes **(11)** have dry flesh that bakes to perfection and fries well, but falls apart when boiled.

13. Corn. Always wait for local crops; corn's natural sugar turns to starch very soon after it's harvested. There are many varieties of fresh eating corn—yellow, white and even hybrids with a mix of colors. Look for firm, plump kernels that fill out the rows to the tip. Store corn in the refrigerator and cook it the day you buy it.

14. Arugula. A pungent and somewhat bitter salad green also known as rocket. Dress with oil and vinegar, coarse salt and freshly ground black pepper. Arugula

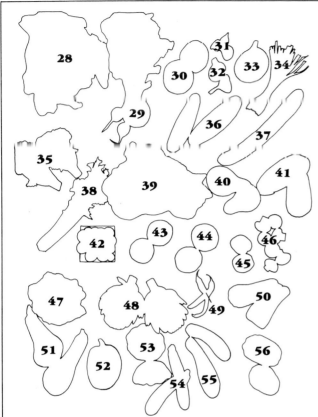

28. Red Cabbage **29.** Beets **30.** Red Onions **31.** Shallots **32.** Garlic **33.** Spanish Onion **34.** Scallions **35.** Broccoli **36.** Cucumbers **37.** Seedless Cucumber **38.** Celery **39.** Green Cabbage **40.** Avocados **41.** Eggplants **42.** Cherry Tomatoes **43.** Beefsteak Tomatoes **44.** Hothouse Tomatoes **45.** Italian Plum Tomatoes **46.** Mushrooms **47.** Cauliflower **48.** Artichokes **49.** Chili Peppers **50.** Sweet Peppers **51.** Butternut Squash **52.** Acorn Squash **53.** Pattipan Squash **54.** Zucchini **55.** Yellow Squash **56.** Green Bell Peppers

mixes well with other salad greens, and can be sautéed like spinach.

15. Rutabaga. A root vegetable with yellow flesh, rutabaga is also known as the yellow turnip. It makes an excellent purée to accompany meats and can also be deep-fried. Rutabaga should be firm, smooth and unblemished.

16. Turnips. White turnips are available year-round, but are most abundant in the fall and winter. Milder and more tender than rutabagas, they can be prepared by many cooking methods. Turnip tops are a favorite cooking green in the South. Boil, steam and then purée firm, round turnips, or eat them raw.

Beans. Many varieties of beans can be cooked pod and all when young and tender. Green beans **(24)**, wax beans **(23)** or fava beans **(20)** should be picked when they are young and at their sweetest for the best flavor. Look for

crisp slender pods with small, barely developed seeds and cook them as soon as possible. Boil or steam and then sauté them with cream, or bathe them in vinaigrette while warm or cool. Try them stir-fried with ginger and garlic.

19. Lima beans. Fresh lima beans are delicate and sweet, but seldom appear in the market anymore. Keep an eye out for them in the summertime; they are worth pursuing. They are good just buttered or in salads.

21. Peas. Fresh peas, like fresh corn, should go from the vine to the cooking pot as quickly as possible or they become starchy and lose their flavor. Look for crisp, bright-colored pods. Snow peas **(18)** are a variety grown for the pod rather than the peas. They, too, should be very fresh. String them before cooking. They are best when still crisp. Both peas and snow peas can be steamed, sautéed, stir-fried, added to a vegetable stew or salad.

Cabbage. One of the oldest cultivated vegetables. Green or head cabbage **(39)**, savoy cabbage **(58)** with its curly leaves and red cabbage **(28)** are the most readily available varieties. Chinese cabbage **(59)** has pale, oval heads. All are available year-round, and are eaten raw as well as cooked. Look for crisp, firm heads and unblemished leaves. Basic to braises, stews and soups, cabbages go well with pork, duck, beef and such flavorings as chestnuts and apples.

29. Beets. Bright-red root vegetables, beets are available all year but are best in the summer. Beet greens have a lovely sweet flavor and should be stir-fried in butter or oil. Bright greens are a clue to the freshness of the beets, which should be firm and round. Don't trim the root or cut the greens off too close to the bulb, or they'll bleed while cooking. Use in borscht or boil and marinate in oil and vinegar.

Onions. Scallions **(34)**, garlic **(32)**, shallots **(31)** and other onions **(30, 33)** are used as a seasoning and as a vegetable. Yellow onions are best for stocks, soups, meats and vegetable stews and braises. Red onions are sweet, and Bermuda onions are big and mild; both are great in salads. Small white or pearl onions glaze easily. Scallions are milder than the other members of the onion family. Robust garlic and delicate shallots are important members, too. Onions are sold all year. All except scallions are dried after harvesting and have a papery outer skin. Onions should not be stored in a damp refrigerator. Store them in a cool, dark, dry place with plenty of air to keep them from getting mushy. Choose onions that feel firm and dry and have no green sprouts.

35. Broccoli. Available year-round and a member of the cabbage family, broccoli is the stem and flower of its plant and must be picked when the heads are immature. Look for a tight, compact head, firm stems and a deep green or purple color. Boil, steam, stir-fry with garlic and sesame oil or purée as a creamy soup.

36. Cucumbers. Available all year, cucumbers are best in the summer. Pick firm, dark, undamaged cucumbers that are long and narrow. Marinate thin slices in cream with dill. Poach or sauté lightly with butter and dill or use in soup in place of summer squash.

38. Celery. Another staple vegetable, celery is available all year. Good celery should be crisp with bright green leaves. Braise celery in a rich stock, or use in a gratin.

40. Avocado. Actually a fruit, these creamy Central American alligator pears are used in salads, sautéed with fish or chicken, puréed for soups and mashed for guacamole. When they are halved, they are natural containers for shellfish, composed salads and herbal vinaigrettes. Ripe avocados are soft to the touch. Brush the cut flesh with lemon or lime juice to prevent darkening.

41. Eggplant. Eggplants come to us from Italy and the Middle East with a rich legacy of preparations. They are available all year. Look for a glossy, deep purple color and smooth skin. Occasionally you will find small white or purple ones. Eggplants can be stewed or braised, alone or with oil, garlic, onions, tomato, zucchini and peppers as in ratatouille. They can be mashed into thick, creamy, caviar-like salads or sautéed lightly by themselves. They take well to batters for fritters or tempura.

42, 43, 44, 45. Tomatoes. Fresh, ripe tomatoes right off the vine are one of the best things about late summer. The tomatoes available the rest of the year are grown and harvested while still green and have no flavor. There are hundreds of varieties of tomatoes, from the tiny cherry tomatoes (**42**) to the juicy beefsteaks (**43**). Italian plum tomatoes (**45**), with a rich flavor and fewer seeds, are best for canning tomatoes and making sauce. Look for heavy tomatoes that are well colored and firm, with no soft spots. Keep them outside the refrigerator; cold stops the ripening. Treat them to lots of basil and olive oil, stew them, stuff them or simply sauté them with herbs.

46. Mushrooms. Cultivated mushrooms, a subtle and faintly earthy-tasting variety, are grown indoors, so their season is year-round. Tan, white and cream-colored, they come in many sizes. Look for smooth, unblemished mushrooms with closed caps over the gills. Store them in the refrigerator unwashed. Wipe them with a damp towel before cooking. Marinate them raw, stuff and bake or sauté in butter, perhaps adding lemon and cream. Cèpes (French) and porcini (Italian) are large and meaty wild mushrooms that are usually sautéed or braised with butter or oil and added to rich rabbit stew. You can also thinly slice these or any mushroom, combine them with thin shavings of Parmesan and sprinkle with olive oil and freshly ground black pepper. Since these mushrooms are rarely found fresh in this country, look for the dried varieties, loose or packaged.

Truffles are the *crème de la crème* of fungi. Extremely expensive and available fresh only during a few weeks in the fall, black and white truffles are still impossible to mass-cultivate and are rooted out by trained dogs and pigs. They elevate pâtés, risottos, pastas and even scrambled eggs to glorious new heights with their woodsy flavor and indefinable texture.

47. Cauliflower. A member of the cabbage family, cauliflower is at its peak in the fall. Good cauliflower has firm, white, compact heads. Home-grown cauliflower often has a purple cast; commercially, it is shielded from the sun to keep it white. Classic in a gratin or browned in butter with sieved egg on top; puréed or creamed in a soup. Combine cauliflower with Brussels sprouts or sauce with a vinaigrette.

48. Artichokes. Considered a type of thistle, the artichoke is the flower of a plant native to North Africa. The bulk of our crop comes from Castroville, California, where the warm, misty climate is perfect for the sensitive plant. The delicate flesh at the bottom of the leaves and the

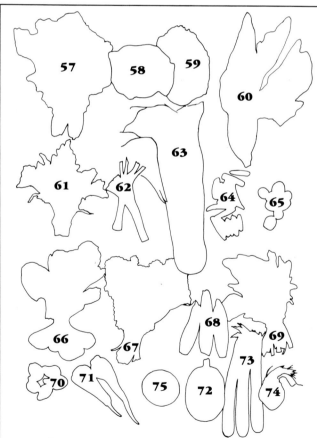

57. Kale **58.** Savoy Cabbage **59.** Bok Choy **60.** Collard Greens **61.** Broccoli Rabe **62.** Leeks **63.** Fennel **64.** Okra **65.** Brussels Sprouts **66.** Kohlrabi **67.** Mustard Greens **68.** Belgian Endive **69.** Dandelion Greens **70.** Jerusalem Artichoke **71.** Parsnips **72.** Spaghetti Squash **73.** Salsify **74.** Celery Root **75.** Rutabaga

succulent meaty bottoms of mature artichokes are consumed. Tiny, young ones are eaten whole. Trim the prickly points off the leaves, then boil or steam and serve them hot with butter, hollandaise or bagna cauda, or cold with herbed mayonnaise or vinaigrette. Stuff and bake them with mushrooms or sausage meat. Sauté the bottoms in butter and cream or turn them into fritters. High season is March through May.

49, 50. Peppers. Most peppers are available year-round, but they abound in summer months. Good peppers, whatever the variety, have bright color and smooth, shiny, firm shells. Broil green, red or yellow peppers until their skins are black, peel and bathe them in olive oil. Peppers combine naturally with tomatoes, eggplant and zucchini.

Squash. There are two basic kinds of squash: tender summer varieties like zucchini **(54)**, yellow **(55)** and scalloped-edged pattypan **(53)** and hard-skinned winter squash like acorn **(52)**, butternut **(51),** turban squash and giant Hubbards. Summer squash peak in the summer, as you would expect, but are now available all year. They should be picked early, before they get too large and their skins harden. Mild in flavor and incredibly versatile, they mix well with herbs and can be eaten raw, steamed, sautéed, puréed or stuffed. Choose small, firm squash with good color and smooth skins. A relatively new squash recently brought into the country from China is the large, oval spaghetti squash **(72)**, with a pulp that naturally shreds into spaghettilike strands. The winter squashes come in about August and hold through the winter because of their hard protective shells. Look for firm, heavy winter squash that can be boiled and puréed or baked. Summer squash needs refrigeration and should be used right away. Winter squash can be kept cool in a dry place for many weeks.

59. Bok choy. Like celery and fennel, bok choy has tender, sweet stalks as well as delicious dark green leaves, which are cooked with the stalk or by themselves. Available year-round, bok choy should have firm stalks and bright, unblemished leaves. Bok choy can be braised or stir-fried. It is similar in cooking quality to Swiss chard.

62. Leeks. A favorite with the New American Cuisine and available year-round, leeks are a member of the onion family. They are used both as a seasoning and as a vegetable, often braised or served with vinaigrette, but we've expanded our repertoire with Leek and Potato Pâté (see page 226). Leeks grow underground, so they are often sandy and need careful cleaning. Good leeks are flexible and have fresh, green tops.

63. Fennel. A bulbous stalk plant with a licorice taste, fennel was cultivated by the Italians for its bulb while other cultures opted for the feathery top herb. Now we're learning to use this autumn/winter vegetable. Pick firm stalks with fresh leaves, and treat fennel as you would celery. Use it raw in salads, sauté it with oil or butter, braise or purée it to accompany pork; grill it with fish; or serve hot or cold in an antipasto.

64. Okra. The immature seed pod of the okra plant, this vegetable is popular in the South. Pick out small, unblemished pods. Okra is a major ingredient in gumbos and its glutinous quality excels in tomato stews. It can be coated with cornmeal for deep-frying.

65. Brussels sprouts. These miniature cabbages were found in prehistoric sites near the city of their name. Available in the autumn and winter, look for good color, tight heads and unblemished leaves. They have a strong flavor that goes well with smoked pork and chestnuts.

66. Kohlrabi. A member of the cabbage family, this bulbous stem looks a little like a turnip but grows above the ground. The color is purple or pale green. It tastes like a mild turnip and can be eaten raw or cooked. Pick out small tender kohlrabi that have fresh-looking leaves and prepare them in a cream sauce.

68. Belgian endive. As its name implies, this tender, pale vegetable comes from Europe. Its careful cultivation under sand makes it unprofitable to American farmers. Available in the winter months. Braise it with broth, simmer with butter and cream or serve with a simple vinaigrette.

70. Jerusalem artichoke. Neither an artichoke nor from Jerusalem, this gnarled North American tuber has a wonderfully nutty flavor. Look for firm, hard Jerusalem artichokes with no soft spots. Try boiling and then sautéing them in butter and lemon or grate raw with lemon in salads.

71. Parsnips. Parsnips look like white carrots but have a sweeter taste. Available year-round, they are best when young and tender, which means under 8 inches long. Good raw, parsnips are often served glazed or are added to soups and stews. Store unwashed and unscraped in the refrigerator.

73. Salsify. A long, slim root plant—at its peak in autumn but available throughout the year in specialty stores—salsify is sometimes called the oyster plant. Its delicate flavor is somewhat similar to that of a parsnip. Salsify should be firm and smooth with no blemishes. Its flavor diminishes with age, so choose smaller ones and use them immediately. After peeling, rub with lemon or they will turn dark. Braise them in stock or broth; simmer in cream after steaming; or sauté.

74. Celery root. Also called celeriac, it's a year-round vegetable that is best in winter. Celery root is a kind of celery that is grown for its round, knobby root rather than its stalk. It is delicious raw with cold mustard sauce and has a rich earthy flavor when boiled and braised or puréed with potatoes.

COOKING TECHNIQUES

Most vegetables can be prepared by any of the seven techniques described below. Obviously, the cooking time depends on the quantity you're planning to cook. (Check the individual recipes.) We offer some suggested vegetables for each method, but by no means should this be considered a definitive list.

Boil. For tough fibrous vegetables such as asparagus and green beans; cook them in a covered pot of salted and rapidly boiling water. Boil until tender yet still firm.

Braise. Cook Belgian endive, fennel, onions and others in a covered pot with butter and water or stock.

Gratin. Cover partially steamed or boiled leeks, cauliflower, salsify or other vegetables with Parmesan or bread crumbs. Bake or broil the vegetables until a brown crust forms.

Purée. Drain steamed or boiled peas, carrots or turnips, then purée them in a food processor or blender or press them through a sieve or food mill for a thick, smooth mixture.

Sauté. Cook julienne or bite-size pieces of zucchini, peppers or mushrooms in a small amount of butter or oil in an uncovered skillet over moderate heat stirring occasionally, until they are *al dente*.

Steam. Put snow peas, acorn squash or chunks of broccoli in a covered colander or steamer basket placed above boiling water.

Stir-fry. Cook bite-size pieces of bok choy, spinach and eggplant in a small amount of oil over high heat and stir constantly until the vegetables are tender but still crisp and their colors are bright.

STUFFED ARTICHOKES

Serves 2

2 artichokes
juice of 1 lemon
¼ pound bulk sausage
1 clove garlic, minced
1 cup chopped, squeezed-dry cooked fresh or frozen
    chopped spinach, thawed and squeezed
    dry in a towel
½ cup dry bread crumbs
salt
freshly ground black pepper
2 tablespoons freshly grated Parmesan

1. Bring 2 quarts of water to a rolling boil in a large pot.

Cut the stems off the artichokes, snip off the prickly points of the leaves and halve lengthwise. Add the lemon juice to the water and drop in the artichokes. Boil for 15 to 20 minutes, or until they are easily pierced with a fork.

2. While the artichokes are cooking, fry the sausage in a heavy skillet over medium heat until well browned—about 10 minutes. Pour off all but about 1 tablespoon of fat and add the garlic. Sauté the garlic with the sausage for another 5 minutes. Add the spinach and bread crumbs and stir until the mixture is blended and heated through. Stir in salt and pepper to taste and remove from the heat.

3. Preheat the broiler. Drain the artichoke halves and dig out the fuzzy-looking choke in the middle. Fill this cavity and the cut surface of the artichoke with the stuffing and put the artichokes, stuffing side up, in a shallow roasting pan. Sprinkle the top of the stuffing with Parmesan and put the pan under the broiler, 6 inches from the heat, until the cheese is browned. Serve hot.

ASPARAGUS MOUSSE

Serve 8

2½ pounds asparagus
1 quart milk
6 eggs, well beaten
1 teaspoon salt
¼ teaspoon pepper
¼ teaspoon nutmeg
juice of 2 oranges
Juice of ½ lemon
2 cups butter
cooked asparagus tips (optional)

1. Boil or steam the trimmed asparagus until tender, then purée in a blender or food processor.

2. Preheat the oven to 400°F. Mix the asparagus and the next 5 ingredients in a bowl until well blended. Pour the mixture into 8 well-buttered 1-cup ramekins. Put the cups in a larger pan and add hot water to the large pan to a depth of 1 inch. Bake until the mousse is puffed and brown, about 20 to 25 minutes.

3. To prepare the sauce, boil the orange and lemon juice until it is reduced by half. Stir in the butter over low heat, 1 tablespoon at a time. Salt to taste.

4. Spoon the sauce on the serving plates and unmold the custard on top of the sauce. Garnish with additional cooked asparagus tips arranged like spokes around the mousse.

Chilled Asparagus with Mousseline Sauce

CHILLED ASPARAGUS

1 pound trimmed asparagus

1. Cook asparagus in simmering salted water for 5 minutes, or until tender yet still firm. Pour ½ cup Vinaigrette Dressing (see page 80) over the hot asparagus and refrigerate until ready to serve.

Cold Mousseline Sauce. Fold ½ cup whipped heavy cream into ½ cup Mayonnaise (see page 78). Gently stir in your choice of seasonings, choosing from a dash of curry, ½ teaspoon of dried mustard or 1 tablespoon finely chopped mint, chives or other herbs.

GREEN BEANS VINAIGRETTE

Serves 8

2 pounds green beans, trimmed
2 red onions, thinly sliced
1 4-ounce jars large capers, drained
1½ cups olive oil
½ cup red wine vinegar
1 tablespoon sugar
1 clove garlic, minced
salt
freshly ground black pepper

1. In a saucepan, cook the green beans in boiling salted water or steam for 5 minutes. They should be tender but still very crisp. Drain.

2. While the beans are still hot, add the onions and capers.

3. In a small bowl, combine the olive oil, vinegar, sugar

and garlic and beat until thick. Pour the dressing over the green beans and season with salt and pepper. Chill, stirring occasionally.

MARINATED BEETS

Serves 4

12 baby beets with greens attached
¼ cup finely chopped shallots
¼ cup red wine vinegar
pinch ground mace
¼ teaspoon crumbled dried thyme
⅔ cup safflower oil
salt
freshly ground black pepper

1. Trim the beets; remove the smallest young beet leaves and set them aside.

2. In a medium saucepan, cover the beets with salted water and boil, covered, until tender, about 25 to 30 minutes. Drain the beets.

3. While the beets are still warm, slip off the skins and cut the beets in ¼-inch-thick slices and put them in a bowl. Shred the reserved beet leaves and add them and the shallots to the beets.

4. In a small bowl, mix the vinegar, mace and thyme and let stand for 20 minutes. Slowly beat in the oil, beating until thick. Toss the beets with the dressing. Refrigerate, then toss again before serving. Season with salt and pepper.

SWEET AND PUNGENT BOK CHOY

Serves 2 to 4

1 tablespoon oil
1 small clove garlic, minced
4 scallions, sliced diagonally
½ cup slivered green pepper
1 carrot, shredded
4 tomatoes, peeled, seeded and chopped
4 cups 2-inch bok choy pieces, both white part and leaves
½ cup Chicken Stock (see page 58) mixed with
    1 tablespoon cornstarch
2 tablespoons red wine vinegar
2 tablespoons sugar
salt

1. In a wok or heavy skillet, heat the oil over medium high heat. When it is hot, stir-fry the garlic, scallions, green pepper and carrot for 1 to 2 minutes.

2. Add the tomatoes and bok choy and stir-fry for 1 to 2 minutes. Reduce the heat, add the stock mixed with cornstarch, vinegar and sugar and simmer, stirring, for no more than 5 minutes, or until the bok choy is tender-crisp and the sauce has thickened slightly. Season with salt.

STUFFED SAVOY CABBAGE

Serves 4 to 8

3 cups ½-inch bread cubes
¾ teaspoon chopped fresh or ¼ teaspoon dried marjoram
¾ teaspoon chopped fresh or ¼ teaspoon dried thyme
¾ teaspoon chopped fresh or ¼ teaspoon dried sage
¼ teaspoon salt
dash white pepper
8 large outer leaves from a savoy cabbage
2 tablespoons butter
1 onion, chopped
½ cup minced celery
1 carrot, shredded
2 cups shredded savoy cabbage
1 cup Chicken Stock (see page 58)
1 egg
salt
freshly ground black pepper
4 tomatoes, peeled and chopped
½ teaspoon celery seeds
2 tablespoons minced onion

1. To make the herb stuffing, bake the bread cubes in a 300°F oven for 30 minutes, or until dry and toasted. In a large bowl, toss the bread cubes with the marjoram, thyme, sage, salt and pepper. Set aside.

2. Preheat the oven to 350°F. Plunge the large cabbage leaves into boiling water for 1 to 2 minutes, just long enough to wilt them and make them flexible. Cool in cold water and trim off the thick rib at the bottom of each leaf.

3. In a heavy skillet or saucepan, melt the butter over medium heat. Add the onion, celery, carrot and shredded cabbage and sauté for 5 minutes. Remove from heat and stir in the herb stuffing and ½ cup of the stock. Beat the egg in a small bowl and add it to the stuffing. Season with salt and pepper, mix well and divide into 8 portions.

4. Butter a 9 × 13 × 2-inch shallow casserole or baking dish. Put stuffing in the center of each large cabbage leaf. Roll up the leaves, tucking in the sides to hold the stuffing, and put seam side down in the casserole in a single layer.

5. In a small bowl, mix the remaining stock and ingredients. Spoon over the cabbage rolls. Cover and bake for 35 to 40 minutes.

Steamed Cabbage and New Potatoes

STEAMED CABBAGE AND NEW POTATOES

Serves 4

1 small head green cabbage, cored and cut into 8 thin wedges
1 pound small new potatoes
⅓ cup butter
¼ cup lemon juice
1 tablespoon chopped fresh or 1 teaspoon dried dill
½ teaspoon salt
½ cup walnut oil
¼ cup red wine vinegar
1½ teaspoon fresh or ½ teaspoon dried tarragon
1½ teaspoon fresh or ½ teaspoon dried sage
2 tablespoons grated walnuts
salt

1. Put the cabbage and the potatoes into the top part of a steamer. Put them over boiling water, cover and steam until the vegetables are tender, about 15 to 18 minutes.

2. To prepare the lemon butter, combine the butter, lemon juice, dill and salt in a small saucepan and stir over low heat until the butter is melted and hot.

3. Combine the walnut oil, vinegar, tarragon, sage and walnuts in a small bowl and beat until thick. Season to taste with salt. The vinaigrette can be served cold or hot.

BRAISED CHINESE CABBAGE

Serves 2

1 head Chinese cabbage
4 teaspoons peanut oil
1 small clove garlic, chopped
4 teaspoons soy sauce
4 teaspoons dry sherry

1. Remove the tough outer leaves of the cabbage and cut the head into quarters lengthwise.

2. Heat the oil in a wok or heavy skillet over medium high heat. Add the garlic and stir-fry for 2 to 3 minutes. Add the cabbage and stir-fry for no more than 5 minutes, or until it is just wilted. Stir in the soy sauce and sherry.

CAULIFLOWER AND BRUSSELS SPROUTS WITH CREAM SAUCE

Serves 6

1 head cauliflower
1 pound Brussels sprouts
¼ cup butter
2 shallots, chopped
¼ cup flour
⅓ cup French cider or white wine
1½ cups heavy cream
2 teaspoons fresh lemon juice
dash nutmeg
salt
freshly ground black pepper

1. Trim the cauliflower but leave it whole. In a large saucepan, cook the cauliflower and Brussels sprouts in water until both are tender but still crisp. Reserve 1 cup of the cooking liquid.

2. In a small saucepan, melt the butter and sauté the

shallots for 5 minutes. Stir in the flour, then gradually add the cider, cream and finally the lemon juice. Keep stirring over low heat until the sauce thickens. Add the nutmeg and reserved cooking liquid and stir until the sauce coats a spoon.

3. Season with salt and pepper to taste. To serve, put the cauliflower on a serving platter, circle with Brussels sprouts and spoon the sauce on top.

BRAISED CELERY HEARTS

Serves 4

2 tablespoons butter
1 medium red onion, chopped
2 celery hearts, halved lengthwise
¼ teaspoon celery seed
coarsely ground black pepper
¼ cup dry white wine
¼ cup Chicken Stock (see page 58)
salt

1. In a skillet, heat butter and sauté the onion for 5 minutes. Add the celery hearts, celery seed, pepper, wine and chicken stock.

2. Cover and simmer gently over low heat until the celery is tender but still holds its shape, about 15 to 20 minutes. Season with salt to taste. Serve the celery hearts with some of the pan juices spooned over them.

Cauliflower and Brussels Sprouts with Cream Sauce

CHESTNUT PUREE

Serves 10 to 12

4 pounds chestnuts or 4 15-ounce cans whole chestnuts, drained
1 cup heavy cream
2 tablespoons Chicken Stock (see page 58)
¼ cup butter
1 cup finely chopped celery
salt
freshly ground black pepper

1. If using fresh chestnuts, shell and cook the chestnuts (see page 314).

2. In a blender or food processor, combine the chestnuts, cream and stock. Process until smooth.

3. In a saucepan, melt the butter and sauté the celery for 10 minutes, or until tender. Stir in the chestnut purée. Season with salt and pepper.

4. Reheat to piping hot, stirring occasionally.

STUFFED EGGPLANT

Serves 2

1 medium eggplant, sliced in half lengthwise
⅓ cup olive oil
2 cloves garlic, chopped
2 tomatoes, seeded and chopped
1½ teaspoons chopped fresh or ½ teaspoon dried basil
1½ cups soft bread cubes
¼ cup pine nuts
¼ cup chopped pitted black olives
1 to 2 tablespoons drained capers
salt
freshly ground black pepper
¼ cup grated Parmesan

1. Preheat the oven to 400°F. Remove the eggplant from its skin, leaving a shell ½-inch thick. Save the shell halves and dice the flesh.

2. In a skillet, heat the oil and sauté the eggplant and garlic for 5 minutes. Add the tomatoes and basil and cook 5 minutes more, stirring, until the eggplant is soft. Stir in the bread cubes, pine nuts, olives and capers. Season with salt and pepper.

3. Mound the stuffing in the shells. Put the stuffed shells in ½ inch water in a shallow baking pan. Top with Parmesan and bake for 15 to 20 minutes, or until brown.

RATATOUILLE

Serves 2

⅓ cup olive oil
1 clove garlic, chopped
1 large onion, sliced
1 small eggplant, peeled and cut into ½-inch cubes
1 red or green bell pepper, cored, seeded and diced
2 small zucchini, sliced
2 large tomatoes, peeled, seeded and chopped
1½ teaspoons each chopped fresh or ½ teaspoon each dried thyme, chervil and summer savory
¼ teaspoon ground coriander
salt
freshly ground black pepper

1. In a large heavy skillet, heat the oil over medium heat. Add the garlic and onion and sauté 5 minutes. Add the eggplant, pepper and zucchini and sauté 5 minutes.

2. Add the tomatoes and seasonings and stir for 2 minutes, then reduce the heat, cover and simmer for 10 to 15 minutes, or until the vegetables are tender. Stir occasionally. Check the seasoning for salt and pepper and serve hot, at room temperature or cold.

EGGPLANT SALAD WITH ROASTED PEPPERS

Serves 4 to 6

2 large eggplants
½ cup olive oil
1 clove garlic, crushed
juice of 1½ lemons
¼ cup chopped parsley
2 red or green sweet peppers
salt
freshly ground black pepper

1. Broil the eggplants whole until soft and slightly charred on both sides. Let cool and remove the skin.

2. Cut the eggplant into ½-inch chunks and put them in a bowl. Add 6 tablespoons of the oil, the garlic, lemon juice and parsley. Chill.

3. Broil the peppers until golden brown on all sides. Dip in cold water and peel the skins. Cut in halves and remove the seeds, then cut them into ¼-inch strips.

4. Mix the peppers with the remaining oil and season with salt and black pepper. Season the eggplant mixture with salt and pepper and spread the peppers on top.

Bubbly and browned Fennel au Gratin

FENNEL AU GRATIN

Serves 4

3 cups thinly sliced fennel (or peeled, thinly sliced
   kohlrabi)
1½ cups water
½ teaspoon salt
¼ cup butter
¼ cup flour
1 cup light cream
1 teaspoon paprika
salt
½ cup grated Parmesan

1. In a saucepan, combine the fennel, water and salt. Cover and simmer until tender, about 10 to 15 minutes. Drain and reserve the cooking liquid.

2. Preheat the oven to 350° F. Return the cooking liquid to the saucepan and reduce it by boiling until there is 1 cup left. In a clean saucepan, melt the butter and stir in the flour. Gradually stir in the cooking liquid, cream and

paprika. Stir over medium heat until the sauce bubbles and thickens. Season to taste with salt.

3. Stir in the fennel and spoon the mixture into 4 individual baking dishes. Sprinkle with the Parmesan and bake until it is bubbly and browned, about 15 minutes.

SAUTEED FENNEL

Serves 6

3 large fennel
¼ cup butter
salt
pinch freshly ground black pepper

1. Wash and trim off the fennel stalks (which you can save for cooking with fish or soup or hang to dry as an herb). Cut the bulbs into quarters.

2. In a heavy saucepan, melt the butter over medium heat. Add the fennel and sauté until tender but still crisp— about 5 to 10 minutes. Season with salt and pepper.

Note. Sautéed in oil, fennel is succulent cold as a first course with fresh mozzarella, roasted red peppers, olive oil and freshly ground pepper.

BASIC BOILED GREENS

Serves 2 to 4

There are a few greens that take better to boiling than to gentle steaming. Strip the leaves off the rough stringy stems of kale, collard greens, beet, turnip and/or mustard greens and cut tender stems into 1-inch pieces.

1 pound greens
¼ teaspoon salt
pinch freshly ground black pepper

1. Put ½ inch of water in a large pot. Greens shrink incredibly during cooking, so fit them into the pot tightly. Add the salt. Bring the water to a boil.

2. Cover the pot and simmer over low heat, stirring occasionally, until just tender and still green. Beet tops and mustard greens take 7 to 9 minutes. Dandelion greens, arugula and Swiss chard take 10 to 12 minutes. Kale, collard greens and turnip greens take 20 to 25 minutes.

3. Season the greens with salt and pepper. Serve them plain, buttered, with crumbled bacon or splashed with vinegar or lemon juice.

GREENS WITH POT LIQUOR

Serves 2 to 4

In the South this is the only acceptable way to fix collard, turnip, and/or mustard greens.

1 ham hock or 4 strips of bacon or 2 ounces diced salt
   pork
2 cups Chicken Stock (see page 58)
1 pound collard or turnip greens
freshly ground black pepper

1. If you are using a ham hock, combine it with the stock in a heavy saucepan and bring to a boil. Reduce the heat and simmer, covered, for 1 hour, or until tender. If necessary, add stock from time to time to keep up the liquid level.

2. If you are using bacon or salt pork, fry it until crisp in a heavy saucepan. Remove crisp pieces and reserve. Add the stock.

3. Add the greens and simmer, covered, 20 to 25 minutes. Season with pepper.

4. If you've used the ham hock, remove the skin and bones and cut the meat in pieces. Serve the greens and ham or crisp bacon or pork with the pot liquor in bowls alongside.

BRAISED ARUGULA OR DANDELION GREENS

Serves 2 to 4

6 slices bacon, cut in half
1 clove garlic, minced
1 pound arugula or dandelion greens, chopped
½ cup Chicken Stock (see page 58)
1 tablespoon red wine vinegar
salt
freshly ground pepper

1. In a heavy saucepan, fry the bacon over medium high heat until crisp. Remove the bacon, drain it on paper towel and reserve.

2. Sauté the garlic for 1 minute. Add the greens, stock and vinegar and stir until the liquid begins to simmer. Cover and simmer 1 to 2 minutes.

3. Season with salt and pepper and sprinkle the greens with crumbled bacon.

JERUSALEM ARTICHOKES WITH LEMON

Serves 6

2 pounds Jerusalem artichokes
salt
¼ cup butter
¼ cup lemon juice
⅓ cup chopped parsley
salt
pinch freshly ground black pepper

1. Put the unpeeled Jerusalem artichokes in a saucepan and add water to cover and 1 teaspoon salt. Bring the water to boil over high heat. Reduce the heat slightly and let boil, covered, for 15 to 20 minutes, or until just tender and easily pierced with a fork. (Don't overcook or they will get tough.)

2. Drain, cool to lukewarm and peel. If they are small, leave whole; slice if they are large. In a heavy saucepan melt the butter over medium heat. Add the artichokes, lemon juice and parsley. Stir until they are hot. Season with salt and pepper and serve.

KOHLRABI IN CREAM SAUCE

12 kohlrabi
salt
⅓ cup butter
⅓ cup flour
1 cup light cream
pinch freshly ground black pepper

1. Trim and peel the kohlrabi and cut into ½-inch slices. Chop some of the young green leaves. Put slices and chopped leaves in a saucepan with water to cover. Salt lightly. Bring the water to a boil, reduce the heat slightly and boil, uncovered, for 10 to 15 minutes, or until the kohlrabi is tender and easily pierced with a fork.

2. Lift out the kohlrabi with a slotted spoon. Boil the cooking liquid until it is reduced to 1 cup.

3. In a heavy saucepan, melt the butter over medium heat. Add the flour and cook for 2 minutes, stirring all the while. Gradually stir in the reduced cooking liquid and the cream. Keep stirring until the sauce begins to simmer and thicken.

4. Add the kohlrabi to the sauce and cook until the vegetable is hot. Season with salt and pepper and serve hot.

BRAISED LEEKS

Serves 6

Leeks look like large scallions and taste like very young onions. Braising in stock brings out their mild flavor.

12 leeks
1 cup Chicken Stock (see page 58)
2 tablespoons butter
salt
freshly ground black pepper

1. Trim off the roots and tough green leaves of the leeks, saving the green leaves to use in soup another time. Wash the leeks carefully; they tend to be very sandy.

2. In a heavy saucepan, bring the stock and butter to a boil. Add the leeks, reduce the heat and simmer, covered, for 15 minutes, or until tender.

3. Drain and season with salt and pepper and serve hot.

Note. Cold braised leeks are good with Vinaigrette Dressing (see page 80).

LEEK AND POTATO PATE

Makes 1 9 × 5 × 3-inch loaf

A silken package, wrapped with pale green leeks, tempting on even the hottest summer days.

6 large Idaho potatoes
1 teaspoon salt
8 leeks
½ cup dry white wine
2 envelopes unflavored gelatin
1 cup melted butter
1 cup plain yogurt
6 scallions, sliced crosswise
¼ cup chopped chives
salt
¼ teaspoon ground white pepper

1. Put the potatoes in a saucepan. Add 1 teaspoon salt and water to cover. Bring to a boil over high heat, lower the heat to medium and cook, uncovered, for 20 minutes, or until the potatoes are easily pierced with a fork. Remove the potatoes from the water and let them cool. Peel and press through a ricer or food mill into a large bowl (a food processor makes the potatoes too sticky). Cover and keep in reserve.

2. Trim the leeks and wash carefully to remove sandy particles. Bring a saucepan of water to a boil and add 2 whole leeks. Let them boil until soft and flexible—about 10 minutes. Cool and separate into leaves for lining the pâté pan.

3. Slice the remaining leeks and put in a saucepan with water to cover. Bring to a boil, reduce the heat and simmer, covered, for 20 minutes, or until the leeks are tender. Drain, mince and add to the potatoes.

4. Oil a 9 × 5 ×3-inch loaf pan and line it with the separated leek leaves, reserving enough to cover the top.

5. Put the wine in a small saucepan. Add the gelatin and let it soften for a minute, then put the pan over low heat and stir until the gelatin is completely dissolved.

6. Add the dissolved gelatin, butter, yogurt, scallions and chives to the potato-leek mixture. Stir until well blended. Add salt to taste and pepper and stir again. Pack this mixture into the leek-lined pan. Cover the top with leek leaves and cover the pan with foil. Chill for 5 to 6 hours, or until the loaf is firm.

7. To serve, unmold the loaf onto a platter and cut into thick slices. Garnish with watercress and serve with Mustard Vinaigrette (see page 80).

FRIED OKRA

Serves 2

Cooked slowly, this Southern specialty should be crisp and brown outside, soft and succulent inside.

1 pound okra
1 egg, beaten
approximately ⅓ cup yellow cornmeal
2 tablespoons butter
¼ cup corn oil
salt

1. Wash the okra and trim off the stems. Coat each piece with beaten egg, then cornmeal.

2. In a heavy skillet, large enough to hold the okra comfortably, combine the butter and oil. When the butter and oil are hot, add the okra. Sauté gently until the okra is brown and easily pierced with a fork—about 5 to 6 minutes. It may be necessary to fry in batches to keep from crowding.

3. Drain on paper towel and salt to taste. Serve hot or cold.

Yogurt adds smoothness to a cooling Leek and Potato Pâté.

STEWED OKRA AND TOMATOES

Serves 6

2 tablespoons butter
¼ cup chopped onion
3 cups diced fresh tomatoes
2 cups sliced okra
1 tablespoon chopped fresh or 1 teaspoon dried basil

1. In a skillet, melt the butter and sauté the onion. Add the tomatoes, okra and basil and simmer, stirring frequently, for 20 minutes.

SWEET AND SOUR ONIONS

Serves 6

1½ pounds small white onions
2 teaspoons sugar
1 cup white vinegar
1 cup Brown Stock (see page 57)
salt

1. In a bowl, cover the onions with cold water and let stand for 1 hour. Drain.

2. In a saucepan, combine the onions and the remaining ingredients. Cover and simmer for 40 minutes and season with salt to taste. Drain and serve hot.

GLAZED PARSNIPS

Serves 4

6 parsnips
salt
¼ cup orange marmalade
¼ cup apricot preserves
¼ cup butter
juice of 1 lemon

1. Trim and peel the parsnips. Keep young parsnips whole but slice the larger parsnips. Put them in a saucepan. Add water to cover and ½ teaspoon salt. Bring to a boil, reduce the heat and simmer, covered, until the parsnips are tender—about 15 to 20 minutes. Drain.

2. In a heavy skillet, combine the marmalade, preserves, butter and lemon juice. Stir over medium heat until the glaze begins to bubble. Add the parsnips and reduce the heat to low. Turn the parsnips gently to coat them. Simmer for 10 minutes, occasionally turning the parsnips. Season with salt. Serve hot.

STIR-FRIED PARSNIPS

Serves 4

¼ cup Oriental sesame oil
1 tablespoon sesame seeds
4 scallions, cut into 1-inch pieces
1 clove garlic, chopped
2 parsnips, scraped and thinly sliced
4 ounces snow peas, trimmed and halved lengthwise
salt
freshly ground black pepper

1. In a large skillet, heat the oil and sauté the sesame seeds until they are golden brown.

2. Add the scallions, garlic and parsnips and stir-fry for 5 minutes or until the parsnips are tender but still slightly chewy. Add the snow peas and stir-fry for another 2 minutes. Season to taste with salt and pepper.

POTATOES LYONNAISE

Serves 4

4 large boiling potatoes
⅓ cup butter
1 large onion, thinly sliced
salt
pinch freshly ground black pepper

1. Boil and peel the potatoes. Cut into ¼-inch-thick slices.

2. In a heavy skillet, melt the butter over medium heat. Add the potatoes and sauté until pale golden brown—about 5 minutes.

3. Add the onion to the skillet and sauté until the potatoes are a rich brown, an additional 8 to 10 minutes. Season with salt and pepper and serve hot.

POTATO SALAD

Serves 6

A classic with mayonnaise, but even better with a lemon-flavored vinaigrette.

6 potatoes, peeled
½ cup dry white wine
salt
freshly ground black pepper
½ cup Mustard Vinaigrette (see page 80)
juice of 1 lemon

1. In a large saucepan, boil the potatoes until they are easily pierced with a fork. Be careful not to overcook them.

2. Cut them into chunks and let them steam in a colander for a few minutes. While they are still warm, toss them in a large bowl with the wine. Then let them rest to absorb the wine.

3. Season with salt and pepper, then toss with the vinaigrette and lemon juice. Serve warm or cold.

BOURBON SWEET POTATOES

Serves 6

Sweet potatoes come deep orange to pale yellow; any shade tastes good with bourbon and brown sugar.

6 medium sweet potatoes
¼ cup butter
3 tablespoons bourbon
3 tablespoons milk
1 tablespoon firmly packed brown sugar
½ teaspoon nutmeg
salt
dash freshly ground black pepper
6 pecan halves (optional)

1. In a 400°F oven, bake the sweet potatoes for 50 minutes, or until they can be easily pierced with a fork. Cut a slice off the top of each and scoop out the inside, taking care not to break the shell.

2. In a bowl, mash the potatoes and add all the ingredients except the salt, pepper and pecans. Beat together until well blended, then season with salt and pepper.

3. Spoon the mixture into the shells. Garnish with the pecan halves. Bake the potatoes in a 350°F oven for 15 to 20 minutes.

FRIED RUTABAGA

Serves 4

A refreshing and somewhat tart orange and chive sauce sets off the deep-fried vegetable.

1 large rutabaga, about 2 pounds, peeled and cut into
   ¼-inch-thick slices
milk
flour
deep fat or oil heated to 360°F

¼ cup butter
¼ cup flour
2 cups orange juice
2 tablespoons chopped chives
¼ cup slivered orange rind
2 navel oranges, cut into sections
salt

1. Cut the slices of rutabaga into 1 × 2-inch oblong pieces. Coat them with milk, then with flour. Drop the pieces into hot fat and fry for 6 to 8 minutes or until golden brown on all sides. Drain on paper towel.

2. To prepare the sauce, heat the butter in a skillet and stir in the flour. Next, stir in the orange juice and chives. Continue stirring over medium heat until the sauce is thickened. Fold in the rind and orange sections. Reheat slightly and season to taste with salt.

Fried Rutabaga

Puréed Turnips and Chestnuts

2. Press the turnips and chestnuts through a food mill or purée in a food processor until smooth. Return them to the saucepan and simmer over low heat until thick. Stir in the 2 tablespoons butter, peppercorns and salt to taste.

3. In a skillet, melt the 3 tablespoons butter and sauté the artichoke bottoms until they are heated through. Remove them from the pan, spoon the purée into the bottoms and garnish with parsley.

YAM AND LEEK PIE

Makes 1 9-inch pie

2 cups unsifted all-purpose flour
½ teaspoon salt
½ cup minced smoked ham
⅔ cup shortening
ice water, about ½ cup
3 yams, about 1½ pounds, cooked and peeled

¼ cup butter
4 leeks, white part only, washed and thinly sliced
4 egg yolks
4 egg whites, stiffly beaten
salt

1. In a large bowl, mix the flour, salt and ham. Cut in the shortening until particles are very fine. Stir in the water and continue stirring until a ball of dough is formed. Wrap in plastic wrap and chill for 30 minutes.

2. Roll out the dough large enough to cover the bottom and sides on an ungreased 9-inch pie pan. Flute the edges and chill.

3. Preheat the oven to 350°F. Mash the yams until they are smooth and fluffy. In a skillet, heat the butter and sauté the leeks for 5 minutes. Set aside half the leeks to use as a garnish for the finished pie.

4. Stir the remaining leeks and the pan juices into the yams, then stir in the egg yolks. Fold the beaten egg whites into this mixture and season to taste with salt. Spoon this filling into the pie shell and bake until the pie is lightly browned and puffed, about 40 to 45 minutes. Spoon the extra leeks around the edge of the pie and serve hot.

FRIED ZUCCHINI WITH GREEN PEPPERCORN BUTTER

Serves 6

¼ cup butter
1 tablespoon chopped fresh parsley
1 tablespoon chopped fresh chives
1 tablespoon crushed green peppercorns
1 tablespoon fresh chopped or 1 teaspoon dried, crushed rosemary
¼ cup vegetable oil
6 zucchini, trimmed and cut into 1-inch-thick slices

1. In a bowl, cream the butter with the parsley, chives, peppercorns and rosemary.

2. In a skillet, heat the oil and sauté the zucchini until golden brown on each side. Drain on paper towel.

3. Toss the hot zucchini with the herb butter. Serve hot.

VEGETABLE KARI

Serves 4

Kari is the Indian word for sauce, which was modified by the English to curry *(which in turn means sauce).*

½ cup Clarified Butter (see page 79)
½ teaspoon ground cumin
¼ teaspoon ground ginger
1 teaspoon turmeric
¼ teaspoon ground fenugreek
4 small potatoes, peeled and diced
1 small cauliflower, cut into pieces
1 cup fresh green beans, cut into 1-inch pieces
4 small carrots, cut into julienne strips
1 medium onion, chopped
salt

1. In a saucepan, heat the butter and sauté the spices for 2 minutes.

2. Add the potatoes and cauliflower and sauté for 5 minutes. Then add the beans, carrots and onions and stir-fry over high heat until the vegetables are tender but still crisp, about 5 or 6 minutes. Season with salt.

VEGETABLE TERRINE

Serves 8

1 cup rendered duckling or chicken fat
1 small eggplant, peeled and cut into ½-inch-thick slices
4 zucchini, cut into thin slices
4 red peppers, broiled until black on all sides, peeled and cut into thin strips
1 pound tiny white onions, sliced
4 carrots, thinly sliced
4 tomatoes, seeded and chopped
3 envelopes unflavored gelatin
4 cups tomato purée (about 6 to 8 peeled and seeded tomatoes)
salt
freshly ground black pepper
1½ cups olive oil
½ cup fresh lemon juice
1 tablespoon Dijon mustard
1 egg yolk
1 tablespoon raspberry vinegar
2 tablespoons chopped chives

1. Divide the fat, using fresh fat for each vegetable. In a large skillet, heat the fat and sauté the vegetables separately until wilted. Remove each batch with a slotted spoon to drain the excess fat.

2. Layer the vegetables into a 2½-quart terrine in the following order: eggplant, zucchini, red peppers, onions, carrots and tomatoes.

3. In a saucepan, combine the gelatin and 1 cup of the tomato purée. Stir over low heat until the gelatin is dissolved. Stir in the remaining purée, 1 teaspoon salt and ¼ teaspoon pepper. Pour the purée into the terrine over the vegetables slowly and run a knife around the edge to allow the gelatin to settle down to the bottom of the terrine. It may not be necessary to use all the purée; there should be enough gelatin to just hold the mold together and to coat the outside thinly. Refrigerate for several hours or overnight, until firm.

4. Dip the terrine into lukewarm water for a few seconds, tap loose and unmold the terrine onto a serving platter. To make a chive vinaigrette, combine the remaining ingredients and beat until thick and well blended. Season with salt and pepper. Cut the mold into slices and spoon the dressing over it.

SALADS

Greens should be washed in a generous amount of cold water to remove all the grit and sand. Discard discolored or wilted leaves. Washed greens must be carefully dried with dish towels or in a salad spinner—wet greens simply will not hold a dressing. The dried greens, wrapped in towels or in a plastic bag, will be at their crispest if refrigerated for an hour or more.

Often the most simple things require the most care. The best green salad has a carefully chosen balance of greens, with textures, colors and flavor in simple harmony. A perfect salad deserves to be a course unto itself. Europeans claim it aids the digestion if it follows the main course, before cheese and dessert. We think it's up to the individual.

Start with a yellow, buttery Boston lettuce, add flat crisp romaine and finish the composition with some strands of peppery, dark green watercress. Or match two strong contenders—smooth Belgian endive and bitter, curly escarole. Elaborate on a theme, especially if the salad is to be the main dish. Add raw vegetables that have been cut into small slices or wedges: tomatoes, cucumbers, carrots, fennel stalk, beans, broccoli, avocado and mushrooms are good candidates. Cold cooked vegetables like artichoke hearts, hearts of palm, asparagus, pimento, snow peas and beets are also good in salads. Try cold cooked meats or croutons made from sautéed cubes of French bread.

Tear the greens into bite-size pieces and use a serving bowl large enough to allow for comfortable tossing. Toss the greens with dressing just before serving; sitting in oil for any length of time will wilt them. Use any of the following vinaigrette dressings or check the Index for other choices.

The perfect green salad: tart Belgian endive, buttery Boston lettuce, crisp romaine and dark watercress

CHICKEN AND AVOCADO SALAD

Serves 4

A salade composée can be made from anything you choose to "compose," so try variations on this theme.

2 avocados
1 tablespoon lemon juice
2 whole chicken breasts, skinned, boned, poached (see page 131) and cut into chunks
1 tomato, cored, seeded and chopped
10 water chestnuts, cut in half
1 recipe Vinaigrette Dressing (see page 80)
4 slices bacon
2 cups trimmed watercress

1. Peel and seed the avocados and cut the meat into pieces. Sprinkle the avocado with lemon juice and put in a large bowl. Add the chicken pieces, tomato and water chestnuts.

2. Pour the vinaigrette over the chicken and avocado mixture. Toss gently until all the ingredients are coated. Cover the bowl and chill for at least an hour. While it

chills, cook the bacon over medium heat in a heavy skillet until brown and crisp. Drain on paper towel and crumble.

3. To serve, make a bed of watercress leaves on 4 plates. Spoon the chicken-avocado salad onto each. Sprinkle with crumbled bacon.

AVOCADO SALAD WITH YOGURT DRESSING

Serves 2

Yogurt and mint make a refreshingly simple dressing.

1 large avocado
1 teaspoon lime juice
1 tablespoon chopped fresh mint leaves
½ cup plain yogurt
2 lime wedges

1. Cut the avocado in half and remove the seed. Brush the cut edges with lime juice and chill.

2. Mix the mint and yogurt in a small bowl and spoon into the avocado halves. Garnish with the lime wedges.

SALADE NICOISE

Serves 4

Boston lettuce leaves
2 7½-ounce cans tuna, drained
1 2-ounce can flat anchovy filets, drained
2 cups boiled, peeled and halved new potatoes
2 tablespoons chopped fresh parsley
¼ cup drained capers
2 cups whole cooked green beans
2 shallots, minced
½ cup Niçoise black olives
1 4-ounce jar pimentos, drained and cut into large pieces
4 hard-boiled eggs, peeled and halved
2 tomatoes, cut into wedges
1 lemon, cut into wedges
Vinaigrette Dressing (see page 80)

1. Prepare a bed of lettuce leaves on a large platter. In a small bowl, mix the tuna and anchovies and arrange in the center of the platter. Mix the potatoes, parsley and capers in a separate small bowl and put on one side of the tuna mixture. Mix the beans and shallots and put them on the other side.

2. Add the olives, pimentos, eggs, tomatoes and lemon to the platter, tucking them in groups between the tuna, potatoes and beans.

3. Pour the vinaigrette evenly over the salad.

Salade Niçoise

WARM GOAT CHEESE SALAD

Serves 4

1 head red-leaf lettuce
2 spears Belgian endive
4 2-ounce packages goat cheese
¼ cup white wine vinegar
¾ cup walnut oil
2 tablespoons Dijon mustard
salt
white pepper

1. Arrange the washed and dried lettuce and endive on serving plates.

2. In a 350°F oven, bake the cheese on a baking sheet for 5 minutes, or until melted. Put the hot cheese in the center of the salad.

3. In a small bowl, combine the vinegar, oil and mustard and beat until thick. Season with salt and pepper and spoon the dressing in a ring around the cheese.

TOMATO AND CELERIAC SALAD

Serves 4

8 Italian plum tomatoes, cut into thin wedges
1 celery root, shredded coarsely
1 bunch watercress
½ cup olive oil
¼ cup white wine vinegar
1 teaspoon salt
1 teaspoon sugar
¼ teaspoon white pepper
1 teaspoon chopped fresh or ¼ teaspoon dried marjoram
1 teaspoon chopped fresh or ¼ teaspoon dried chervil
2 scallions, minced
¼ cup finely chopped celery leaves

1. Arrange the tomatoes, celeriac and watercress on salad plates and chill.

2. Combine the remaining ingredients and beat until thick. Let the dressing stand at room temperature for 1 hour, then beat again. Spoon the dressing over the salad when ready to serve.

GREEK SALAD

Serves 6

Feta cheese, olives and tomatoes, traditional glories of the Mediterranean, are the basis of a Greek salad, here updated with green peppercorns.

½ cup olive oil
¼ cup lemon juice
1 teaspoon sugar
1 tablespoon Dijon mustard
1 tablespoon green peppercorns
salt
8 cups assorted greens, torn into bite-size pieces
2 tomatoes, cored and cut into wedges
1 4-ounce jar pimentos, drained and diced
1 cucumber, peeled and sliced
24 black Mediterranean olives
1 cup (4 ounces) crumbled feta cheese

1. In a small bowl, beat the oil, lemon juice, sugar, mustard, peppercorns and salt to taste until well blended. Let stand at room temperature to develop the flavors.

2. In a salad bowl, mix the remaining ingredients and chill until ready to serve. Pour the dressing over the salad, toss gently to coat all the ingredients and serve at once.

HAM AND BEET SALAD

Serves 2

½ cup diced smoked ham
¼ cup shredded young beet or spinach leaves
2 beets, boiled, peeled and diced, or 1 8-ounce can diced beets, drained
4 new potatoes, boiled, peeled and sliced
½ cup plain yogurt
2 tablespoons minced onion
2 teaspoons prepared horseradish
2 teaspoons Dijon mustard
salt
freshly ground black pepper
sorrel or Boston lettuce leaves

1. In a large bowl, mix the ham, shredded leaves, beets and potatoes.

2. In a small bowl, blend the yogurt, onion, horseradish, mustard, salt and pepper, then pour this dressing over the ham and vegetables. Toss gently until all the ingredients are coated.

3. Cover the bowl and chill for at least 1 hour. Serve on a bed of sorrel or lettuce leaves.

Fruit

The New American Cuisine upsets the fruit basket with new notions of how to serve what and when. The possibilities are myriad: from almost out of nowhere, the kiwi emerges as a prime accompaniment to fish and a major new fruit flavor in fresh sherbet.

Raspberries turn up nestled around broiled chicken and squab, and in the first new vinegar flavor since apple. The pear, it turns out, is as versatile as the potato, succumbing with grace to poaching in wine, being stuffed with cheese and puréeing as a thickener for sauces.

Fruit sherbets abound in new flavors, from honeydew melon to mango. Replacing tortured curls of lemon rind and ubiquitous sprigs of parsley are whole or halved blue plums, pomegranates, persimmons, lady apples, Seckel pears and clementines. Fruit as the new garnish is, like the best new ideas, instantly and obviously right.

THE ESSENTIALS

The following list of fruits is designed to help you recognize the many varieties of fruits, their best seasons, their best uses and clues to their states of ripeness or flavor.

1, 8, 12. Grapes. We've been eating grapes at least since recorded history and, at least since Roman times, have distinguished between grapes for wine, for eating and for raisins. North American eating grapes include the tiny Concord grapes of New England with their tough, blue pop-off skins. The popular green seedless Thompson grapes come into season in early summer and are followed through the fall and winter by red Tokays, Cardinals and Emperors and the deep purple Malagas. Good-quality grapes are firm and unblemished, particularly around the stem. Dried grapes, of course, are raisins and come in brown and golden varieties. Grapes accompany pheasant,

1. Ribier Grapes 2. Figs 3. Santa Rosa Plums 4. Nubiana Plums 5. Duarte Plums 6. Raspberries 7. Black Raspberries 8. Thompson Seedless Grapes 9. Cranberries 10. Currants 11. Gooseberries 12. Tokay Grapes 13. Blueberries 14. Bing Cherries 15. Strawberries 16. Nectarines 17. Apricots 18. Sour Cherries 19. Peaches

small fowl and lightly sauced fish; use concentric circles of different varieties on delicate puff pastries.

2. Figs. The fresh figs grown in California are the descendants of early stock brought in by sixteenth-century Spanish missionaries. They are purple or pale green outside and pink inside, shaped like tiny, heavy-bottomed pears. Buy them slightly soft. Fresh ripe figs, a summer fruit, are a lusciously exotic experience. Cut them open and scoop out the sweet pink-seeded flesh or wrap them with prosciutto. Whip them into a heady purée to enhance fowl or pork. Use dried figs in puddings, stewed fruit compotes and baked goods.

3, 4, 5. Plums. Succulent fresh plums are one of the joys of summer. There are many varieties, ranging from the dark purple presidents and red Santa Rosas to the interestingly sweet plump greengages. Good plums should be plump, smooth-skinned and slightly soft. Damsons are small and tart, good for making jams and prunes. Plums are a lovely edible garnish and make fragrant sauces for meat and game birds. They can be lightly poached in wine and plumped on top of tarts.

6, 7. Raspberries. The raspberry is known for its exquisite flavor and fragile fragrance. Traditional with cream and custards, they flavor fantastic vinegars, puréed sauces, syrups and sorbets. They combine with great delicacy with chicken, duck and game birds. Raspberries are highly perishable and should be handled lightly. Dry-packed frozen raspberries are good when fresh aren't available.

9. Cranberries. The first cranberry sauce was made with maple sugar by the Indian tribes of what's now the northeastern United States. Traditionally they are cooked with sugar until their skins pop to make a sauce for turkey. We are now refining cranberry sauce into delicate purées to accompany venison, duck and other game birds. We've taken these tart berries one step further and expanded our repertoire by including them in delicate, frothy soufflés and crisp, refreshing ices. That's not to say that we've lost our love for breads, muffins and jellies filled with firm, unblemished red berries. Available fresh from September to February, cranberries keep up to 1 year in the freezer.

10. Currants. Tiny, bright red, almost translucent, currants have a tart flavor that encourages that of other fruits and makes the best jellies, glazes and sauces for game. Currants ripen in midsummer. So-called dried currants are really a kind of raisin and have nothing to do with the berry.

11. Gooseberries. Large green berries with an almost translucent skin, pale with white stripes, gooseberries have a distinctive tart flavor—perfect for jams and preserves. Available only in midsummer, they are splendid stewed with sugar and covered with custard sauce.

14, 18. Cherries. Sweet eating cherries—Bings, Windsors and Lamberts—are usually deep red or reddish-brown plump spheres that are sold with the stems still attached. Sweet cherries, stemmed and pitted, are marvelous in compotes, but the small and pale sour cherries are better for tarts and jellies. Fresh cherries come into season in June and last throughout the summer.

15. Strawberries. The legendary wild strawberries have grown around the world since ancient times. Early explorers raved about the size and abundance of North American varieties, but cultivation of these delicate berries didn't really take place until the sixteenth century, and commercial production had to wait for railroads in the nineteenth century. Strawberries are available year-round, although the height of the season is still May and June. Wild strawberries can still be found in rural areas, and plants are available from seed companies. More aromatic and musky-tasting than commercial strawberries, they are too delicate for shipping but are easy to grow in a sunny spot for the luxury of picking them yourself minutes before a meal. Good strawberries are bright red, plump, firm and dry, but with some sheen. Wash and hull them at the last minute for covering with cream or in compotes, or leave the stems on and set out with a dish of sugar to dip them in. Float them in wine or sauce them with raspberry purée. Heap them on shells of fresh puff pastry for a glorious finale to a meal.

16. Nectarines. A smooth-skinned peach, nectarines are poached in compotes or covered with lovely thick cream or custard. They marry well with duck and game birds, make delicious flans and ice cream. Available from June to September, nectarines should be plump, orange-yellow and red in color and a bit soft along the seam.

17. Apricots. A temperate-climate fruit that came to us from China, apricots are small and orange-yellow with a tart-sweet flavor. Fresh apricots are available in June and July, should be plump and juicy and should give a little when you press them. Apricots are grown in California, but only 5 percent of the crop is sold fresh. Dried apricots are good substitutes for fresh in cooking, and apricot preserves or jam can be used as a glaze for meat, poultry and game. Fresh, they can be poached whole and covered with cream. They make beautiful fresh tarts and, of course, fresh or dried, they can be served in a wine-laced compote.

19. Peaches. A temperate-zone fruit that must have a dormant period, peaches require warm weather to ripen to their full sweetness. Native to China, they reached Europe via the Middle East and were known as Persian apples. Brought to the New World by the Spaniards, peaches were spread throughout the United States by Indians, who adored them. The best peaches ripen on the trees and are available in summer. Look for heavy yellow peaches, without brown spots, that have some softness.

Hard green peaches will not ripen at home, but firm peaches will ripen in a brown paper bag at room temperature. You can keep cut peaches from turning brown by rubbing them with lemon juice. Peaches (like tomatoes) are easily peeled if they are dipped for 10 seconds in boiling water. Wonderful in tarts and jams, sherbets and ice cream, peaches are also brandied and spiced to go with meat and fowl. Or they can simply be served whole, peeled and bathed in fresh raspberry purée.

20. Bananas. Botanically speaking, bananas aren't fruit but the world's largest herb. They were known in antiquity in the Indus Valley; the Koran identifies the forbidden fruit of the Old Testament as a banana, not an apple. Wild bananas—hard and full of seeds—are a far cry from the sweet bananas we now enjoy. Tropical bananas are available year-round. They can be picked early and ripened off the tree. Ripe bananas are yellow or red and firm, never hard. Slice them and cover with cream, or sauté or bake them with butter, sugar and rum.

21, 22, 23. Pears. A subtle-tasting, versatile fruit, pears are important to the New Cuisine. They are used in purées

20. Bananas **21.** Bartlett Pears **22.** Bosc Pears **23.** Anjou Pears **24.** Pineapple **25.** Rome Apples **26.** Red Delicious Apples **27.** Golden Delicious Apples **28.** Granny Smith Apples **29.** Navel Oranges **30.** Juice Oranges **31.** Lemons **32.** Limes **33.** Honeydew Melon **34.** Cantaloupe **35.** Pink Grapefruit **36.** White Grapefruit **37.** Watermelon

for sauces, salads with goat cheese and greens. Pears replace traditional vegetables—whole or sliced, they can garnish anything. The best pears in the United States come from the Northwest. Our most popular eating pear is the Bartlett, available in the summer. In early autumn Anjou and Bosc pears can be found. The luxury pear is the Comice, tender, sweet and hard to ship without bruising. Look for firm, unbruised pears. Different varieties have different colored skins, ranging from yellow to green to brown. Pears are often sold unripe and should be bought a few days ahead and left at room temperature.

24. Pineapples. In the sixteenth century, this New World native caused a sensation in Europe after its introduction and made its way around the tropical world faster than any other fruit. It was not until the nineteenth century that Americans became familiar with pineapples. Pineapples must ripen on the plant to develop their best flavor. Look for heavy, sweet-smelling fruit with healthy leaves and no soft spots. (Pulling out a leaf to see if the fruit is ripe is an old wives' tale.) The best time for pineapples is spring, although they are available all year. Fresh pineapple, incidentally, has an enzyme that destroys the jelling power of gelatin, so it must be cooked before using in gelatin dishes. They are at their best with a squeeze of fresh lime, but make fine sherbets and ices as well.

25, 26, 27, 28. Apples. They've been around for so long that we've discovered they can do almost anything. They comfort us in homey tarts and baked with cinnamon and raisins; they delight us when prepared with veal, cream and Calvados. Apples make a succulent stuffing alone or with prunes and apricots for a roast loin of pork or goose. Sautéed in butter, they enhance anything from country ham to pheasant. As new garnishes, the gentle lady apple and the Granny Smith, thinly sliced, have replaced lettuce leaves. Red and Golden Delicious apples are large and should have a distinctive sweetness and rather mealy quality; the smaller red or green McIntosh should be crisp and more tangy; while the glorious greenings or Granny Smith are crisp, juicy and somewhat tart. Green apples are particularly good for cooking, and the large round Rome Beauty bakes beautifully. In the late summer or fall, when apples are at their peak, look for firm, unblemished apples in many varieties.

29, 30. Oranges. This ancient fruit is thought to be native to southern China and first introduced to our shores by Hernando de Soto in 1539 near St. Augustine, Florida. Western oranges from Mexican seeds were planted in Arizona by missionaries in the early eighteenth century. There are three basic types: bitter or sour oranges like the Seville, which makes the best, tangiest marmalade; the sweet orange varieties, of which the Valencia is the most prevalent juice orange and the navel and Temple the favorite eating oranges; and the small, loose-skinned, sweet mandarin orange, which we also call the tangerine. Sweet oranges are at their best in fall, winter and spring. All oranges should be heavy and thin-skinned. Green color does not signify lack of ripeness; oranges ripen on the tree or not at all. Discoloration at the stem end of an orange does indicate the beginning of deterioration. Oranges are a natural with fowl, pork, ham and mix beautifully with plump berries and kiwis.

31. Lemons. The origins of the lemon tree are obscure but the fruit has been considered a delicacy since at least Roman times. A tropical plant that produces year-round, our lemons are grown chiefly in California. Good lemons are heavy and firm and have a relatively thin skin. Thick-skinned lemons tend to have little juice. The acidity in lemons makes them a natural meat tenderizer and marinade ingredient; rubbing with a cut lemon will keep some fruits from turning brown. Fresh lemon juice with a good, fragrant oil is lighter and fresher for use on the more

38. Kiwis **39.** Kumquats **40.** Quinces **41.** Papaya **42.** Plantains **43.** Blackberries **44.** Tangerines **45.** Mangoes **46.** Persimmons **47.** Pomegranates

delicate salad greens and cold vegetables than the traditional vinegar and oil pairing. A bit of freshly squeezed lemon brings out the flavor of a cold veal scaloppini, an herb mayonnaise, a silky fish sauce or a summer soup. Fresh lemon juice is the best, but frozen lemon juice can be used as a substitute. Forget bottled lemon juice—it has a flat, bitter taste.

32. Limes. These small green citrus fruits are closely related to lemons, although their flavor is quite distinct and somewhat more exotic—as is their incredible fragrance. Limes are thought to be native to India, and their juice and peel are used as a seasoning in Indian cooking. Tiny, round Key limes are a product of southern Florida and have a more intense flavor than regular limes. Available year-round, limes should be heavy and thin-skinned. You can use lime juice in many of the same ways that you use lemon juice. Deglaze the pan with it after sautéing shellfish, veal, chicken or vegetables. Use them in tarts, lime ices or soufflés and as a garnish.

33, 34, 37. Melons. Melons are native to Persia. Commercial melon production began in the United States at the turn of the century. There are three basic types available to us: muskmelons or cantaloupes, which must ripen on the vine to reach their peak of flavor; winter melons like honeydew and casaba, which have a longer shipping life and continue to mature after being picked; and watermelons, which are not true melons, botanically speaking. Although their skins can vary from relatively smooth to heavily webbed, ripe muskmelons should have lost their greenish cast and the stem end should be soft and fragrant. Honeydews, too, should give off a good melon smell when they are ripe. Casabas and watermelons give off no aroma and are more of a risk to judge. Casabas should have a slightly soft stem end, but watermelons must be cut open to test their ripeness. A good watermelon has firm, red flesh, no white streaks and dark seeds. Musk and winter melons need only a wedge of lemon or lime but combine well with other fruits in salads and compotes or with prosciutto. Watermelon is pure nostalgia when carved in great wedges or churned into ices. Its rind makes a traditional sweet pickle. Muskmelons are available from May through September; the winter melons from July to November; watermelons peak in midsummer.

35, 36. Grapefruit. A relative newcomer to the family of fruits, grapefruit was first reported less than two hundred years ago in Jamaica and seems to have developed spontaneously as a mutant of the pummelo, a citrus fruit brought to the West Indies from Indonesia. It was not cultivated in this country until 1890. Now the United States grows 90 percent of the world supply, half of which is processed for juice. Grapefruit is available year-round, but the summer fruit is the least succulent. Good eating grapefruit are firm and heavy with a smooth, thin rind. The color of the meat—pale yellow or pink—does not affect the flavor.

38. Kiwi. This fuzzy-skinned, light brown little fruit was dubbed "kiwi" in the 1950s, when politics made it unprofitable to ship it to the United States under its native New Zealand name of Chinese gooseberry. Its vivid green interior is stippled with a ring of dark brown edible seeds around a white center. It is a key fruit in the New American Cuisine. Simply peeled and sliced, it is luscious with fish and fowl and on top of fresh, flaky tarts. Chiefly imported from New Zealand, the kiwi is being cultivated increasingly in California. It has a melonlike texture and a flavor similar to strawberries. Look for heavy, unblemished fruit that gives slightly under pressure.

39. Kumquats. The name means "golden orange," and this native of eastern Asia is closely related to citrus fruits, with which it is frequently crossed. It looks like a miniature oval orange. It has a tart-sweet flavor and is eaten raw, rind and all, or used in preserves. Look for fresh kumquats in late fall and early winter.

40. Quinces. The Portuguese word for quince is *marmelp;* it is from Portuguese quince preserves that we get the word "marmalade." An ancient fruit with Middle Eastern origins, the quince is small, tart and has pale yellow pulp that turns pink when it's cooked. It is used mainly for jams and preserves here; a quince sauce made like applesauce is served with meats in Germany.

41. Papaya. A tropical fruit of the West Indies, papaya is melonlike and mild and is often enlivened simply by a wedge of lime. Grown here only in Florida, papaya is usually available in May and June. Look for firm, but not hard, papayas that are not much larger than a pear—the larger papayas have less flavor—and a good orange or yellow color. Papaya juice is a natural meat tenderizer and in many cultures the fruit is cooked like a vegetable. Baked papaya tastes somewhat like winter squash.

42. Plantain. This banana look-alike is a staple of tropical countries, where it is treated like a potato: baked, fried or boiled. It has no natural sweetness, but cooked and served with a coconut sauce, it makes a wonderful dessert.

43. Blackberries. Blackberries, known as brambleberries in England and Scotland (in reference to the thorny nature of their bush), are cultivated here and in the British Isles to be eaten fresh with cream or in compotes. Blackberries are the last summer berry to ripen and should be plump, juicy and dark in color. Splendid in tarts and jams or jellies, they are also used for liqueurs. Frozen blackberries retain their flavor well and make wonderful fresh fruit ice cream.

44. Tangerines. Native to southern China, they are eaten fresh, used in a delicate liqueur or candied.

45. Mangoes. A succulent tropical fruit, mangoes are delicious eaten raw with the skin peeled back and the fruit spooned out from around the seed. They exude an aroma and have a smooth, silky flesh. With a skin that ranges from orange to red to green, good mangoes should be soft to the touch and unblemished. An unripe mango will have a puckering, acid taste. Mangoes, though mostly imported, are grown in Florida as well. Mangoes can grace duck, fowl and fish and are the mainstay of sorbets, ice cream and chutneys. They also make the simplest of garnishes.

46. Persimmons. A round, red-orange fruit native to America, but made popular only after a Japanese variety was introduced by Admiral Perry. Ripe persimmons—soft to the touch—are sweet, tangy and delicious, somewhat like apricots and mangoes in taste. The succulent flesh is tart. They are available in late fall. Buy unblemished persimmons with their stems still attached and they'll ripen at room temperature. Persimmons, whole, halved or thinly sliced, are a stunning garnish.

47. Pomegranates. These brilliant golden-red fruits, called Chinese apples, with their crimson seeds, are one of the most ancient foods known. Native to the Middle East, they are now grown in California and Florida and are available in the fall. The flesh and seeds are luscious eaten raw and exude a beautiful juice. Look for fruit with good color and not too dry a rind.

Rhubarb. (Not shown.) Thought to have come from northern China, rhubarb was known for thousands of years as a medicinal plant before an anonymous adventurer thought to eat it. Its red or green stalks make a tart-sweet dessert when boiled with sugar; its leaves are poisonous. By the late eighteenth century, rhubarb was known as the pie plant in Northern European countries, where it is still a popular dessert either stewed or in tarts, often mixed with strawberries. You'll find rhubarb available from January through June. Look for stalks that are firm, unblemished and not too fibrous (a sign of age).

Ugli fruit. (Not shown.) A hybrid between the tangerine and the grapefruit, ugli fruit has a knobby yellow and green skin and sweet-tasting grapefruitlike flesh. It can be peeled, sectioned and eaten like an orange or added to a compote. Native to the East Indies, the ugli fruit is smaller than a grapefruit and has fewer seeds. Look for heavy unblemished fruit all year.

Dates. (Not shown.) The fruit of a desert palm tree, dates ripen only in the dry, hot air of their native habitat, although the trees grow in other tropical climates. Fresh dates are not readily available beyond one area in California where they are grown, but packaged dried dates from many desert regions are available year-round. The pitted ones are easiest to use in cooking—they make wonderful breads, cookies and candies.

FRESH FRUIT COMPOTE

Serves 4

1 large apple, cored and diced
4 peaches, peeled, pitted and sliced
1½ cups diced fresh pineapple
1½ cups Bing cherries, stemmed and seeded
1 lemon, cut into thin slices
¼ cup sugar
1 cup orange juice
1 cup sauterne or other sweet white wine

1. In a large bowl, mix the fruits.

2. In a saucepan, heat the remaining ingredients until just boiling. Pour over the fruits. Stir, cover and refrigerate until ready to serve.

FRUITS IN CASSIS

Serves 4

1 pint strawberries, hulled
3 cups stemmed seedless green grapes or halved and seeded purple grapes
¼ cup sugar
½ cup crème de cassis
white wine

1. In a large bowl, mix the strawberries, grapes and sugar. Stir in the cassis and add enough white wine to just cover the fruit. Refrigerate.

Melon in Cassis. Omit the strawberries and grapes. Use a combination of 4 cups of honeydew melon or cantaloupe cut into pieces, peeled, pitted peach slices, apricot halves and raspberries.

Fruits in Port Wine. Use port wine in place of the crème de cassis and white wine. Add 2 cinnamon sticks and 4 whole cloves. Refrigerate for several hours.

FRUITS IN CIDER

Serves 4

4 Granny Smith green apples
1 pound sour cherries, stemmed but not pitted
⅓ cup sugar
½ cup Benedictine
2 cups apple cider
2 strips lemon peel
Crème Fraîche (see page 250)

Fresh strawberries with Raspberry Purée

1. Peel and core the apples, then cut them into thick wedges. In a medium saucepan, combine all the ingredients and simmer gently until the apples can be easily pierced with a fork, about 10 to 15 minutes. They should still hold their shape. Serve warm or cold with crème fraîche.

2. Fruits in White Wine. Omit the sugar and Benedictine and use ⅓ cup honey and 2½ cups sweet white wine. Instead of the apples and cherries, use 1 quart coarsely sliced peeled pears, unpeeled plums, tangerine or orange sections, fresh kumquats, seedless grapes. Mix ingredients, do not cook and chill until ready to serve.

FRUIT PUREE

Serves 8

Raspberries and strawberries are top candidates for fruit purées, but don't be afraid to experiment with melon, banana, papaya and other fruits. Serve over other whole fruits or ice cream.

2 tablespoons cornstarch
½ cup raspberry liqueur or port wine
1 pound raspberries
2 pints strawberries, hulled

1. In a small saucepan, combine the cornstarch and liqueur. Stir over low heat until the mixture simmers and thickens.

2. In a blender or food processor, process the raspberries until they are puréed. Add them to the liqueur mixture and heat through.

3. When ready to serve, spoon the sauce over strawberries.

SORBET
Frozen Fruit Ice

Serves 4

Ices replace ice cream as a light, refreshing way to end a meal. Though almost any fruit can be used, apricots and pears are particularly good. The key to its texture: the more you beat the partially frozen mixture, the finer the consistency will be. Ices should be served slightly soft, so remove from the freezer 10 minutes or so before serving.

2 cups fruit, such as apricots, plums, pears, apples,
    peaches, strawberries, honeydew melon or cantaloupe
⅓ cup sugar or honey
½ cup dry white wine, champagne or fruit juice

1. Purée the fruit in a blender, food processor or food mill.

2. In a saucepan, combine the sugar and wine and simmer until the sugar is dissolved. Stir in the fruit purée.

3. Pour into an 8-inch square pan and put in the freezer. Stir every 15 minutes until creamy. Cover and freeze until hard.

4. Scoop into serving dishes and garnish with mint sprigs.

Note. If you have an ice cream freezer, just follow the manufacturer's directions.

CHOCOLATE DIPPED FRUITS

The principle here is the same as a fondue, except the chocolate solidifies before serving. Large strawberries, navel orange sections, small bunches of grapes, pieces of crystallized ginger, whole roasted chestnuts and dried figs are all suitable. This recipe makes about 1 cup of chocolate for dipping.

8 1-ounce squares semisweet chocolate
¼ cup vegetable shortening

1. Melt the chocolate and shortening in the top part of a double boiler set over barely simmering water.

2. Dip the fruits individually and put on baking sheets lined with foil. Chill until the chocolate hardens, then serve.

Note. Water will cause the chocolate to curdle, so make sure all fruit pieces are dry before dipping.

PEACHES WITH CREME ANGLAISE

Makes 2 cups

Another creamy cloak, crème anglaise is actually a vanilla-flavored custard that goes nicely with stewed fruits, or as another version of peaches and cream.

2 cups milk
1 vanilla bean
4 egg yolks
½ cup sugar
½ cup flour
4 peaches
⅓ cup port wine, kirsch or fruit brandy

1. In a heavy saucepan, combine the milk and vanilla bean and bring just to a boil. Remove from the heat immediately and cover.

2. In a separate, heavy 2-quart saucepan, beat the egg yolks and sugar with a wire whisk or electric beater until they are pale and thick enough to make a ribbon when the beater is lifted from the pan, at least 2 or 3 minutes. Beat in the flour. (Omit the flour for a creamlike filling.)

3. Remove the vanilla bean from the hot milk and gradually pour the milk in a thin stream into the egg-sugar mixture, beating constantly. Put the pan over low heat and stir until the sauce thickens. (Without the flour, this could take as long as 20 minutes; with the flour, less time.) Do not let the mixture boil, and stir the bottom and edges of the pan carefully to prevent scorching. The sauce should be just thick enough to coat a spoon.

4. Remove the pan from the heat. If you like, stir in 1 tablespoon wine, liqueur or brandy.

5. Peel, pit and quarter the peaches, then lightly toss them with the wine. Serve in individual bowls with the crème anglaise spooned over them.

Note. You can use 2 teaspoons vanilla extract instead of the vanilla bean. Add it in Step 4.

Clockwise from top: **Refreshing strawberry, pineapple, honeydew and apricot Sorbets**

MERINGUE WITH FRUIT

Makes 1 8-inch meringue tart

6 egg whites at room temperature
½ teaspoon cream of tartar
2 cups sugar
oranges
kiwis
strawberries

1. Preheat the oven to 250°F. In a mixing bowl, beat the egg whites with the cream of tartar until fluffy. Then beat in the sugar, 1 tablespoon at a time, until the mixture is stiff.

2. Line a baking sheet with foil, then spread about 2 cups of meringue into an 8-inch circle on the baking sheet. Put the rest in a pastry bag with a star tip and make rosettes of meringue all around the outside edge. Bake for 1 hour. (Keep the oven door cracked open with a potholder so the moisture escapes.)

3. Let the shell cool and just before serving fill with sliced fruit.

POACHED MERINGUES WITH FRUIT PUREE

Serves 6 to 8

3 egg whites, at room temperature
pinch salt
1 pound sifted confectioner's sugar
2 cups puréed strawberries (about 2½ pints whole berries)
juice of 3 lemons
½ cup kirsch
½ cup granulated sugar
kiwi fruits, peeled and sliced
slivered toasted almonds

1. With an electric mixer, beat the egg whites and salt until stiff. Beat in the confectioner's sugar, 1 tablespoon at a time, until the meringue is stiff and glossy.

2. Using an ice cream scoop or large spoon, float balls of meringue on barely simmering water and poach for 3 minutes on each side. (Poach just a few at a time to keep them from touching and sticking together.) Remove with a slotted spoon and drain on a dry cloth.

3. In a blender or food processor, combine the strawberries, lemon juice, kirsch and granulated sugar and process until smooth. Spoon the sauce into serving dishes and top each with a ball of meringue. Decorate with kiwi fruit slices and slivered almonds. Chill until ready to serve.

Note. Raspberries, fresh currants, blackberries or blueberries may be used instead of strawberries. If the purée is too thick, thin with an appropriate fruit brandy.

FRUIT TART

Makes 1 10-inch tart

Sparkling glazed fruits make tarts look like jewel cases. Choose those that don't need baking—gooseberries, blackberries, seedless grapes, nectarines, kiwis, pears, strawberries, raspberries, bananas. Use only 1 fruit or make stripe or circle designs with several.

1 pound Food Processor Puff Pastry (see page 275)
1 egg yolk, well beaten
¾ cup sugar
4 egg yolks
½ cup unsifted all-purpose flour
1¼ cups milk
1 tablespoon vanilla extract
2 teaspoons butter
3 cups fruit—choose from peeled and sliced peaches, apricot halves, stemmed seedless grapes, melon balls, pitted Bing cherries, poached apple or pear slices, banana slices or orange sections
½ cup strained apricot preserves or currant jelly
1 tablespoon sugar

1. Preheat the oven to 400°F. Roll out the dough on a floured surface to 2 10-inch rounds. Put a round on a baking sheet and brush the edges with water. Cut a ring of dough, 1-inch wide, from the second round and put it around the edge of the round on the baking sheet, forming a rim. Prick the bottom of the round with a fork, brush with beaten egg yolk and bake until the pastry is richly brown, about 20 to 25 minutes. If the pastry puffs in the middle during baking, remove from the oven and prick again to flatten.

2. In a saucepan, mix the sugar, egg yolks, flour and milk and stir constantly over low heat until the mixture thickens and bubbles. Don't let it boil. Remove the saucepan from the heat and stir in the vanilla and butter. Cover, let cool and refrigerate.

3. When ready to serve, put the pastry shell on a serving plate, cover it evenly with the cream and then arrange the well-drained fruit in any pattern you like.

4. In a saucepan, heat the preserves and sugar until bubbly. Cook for 2 minutes. Let the mixture cool until it is just warm and then spoon over the fruit evenly. Once the glaze is set, the tart is ready to serve.

BAKED APPLES WITH BRANDY AND RAISINS

Makes 10

½ cup apple butter
½ cup raisins
10 baking apples, such as Rome Beauty or Granny Smith
1½ cups sugar
¾ cup brandy
¼ cup butter

1. Preheat the oven to 350°F. In a small bowl, mix the apple butter and raisins. Wash, core and peel the apples halfway down from the stem. Put the apples in a shallow baking pan and fill the centers with the apple butter.

2. In a saucepan, combine the sugar, brandy and butter, bring it to a boil and simmer for 5 minutes. Pour over the apples. Bake the apples for 45 to 60 minutes, spooning the pan juices over the apples every 15 minutes.

3. Remove from the oven and spoon the pan juices over the cooling apples several times. Serve warm or cold with sherry cream sauce.

SHERRY CREAM SAUCE

2 tablespoons cornstarch
¼ cup sugar
1 cup cream sherry
2 cups heavy cream
2 teaspoons vanilla extract

1. In a saucepan, mix the cornstarch and sugar. Then stir in the sherry and cream. Stir over low heat until the sauce thickens and begins to bubble.

2. Remove from heat, cool, then stir in the vanilla. Chill.

SAUTEED BANANAS

Serves 2

¼ cup sweet butter
½ cup confectioner's sugar
2 tablespoons slivered orange rind
2 tablespoons slivered lemon rind
¼ cup dark rum
4 firm bananas, peeled and cut in half crosswise

1. In a large skillet, heat the butter and add the sugar, rinds and rum. Bring to a boil and stir until slightly thickened.

2. Add the banana halves and spoon the pan juices over them. Simmer for five minutes, or until hot.

Meringue with Fruit

BANANA FRITTERS

Serves 4

Some restaurants serve them with meat and fish courses; we also like them dusted with confectioner's sugar for dessert.

2 cups unsifted all-purpose flour
4 teaspoons sugar
½ teaspoon salt
(continued)

1 teaspoon baking powder
⅔ cup milk
2 eggs
2 tablespoons melted butter
2 teaspoons dark rum
6 ripe bananas, cut into 1-inch pieces
corn oil
confectioner's sugar

1. In a large bowl, beat all the ingredients except the bananas, oil and sugar together. The batter should be smooth and about the consistency of pancake batter. If it's too thick, thin it with milk. In a frying pan, heat 2 inches of oil to 375°F. (If you use a small pan, you'll need less oil; just don't crowd too many bananas at a time—they won't brown.)

2. Dip the banana pieces in the batter and drop them into the oil. Fry the banana pieces until golden brown, about 5 minutes.

3. Drain on paper towel and serve warm sprinkled with confectioner's sugar.

FIG JAM

Makes 6 half pints

Dried black figs, quinces (or green apples), lemon and walnuts cook down to make a thick, dark jam with great character.

1 cup water
¾ pound dried black Mission figs, stemmed
3 pears, peeled and cored
2 quinces or green apples, peeled and cored
1 lemon, quartered and seeded
¾ cup coarsely broken walnuts
sugar

1. Pour the water into a large, heavy saucepan. In a food mill or processor, grind up the fruit and nuts. Measure the mixture as you pour it into the saucepan. Add 1 cup sugar for every 2 cups fruit.

2. Simmer for 1 hour, stirring occasionally, until the mixture is thick and jamlike. Pour into sterilized jars and seal with melted paraffin.

Note. To sterilize the jars, cover them and a pair of tongs with water. Cover the pan and bring to a full rolling boil. Remove the lid and boil for 10 minutes. Remove the tongs, and let them cool before using them to remove the jars. Use the jars as soon as possible, or leave them in the hot water until ready to use.

MANGO WITH RICOTTA CREAM

Serves 4

1 pound ricotta cheese
1 teaspoon vanilla extract
1 teaspoon grated orange rind
2 tablespoons finely chopped citron (candied citrus rind)
2 tablespoons sugar
4 mangoes, sliced

1. In a medium bowl, combine all the ingredients except the mangoes and mix well. When you're ready to serve, spoon the sauce over the mango slices.

BAKED PAPAYA

Serves 4

The rum and sugar used to coat the papaya is equally successful on baked bananas or mangoes or even apples.

2 papayas
¼ cup dark rum
½ cup firmly packed brown sugar

1. Preheat the oven to 350°F. Cut the papayas in half lengthwise and remove the seeds. Put the halves in a shallow baking dish.

2. In a small bowl, mix the rum and sugar into a paste and spread it evenly over the fruit. Bake in the middle of the oven for 15 to 20 minutes, or until the fruit is easily pierced with a fork. Serve hot.

CREME FRAICHE

Serves 8

Crème fraîche, the slightly tart, thickened cream the French adore, is light but rich. Our version approximates the flavor and consistency of the real thing.

1 cup heavy cream
1 cup sour cream

1. In a small glass bowl, combine the two creams, mix them well and let the mixture stand in a warm place (65°F to 80°F) for about 12 hours, or until the crème fraîche becomes very thick. The time will vary according to the temperature.

2. Chill for at least 24 hours. It will keep in the refrigerator for about a week.

Note. Serve over berries or melon or with any fruit mixture.

Bread

□□□□

At first it's just a messy lump of flour and yeast, but that soon changes as you knead the dough—wonderfully physical work—leaving you with an incredible feeling of accomplishment, not to mention some pretty great-tasting bread.

Making bread is a soul-satisfying experience. And the results are glorious: a lovely browned loaf, steaming and fragrant. By now, you're thinking that anything that sounds this terrific has got to be difficult. Not true. The problem—and there is one—is the rising time required to create these fat loaves. We'll agree that making yeast bread is a bit of a production, but once again, with some well-developed strategies, bread baking can be timed to fit your schedule. Added attraction: bread takes well to freezing. Invest an afternoon in bread making and your freezer will be well stocked. If you're really short on time, quick breads seldom take longer than 15 minutes to mix or an hour to bake.

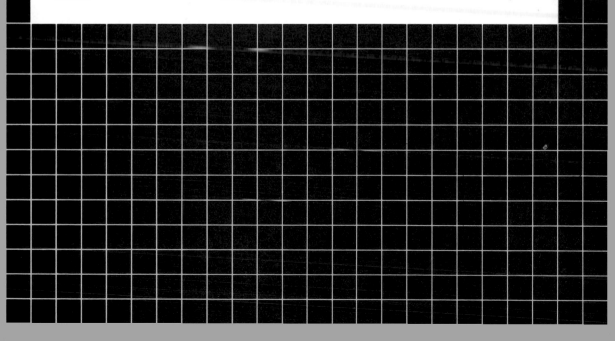

Yeast Breads

THE ESSENTIALS

Confidence in yeast bread baking comes from doing. Only experience can help you develop your own "feel" for dealing with its simple variables.

First, a few facts about yeast. It is a tiny living fungus that thrives on warmth, moisture and sugar. It leavens dough by releasing gases that stretch the elastic gluten in wheat flour and develop the light texture of bread.

Because it's a living organism, yeast's environmental needs must be respected if it is to perform properly. If it's too cold, it remains inactive; if the yeast is exposed to too high a temperature, it's killed. That is why yeast is dissolved in lukewarm liquid and why liquids mixed into a yeast dough must also be lukewarm. The tolerance of active dry yeast—the granular yeast sold in foil-lined packets or jars—is 100° to 115°F. You can recognize this temperature easily—warm but not hot to the tender skin of the wrist. Use a meat thermometer to experiment.

Our recipes use packaged active dry yeast for three reasons: it's universally available, it will keep for several months in a cool dry place and the package is stamped with an expiration date. One ounce of compressed or cake yeast can be used interchangeably with 1 envelope dry yeast, but compressed yeast must be refrigerated and lasts only 10 days. If you have doubts about the viability of a package of yeast, you can "proof" it by dissolving it in ¼ cup warm water with a pinch of sugar. Within 10 minutes it should begin to foam and expand if the yeast is active.

Flour is one of the great variables in bread making. There are different ways of milling wheat and different kinds of wheat as well. And myriad other grains like rye, corn and oats can be made into flour. Flour can differ from one part of the country to another and from one batch to the next. It's also affected by humidity and temperature. That is why yeast bread recipes are never too specific about how much flour to use.

Wheat kernels contain an endosperm that is largely starch, a germ and bran. Almost all the vitamins and minerals are in the germ and bran, which are, unfortunately, milled out of most commercial white flours, and this milling is the motive behind artificial enrichment. Here's a brief primer on the kinds of flour available.

All-purpose enriched flour. A blend of hard- and soft-wheat flours milled without germ or bran, all-purpose flour is chemically bleached and enriched. Known as white flour, it is used for all baking except very fine cakes. In all of our recipes we refer to it as "all-purpose flour."

Unbleached flour. Flour with a yellowish cast that has not been chemically bleached. It can be used interchangeably with all-purpose flour.

Hard-wheat flour. Milled from winter wheat, hard-wheat flour is high in gluten. Used by professional bakers, it is the best choice for bread making. Bread flour is now available in many supermarkets.

Whole-wheat flour. Commercial whole-wheat flour is milled without bran but contains some germ. Less glutenous than white flour, it makes a more compact bread and is often mixed with white flour to make a higher loaf.

Stone-ground whole-wheat flour. This flour contains the whole wheat kernel and is more nutritious than the others. Low in gluten, it's mixed with white flour for bread and gives bread a coarser texture. Similar to stone-ground, cracked-wheat flour is coarsely ground.

Gluten flour. High in protein and low in calories, gluten flour contains no starch. The results are a flat and rubbery bread. It can be used to add gluten to other flours.

Specialty flours. Flours and meals made from corn, barley, rice, soybeans, buckwheats or oats add nutrition and flavor to white flour. They don't interact with yeast, so they can't be used alone. The general rule for combining flours is to use 1 part specialty flour to 3 parts white flour. Whole-rye flour is used for pumpernickel bread and mixed with white flour for rye bread.

The rising process of bread can be manipulated to suit your schedule. Wrapped in a plastic bag or set in a bowl large enough to allow for its rising, the dough can be refrigerated after kneading. Cold slows down the action of the yeast long enough for you to take a break—for work or sleep. After an 8- to 10-hour hiatus, the dough can be kneaded, shaped and set in a warm place for the second rising. Because the bread is cold, this rising will take longer—2 to 2½ hours. If you have to interrupt your bread baking schedule for 2 to 10 hours, you can also refrigerate the dough after shaping it into loaves. When you're ready to continue, remove the dough from the refrigerator and let it finish rising in a warm place.

Glazes are not absolutely necessary, but they supply variety in the color and texture of bread crusts. Before baking, brush on melted butter, milk or cream for a soft crust, or salt water for a firmer crust. Beaten egg yolks give a soft crust a golden brown color. Egg white makes it crisp and shiny. Beaten whole egg thickens the crust.

Nothing is more delectable than freshly baked bread. So it follows that you should freeze whatever bread you aren't using immediately—even half loaves—to preserve its good flavor. Cool the bread completely before wrapping it tightly in aluminum foil. To defrost, let the bread sit out for several hours or heat it, still wrapped in foil, at 300°F for 15 to 20 minutes.

Basic White Bread (see page 254) is delicious when toasted, buttered and sprinkled with cinnamon sugar.

BASIC WHITE BREAD

Makes 2   9×5×3-inch loaves

A good basic recipe, this makes an honest, everyday sandwich and toast bread that tastes and smells better than any bread you ever brought home from the store. It will help you master all the yeast-dough techniques, and then it's no trick to take on the variations.

2 envelopes active dry yeast
¼ cup lukewarm water (100° to 115°F)
2 cups milk
¼ cup sugar
1 tablespoon salt
2 tablespoons butter
7 to 7½ cups unsifted all-purpose flour

1. In a large bowl, mix the yeast with the water and let stand without stirring in a warm place for 5 minutes to dissolve completely. In a saucepan, heat the milk over low heat with the sugar, salt and butter until lukewarm. The butter does not have to melt.

2. Stir the milk into the dissolved yeast with a wooden spoon. Begin adding the flour, 1 cup at a time, and stir to mix it thoroughly. Continue adding flour until the dough is stiff and thick and pulls off the spoon like chewing gum. The amount of flour can vary enormously depending on the weather; stop adding flour—whether it's 6 cups or 7½ cups—when the dough is stiff enough to handle.

3. Turn out the dough on a lightly floured surface. With floured hands, press the dough into an oval, fold it in half and seal it with the heel of your hand, then push it hard, down and away from you. Give it a quarter turn, pull the far end over and fold. Push again with the heel of your hand. Repeat these three steps—fold, push, turn—and you are kneading. If the dough is very sticky, knead for a minute or so and then let it rest for 10 minutes to give the gluten a chance to develop. Knead for at least 10 minutes. Remember, this process distributes the yeast and other ingredients evenly and develops the gluten, which ensures high, light loaves. You will soon feel the dough becoming smooth, elastic and easier to handle.

4. The dough is ready for rising when it forms a soft, elastic ball that springs back when you poke a finger in it. Lightly grease a bowl and brush the dough with oil or melted butter so it will not dry out while rising. Put the dough in the bowl, cover it with a damp cloth or towel and set it in a warm, draft-free place to rise.

5. The dough should double in size during its rising. How long it takes depends on the surrounding temperature—

the process takes more time in a cooler place. Be patient. Many bakers feel a double rising in the bowl makes a better bread with a finer texture. Putting the dough in too warm a spot—an oven with a pilot light, for example—can kill the yeast. At 65° to 70°F, the bread should take 1½ to 2 hours to rise. Stick your finger in the center of the dough. If the depression remains, it has risen enough.

6. Turn the risen dough out onto a lightly floured board and punch it in the middle with your fist to let the trapped gases escape. Knead the dough for 1 minute and then cut it into 2 equal parts with a knife. Roll or pat each half into a 10-inch square.

7. Preheat the oven to 375°F. Grease 2 loaf pans that measure 9×5×3 inches. (If you want taller loaves, use the next smaller size pans—8×4½×2½ inches. The dough won't collapse over the sides, it will just rise higher.) Roll the squares of dough from either side, making a seam in the middle. Pinch ends and fold over slightly. Put the rolls, seam side down, into the pans. Brush the tops of the loaves with your choice of glaze (see The Essentials). Cover the loaf pans with damp towels and let the loaves rise again in a warm, draft-free place. The loaves should double in bulk during this rising, which should take about 30 minutes to 1 hour.

8. Brush the loaves with your glaze once more and bake them in the middle of the oven for 30 to 35 minutes. They will be dark golden brown and will make a hollow sound when thumped on the top. For a crisp crust, remove the loaves from the pans 5 minutes before the end of the baking time and let them finish baking on a baking sheet.

9. Remove the breads from the pans and cool on a wire rack before slicing. Cool completely before wrapping for storage.

Herbed Bread. (Makes 12 small loaves or 2 regular loaves.) Add 2 tablespoons minced fresh herbs—chives, parsley, oregano or basil—and 2 tablespoons toasted sesame seeds to the milk-butter mixture in the basic recipe. Brush the shaped loaves with beaten egg and sprinkle with more sesame seeds. The small loaves should bake for 20 to 25 minutes.

Cheese Braid. (Makes 2 loaves.) Add 2 cups grated sharp Cheddar and 2 tablespoons minced onion to the milk-butter mixture in the basic recipe. Make 2 conventional loaves or divide dough after the first rising into 6 equal parts. Roll each into a 16-inch-long rope. Using 3 bread ropes for each, weave 2 braids. Pinch the ends under and put the braids on individual greased baking sheets for the second rising and baking. Put the baking sheets on separate oven racks so the heat can properly circulate around the loaves. Use beaten egg for the glaze.

MAKING BREAD. To make Basic White Bread there are only eight steps from the time you dissolve the yeast until you slide the loaves into the oven. Brushing the dough with beaten egg and water keeps it from drying out and adds a glaze to the freshly baked bread.

Clockwise from bottom left: **Rye Bread, Whole-Wheat Health Bread, Brioche Loaves, French Bread, Sicilian Pizza, Herbed Bread, Basic White Bread, Cheese Braid, Apple Kuchen and Cinnamon Rolls**

Brioche Loaves. (Makes 2 brioches.) Reduce the milk in the basic recipe to 1½ cups and increase the butter to ½ cup (cut into thin slices). Beat in 4 eggs and proceed with the recipe. After the first rising, cut the dough in half. From each half pinch off enough dough to make a plum-size ball. Shape the remaining dough halves into round loaves by tucking the sides under all around. Put the rounded loaves in buttered 2-quart brioche pans. Shape a point on one end of the smaller balls of dough. Push the points down into the centers of the larger loaves to secure the balls. Brush tops with beaten egg. The dough can also be baked in 2 loaf pans, 9×5×3 inches.

French Bread. (Makes 2 loaves.) Use water instead of milk in the basic recipe and omit the sugar. After the first rising, cut the dough in half and shape each into a 10 × 15-inch rectangle. Roll up the rectangles, starting at the 15-inch side, and put seam side down on a greased baking sheet sprinkled with cornmeal to prevent sticking. With a sharp knife, make ½-inch-deep diagonal slices every 2 inches along the loaves—this not only looks good on the finished loaf, but prevents cracking. Brush loaves with salt water. Preheat the oven to 425°F and bake on the bottom rack for 10 minutes. Reduce the heat to 375°F, brush again with salt water and bake 10 minutes more. Brush with salt water once more and bake an additional 10 to 15 minutes, or until golden brown. Brushing the loaves with salt water makes a crisp, hard crust.

Whole-Wheat Health Bread. (Makes 2 loaves.) Substitute ¼ cup honey and ¼ cup molasses for the sugar in the basic recipe. Use 3 cups whole-wheat flour and 1 cup wheat germ in place of 3 cups of the white flour. (The wheat germ adds texture and nourishment.) Make conventional loaves or shape into 2 round loaves and bake on greased baking sheets on separate oven racks. Brush the loaves with a beaten egg.

Rye Bread. (Makes 2 loaves.) Substitute 3 cups rye flour for 3 cups of the white flour in the basic recipe. If you like, add 2 tablespoons caraway seeds to the milk-butter mixture. Bake in 2 loaf pans or shape the dough into round loaves. Put the ovals seam side down on 2 greased baking sheets and bake on separate racks in the oven. Glaze the loaves with beaten egg.

Beer Bread. (Makes 2 oval loaves.) Substitute warm beer for the milk in the basic recipe and 3 tablespoons oil for the butter. Decrease the salt to 1½ teaspoons. Since you don't have to melt butter, simply heat the beer to lukewarm and add it to the sugar, salt and oil in the mixing bowl and proceed from there. After the first rising, halve the dough and roll each piece into an 8- × 10-inch oval loaf. Make several ½-inch-deep diagonal slashes and put on greased baking sheets for the second rising and baking. Use salt water for the glaze.

Sicilian Pizza. (Makes 2 14-inch pizzas.) Use water instead of milk in the basic recipe. After the first rising, cut the dough in half and roll each into a circle. Put the circles on greased 14-inch pizza pans and, starting from the center, press the dough out to the edges of the pans. On each pizza spread 2 cups Fresh Tomato Sauce (see page 186), 1 cup shredded mozzarella and ½ cup grated Parmesan. Let them rise 30 minutes. If you wish, add any combination of the following to the sauce before adding the cheese: 8 ounces sliced pepperoni, 1 cup chopped green pepper sautéed in 1 tablespoon olive oil, 1 sliced onion sautéed in 1 tablespoon olive oil, 1 2-ounce can drained anchovy filets. Bake in the center of a preheated 400°F oven for 20 minutes, or until the cheese is melted and the crust is browned and crisp. The dough may be frozen after the first rising; defrost before using.

Apple Kuchen. (Makes 2 10 × 15-inch cakes.) Reduce the milk in the basic recipe to 1¾ cups and increase the sugar and butter to ½ cup each. Add 2 eggs to the milk-butter mixture before adding the flour. After the first rising, cut the dough in half and roll each into a rectangle. Put the rectangles into greased 10 × 15-inch jellyroll pans and press the dough out from the middle to fill the pans evenly. For each kuchen, peel and core 4 apples (8 altogether) and cut into thick slices. Overlap the slices in rows across the dough, completely covering it. Mix 1 cup sugar, 2 teaspoons cinnamon and ¼ cup softened butter in a small bowl and spread evenly over the apples. Let rise for 30 minutes. As in the basic recipe, bake in a preheated

375°F oven, but only for 25 to 30 minutes. Bake on separate racks to let the hot air circulate. If you want only a single kuchen, you have three choices: halve the dough recipe to 1 envelope yeast, ¼ cup lukewarm water, ¾ cup milk, ¼ cup sugar, 1½ teaspoons salt, ¼ cup butter, 1 egg and 3 to 4 cups flour; after the first rising, freeze half the dough and use later for kuchen or for cinnamon rolls; or make both kuchens and let the extra one cool completely, wrap it tightly and freeze for later use.

Cinnamon Rolls. (Makes 36 rolls.) Make the basic white bread recipe with the modifications for apple kuchen dough. After the first rising, halve the dough and roll it into 2 9×18-inch rectangles. Spread each with ¼ cup softened butter mixed with ½ cup sugar and 1 teaspoon cinnamon. Starting with the long side, roll up each rectangle of dough and cut into 1-inch slices. Grease 2 10-inch round baking pans and put the slices in the pans so they are touching, flat-side down. Cover and put in a warm place for the second rising. Bake in a preheated 375°F oven for 25 to 30 minutes. Be sure the pans have plenty of room between them for the air to circulate. Cool the rolls in their pans on a rack. While still warm, ice the rolls by drizzling a mixture of 2 cups confectioner's sugar and 1 tablespoon milk over the tops.

KATCHAPURI WITH SALMON

Makes 1 9-inch loaf

Katchapuri is a close cousin to coulibiac; instead of a salmon and rice filling baked in pastry crust, salmon, spinach and Jarlsberg are enclosed in a bread crust.

2 envelopes active dry yeast
1½ tablespoons sugar
1 cup lukewarm milk
3½ to 4 cups unsifted all-purpose flour
2 teaspoons salt
½ cup softened butter
vegetable oil
3 tablespoons butter
1 shallot, finely chopped
1 pound spinach, cooked, squeezed dry and finely chopped
pinch nutmeg
¼ cup heavy cream
salt
freshly ground black pepper
8 1-ounce slices Jarlsberg
2½ pounds poached salmon filet (see page 100)
1 egg, well beaten

1. In a small bowl, sprinkle the yeast and 1½ teaspoons of the sugar into a ½ cup of the milk. Let it stand for 2 minutes, then stir to blend it. In a large mixing bowl, make a deep well in the center of 3 cups of the flour. Pour the yeast mixture, the remaining milk and sugar, the salt and the softened butter into the well and, with a spoon, beat until the dough is well blended and smooth. On a dry surface, put the ball of dough on top of the remaining flour and knead until the dough is smooth and elastic, about 10 minutes.

2. Brush the top of the dough with vegetable oil and put it in a large greased bowl. Cover and let rise in a warm place until the dough doubles in bulk. This will take about 1 hour. Punch it down and let it rise again, covered, until it doubles in bulk again, about 30 to 40 minutes.

3. In a skillet, heat the 3 tablespoons butter and sauté the shallot for 5 minutes. Add the spinach and nutmeg. Sauté for 5 to 6 minutes. Stir in the cream and season with salt and pepper. Cool.

4. Turn out the dough onto a lightly floured surface and knead until it's a smooth ball. Roll out the dough to a circle 22 inches in diameter. Fold the dough into quarters and put the point of the wedge at the center of a 9-inch greased spring-form pan. Unfold the dough, draping the outer rim of the circle over the edge of the pan, making sure the center is smooth.

5. Using half the cheese, arrange an even layer over the bottom. Cover with half the spinach mixture. Arrange a layer of salmon over the spinach. Top with the remaining spinach and cheese.

6. Fold the excess dough over the filling, drawing up the sides and pleating the dough evenly all around on top, turning the pan as you work. Gather the ends of the dough together in the center and twist to form a small knot. Brush with beaten egg and let the loaf rise in a warm place for 30 minutes.

7. Bake in a preheated 350°F oven until the crust is golden brown, about 1 hour. Remove the sides of the pan and let it cool thoroughly on a rack before cutting into wedges.

Quick Breads

THE ESSENTIALS

Quick breads have a cakelike texture. They are leavened with baking powder and/or baking soda and rise in the oven. Ironically, their success often depends on a minimal amount of beating and handling—a warning to the overzealous cook.

Because of their fragile texture, it is important to let quick breads cool completely—5 minutes in the pan, then unmolded on a rack—before slicing or they will crumble. (In the case of hot corn bread, crumbling is part of the experience.) A crack down the middle of a loaf of quick bread is characteristic, not a fault.

Quick bread loaves can be cooked in any kind of ovenproof container—even coffee cans or small molds. Grease them carefully and fill only ¾ full so the loaves have room to rise. Smaller loaves don't need to bake as long, so test them by poking a toothpick into the loaf. If the dough doesn't stick, the loaves are done.

Quick-breads, tightly wrapped, keep for up to 10 days in the refrigerator or up to 6 months in the freezer. Just be sure they have cooled completely before wrapping and freezing. They make traditional holiday gifts.

BASIC NUT BREAD

Makes 1 9×5×3-inch loaf or 2 8×4½×2½-inch loaves

3 cups unsifted all-purpose flour or 2 cups whole-wheat flour and 1 cup all-purpose flour
¾ cup sugar
3 teaspoons baking powder
½ teaspoon baking soda
1 teaspoon salt
2 tablespoons melted butter or vegetable oil
1 egg
1½ cups milk
1½ cups coarsely chopped nuts

1. Preheat the oven to 350°F. Grease a 9×5×3-inch loaf pan or 2 8×4½×2½-inch pans.

2. In a large bowl, thoroughly mix the dry ingredients—flour, sugar, baking powder, baking soda and salt—with a wooden spoon. Add the butter, egg and milk and stir until just blended. Fold in the nuts.

3. Pour this batter into the greased pan(s) and bake in the middle of the oven for 1 hour, or until a toothpick stuck in the center comes out clean. Check the smaller loaves after 45 to 50 minutes. Cool in the pan 5 minutes, then unmold and cool on a rack.

Apricot Bread. Fold in 1 cup chopped dried apricots (or any dried pitted fruit).

Banana Bread. Add 1 cup mashed bananas (2 very ripe bananas).

Cranberry-Orange Bread. Fold in 2 cups fresh cranberries and the grated rind of 1 orange.

Carrot Wheat-Germ Bread and Cheese Bread

CARROT WHEAT-GERM BREAD

Makes 1   9×5×3-inch loaf

Carrots give this loaf texture and character and a slightly sweet flavor.

3 cups unsifted all-purpose flour
½ cup wheat germ
1 teaspoon salt
1 teaspoon baking powder
¼ teaspoon baking soda
1 teaspoon ground cinnamon
1 teaspoon ground nutmeg
1 cup firmly packed light brown sugar
3 eggs
1 cup corn oil
1 cup very finely grated raw carrot (about 2 or 3 medium
   carrots)

1. Preheat the oven to 350°F. Grease a 9×5×3-inch loaf pan. In a large bowl, combine the dry ingredients and mix thoroughly with a wooden spoon.

2. Add the eggs and oil and stir until the batter is just blended. Fold in the carrots. Pour the batter into the prepared pan and bake in the middle of the oven for 1 hour, or until a toothpick inserted in the center comes out clean.

CHEESE BREAD

Makes 1   9×5×3-inch loaf

Sharp Cheddar gives this bread an almost sweet and mellow flavor; chèvre adds tartness.

3 cups unsifted all-purpose flour
4 teaspoons baking powder
1 teaspoon salt
6 ounces grated sharp Cheddar, chèvre or feta
½ cup chopped nuts
2 eggs
1⅓ cups milk
¼ cup vegetable oil

1. Preheat the oven to 350°F. Grease a 9×5×3-inch loaf pan. In a large bowl, combine the flour, baking powder and salt (omit salt if feta is used). Mix in the cheese and nuts. Add the eggs, milk and oil, but stir only until the dry ingredients are moistened. The batter should be lumpy.

2. Pour the batter into the greased pan and bake in the middle of the oven for 1 hour, or until a toothpick inserted in the center comes out clean. Turn out and cool thoroughly before slicing.

PROSCIUTTO AND ONION BREAD

Makes 1 round loaf

This is a quick-yeast bread. It must rise once before baking, but no kneading is necessary. The salty ham and the sweet bite of onion give the bread its unusual flavor.

1 envelope active dry yeast
¼ cup lukewarm water
1 cup milk
½ cup butter
2 eggs, well beaten
½ teaspoon salt
2 ounces prosciutto, finely chopped
2 tablespoons minced onion
4 cups unsifted all-purpose flour
1 tablespoon milk
2 tablespoons sesame seeds

1. In a large bowl, stir the yeast into the water and let stand 5 minutes to dissolve. In a small saucepan, heat 1 cup milk with the butter over low heat until lukewarm. The butter does not have to melt.

2. Add the lukewarm milk, eggs, salt, prosciutto and onion to the yeast. Add the flour and beat with a spoon until the ingredients are well blended and the dough pulls cleanly away from the spoon.

3. Grease a 1½-quart round baking pan. Scrape the dough into the dish and spread it out evenly. Brush the top of the dough with 1 tablespoon milk and sprinkle on the sesame seeds.

4. Let the dough rise, uncovered, in a warm place until it comes to the top of the baking dish—about 1 hour. Preheat the oven to 350°F and bake the bread on the center rack for 25 to 30 minutes, or until it is nicely browned and sounds hollow when you tap the top. Cool in the pan on a rack and serve warm.

IRISH SODA BREAD

Makes 1 long or round loaf

A traditional Irish loaf, raisin-rich and caraway-flavored, soda bread is usually round. However, it can also be shaped in a long loaf for more manageable slices.

3 cups unsifted all-purpose flour
¼ cup sugar
1 tablespoon baking powder
½ teaspoon baking soda
½ teaspoon salt

1½ cups raisins or currants
1 teaspoon caraway seeds
1½ cups buttermilk

1. Preheat the oven to 350°F. Grease a baking sheet.

2. In a large bowl, combine the dry ingredients. Add the raisins, caraway seeds and buttermilk and stir until a soft dough is formed that clings to the spoon.

3. Turn the dough out on a floured surface and knead 3 or 4 times, until it forms a smooth ball. Less kneading produces a more tender loaf. For a round loaf, keep the ball shape and put it on the baking sheet. For a long loaf, shape the dough into a 10-inch roll. To allow the loaf to spread without cracking, make a ¼-inch-deep cross with a sharp knife in the center of the round loaf or several slashes across the long loaf.

4. Bake in the center of the oven for 40 to 45 minutes, or until the loaf is well browned and a toothpick inserted in the center comes out clean.

SKILLET CORN BREAD

Serves 6

Good Southern corn bread is made only with white cornmeal, prefereably stone-ground, and never has sugar in it.

3 tablespoons bacon grease or lard
2 cups white cornmeal
3 teaspoons baking powder
½ teaspoon baking soda
½ teaspoon salt
1 egg
1¼ cups buttermilk

Sausage in Corn Bread

1. Preheat the oven to 400°F. Put the grease in a 9-inch iron skillet and put the skillet in the hot oven to melt the grease and preheat the pan. Rotate the skillet to cover the bottom with melted grease.

2. In a large bowl, combine the dry ingredients. Add the egg and buttermilk. Pour in excess melted grease from the skillet and stir until the batter is well blended.

3. Pour the batter into the hot skillet and bake in the middle of the oven for 20 to 25 minutes, or until the bread begins to draw away from the sides of the pan and the top is lightly browned. If the top isn't brown enough, put the pan under the broiler for a minute. Cut into wedges and serve hot with butter.

SAUSAGE IN CORN BREAD

Makes 1   8½×4½×2½-inch loaf

Sausage is traditionally wrapped in brioche, but highly textured corn bread offers a strong (and earthy) contrast.

1 1-pound cotechino sausage, 8 inches long
½ cup unsifted all-purpose flour
1½ cups yellow cornmeal
1 teaspoon salt
2 teaspoons sugar
1 tablespoon baking powder
3 eggs
3 tablespoons melted butter or lard
1 cup milk
¼ cup heavy cream
1 tablespoon Dijon mustard

1. In a large saucepan, poach the sausage in boiling water until it rises to the surface, about 15 minutes. Let it cool, then peel the sausage.

2. Preheat the oven to 425°F. In a bowl, mix the dry ingredients. In another bowl, beat the eggs, then mix in the butter, milk and cream. Stir the egg-butter mixture into the dry ingredients, making sure all the particles are moistened. Grease an 8½×4½×2½-inch loaf pan and pour in the batter, making sure the top of the batter is 2 inches below the top of the pan.

3. Brush the sausage with mustard and put it on top of the batter. Push the sausage down until it is under the batter. Bake the loaf until it is a rich golden brown, about 45 to 50 minutes. Let the loaf rest, out of the oven, for 15 to 20 minutes. Turn out onto a baking sheet and turn right side up. Put the loaf back in the oven and bake another 5 to 10 minutes. Cool thoroughly before cutting into thick slices with a very sharp knife.

BAKING POWDER BISCUITS

Makes 16 2-inch biscuits

Sausage and eggs seem to beg for these flaky little hot breads on a Sunday morning. They are quick and easy to make and at their best with the least amount of mixing and handling.

2 cups unsifted all-purpose flour
2 teaspoons baking powder
½ teaspoon salt
½ cup butter or vegetable shortening
⅔ cup milk

1. Preheat the oven to 425°F. Grease a baking sheet. Combine the dry ingredients in a large bowl. Using a pastry blender or two knives, cut the butter into the flour mixture until the texture resembles coarse meal. Add the milk and stir just long enough to make a soft dough.

2. Turn out the dough on a lightly floured surface and knead 5 or 6 times—just enough to make the dough smooth and manageable for rolling. Gently roll out the dough to a ½-inch thickness. Cut out 2-inch rounds with a biscuit cutter or the rim of a glass. Gather the scraps into a ball and roll out and cut again until all the dough is used.

3. Arrange the biscuits on an ungreased baking sheet, leaving 1 inch between each biscuit. Bake on the middle rack of the oven. Bake for 15 to 20 minutes, or until golden brown.

Cheese Biscuits. Add ½ cup grated sharp Cheddar to the dry ingredients.

BUTTERMILK BISCUITS

Makes 12 2½-inch biscuits

2 cups unsifted all-purpose flour
½ teaspoon salt
2 teaspoons baking powder
½ teaspoon baking soda
½ cup vegetable shortening
⅔ cup buttermilk

1. Preheat the oven to 450°F. Combine the dry ingredients in a large bowl and mix thoroughly.

2. With two knives or a pastry blender, cut the shortening into the flour, working until the mixture looks like coarse meal.

3. Pour in the buttermilk and stir just long enough to form a ball of dough. Remember: the less you handle the dough, the more tender the biscuits. Turn the dough out on a floured surface and knead 3 or 4 times into a smooth ball.

4. Roll out the dough until you have a large circle, ½-inch thick. Cut as many rounds as you can with a biscuit cutter or the rim of a glass. Reroll scraps, cutting more rounds until the dough is used up.

5. Put the biscuits at least 1 inch apart on an ungreased baking sheet and bake in the middle of the oven for 12 minutes, or until golden.

POPOVERS

Makes 6

Popovers are true to their name—they puff up and over the sides of their pans and look like miniature brown chef's hats. Crusty on the outside and moist and tender on the inside, they are one of the easiest quick breads. Cast-iron popover pans require preheating in the oven for 10 minutes but Pyrex custard cups do not. Mix the batter with cold ingredients—the high heat makes them "pop."

2 cold eggs
1 cup cold milk
1 tablespoon melted butter
1 cup unsifted all-purpose flour
½ teaspoon salt

1. Preheat oven to 425°F. Grease 6 deep custard cups or muffin or popover holders.

2. In a large bowl, beat all the ingredients until the batter is smooth. Pour immediately into the containers, filling each ¾ full. Bake for 35 to 40 minutes.

Herb-Cheese Popovers. Add 1 tablespoon minced fresh herbs and 2 tablespoons grated Parmesan to the batter.

Dill Popovers. Add 1 tablespoon minced fresh or 1 teaspoon dried dill to the batter.

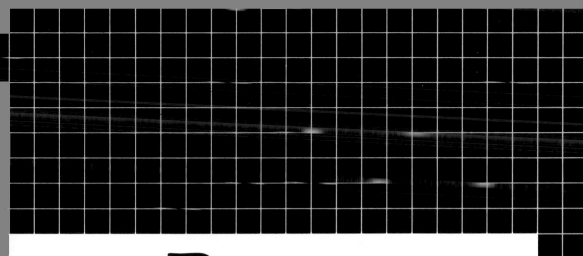

Pastry

There's been a renaissance of the pastry chef—both in restaurants and at home. Our urge to create a brightly glazed tart or a richly colored pâté en croûte has become irresistible. Cooking schools are offering courses on just puff pastry, and big-name food companies are distributing packaged frozen sheets of pastry, many kinds of premade pie shells, refrigerated doughs and dry mixes.

We've rediscovered how simple pastry can transform mundane foods into ethereal delicacies. We've remembered the timelessly wonderful aroma of a freshy baked apple pie; reawakened to the age-old satisfaction of hands-on pastry work. It certainly makes sense that we who love the first fresh spear of spring asparagus, steamed and unadorned, can also love an equally flawless stuffed trout in a crust: both are honest presentations that glorify the food itself.

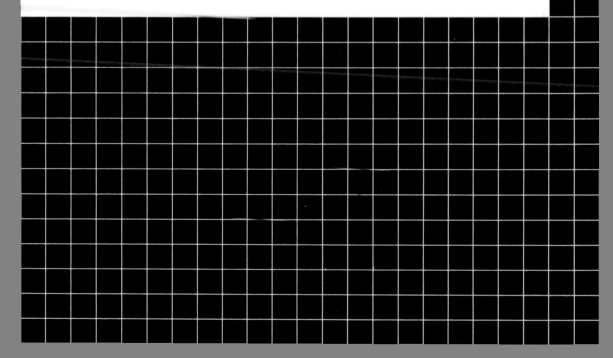

THE ESSENTIALS

The first easy-as-pie truth is that all crusts (even the most complex) are made from the same basic ingredients: flour, shortening (be it lard, butter or vegetable oil) and water. But the final results are far from similar. Understanding the differences is the key to making good pastry and using it to its best effect. Crusts vary in texture, structure and taste. They can range from flaky, light and multilayer to crumbly and sturdy enough to hold a filling. They can be flavored with cheese or herbs or sweetened with sugar. From the simple to the complex, here's a pastry primer.

Basic pastry. It's made with vegetable shortening or lard and is flaky, tender and light. You'll find it most often used for fruit and other classic dessert pies. Best hot from the oven.

Tart pastry. Butter (instead of vegetable shortening or lard) gives it flavor and the strength to stand on its own without a pan. More crumbly than flaky, tart dough holds up quiches and individual dessert tarts.

Combination pastry. Equal portions of butter and lard give this dough the best of both worlds: the flakiness of basic pastry and the buttery strength of tart pastry. Try it in turnovers and meat pies.

Mock puff pastry. A quick method that incorporates extra butter into basic pastry to make it "puff."

Puff pastry. Queen of the pastry world, *pâté feuilletée* is the most elegant and time-consuming of pastries. You'll find its crisp, butter-filled, paper-thin layers gracing the long, rectangular fruit tarts in French bakeries as well as in the more pedestrian Napoleons. Wrapped around cheese, meat or fish, or as a bed for seasonal vegetables, puff pastry makes a glorious hors d'oeuvre as well.

Crumb and bread crusts are not truly pastry, although bread doughs make fine wrappers.

Great culinary wars have been fought over which pastry should be used for what, but whether to use puff or basic for sausage en croûte is not the point; experimenting is. Puff or basic pastry should always be crisp. For the ultimate crust, keep these guidelines in mind:

If you're making a butter crust, always be sure the butter is very well chilled.

It's timesaving to double a pastry recipe and freeze half the raw dough. Wrap well in foil.

Always preheat the oven for at least 15 minutes before baking.

Put pies on the lowest rack to ensure crisp bottoms.

Pie pans with white nonstick coatings tend to keep crust from browning properly.

Assemble and fill pastries just before baking so liquids won't be absorbed by the crust.

It's safer to bake unfilled shells with dried beans, rice or the metal pellets sold in housewares stores. This keeps the bottom crust flat in the middle. Prick the bottom thoroughly with a fork (every ½ inch), line the shell with cheesecloth, fill with beans, rice or pellets (all reusable for years) and bake until the edge of the shell is brown. If the crust contains sugar, this will take about 8 to 10 minutes at 400°F; a sugarless crust will take a few minutes more. Remove the cheesecloth and beans and bake another 5 minutes for a sweetened crust, 10 to 12 minutes more for a pastry shell without sugar; the crust should be nicely browned and dry. You can also start with a solidly frozen shell, and not use any weights—but do be sure to prick it well. If it starts to rise while baking, simply reprick the bottom. Bake for 10 minutes (crust with sugar) to 20 minutes (unsweetened crust) at 400°F.

Always allow a baked pie shell to cool completely on a rack before filling it; this also prevents the bottom crust from becoming soggy.

EMERGENCY PASTRY

When you need to save time, or simply want to experiment with ease, there's a wide variety of packaged doughs to choose from. Puff pastry, for example, which is very time-consuming and somewhat tricky, comes frozen in patty shells or in sheets, which can be used as is or defrosted and rolled out to suit the recipe. Fresh or frozen phyllo dough (the Middle Eastern version of puff pastry, see page 50) is an excellent substitute and a nice change. In the following recipes, one recipe of food processor puff pastry is the equivalent of 1½ packages of frozen puff pastry sheets or 2½ packages of frozen patty shells stacked, then rolled out together.

Refrigerated or frozen pie doughs offer good quality and can be used when basic pastry is called for. Commercially frozen pie crusts are good for emergencies, but hold less filling, so adjust your recipe accordingly. Let a frozen crust defrost enough to flute the edges before you bake it; this will help to hold the filling more securely. The "deep-dish" variety is closer to homemade size.

Packaged dry pie crust mixes are made with flour that has a high gluten content, which makes the dough easier to roll evenly (more tensile and elastic) than homemade. It can be handled a great deal and still be tender. Herbs, lemon rind, sugar, cheese or other seasonings can be added while mixing.

Homemade Ice Cream (see page 303) on freshly baked Apple Pie (see page 268)

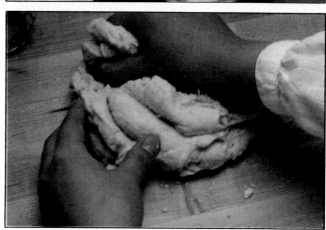

MAKING PASTRY. Cut shortening into the dry ingredients, then moisten with water. Lightly knead the lumps of dough into a ball, then roll it out on a floured surface. Fold into quarters so it can easily be placed in pie pan.

BASIC PASTRY

Makes 2 9-inch pie shells or a 2-crust 9-inch pie

Variations on this basic homemade crust are simple: just change the shortening. Vegetable shortening makes the flakiest crust; butter the crumbliest and sweetest. Lard makes a durable crust on the flaky side, and a mixture of vegetable shortening and butter makes a similarly durable crust with a buttery flavor.

Crusts can be seasoned. Try adding sugar, grated lemon or orange rind, grated cheese or ground spices to the flour and shortening mixture before you add the water.

2 cups unsifted all-purpose flour
1 teaspoon salt
⅔ cup cold shortening (vegetable shortening, lard, butter or a combination)
approximately ⅓ cup cold water

1. In a large bowl, mix the flour and salt. Cut in the shortening with a pastry blender or two knives, one held in each hand, worked in opposite directions. You literally "cut" the shortening into little pieces in the flour mixutre. Keep cutting the larger lumps of shortening and soon the mixture will be like coarse meal. The texture of the flour-shortening mixture should not be uniform, since it's the tiny bits of shortening, which melt during baking, that crisp the thin rolled-out layers of flour and water. Water creates steam, which puffs and lightens the dough.

2. Sprinkle a little cold water over the flour mixture. Toss the sprinkled layer of the mixture lightly with a fork until large lumps of dough form. Push these to the side of the bowl and sprinkle a second layer of water on the flour mixture. Repeat this process until all the flour is moist.

3. Gather all the lumps of dough together into a loose ball. The dough shouldn't be too sticky, but if it's hard to handle, dust your hands with flour to finish making the ball.

4. Turn out the dough on a lightly floured surface and knead lightly with the heel of your hand just until it makes a smooth ball. Even the heat from your palm melts some of the shortening, and since breaking down the tiny globules of shortening will toughen the pastry, don't get carried away in your kneading. Wrap the ball of dough and chill it for at least 30 minutes in the refrigerator.

5. Lightly flour a flat work surface. Since marble is 10 degrees cooler than room temperature, it's the best, but any smooth surface is fine. Cut the chilled dough in half and shape each into a flattened ball.

6. Roll out 1 piece of dough at a time. Work from the center out, lifting the rolling pin as you reach the edges to keep them from getting too thin. With each roll, change the direction of the rolling pin by about 60 degrees. This will maintain a uniform thickness. For a 9-inch pie shell, the diameter of the finished circle of dough should be at least 12 inches, in order to cover both the bottom and sides of the pan comfortably and allow for edge crimping.

7. Carefully fold the finished circle of dough into quarters so that it can be lifted into the pan without tearing. Put the corner of the folded dough at the center of the pan and gently unfold it. (An alternative method is rolling the circle of dough loosely around the rolling pin and undraping it in the pan, but it's a bit harder to get the dough centered properly this way.) Press the dough lightly against the sides of the pan, being careful not to stretch it. Trim the edges if necessary, then finish them by crimping or fluting.

8. For a top crust, roll in the same fashion and fold into quarters. Center the folded dough over the filling just as you centered the bottom crust in the pan. Unfold, trim to allow a 1-inch overhang and seal the edges of the pie by folding the bottom and top crusts together, turning them under the edge and fluting or pressing them together with the tines of a fork. This seals the pie and makes an attractive pattern. With a sharp knife, cut a few slits or small holes to vent steam during baking.

9. For a baked pie shell, prick the dough in the bottom of the pan every ½ inch with the tines of a fork to keep it from puffing up too much. Chill for an hour or freeze for 30 minutes. Preheat the oven to 400° F. Line the shell with cheesecloth and fill with beans, rice or metal pellets and bake for 12 to 15 minutes, or until the sides are brown. Remove the beans and bake another 10 to 12 minutes, or until the crust is brown and dry. If the bottom does swell, enlarge the fork holes and push down with a wooden spoon.

Note. For a partially baked pie shell, proceed as above, but reduce the baking time to 10 minutes.

Cook pie crusts on a rack to let air circulate underneath; this prevents soggy bottoms.

If you have a food processor, put the flour, salt and very cold butter or vegetable shortening in the bowl and process for 3 seconds. Turn the machine on again and add the ice water in a slow, steady stream. A ball of dough will form. Remove the dough and chill for 30 minutes before using. This type of pastry will have plenty of tensile strength and will be easy to roll and shape, but it will not be as flaky as handmade.

APPLE PIE

Makes 1 9-inch pie

Flaky, tender crust, firm sweet apples and the telltale hot cinnamon aroma—"as American as apple pie."

1 recipe Basic Pastry (see page 267) made with vegetable shortening
¾ cup sugar
2 tablespoons flour
1 teaspoon cinnamon
2 tablespoons melted butter
7 cups peeled, cored and sliced tart cooking apples (about 6 medium-size apples such as Granny Smith or greening)

1. Preheat the oven to 400°F. Roll out half the dough into a 13-inch circle and put it carefully in an ungreased 9-inch pie pan.

2. In a large bowl, mix the sugar, flour, cinnamon and butter. Add the apples and toss gently until they are coated. Pour evenly into the pie pan.

3. Roll out the remaining dough into an 11-inch circle. Put it over the apples and press the edges of the top and bottom crusts together to seal them. Fold the dough under and then crimp the edges.

4. Cut several slits in the center of the top crust for steam vents during cooking. For a sweet glaze, brush the crust with water and sprinkle lightly with sugar. Bake for 50 to 60 minutes, or until the crust is brown. Cool briefly and serve warm.

RUM MINCE PIES

Makes 12 6-inch pies

These are small pies, perfect for holiday gifts. If you want to make 1 9-inch pie, halve the recipe.

2 recipes Basic Pastry (see page 267)
2 28-ounce jars mincemeat
1 14-ounce jar cranberry-orange relish
⅔ cup dark rum
2 cups chopped walnuts or pecans

1. Preheat the oven to 400°F and prepare the pastry for pie crust.

2. Divide the dough into 12 pieces. Roll out ⅔ of each piece into rounds, large enough to line the bottom and the sides of 12 6-inch flan pans, 1 inch high. Or, using 1 batch of basic pastry, line a 9-inch pie pan.

3. Mix the mincemeat, relish, rum and nuts and pour into the dough-lined pans. Roll out the remaining dough, cut into ½-inch-wide strips and make a lattice top across each pie. Use 8 strips per small pie, 4 across and 4 down. Use 12 strips for the larger pie, 6 each way. Bake for 40 to 45 minutes.

PECAN PIE

Makes 1 9-inch pie

½ recipe Basic Pastry (see page 267)
¼ cup butter, melted
¾ cup sugar
1 cup white corn syrup
3 eggs
1 teaspoon vanilla extract
1 cup whole pecans

1. Preheat the oven to 350°F and prepare the pastry for pie crust.

2. Mix the melted butter and sugar and add the corn syrup, then beat well. Beat in the eggs, 1 at a time. Stir in the vanilla and pecans.

3. Pour into the unbaked pie crust. (Don't worry, the pecans will rise to the top during baking.) Bake for 45 to 50 minutes. Let it cool so the center won't run.

CHERRY PIE

Makes 1 10-inch pie

Juicy and tart-sweet with a whiff of almond and cinnamon, lattice-top cherry pie falls in the tradition of all-time, all-American greatness.

1 recipe Basic Pastry (see page 267) made with vegetable shortening
6 cups fresh pitted sour cherries or 3 16-ounce cans pitted sour cherries
1 cup sugar (½ cup if using canned cherries)
3 tablespoons quick-cooking tapioca
¼ teaspoon almond extract
¼ teaspoon vanilla extract
1 egg white, slightly beaten

1. Roll out ⅔ of the dough into a 13-inch round to fit a 10-inch pie pan. We use a straight-sided flan pan, but any pie pan is fine. Put the dough in the pan and fold down the top edges of crust to make an even rim all around to support the lattice strips.

2. For fresh cherries, in a large bowl mix the sugar,

Cherry Pie with a lattice top shows off the juicy, tart fruit.

tapioca and almond extract. Add the fresh cherries and toss until they are well coated. Put the coated cherries in the pie shell. (For canned cherries, drain but reserve ¾ cup juice and put the drained fruit in the pie shell. In a bowl, mix the cherry juice, ½ cup sugar, the tapioca, almond extract, vanilla extract and cinnamon until the sugar is dissolved. Pour this mixture evenly over the cherries.)

3. Preheat the oven to 425°F. Roll out the rest of the dough and cut into 12 ½-inch-wide strips for making the lattice top. Weave these strips in a lattice over the cherries. Trim lattice ends and roll out trimmings to make a ½-inch-wide strip to go around the outer edge of the pie.

4. Brush the lattice with beaten egg white to ensure a glossy crust. Bake for 40 to 45 minutes, or until the top is golden brown. Put a pan under a lattice fruit pie to catch the sticky drips.

The crust for Baked Apples or Pears en Croûte is light and flaky, the fruit warm and sweet.

BAKED APPLES OR PEARS EN CROUTE

Makes 4

When thinking about this charming concoction, it's fun to let your mind wander to all the fruits you might wrap. Here, cored apples or pears are filled with raisins mixed with marmalade. Customize the pastry with sugar and grated lemon rind.

1 recipe Basic Pastry (see page 267) made with vegetable shortening and 1 tablespoon sugar and the grated rind of 1 lemon mixed into the flour-salt mixture
4 medium-size tart cooking apples or firm pears
juice of ½ lemon
⅓ cup raisins
⅓ cup orange marmalade
1 egg, beaten

1. Preheat the oven to 375°F and grease a shallow baking dish. Divide the pastry dough into 4 equal parts and roll each into an oval about ¼-inch thick.

2. Peel and core the fruit, sprinkle lightly with lemon juice to prevent darkening and set aside.

3. In a small bowl, mix the raisins and marmalade. Fill the core cavity of each fruit with this mixture.

4. Put an oval of dough over each piece of fruit and pull it down to completely cover the fruit. Make a seam underneath. With kitchen shears, trim the edges of the dough to fit the shape of the fruit and pinch the seam edges together. Use the pastry scraps for decorative stems and leaves and "glue" them to the wrapped fruits with a little water.

5. Stand the pastry-wrapped fruits in a shallow baking pan, brush them with beaten egg and bake for 35 to 40 minutes, or until the fruit is easily pierced with a fork.

CHOCOLATE-ORANGE TORTE

Chocolate-Orange Torte

Serves 10

Call it 10-layer cake—this luscious, rich, extravagant Austrian waltz of egg yolks, sugar and orange rind and a rich, creamy chocolate filling takes time and patience but it's not difficult.

2 recipes Basic Pastry dough (see page 267), made with vegetable shortening (before preparing, see Step 1)
grated rind of 1 orange
2 tablespoons granulated sugar
2 egg yolks
approximately ½ cup orange juice
¾ cup granulated sugar
¼ cup cornstarch
¾ cup unsweetened cocoa
3 cups half-and-half
2 cups heavy cream
¼ cup confectioner's sugar
1 teaspoon vanilla extract
1 teaspoon instant coffee

1. In making the basic pastry, add the grated orange rind and 2 tablespoons sugar to the flour and salt mixture. Cut in the shortening, then mix in the egg yolks and use the orange juice in place of water. Wrap the dough and let it chill 10 minutes in the refrigerator before rolling.

2. Preheat the oven to 375°F. Divide the dough into 10 equal pieces and roll each into a 9-inch round. Using a 9-inch dinner plate as a guide, trim each round into a perfect circle with a sharp knife. Put the rounds on ungreased baking sheets and prick all over with a fork to keep them flat while baking.

3. You may have to bake the rounds in batches, depending on the size of your oven. No 2 baking sheets should touch. Bake for 12 to 15 minutes, or until the pastry is lightly browned. Cool on racks.

4. To make the filling, mix the ¾ cup sugar, cornstarch and cocoa in a large heavy saucepan. Put the pan over medium heat and, using a wire whisk, gradually beat in the half-and-half. Keep stirring over medium heat until the pudding thickens. Remove the pan from the heat and cover it while the pudding cools to prevent a skin from forming.

5. When the pudding is cool, whip it with a whisk until it is quite smooth. In a separate bowl, whip the cream until it forms soft peaks. Fold half the whipped cream into the pudding with a rubber spatula. Reserve the rest of the whipped cream.

6. To assemble the torte, put a pastry round on a flat serving plate and cover it with an even layer of pudding mix. Add a second pastry round, aligning it carefully over the first, and cover with pudding mix. Continue stacking and covering. Top the torte with the tenth round of pastry.

7. Mix the confectioner's sugar and vanilla into the reserved whipped cream and spoon little mounds of whipped cream around the edge of the top pastry round. Dust the whipped cream mounds with instant coffee and chill the torte for at least 2 hours before serving.

Ricotta Cheesecake is garnished with lime slices.

RICOTTA CHEESECAKE

Makes 1 cake

Amaretto liqueur adds its nutty flavor to this creamy Italian classic.

½ recipe Basic Pastry (see page 267) made with butter
2 pounds ricotta
¼ cup flour
½ cup sugar
⅓ cup Amaretto liqueur
1 teaspoon vanilla extract
6 eggs
1 cup heavy cream

1. Preheat the oven to 400°F. Roll out the dough to a 13-inch round and place it carefully across the bottom and 2 inches up the sides of a 9-inch spring-form pan with 3-inch-high straight sides. Prick the bottom all over with a fork. Line with cheesecloth and weight with rice or beans. Bake on the lowest rack of the oven for 10 minutes. Remove cheesecloth and beans. Let cool on a rack.

2. Reduce the oven heat to 325°F. In the large bowl of an electric mixer or in a large mixing bowl, combine the remaining ingredients. Beat by machine or by hand until the mixture is smooth. Pour into the cooled pastry shell and bake in the lower third of the oven for 1½ to 2 hours, or until firm in the center. The center always sinks a little when cooling, so don't worry about it.

3. Chill the cooled cake, covered, in the refrigerator for at least 2 hours or overnight. When ready to serve, release the lock on the side ring and remove it. If you use the bottom of the base of the cake pan as a serving plate, the cake will be easier to cut. Garnish with lime slices.

SALMON STUFFED TROUT EN CROUTE

Serves 4

Trout and salmon are both elegant fish. A combination punctuated with chives, parsley and lemon juice and wrapped with a lemony, dill-flavored crust is especially beautiful.

1 7-ounce can salmon
2 tablespoons chopped fresh or 2 teaspoons dried chives
2 tablespoons chopped fresh parsley
2 tablespoons lemon juice
4 slices fresh white bread, trimmed of crust and made into crumbs
1 egg
salt
freshly ground black pepper
4 trout (approximately 8 to 10 ounces each), heads and tails removed
dry white wine
1 recipe Basic Pastry (see page 267) made with lard as the shortening and seasoned with 2 tablespoons chopped fresh dill and the grated rind of 1 lemon
1 egg, beaten

1. Preheat the oven to 350°F. Drain the salmon and discard any skin and bones. Flake the salmon meat into a small bowl and stir in the chives, parsley, lemon juice, bread crumbs and egg.

2. Salt and pepper the trout inside and out and fill the body cavities with stuffing. Put the fish in a shallow baking dish and add enough wine to half cover the fish. (Supplement with water if necessary.) Cover the pan with foil and bake in the middle of the oven for 15 to 20 minutes, or until the fish are barely tender. Don't overcook—they must retain their shape. Cool the fish in the cooking liquid.

3. Divide the dough into four pieces and, on a floured surface, roll each into a rectangle big enough to completely envelop a trout.

4. Preheat the oven to 375°F and grease a baking sheet. Drain the cooled trout and gently remove the skin from the outside and the backbone from the inside. Loosen the backbone at the tail end first and pull it out along the length of the fish. Tuck in any dislodged stuffing. Dry trout well with towels to keep pastry from becoming soggy.

5. Using a long spatula, gently lift a cooked trout onto the center of 1 of the rectangles of dough. Pull the side pieces together and make a seam down the middle. Seal it with beaten egg. Make neat corner folds at the ends and seal them with beaten egg. Turn the trout seam side down and glaze the top of the dough with beaten egg. Make "scales" with a melon baller or sharp-edged spoon and put the finished trout on the baking sheet. Repeat with each trout.

6. Bake the pastry-wrapped trout on the lowest rack in the oven for 25 to 30 minutes, or until the crusts are well browned. Serve hot with lemon wedges.

PATE MAISON EN CROUTE

Serves 10 to 12

Visions of simple roadside picnics, tastes of rich pâté, golden crust and tiny cornichons—this represents a perfect combination of tastes and textures.

¾ pound ground beef
¾ pound ground veal
¾ pound ground pork
1 large onion, chopped
1 clove garlic, minced
1 tablespoon chopped fresh or 1 teaspoon crumbled dried sage
1 tablespoon chopped fresh or 1 teaspoon crushed dried rosemary
2 teaspoons salt
3 eggs
3 cups fresh rye bread crumbs
⅓ cup milk
2 recipes Basic Pastry (see page 267) made with lard
1 egg, beaten

1. Preheat the oven to 350°F. In a large bowl, mix the meats, onion, garlic, herbs, salt, eggs, bread crumbs and milk. Pack this mixture into a 10×3×3-inch loaf pan or shape the loaf by hand into a similar size and set it in a shallow roasting pan. Bake in the middle of the oven for 1 hour. Remove from the oven and drain off any accumulated fat. Let the pâté cool completely.

2. Meanwhile, prepare the basic pastry. Roll out ¾ of the dough into a rectangle large enough to completely wrap the pâté.

3. Wrap the pâté as you would a gift package. Put the loaf upside down in the middle of the rolled dough. Bring the sides together in the middle and brush the beaten egg on the seam to seal it. Make neat corners on the ends and seal them with beaten egg. Turn the pâté right side up with the seam underneath and put it on a greased baking sheet.

4. Roll out the remaining dough and cut it into ½-inch-wide strips with a sharp knife or pizza cutter. Brush the loaf with beaten egg and use the strips to decorate the top

Pâté Maison en Croûte

of the loaf with a lattice or other design. Brush the finished loaf with beaten egg to glaze.

5. Preheat the oven to 400°F. Put the enclosed pâté on a greased baking sheet and bake on the lowest rack of the oven for 35 to 40 minutes, or until the crust is richly browned. Cool on a rack and serve warm or cold, with cornichons and Dijon mustard.

CUSCINETTI
Cheese in Crust

Makes 6

1 recipe Basic Pastry (see page 267) made with a dash of nutmeg in the flour and dry white wine in place of the water
6 pieces Gruyère, cut 3 inches square and ½-inch thick
1 clove garlic, cut in half
1 egg, beaten

1. Roll out the pastry dough into a rectangle roughly 12×18 inches. With a sharp knife or pizza cutter, cut out 6 6-inch squares. Save the dough trimmings.

2. Preheat the oven to 375°F and grease a baking sheet. Rub each piece of cheese with a cut side of the garlic clove and then put the cheese in the center of a square of dough. Wrap the dough carefully around the cheese, sealing the seams with beaten egg. Melted cheese will leak out of any opening, so be thorough! Put the wrapped squares seam side down on the baking sheet.

3. Reroll the dough trimmings and cut into ½-inch-wide strips. Brush the dough squares with beaten egg and arrange the strips across the top to look like the strings on a package. Brush the strips with beaten egg and bake in the lower third of the oven for 35 to 40 minutes, or until nicely browned. Serve at once.

CHICKEN AND SAUSAGE POT PIES

Makes 6

Some call it mock puff pastry, but we see no joke in adding butter and "turns" to basic pastry to enrich it and puff it into something special.

1 recipe Basic Pastry (see page 267) made with vegetable shortening
¼ cup firm butter
1 pound bulk sausage
1 large onion, chopped
2 cups sliced celery and leaves
½ pound mushrooms, sliced
½ cup flour
2 cups Chicken Stock (see page 58)
4 cups diced cooked chicken
4 carrots, sliced and cooked
2 cups 1-inch pieces cooked green beans
salt
freshly ground black pepper

1. Roll out the pastry into a large ¼-inch-thick oval. Under cold running water at the sink, knead the butter with your fingers until it is malleable but still cold. If you can work quickly, knead with the heel of your hand on a smooth surface. Dry the butter briefly on paper towel and dot the rolled-out dough evenly with teaspoon-size bits of butter. Fold the dough in thirds, then in half. Wrap it in foil or plastic wrap and chill it for an hour.

2. With moist hands to prevent sticking, shape the sausage into small balls. In a large heavy skillet over medium heat, brown the sausage balls thoroughly. Drain off all but 2 tablespoons of the fat and push the sausage to the edges of the skillet. Add the onion and celery and sauté for 5 minutes. Add the mushrooms and flour and sauté another minute. Gradually add the stock, stirring over medium heat until it simmers and the sauce thickens.

3. Stir in the chicken, carrots, green beans and salt and pepper to taste. Divide the mixture equally among 6 1-cup ovenproof baking dishes.

4. Preheat the oven to 400°F. Cut the dough into 6 pieces and roll out each piece, large enough to cover the top of each crock with a 1-inch overhang.

5. Gently top each baking dish with pastry, tucking the edges of the dough over the sides of the dishes. Trim the edges.

6. Reroll the pastry scraps and cut into 2-inch triangles for decorating the top. Overlap the triangles of dough in a strip down the middle of each.

7. Put the dishes on a baking sheet or jellyroll pan to catch any drippings. Bake in the middle of the oven for 35 to 40 minutes, or until the tops are brown and the filling is simmering.

Note. For a 1½-quart pie, roll out all of the dough and cover the baking dish. Bake at 400°F for 35 to 40 minutes, or until brown.

QUICHE AU FROMAGE
Cheese Tart

Makes 1 10-inch quiche

Quiche is a silken French custard tart made of cream, eggs and a host of variables—vegetables, fish, meat, any combination that suits. A cheese quiche makes an ideal base for variations.

1½ cups all-purpose flour
½ teaspoon salt
¼ cup vegetable shortening
¼ cup chilled butter
2 cups grated Gruyère
5 eggs
2 cups half-and-half
1 teaspoon salt
¼ teaspoon cayenne pepper

1. Make the pie crust according to the Basic Pastry recipe techniques (see page 267) but using the ingredient amounts above. Line a 10-inch pie pan with the crust and flute the edges.

2. Preheat the oven to 375°F. Sprinkle the grated cheese across the bottom of the pie shell. In a bowl—or in a blender or food processor—beat the eggs with the half-and-half and seasonings until well mixed (this will take only a few seconds in a machine). Pour this mixture into the pie shell over the cheese. It should come a little short of the top of the pie shell to allow for expansion.

3. Bake in the middle of the oven for 40 to 45 minutes, or until the custard is set and the top is browned. Cool for approximately 15 minutes to firm and to make cutting easier.

Vegetable Quiche. Decrease the cheese to 1½ cups and add any combination of vegetables to the pie shell before pouring in the egg mixture: 1 cup diced parboiled or steamed broccoli or cauliflower tops, zucchini or sliced green beans, or ½ cup minced cooked and squeeze-dried spinach. Season egg-milk mixture with 2 tablespoons chopped fresh dill, parsley or chives.

Vegetable Quiche with zucchini

Chicken and Sausage Pot Pies

Bacon-Cheese Quiche. Line the pie shell with 8 crumbled slices of crisply cooked bacon before adding the cheese. Decrease the salt to ½ teaspoon or less.

Onion Quiche. Chop 1 medium onion and sauté it in 2 teaspoons butter over medium heat for 5 minutes, then spread over the bottom of the pie shell before adding the cheese.

FOOD PROCESSOR PUFF PASTRY

Makes 1½ pounds

This is a simple way to take a lot of the scare out of making puff pastry. It will take time and a bit of easily developed talent, but the results are well worth it. It is not as flaky as a classic or commercially made puff pastry.

3 cups unsifted all purpose flour
1 teaspoon salt
1½ cups very cold butter, cut into ½-inch slices
⅓ cup very cold water

1. Put all ingredients in a food processor and process until a ball of dough forms. Wrap the dough in foil and chill 30 minutes.

2. Roll the dough out on a floured surface to an 8×18-inch oblong. Fold dough into thirds, as you would a letter. Turn the dough so that it looks like a book ready to be opened. Roll again to an 8×18-inch oblong and fold into thirds. You have just completed 2 "turns" of the dough. Chill the dough covered lightly with foil on a plate for 30 minutes.

3. After dough has chilled, make 2 more turns. Chill again for at least 1 hour before using.

Note. Do not make less than this amount of dough; the results will not be as good. If you need less than the full amount, freeze the remainder. Wrap folded dough in foil and freeze, unbaked, until ready to use; then thaw in foil in the refrigerator overnight.

SAUCISSON EN CROUTE
Sausage in Crust

Serves 6 to 8

The French wrap sausage in every imaginable dough, including the butter-filled brioche. The pungent meat is a nice match for the richness of multilayered puff pastry.

1 Polish sausage, cut in thirds, or 1 pound sweet or hot Italian sausage
¾ recipe Food Processor Puff Pastry or
 1 17½-ounce package frozen puff pastry, thawed overnight in the refrigerator
Dijon mustard

1. In heavy skillet over medium high heat, fry the Italian sausage until browned and cooked through. Drain on paper towel and let cool. (If you use Polish sausage, it's already cooked.)

2. Roll out the dough onto a sheet ⅛-inch thick. If using packaged sheets, unfold and roll. Cut the dough into pieces large enough to encase the sausage.

3. Preheat the oven to 400°F. Wrap the sausages in the pastry, enclosing them completely and sealing the edges with water. Put on an ungreased baking sheet with plenty of space in between and bake in the middle of the oven for 20 to 25 minutes, or until brown and crusty. Let cool on a rack for 10 minutes, then slice into ½-inch pieces and serve with mustard.

SCALLOP AND OYSTER PIE

Serves 6

Another puff pastry glory, this hearty one-crust pie combines seafood, mushrooms, sherry and cream under an ethereal crust. The crust is baked separately and put on top of the filling at the last minute to keep it crisp.

⅓ recipe Food Processor Puff Pastry (see page 275) or
    ½ 17½-ounce package frozen puff pastry, thawed
    overnight in the refrigerator
1½ pounds scallops
18 oysters, shucked, with their liquid
1½ cups dry white wine (approximately)
⅓ cup butter
½ pound mushrooms, sliced
⅓ cup flour
⅓ cup dry sherry
1 cup heavy cream
salt
freshly ground black pepper

1. Preheat the oven to 350°F. Roll out ⅔ of the puff pastry until it's large enough to cover the top of a 1½-quart serving dish. Trim the edges neatly and put the dough on an ungreased baking sheet. Roll out the remaining pastry and cut out 10 crescent shapes. Arrange them on the large circle of dough in a pinwheel pattern, securing them with a little water. Bake the dough in the middle of the oven for 20 to 25 minutes, or until puffed and brown. While it bakes, prepare the seafood.

2. In a medium skillet, combine the scallops, oysters and their liquid and enough white wine to just cover the seafood. Bring to a boil over high heat, then lower the heat and simmer, covered, for 5 to 7 minutes, or until the seafood is cooked. Remove from heat and let the seafood cool in the liquid.

3. In a large, heavy saucepan, melt the butter over medium heat. Add the mushrooms and sauté 1 to 2 minutes. Stir in the flour and cook 1 minute, then gradually stir in the sherry, cream, and 1 cup of the seafood cooking liquid. Keep stirring over low heat until the sauce thickens—about 3 to 4 minutes. Drain the scallops and oysters and add to the sauce. Season with salt and pepper to taste.

4. When the top crust is done, transfer the hot seafood and sauce to the warm serving dish. Arrange the crust on top and take it straight to the table.

POACHED EGGS IN PATTY SHELLS

Serves 6

For a dazzlingly different breakfast or a refreshing lunch, make poached eggs in patty shells with a fresh tomato-pepper-mushroom sauce.

½ recipe Food Processor Puff Pastry (see page 275)
    formed into 6 patty shells or 1 10-ounce package frozen
    patty shells
6 tablespoons Mayonnaise (see page 78)
2 tablespoons lemon juice
¼ cup butter
¼ pound mushrooms, sliced
6 scallions, trimmed to include 1 inch of green part,
    sliced
1 small green pepper, cored and chopped
4 large tomatoes, seeded and chopped
salt
freshly ground black pepper
6 eggs

1. Roll out homemade dough on a floured surface to ¼-inch thickness. Cut into 18 3-inch rounds. Put 6 of the rounds on ungreased baking sheets. Cut out the centers of the remaining rounds to make rings ¾-inch wide. Put 2 rings on each round to form sides, securing them with a little water. Bake at 400°F for 15 to 20 minutes or until puffed and brown. If using frozen patty shells, bake according to package directions, cool and proceed as for homemade.

2. In a small saucepan, mix the mayonnaise and lemon juice and cook over very low heat until very, very hot but not boiling. Set aside.

3. In a heavy skillet, melt the butter over medium heat. Add the mushrooms, scallions and green pepper and sauté 5 minutes. Add the tomatoes and salt and pepper to taste and cook, uncovered, stirring occasionally, until the sauce is thick—about 5 to 6 minutes.

4. While the sauce is cooking, poach the eggs (see page 83). To assemble, put the patty shells on a serving platter. Spread the inside of each shell with the lemony mayonnaise. Put the warm eggs in the shells and top with sauce.

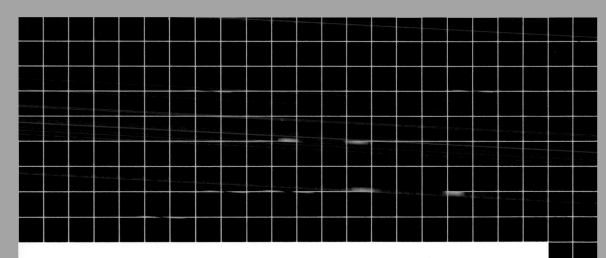

Last Courses

Desserts are no longer an everyday occurrence, an expected finish to each meal. But when we do indulge, we can choose the spectacular or the simple.

Even in these weight-conscious days, our eyes pop and our mouths water at the sight of a rich, smooth chocolate mousse cake. Or we can equally enjoy some fresh fruit and a tray of perfect cheeses. We've come back to the pleasures of the last course, whether it's a triple-crème cheese and ripe pears or a delicate walnut torte.

We offer a selection of desserts and a guide to buying and serving cheese. The cheese glossary will help you choose the right ones, whether you're serving cheese as a dessert, a first course or alone with wine and fruit.

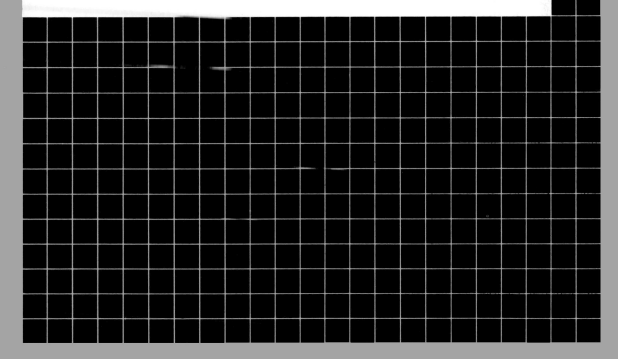

Cheese

THE ESSENTIALS

Our love of cheese has driven us to eat it not just before a meal, as something to go with wine or cocktails, but after the main course and salad, as a dessert by itself or with fruit or as a prelude to sweeter things to come. We now import a palate-boggling array of the finest cheeses—enough to keep us tasting for years to come. New varieties seem to arrive almost daily; never has there been such an interest in cheese. Take joy in experimenting, but beware —cheese is addictive.

Buying cheese is not difficult, but making choices from the hundreds of cheeses available might be. No cheese, even a well-aged one, should smell bitter or rank. An ammonia odor means the cheese is overaged and quite strong—no longer good to most tastes. Next, check the rind. On a soft cheese like Camembert, the rind should be uniformly colored and somewhat moist. On a firm cheese the rind should be free of cracks or bulges, which indicate problems in the ripening process. Press whole cheeses gently with your fingers; there should be no soft spots. A firm cheese should feel slightly elastic. When the cheese is sliced, look for uniform color—except, of course, in blue cheeses, which should be well veined. Ask to taste any cheese sold in bulk; it's the surest way to judge quality. When tasting isn't possible, check the wrapper. If it looks sticky or gummy, or if the cheese has shrunk in its rind, pass it up. One last tip: buy your cheese in a busy shop where the turnover is quick.

To store cheese, wrap it carefully in plastic wrap to keep it from drying out. To slow down its development, refrigerate (all cheeses continue to ripen, eventually to the point of spoiling, even in the refrigerator).

Even under the best of circumstances, stored cheeses can develop surface mold. Simply slice it off; it's not harmful.

Refrigeration is essential to cheese longevity, but it does mute the flavor and harden the texture. Allow cheese to warm to room temperature for an hour or so before serving.

Cheese is a very simple by-product: the once soft, now solid curd of curdled milk (the liquid is whey). The milk may be goat's, sheep's or buffalo's, or the more readily available cow's milk mixed with one of the others, curdled, perhaps heated and ripened in varying degrees. The quality of any cheese can be judged by how clearly that fresh-milk taste echoes in every bite.

Hundreds of cheeses fall into four main categories, based on texture: soft, semisoft, firm and hard, with occasional overlapping allowing for changes wrought in cheese by aging and ripening.

There are several types of soft cheese. The simplest are the soft fresh cheeses (cottage cheese, ricotta and Petit Suisse), which should be eaten within a week or so after they're made. Soft-ripened mild cheeses with a butterfat content of 40 to 50 percent (Brie and Camembert) appeal to those who prefer a somewhat bland, light-flavored cheese. They are ready to be eaten after about a month's curing. Then there are the crèmes, with a higher butterfat content. Double-crèmes with 60 percent butterfat (Suprême and Caprice des Deux) and triple-crèmes at 75 percent butterfat (L'Explorateur and Boursin) are increasingly popular. This soft class also includes the array of goat's milk cheeses (chèvres in French), which look and spread like cream cheese but have a distinctly peppery zing, as well as sheep milk cheeses (feta).

Semisoft mild cheeses (muenster and St. André) are often called monastery cheese because so many were created by religious orders. Characterized by a light, milky taste and a slightly fermented tang, with rinds that range from pale beige to reddish brown, they have an elastic feel and an almost spreadable texture. The semisoft blues (Roquefort and Stilton) are easily identifiable by the bluish-green vein of mold that runs through them.

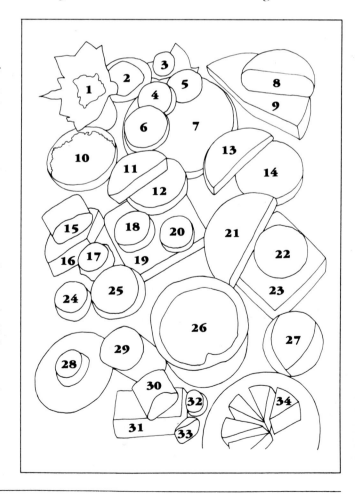

Somerset, England, where it was first made, Cheddar cheese has been made on farms in America since colonial times. The first factory was established in 1851 near Rome, New York, and Cheddar has been a major product of the state ever since. Colored with annatto dye to achieve an appealing orange color, New York Cheddar ranges from mild, 2 to 3 months old, to extra-sharp versions, aged for more than a year. Excellent firm Cheddars are also produced in Wisconsin, Oregon and Vermont. The Vermont Cheddar is not dyed and has a pale cream color.

50. Castello. A very creamy Danish blue cheese rich in butterfat (about 75 percent) with a tangy, slightly sweet taste. Excellent with fruit.

51. Caerphilly. A firm, flaky Welsh cheese at its best in late summer. Mild with a slightly salty taste.

52. Chèvre Cendré. A soft French goat cheese sold in logs ripened in ashes.

53. Brin d'Amour. Aromatically blanketed with rosemary and savory, these soft-ripened goat milk squares are also called Fleur de Maquis. They are still made in small Corsican mountain dairies.

54. Feta. A white, crumbly soft Greek cheese with a salty, tangy flavor. Made from cow's, ewe's or goat's milk.

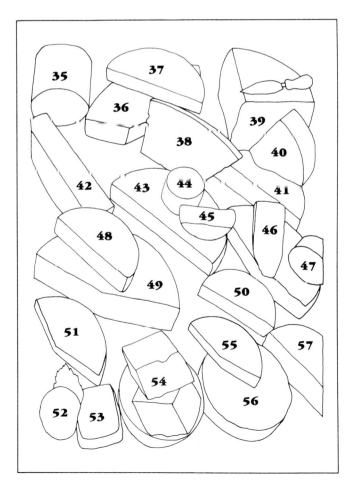

Cheese comes in many shapes and sizes, from bell- and heart-shaped to logs and domes.

Its shape comes from the rectangular boxes in which it is cured.

55. Roquefort. One of the prides of French cheese-making. By law the name Roquefort can be stamped only on the ewe's milk blue cheeses aged in the ancient limestone caves of the Causses region where shepherds first set their curds to cure some two thousand years ago. Semisoft Roquefort has a sharp, peppery flavor and a slightly crumbly consistency. Its peak season runs from June to October.

56. Stilton. A hard, mild blue cheese that is thought by many to be the best English cheese. Its making dates from the 1700s, and its rich, mellow, slightly piquant flavor is much a part of English literature and is often accompanied by a glass of port.

57. Bleu d'Auvergne. A soft Roquefort-type blue-veined cheese from the Massif Central region of France. It is less piquant than Roquefort, but still sharp.

Pears Stuffed with Cheese

Desserts

PEARS STUFFED WITH CHEESE

Serves 6 to 8

4 large firm but ripe green pears
8 ounces Roquefort, Gorgonzola or other blue-veined
  cheese

1. Wash the pears and pat dry. With an apple corer, cut out the center of each pear, making sure you remove all the seeds.

2. In a small bowl, work the cheese with a fork until soft. Fill each pear with a quarter of the cheese. Wrap the stuffed pears in foil or plastic wrap and chill.

3. Just before serving, take out the pears and cut them into ½-inch-thick crosswise slices.

COEUR A LA CREME

Serves 6

A traditional Valentine's Day dessert, coeur à la crème is a thick, creamy cheese mixture molded into a heart shape.

1 8-ounce package cream cheese
1¼ cups creamed cottage cheese, pressed through a sieve
  with the back of a wooden spoon
½ cup sour cream
½ teaspoon vanilla extract
2 tablespoons confectioner's sugar
1 quart strawberries, washed and hulled

1. In a medium bowl, beat the cream cheese until soft, then beat in the remaining ingredients except the strawberries.

2. Spoon the mixture into a heart-shaped mold that has been lined with a layer of damp cheesecloth. Chill several hours, or until firm.

3. Invert the mold on a serving platter. Remove the mold and cheesecloth and surround with fresh strawberries.

PINE NUT COOKIES

Makes about 4 dozen

4 cups unsifted all-purpose flour
1 cup sugar
1 tablespoon baking powder
¼ teaspoon salt
1 cup softened sweet butter
2 eggs
½ cup strong cold coffee
1 teaspoon vanilla extract
1 teaspoon almond extract
warm honey
2 cups pine nuts

1. Preheat the oven to 375°F. In a bowl, mix the flour, sugar, baking powder and salt. Cut in the butter until the particles are like coarse cornmeal. Stir in the eggs, coffee and vanilla and almond extract.

2. Shape the dough into 1-inch balls and bake on ungreased baking sheets until lightly browned, about 12 to 15 minutes. When the cookies have cooled, brush the tops with warm honey and then dip them into pine nuts.

Sesame Seed Cookies. Shape the dough into 2-inch logs about ¾ inch in diameter and roll them in sesame seeds before baking. Bake as above.

TUILES AUX AMANDES
Chocolate-filled Almond Cookies

Makes 30 cookies

1 cup butter
½ cup granulated sugar
1 5-ounce can unblanched almonds, finely grated
   (in a blender or food processor)
2 teaspoons vanilla extract
2 cups unsifted all-purpose flour
1 6-ounce package semisweet chocolate pieces
1¼ cups heavy cream
2 tablespoons instant coffee
1 pound confectioner's sugar

1. Preheat the oven to 350°F. In a medium bowl, cream the butter and granulated sugar. Stir in the almonds, vanilla and flour. Turn out the dough on a floured surface and knead a few times until smooth. Divide it into 60 pieces, roll each into a ball and put them on ungreased baking sheets. Using your fingers, flatten each ball into a 2½-inch round. Bake until lightly browned, about 8 to 10 minutes.

2. While the cookies are cooling, mix the chocolate and cream in a small saucepan. Stir over low heat until the chocolate is melted and the mixture smooth. When the chocolate mixture has cooled, add the coffee and confectioner's sugar.

3. Spread 30 of the cookies with a thick layer of filling, then top with the remaining cookies to make "sandwiches." Refrigerate. Just before serving, sprinkle with confectioner's sugar.

BANH CAM
Sesame Cakes

Makes 20

These golden brown sesame-coated balls from Vietnam look surprisingly egglike when broken open. Their yellow core is made from mung beans, and the "white" is a sweetened combination of rice flour and potato. Packaged dried yellow mung beans without husks and rice flour are available at Oriental groceries.

1 cup yellow mung beans without husks
1 teaspoon all-purpose flour
1 teaspoon water
1 cup sugar
2 cups glutinous rice flour or sweetened rice flour
1 teaspoon baking powder
1 medium potato (about 5 ounces), boiled and mashed

½ cup boiling water
½ cup sesame seeds
2 cups oil

1. Rinse the mung beans and remove any small stones. In a small saucepan, put the beans in just enough water to cover and bring to a boil. Lower the heat and simmer, uncovered, until the water has evaporated and the beans are tender and dry—about 15 minutes; watch carefully so the beans don't scorch. It's equally important that the water completely evaporate, or the beans will be mushy. Mash the cooked beans.

2. In a small bowl, mix the all-purpose flour with the water. In a skillet, combine the mashed beans, ½ cup of the sugar and the flour mixture and stir over medium heat for 5 minutes. Let cool, then divide into 20 portions and shape into balls. Set aside.

3. In a large bowl, combine the rice flour, baking powder, remaining sugar and mashed potato. Add the boiling water and knead until it forms a smooth ball. Divide into 20 pieces, roll into balls, then flatten into 3-inch rounds. Spoon a portion of the mung bean filling on the center of each circle. Gather the wrapper around the filling to enclose it, shaping the whole thing into a ball. Roll the balls in the sesame seeds to coat them.

4. In a medium saucepan, heat the oil to 300°F. One at a time, drop the balls into the hot oil. (The pan should be full but not crowded.) Fry until golden brown, about 15 to 20 minutes.

Banh Cam and Sautéed Bananas (see page 249)

BUNUELOS

Makes 40

Originally from Mexico, these thin, crisp cookies, dusted with cinnamon and sugar, have deep-fried relatives in every nation.

2 eggs
1 cup milk
¼ cup melted butter
⅓ cup sugar
4 cups sifted all-purpose flour
2 teaspoons baking powder
½ teaspoon salt
deep fat or oil heated to 360°F
1½ cups sugar
2 teaspoons cinnamon

1. In a bowl, mix the eggs, milk, butter and ⅓ cup sugar, then stir in the flour, baking powder and salt. Turn the dough out on a lightly floured surface and knead until smooth. It will have the consistency of a pie crust. Let stand for 30 minutes, then knead again.

2. Cut the dough into 40 pieces and roll each piece into a ball. Roll out each ball (using a floured rolling pin) on a floured surface to a 4- to 6-inch round, as thin as possible. Drop the rounds into the hot fat and fry 2 to 3 minutes on each side, until golden brown. Drain on paper towel. In a small bowl or shallow dish, mix the remaining sugar with the cinnamon. After draining the cookies, coat them in the cinnamon sugar.

TARTE TATIN
Upside-down Apple Tart

Makes 1 9-inch tart

The most elegant of apple pies, with swirled sliced fruit peering out from a crunchy coating of caramelized sugar.

2 tablespoons butter
½ cup sugar
5 tart cooking apples, peeled, cored and thinly sliced
¼ cup sugar
2 tablespoons Calvados
1½ cups unsifted all-purpose flour
¼ teaspoon salt
6 tablespoons butter
1 small egg
2 to 3 tablespoons cream or milk

1. Spread 2 tablespoons butter thickly over the bottom and sides of a 9-inch layer cake or spring-form pan. In a

Tarte Tatin—an upside-down apple tart

skillet, heat the sugar until it becomes clear and golden brown. Watch carefully to make sure it does not burn. Pour the syrup into the buttered pan, gently rotating it so the bottom is evenly covered. Arrange the apples decoratively on top of the melted sugar, then sprinkle with sugar and Calvados.

2. Preheat the oven to 350°F. In a small bowl, mix the flour and salt and cut in the 6 tablespoons butter until the particles are very fine. Stir in the egg, then add cream and blend until a dough ball forms. Knead until smooth, roll out on a floured surface to a 9-inch round and fit it into the pan on top of the apples.

3. Bake until the crust is golden, about 40 to 45 minutes. Unmold the hot tart on a serving platter, apple side up. Scrape pan juices over the top and serve warm or cold topped with Crème Fraîche (see page 250).

WALNUT TORTE

Makes 1 10-inch cake

This cake is made without flour. Cakes using ground nuts and/or bread crumbs in place of some or all the flour are called tortes. Walnuts and almonds are the most popular.

12 egg whites
1¼ cups sugar
12 egg yolks
grated rind of 1 lemon
¼ teaspoon salt

¾ cup plus 3 tablespoons dried bread crumbs
2½ cups finely ground walnuts
1 recipe chocolate filling

1. Preheat the oven to 350°F. In a large bowl, beat the egg whites until stiff. Gradually beat in ½ cup of the sugar, 1 tablespoon at a time, until the whites are stiff and glossy. In another bowl, beat the egg yolks with the remaining sugar and lemon rind until thick and fluffy. Fold them into the egg whites, then fold in the salt, ¾ cup bread crumbs and walnuts.

2. Grease 2 10-inch layer cake pans or spring-form pans and sprinkle each with the remaining bread crumbs. Divide the batter equally between the two and bake until the center of the torte is firm to the touch, about 45 to 50 minutes.

3. Loosen the edges and unmold onto cake racks; cool thoroughly. Spread chocolate filling between the layers and on the sides and top of the cake. Chill until the frosting hardens and cut into thin slices to serve.

CHOCOLATE FILLING

1½ cups softened butter
2 cups sifted confectioner's sugar
3 egg yolks
5 squares (5 ounces) semisweet chocolate, melted
3 tablespoons brandy

1. In a medium bowl, combine the butter and sugar and beat until fluffy.

2. Beat in the eggs, 1 at a time, then stir in the cooled chocolate and brandy and leave at room temperature until ready to use.

CHOCOLATE MOUSSE CAKE

Makes 1 8-inch cake

Triple-layered chocolate upon yet more dark goodness—this cake alternates its fine layers with an intensely rich mousse.

6 large eggs at room temperature
1½ cups sugar
½ cup unsifted all-purpose flour
½ cup sifted cocoa
½ cup Clarified Butter (see page 79)
1 teaspoon vanilla extract
8 egg yolks
½ cup water
12 ounces semisweet chocolate, melted over hot water

2 cups heavy cream, whipped until stiff
chocolate shavings
confectioner's sugar

1. Preheat the oven to 350°F. In a large bowl, beat the eggs and 1 cup of the sugar until thick and tripled in volume. In a small bowl, mix the flour with the cocoa and fold into the egg-sugar mixture. Fold in the butter and the vanilla.

2. Pour into 3 greased and floured 8-inch layer cake pans. Bake for 20 to 25 minutes, or until it springs back when you touch the center. Unmold and cool on racks.

3. Beat the egg yolks until thick. In a small saucepan over medium heat, bring the water and remaining sugar to a boil. Boil for 5 minutes, then remove from the heat and add to the egg yolks, pouring in a thin stream. Beat until cool. Fold in the melted chocolate and ½ of the whipped cream. When smooth, fold in the remaining cream.

4. Put 1 of the layers on a serving plate. Spread it with a ¾-inch-thick layer of chocolate mousse. Repeat with remaining layers. Spread the remaining mousse over the sides and top of the cake. Sprinkle with chocolate shavings and confectioner's sugar and chill until ready to serve.

This Fruit Tart (see page 248) is made with strawberries. Try kiwi, pears or blackberries.

FIGGY PUDDING

Makes 2 puddings in charlotte pans (5¾ inches × 3 inches)

1 pound ground suet
⅔ cup sugar
5 eggs
½ cup milk
¼ cup brandy
1 cup dry bread crumbs
1 cup unsifted all-purpose flour
1 teaspoon baking powder
¼ teaspoon salt
1 teaspoon nutmeg
1 pound figs, chopped
rind of 1 orange, grated

1. Preheat the oven to 350°F. In a large bowl, combine the suet, sugar, eggs, milk and brandy. Mix well, then stir in the bread crumbs, flour, baking powder, salt and nutmeg. Beat until smooth.

2. Fold in the figs and orange rind, then pour into greased pans. Cover with greased foil and put the pans in shallow baking pans with 1 inch of water. Bake for 1 hour, or until firm in the center.

CREPIERE

Serves 8

A concoction of fruits, custard and crêpes (brought to new life) baked in a delicious peach crème anglaise.

CUSTARD

9 egg yolks
3 eggs
1¼ cups sugar
1¼ cups flour
½ teaspoon salt
1 quart milk
2 envelopes unflavored gelatin
1½ cups heavy cream
⅓ cup sugar
2 tablespoons raspberry liqueur

CREPES

½ cup unsifted all-purpose flour
1 egg
¼ teaspoon salt
½ cup milk
3 tablespoons melted butter
¼ cup cold water

FRUIT

4 peaches, peeled, pitted and sliced
6 kiwis, peeled and sliced
1 pint strawberries, hulled and left whole

SAUCE

3 cups milk
1 2-inch piece vanilla bean
12 egg yolks
1 cup sugar
1 cup puréed peaches (about 2 or 3 peaches)

1. To make the custard: in a saucepan, beat the egg yolks and eggs with 1¼ cups sugar until thick and lemon-colored. Add the flour and salt. In a small bowl, mix the milk and gelatin, and stir into the egg-sugar mixture. Stir over medium heat until the mixture thickens, but don't let it boil. Cover and let it cool at room temperature. Whip the cream with ⅓ cup sugar until thick. When the custard has cooled, fold in the whipped cream and the liqueur.

2. In a large bowl, combine the crêpe ingredients and beat until smooth. Lightly glaze a 9-inch skillet or crêpe pan with additional melted butter. For the first crêpe, ladle about ½ the batter into the skillet, tilting to coat the bottom of the pan evenly with batter, and cook over moderate heat until the bottom of the crêpe is lightly browned and the edges are easily lifted. Turn the crêpe, using a spatula or simply your fingers, and cook on the other side until it, too, is brown. Repeat for the second crêpe.

3. Line the bottom of a 9-inch spring-form pan with parchment paper cut to fit. Spread enough of the custard in the pan to make a ¼-inch-deep layer. Put the peach slices on top of the custard in an even layer, then cover with another layer of custard, a crêpe, more custard, the kiwis, more custard, the second crêpe and more custard. Stand the strawberries in the custard, point side up, then cover with the remaining custard. Refrigerate at least 4 hours or overnight.

4. To make the sauce: in a saucepan, mix the milk and vanilla bean and scald the milk. In a small bowl, beat the egg yolks and sugar until thick. Gradually beat in the scalded milk. Put this mixture back in the saucepan and cook over low heat, stirring constantly, until the sauce coats the spoon. Be careful not to let it boil. Remove the vanilla bean, cover and cool. Remove the sides of the pan. Fold in the puréed peaches. When you're ready to serve, cut the crêpes into wedges and spoon the sauce over each serving.

GERMAN PANCAKE

Makes 1 12-inch pancake

German pancakes are an egg-filled and thick but raised version of a crêpe. As good for dessert as for brunch, they go well with lemon and a dusting of confectioner's sugar or with a fruit purée or sauce.

4 eggs
⅓ cup sugar
2 cups milk
2 cups unsifted all-purpose flour
1 teaspoon salt
1 teaspoon vanilla extract
butter
confectioner's sugar

1. Preheat the oven to 375°F. In a large bowl, beat the eggs until fluffy and pale-colored. Mix in the sugar, milk, flour, salt and vanilla. Beat until the batter is smooth.

2. Butter a 12-inch skillet with a heatproof handle or a 12-inch paella pan. Pour in the batter and bake for 40 to 45 minutes. The finished pancake will be brown and puffy in the middle (the puff will fall when the pancake is removed from the oven) and curled over at the sides like a Yorkshire pudding.

3. Slide the pancake onto a serving platter, sprinkle with confectioner's sugar and cut into wedges. Serve with wedges of lemon or apricot liqueur sauce.

APRICOT LIQUEUR SAUCE

¼ cup butter
¼ cup flour
½ cup Drambuie
1 cup white wine
12 finely chopped apricots, fresh or dried

1. In a heavy saucepan, melt the butter over medium heat and add the flour to make a roux. Cook with a wooden spoon for 1 minute without browning. Keep stirring as you slowly add the liqueur and wine. Cook over medium heat until the sauce bubbles and thickens.

2. Add the apricots and let the sauce simmer for 5 minutes. Serve warm.

FROZEN COFFEE MOUSSE WITH AMARETTO-ORANGE SAUCE

Serves 12

Make the mousse in a 2-quart soufflé dish with a 3-inch aluminum foil collar tied around the edge. This will allow the frozen mousse to show over the edge of the dish when the foil is removed.

4 cups strong coffee
2 cups granulated sugar
1 tablespoon vanilla extract
2 envelopes unflavored gelatin

4 cups heavy cream, whipped
½ cup cornstarch
1 6-ounce can frozen orange juice concentrate, thawed
1 cup Amaretto
2¼ cups water

1. In a 1½-quart saucepan combine 1 cup of the coffee with 1 cup sugar, the vanilla and the gelatin. Stir over low heat until the sugar and gelatin are completely dissolved. Stir in the remaining coffee and remove from the heat. Chill in a large bowl until it has thickened slightly and is syrupy—about 1 hour.

2. Prepare a 2-quart soufflé dish with an aluminum collar. Whip the cream.

3. Fold the whipped cream into the thickened coffee-gelatin mixture and pour into the soufflé dish. Freeze until firm—at least 8 hours or overnight.

4. To prepare the sauce, mix the cornstarch with 1 cup sugar in a 1½-quart saucepan. Stir in the orange juice, Amaretto and water. Cook over medium heat, stirring constantly, until the sauce thickens and begins to bubble —about 8 to 10 minutes. Cool in a covered dish and refrigerate for several hours or overnight.

5. Take the mousse out of the freezer and remove the aluminum collar 30 minutes before serving. Serve with the sauce.

CASSIS MOUSSE TORTE

Makes 1 9-inch torte

6 egg yolks
1 cup sugar
grated rind and juice of 1 lemon
1 cup sifted all-purpose flour
6 egg whites
½ teaspoon cream of tartar
½ teaspoon salt

3 egg yolks
⅓ cup sugar
⅓ cup crème de cassis
2 teaspoons unflavored gelatin
3 egg whites, stiffly beaten
1 cup heavy cream, whipped

3 egg yolks
3 tablespoons sugar
1 tablespoon vanilla extract
1 cup softened unsalted butter
1 tablespoon crème de cassis
¼ cup black currant preserves or jelly

1. To make the sponge cake, beat 6 egg yolks and 1 cup sugar in a large bowl until very thick, about 5 minutes. Fold in the lemon rind and juice, then the flour. Beat 6 egg whites with cream of tartar and salt until stiff. Gently fold them into the batter. Grease and flour 2 9-inch layer cake pans and pour in the batter. Bake at 325°F for 35 to 40 minutes or until the cake springs back when touched lightly in the center. Cool the cake in the pan for 10 minutes, then loosen the edges and unmold.

2. For the mousse, beat 3 egg yolks with ⅓ cup sugar and ⅓ cup crème de cassis. Stir in the gelatin. Beat over a low heat until the mixture is lukewarm and the gelatin dissolves. Cool until slightly thickened. Fold in 3 beaten egg whites and whipped heavy cream. Chill until the mixture holds its shape.

3. Put 1 layer of the sponge cake on a serving platter and spread it with a thick layer of cassis mousse. Top with the second layer of sponge cake and chill.

4. In a blender or food processor, blend 3 egg yolks, 3 tablespoons sugar and vanilla for 3 minutes. Add the butter 1 tablespoon at a time and continue to blend until creamy; then blend in 1 tablespoon crème de cassis. Transfer the butter cream to a bowl, fold in the preserves, then spread it on top of the cake. Chill the cake until ready to serve.

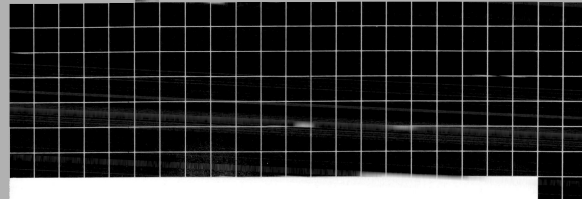

Comfort Foods

There is food for the body and food for the soul. One keeps you alive, the other makes you happy. When you're looking for a little consolation, familiar foods that trigger memories of being loved and cared for can be most reassuring. These foods have magical healing properties that no doctor or chemist could concoct.

Comfort foods remind us of childhood and sustain us still. The simplicity and goodness of comfort foods give us emotional nourishment when life gets more than a little overwhelming. The very ritual of making these humble staples is a tonic in itself.

We don't all get comfort from the same foods. One person's chicken soup is another's oatmeal (with butter and cinnamon, of course). But there are a surprising number of honest, basic, home-cooked foods that seem to universally evoke a smile or a sigh, if not a lump in the throat. The only way they could be more effective is if someone else made them for us.

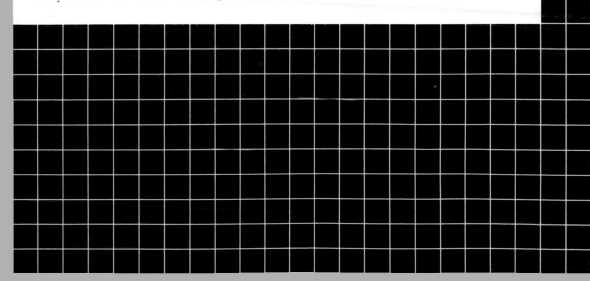

OATMEAL

Serves 4

It's butter melting and brown sugar still slightly crackling on top. It's salt and sweet playing against each other, and heavy cream dancing across the top of hot, soft oats.

2⅔ cups cold water
½ teaspoon salt
1⅓ cups regular or quick-cooking rolled oats

1. In a 1½- or 2-quart saucepan, mix the water, salt and oats. Bring to a boil over high heat, lower the heat and boil gently, 1 minute for quick-cooking oats or 5 minutes for regular.

2. Remove the pan from the heat and let sit 2 or 3 minutes, covered to prevent a crust from forming. Stir and serve with your choice of butter, brown sugar, jam or honey.

FRENCH TOAST

Serves 2

What could be better on a cold gray morning than the smell of French toast and the sizzle as the egg-drenched bread hits the hot butter in the pan? In France, stale bread (pain perdu—"lost bread") is dipped in an egg batter, fried and simply sprinkled with sugar.

1 egg
½ cup milk
1 teaspoon sugar
1 teaspoon vanilla extract
1 tablespoon butter
4 1-inch-thick slices challah or egg bread

1. In a shallow bowl, beat the egg, milk, sugar and vanilla. In a heavy skillet, melt the butter over medium heat until it foams, but don't let it brown.

2. Soak both sides of the bread in the egg mixture and fry in the butter over medium heat until both sides are brown and crisp. Serve hot with more butter and hot syrup.

PANCAKES

Makes 24 4-inch pancakes

2 eggs
2 cups buttermilk
1½ teaspoons baking soda
1½ teaspoons baking powder
2 cups unsifted all-purpose flour
1 tablespoon sugar
½ teaspoon salt
3 tablespoons melted butter
oil

1. In a bowl, beat the eggs with the buttermilk. Add the remaining ingredients except the oil and beat until smooth and well blended.

2. Brush a griddle lightly with oil and heat until a drop of water skitters around when dripped on the griddle.

3. Drop the batter by ¼ cupfuls onto the griddle. Cook until brown on the bottom and bubbles appear on the top surface. Turn the pancakes and brown the other side. Stack the pancakes and serve with pats of butter and heated maple syrup.

Blueberry Pancakes. Fold 1 cup of fresh or dry-pack frozen blueberries into the batter.

French Toast *(left)* and **Oatmeal** *(opposite)*

CORN MUFFINS

Makes 12

Muffins are so easygoing that making them is a no-nonsense matter; other confections might need to be fussed over, but the less you mix a muffin batter, the better the results will be.

1 cup unsifted all-purpose flour
1 cup yellow cornmeal
2 tablespoons sugar
1 tablespoon baking powder
½ teaspoon baking soda
1 teaspoon salt
1 egg
1½ cups buttermilk
¼ cup melted butter

1. Preheat the oven to 450°F. Grease a 12-cup muffin tin for 2½-inch muffins. In a large bowl, mix the dry ingredients. In a separate, smaller bowl, mix the egg, buttermilk and butter.

2. Make a depression in the middle of the dry ingredients and pour the egg-buttermilk mixture into it all at once. Quickly stir until the dry ingredients are moistened, but don't beat. The batter should be lumpy.

3. Fill the muffin tins ¾ full of batter and bake in the middle of the oven for 10 to 15 minutes, or until the muffins are puffed and firm to the touch. (They will not be very brown on top.) Serve hot.

BRAN MUFFINS

Makes 12

Whether made with all-bran (sold in the cereal section at the grocery store) or miller's bran (found in health-food stores), bran muffins come from the oven nutty-tasting and tender, with big wide tops.

1 egg
1 cup buttermilk
⅓ cup melted butter
3 cups bran
⅓ cup firmly packed brown sugar
1 cup unsifted all-purpose flour
2 teaspoons baking powder
½ teaspoon baking soda
1 teaspoon salt

1. Preheat the oven to 400°F. Grease a 12-cup muffin tin for 2½-inch muffins. In a medium-size bowl, mix the egg,

***Clockwise from bottom:* Corn, Bran and Blueberry Muffins served with honey**

buttermilk and butter. Stir in the bran. In a larger bowl, mix the sugar, flour, baking powder, baking soda and salt.

2. Make a depression in the center of the flour mixture and pour in the egg-buttermilk-bran mixture all at once. Stir just until the dry ingredients are moistened. The batter should be lumpy.

3. Fill the tins ¾ full and bake in the middle of the oven for 20 to 25 minutes, or until firm to the touch and slightly brown. Serve hot with butter, honey or marmalade.

BLUEBERRY MUFFINS

Makes 12

Blueberry muffins, plump and steaming, are particularly special when made with tart fresh berries, but the dry-pack frozen ones work just fine.

2 cups unsifted all-purpose flour
½ cup sugar
1 tablespoon baking powder
½ teaspoon salt
1 egg
1 cup milk
¼ cup melted butter
1½ cups fresh or dry-pack frozen blueberries

1. Preheat the oven to 400°F. Grease a 12-cup muffin tin for 2½-inch muffins. In a large bowl, mix the dry ingredients. In a smaller bowl, mix the egg, milk and butter.

2. Make a depression in the center of the flour mixture and pour in the egg-milk mixture all at once. Stir just until the dry ingredients are moistened and the batter is still lumpy. Fold in the blueberries.

3. Fill the muffin tins ¾ full and bake in the middle of the oven for 20 to 25 minutes, or until the muffins are firm to the touch and slightly brown on top. Serve hot with butter.

CINNAMON TOAST

Makes 4 slices

Sometimes the only thing that could pull you out of bed was the smell of cinnamon toast: thick slices of homemade bread smeared with cinnamon, sugar and lots of butter— broiled until crinkly, brown and crisp.

4 slices white or raisin bread
¼ cup softened butter
¼ cup sugar
1 teaspoon ground cinnamon

1. Preheat broiler. Lightly toast the bread on both sides.

2. In a small bowl, mix the butter, sugar and cinnamon. Spread on one side of the toast. Put buttered side up under the broiler to melt the butter and bubble the sugar—30 seconds.

COCOA

Serves 6

6 ounces semisweet chocolate or semisweet chocolate bits
6 cups milk
1 teaspoon ground cinnamon

1. Grate the chocolate in a blender or food processor. In a heavy 1½- or 2-quart saucepan, heat the milk and grated chocolate over low heat until the chocolate is melted and completely blended with the milk.

2. Add the cinnamon and beat with a whisk. Beat longer if you like your cocoa frothy. Serve in mugs.

BAKED POTATO

Serves 1

The homely potato is comfortable in all kinds of company, but it secretly longs to be a star. No potato is a better candidate than the baked one, waiting for someone to come and butter it up. And despite its reputation, the much-maligned spud weighs in at a mere 90 calories. It's the sour cream, bacon or blue cheese that gives the venerable potato a bad name. Try yogurt instead.

1. To bake a potato, preheat the oven to 350°F. With a sharp knife, cut a small cross in the middle of one side to let out any steam. (Potatoes have been known to explode in the oven.) Use the middle oven rack and bake for 1 hour, or until the potato can be easily pierced with a fork. Press open at the cross and serve with whatever you like.

Baked Potato with butter and bacon

STANDING RIB ROAST OF BEEF

Serves 4

A plump roast of beef fairly reeks of well-being. The roast is borne triumphantly to the table with generous bowls of stewed tomatoes, mashed potatoes and gravy, bespeaking prosperity and a life settled enough for a big dinner.

1 4-pound standing rib roast of beef
1 clove garlic, mashed
salt
freshly ground black pepper

1. Preheat the oven to 350°F. The roast needs a good covering of fat over the top to keep it basted during cooking, but trim off excess fat (more than 1 inch thick). Rub the exterior of the roast—fat, too—with the mashed garlic, and sprinkle with salt and pepper to taste.

2. Put the beef, fat side up, in a shallow roasting pan. The ribs act as a rack. Put a meat thermometer into the meatiest part of the roast, making sure its tip is not resting on bone or fat. Cook in the center of the oven for approximately 1 hour, or until the thermometer registers 140°F for rare. Start checking at 45 minutes.

3. Allow the roast to stand 15 or 20 minutes before carving. This will give the juice time to settle and allow the meat to firm. To carve, put the roast on a carving board, meat side up, and anchor it under the first rib with a fork. With a large, very sharp knife, slice across the face of the roast toward the ribs. Cut along the rib bone with the tip of the knife to release the slice of meat, or cut under the rib for a slice that includes the bone.

OLD-FASHIONED BEEF GRAVY

Makes 2 cups

2 tablespoons beef drippings spooned from roasting pan
2 tablespoons flour
drippings from 1 roasting pan
2 cups Brown Stock (see page 57)
salt
freshly ground black pepper

1. In a heavy saucepan, mix the 2 tablespoons drippings with the flour. Stir over medium heat to make a roux. Cook the roux 2 to 3 minutes. Set aside.

Standing Rib Roast of Beef with Mashed Potatoes, Old-Fashioned Beef Gravy and Stewed Tomatoes

2. Pour off the remaining beef fat from the roasting pan and discard. Put the pan on the burner. Using medium heat, add the stock and bring to a boil, scraping the pan to loosen all the brown particles. Keep stirring and scraping until the pan is completely deglazed.

3. Stir this liquid into the roux. Continue stirring over medium heat until the gravy thickens—about 5 minutes. Season to taste with salt and pepper.

MASHED POTATOES

Serves 4

Thick and creamy mashed potatoes are smoothly soothing. Whether drenched in a brown or cream gravy, the richness is all homemade.

4 medium Idaho potatoes
¼ cup butter
¼ to ⅓ cup milk
salt
white pepper

1. Scrub the potatoes and put them in a saucepan with enough salted water to cover. Bring the water to a boil over high heat, reduce the heat and boil gently for 25 to 30 minutes, or until the potatoes are tender.

2. Briefly cool the potatoes in cold water until they can be handled for peeling. In a bowl, mash the peeled potatoes with a potato masher (or use a potato ricer or food mill). Mix in the butter and enough milk to reach the consistency you like. Season with salt and pepper to taste and beat the potatoes with a wooden spoon until fluffy.

STEWED TOMATOES

Serves 4

4 large tomatoes
1 small onion, chopped
2 tablespoons butter
salt
freshly ground black pepper

1. Core the tomatoes and cut them into wedges. Put in a heavy nonaluminum saucepan with the onion and cook over low heat until both are soft—about 10 minutes.

2. Stir in the butter, season to taste with salt and pepper and serve hot. Tomatoes can be peeled before cooking. Just dip them into boiling water for 30 seconds and pull off the skin.

CORNED BEEF HASH AND EGGS

Serves 1

Corned beef hash was probably discovered on a Sunday night when the pantry and the coin purse were pretty bare.

1 tablespoon butter
1 small onion, chopped
¼ cup chopped green pepper
½ cup minced cooked corned beef
1 small potato, boiled, peeled and diced
⅓ cup Brown Stock (see page 57)
2 eggs
salt
freshly ground black pepper

1. In a small, heavy skillet, melt the butter over medium heat and sauté the onion and green pepper for 5 minutes, or until soft. Add the corned beef, potato and stock and stir until heated through.

2. With the back of a spoon, make a hollow in the center of the hash. Break the eggs into a cup and carefully slip the eggs into the hollow. Salt and pepper the eggs. Cover the pan and cook over low heat about 10 minutes, or until

Corned Beef Hash and Eggs

the eggs are set. Serve hot, and of course, don't forget to add ketchup.

Red Flannel Hash. Add 1 cup diced beets to the beef mixture.

CHOCOLATE CHIP COOKIES

Makes 6 dozen cookies

For all their current pseudogourmet popularity, there will never be a chocolate chip cookie as good as the first ones your pudgy fingers put together with chocolate bits from the yellow package.

1 cup butter
2¼ cups firmly packed dark brown sugar
2 eggs
½ cup buttermilk
3½ cups unsifted all-purpose flour
½ teaspoon salt
1 teaspoon baking soda
12 ounces semisweet chocolate pieces
6 ounces pecans, chopped

1. Preheat the oven to 400°F. Grease the baking sheets. In a large bowl, cream the butter with the sugar. Beat in the eggs and buttermilk.

2. In another bowl, mix the flour, salt and baking soda together. Beat this mixture into the butter-egg mixture until smooth. Fold in the chocolate chips and pecans.

3. For small, crisp cookies, drop heaping teaspoons of dough onto the greased baking sheets about 2 inches apart. For larger, chewier cookies, use tablespoons of dough.

4. Bake in the middle of the oven for 8 to 10 minutes, or until the cookies are golden brown. Don't let the baking sheets touch (the air needs to circulate freely) or the cookies won't bake evenly. Bake as many batches as it takes to use up the dough.

5. Cool the cookies on the baking sheets for 2 or 3 minutes, then remove them with a spatula to finish cooling on racks.

OATMEAL COOKIES

Makes 5 dozen cookies

You almost don't have to eat these plump cookies to enjoy their goodness. Just let the smell of cinnamon, raisins, dates and nuts fill the kitchen.

½ cup butter
1½ cups firmly packed dark brown sugar
2 eggs
½ cup honey
2 cups unsifted all-purpose flour
1 teaspoon baking soda
½ teaspoon salt
1 teaspoon ground cinnamon
2 cups regular or quick-cooking rolled oats
8 ounces pitted dates, chopped
1 cup raisins
6 ounces walnuts, chopped

1. Preheat the oven to 400°F. Grease the baking sheets. In a large bowl, cream the butter with the sugar. Beat in the eggs and honey.

2. In another bowl, mix the flour, baking soda, salt and cinnamon. Stir this into the butter-egg mixture until the dough is smooth. Fold in the remaining ingredients.

3. For small, crisp cookies, drop heaping teaspoons of dough on the greased baking sheets, about 2 inches apart. For larger, chewier cookies, use tablespoons. Bake in the middle of the oven—baking sheets should not touch—for 8 to 10 minutes, or until golden brown. Bake in batches until all the dough is used.

4. Let the cookies cool 2 to 3 minutes on the baking sheets, then remove with a spatula to finish cooling on racks.

PEANUT BUTTER COOKIES

Makes 4 dozen cookies

And to think that there could be anything more comforting than a peanut butter and jelly sandwich! This recipe takes the peanut butter predilection one step farther. As you sit down with two or three and a glass of milk, you can ponder the reason why all peanut butter cookies have a crisscross pattern.

½ cup butter
1 cup firmly packed dark brown sugar
½ cup peanut butter, smooth or chunky
1 egg
2 cups unsifted all-purpose flour
½ teaspoon baking powder
½ teaspoon baking soda
¼ teaspoon salt

1. Preheat the oven to 375°F. Grease the baking sheets.

Homemade cookies, no matter what kind, definitely require a complementary glass of milk.

Cream the butter and sugar in a large bowl. Beat in the peanut butter and egg.

2. In a separate bowl, mix the flour with the other ingredients. Then stir this mixture into the butter-egg mixture until the dough is smooth. It should be a little stiff.

3. Lightly flour your hands and shape the dough into 1-inch balls. Put the balls 2 inches apart on baking sheets and press flat with the tines of a fork, making a crisscross pattern.

4. Bake in the middle of the oven—baking sheets should not touch—for 10 to 12 minutes, or until lightly browned. Bake in batches until the dough is used up.

5. Cool the cookies 2 to 3 minutes on the baking sheets, then remove with a spatula to finish cooling on racks.

BROWNIES

Makes 20 squares

The rich, chewy squares were constant childhood companions on picnics, in lunch boxes and when friends stayed over. When the "care packages" arrived at camp, homesickness disappeared almost as fast as the brownies.

3 1-ounce squares unsweetened chocolate
⅓ cup butter
1 cup sugar
2 eggs
1 cup all-purpose flour
½ teaspoon baking powder
½ teaspoon salt
1 cup coarsely chopped walnuts

1. Preheat the oven to 350°F. Grease an 8-inch-square baking pan. In a large heavy saucepan, melt the chocolate and butter over very low heat. Remove the pan from the heat and beat in all the remaining ingredients except the nuts. Fold in the nuts.

2. Spread this mixture evenly in the pan and bake in the middle of the oven for 30 to 35 minutes, or until the sides begin to draw away from the pan and the top looks dull.

3. Cool in the pan on a rack before cutting into squares.

APPLE BROWN BETTY

Serves 4

Apple pie may be an archetypal comfort food, but consider the alternative: Apple Brown Betty.

2 cups soft bread crumbs
¼ cup melted butter
½ cup firmly packed brown sugar
½ teaspoon ground cinnamon
3 or 4 tart cooking apples, peeled, cored and chopped
½ cup water
½ cup heavy cream

1. Preheat the oven to 325°F and grease a 1½-quart baking dish. In a bowl, mix the bread crumbs, butter, sugar and cinnamon.

2. Make alternate layers of apples and the crumb mixture in the baking dish, finishing with the crumbs. Drizzle the water over the top and bake in the middle of the oven for 35 to 40 minutes, or until the apples are tender and the top is brown and crisp. Serve warm, but not hot, with heavy cream, plain or whipped.

PEACH COBBLER

Makes 1 1-quart cobbler

Memories of childhood and the abundance of fresh fruit at harvest makes us crave thick cobblers and heavy cream.

4 cups sliced peeled peaches
½ cup sugar
¼ cup cornstarch
½ teaspoon salt
2 tablespoons melted butter
½ recipe Basic Pastry (see page 267)

1. Preheat the oven to 375°F. In a bowl, mix the peaches, sugar, cornstarch, salt and butter. Pour into a 1-quart baking dish.

2. On a floured surface, roll out the pastry into a square long enough to cover the widest part of the baking dish. Cut the square into 1-inch-wide strips. Put the strips over the filling, weaving a lattice. Press the edges firmly to the edge of the baking dish and trim off the excess dough.

3. Bake for 35 to 40 minutes, or until richly brown and bubbly. Serve warm. If you wish, top the cobbler with thick cream or Vanilla Ice Cream (see page 303).

FLAN

Serves 6 to 8

Add a clear glaze of caramelized sugar to the cups of custard before baking, and it is transformed into flan, a dessert so elegant it appears on the finest menus.

1½ cups sugar
8 eggs
1 quart milk
1 tablespoon vanilla extract

1. Preheat the oven to 350°F. In a heavy skillet (nonstick, if possible), heat ¾ cup of the sugar over low heat without stirring until it melts and turns a clear golden brown. Watch carefully that it doesn't burn. Pour this caramelized sugar into a 1½-quart ovenproof mold, using an oiled scraper to get it all out of the skillet.

2. Rotate the mold until the entire inside is coated with a thin layer of caramelized sugar. Set aside.

3. Break the eggs into a large bowl and gradually beat in the remaining sugar, milk and vanilla. Pour this into the caramel-coated mold and set the mold in a baking pan holding 1 inch of warm water. Bake the flan in the middle of the oven for 1 hour and 20 minutes, or until it is set.

Custard with a sprinkling of nutmeg

Rice Pudding, creamy and filled with raisins

4. Cool the baked flan to room temperature, then chill in the refrigerator for at least 2 hours. To serve, loosen the edges of the mold with a sharp knife, cover it with a serving plate and invert. The flan will unmold and the caramelized sugar will have melted into a sauce.

CUSTARD

Serves 4

Smooth, simple and supremely old-fashioned, baked custard is a concoction that is nothing more than eggs, milk, sugar and vanilla.

3 eggs
⅓ cup sugar
2 cups milk
1 teaspoon vanilla extract
¼ teaspoon ground nutmeg

1. Preheat the oven to 350°F. In a bowl, beat all the ingredients except the nutmeg until smooth and blended. Pour into 4 individual custard cups. Sprinkle each with nutmeg.

2. Put the filled cups in a baking pan. Add hot water to the pan to a depth of 1 inch. Bake in the middle of the oven for 30 to 35 minutes, or until the custard is set.

3. Cool the baked custard to room temperature, then chill in the refrigerator for at least 1 hour before serving.

RICE PUDDING

Serves 4

There's old-time feeling in each grain of rice, just in the

way it naturally expands to absorb its share of the riches. In a time of instant everything, it's comforting that no one has figured out how to make good instant rice pudding.

1 egg, well beaten
¼ cup sugar
¼ teaspoon salt
1 cup half-and-half or ½ cup milk and ½ cup cream
1 cup cooked rice (don't use converted rice)
¼ cup raisins
1 small apple, peeled, cored and diced
1 teaspoon vanilla extract
dash ground nutmeg

1. Preheat the oven to 350°F. Butter a 1-quart baking dish. In a large bowl, combine all the ingredients and stir until well blended. Pour into the baking dish.

2. Bake the pudding in the middle of the oven for 20 minutes. Remove the pudding and stir, then return it to the oven and bake another 15 or 20 minutes, or until firm.

3. Cool to room temperature and serve, or chill for 2 hours first. For a creamier pudding, stir in ½ cup heavy cream after the pudding is baked.

BIRTHDAY CAKE

Makes 1 9-inch layer cake

It was a tradition: special family birthdays at grandmother's house. There was always the relative-of-honor's favorite food, but you really looked forward to the birthday cake and hoped that there were enough butter cream roses to go around.

Birthday Cake, complete with butter cream roses

2 cups sifted all-purpose flour
1½ cups sugar
1 tablespoon baking powder
1 teaspoon salt
½ cup oil
7 egg yolks
2 teaspoons vanilla extract
2 teaspoons grated orange rind
2 teaspoons grated lemon rind
1 cup egg whites (about 7 or 8 eggs)
½ teaspoon cream of tartar

1 12-ounce jar apricot preserves

⅓ cup softened butter
6 tablespoons heavy cream
⅓ cup vegetable shortening
1 tablespoon vanilla extract
6 cups confectioner's sugar, approximately
yellow and green food coloring

decorating tips—star tip for rosettes, leaf tip for leaves, rose tip (large) for full-blown roses, flower nail

1. Preheat the oven to 350° F. Grease and flour just the bottom of 2 9-inch layer cake pans with 2-inch sides.

2. In a bowl, mix the flour, sugar, baking powder and salt. Add the oil, egg yolks, vanilla and orange and lemon rind. Beat until smooth.

3. In another bowl, beat the egg whites and cream of tartar until stiff.

4. Pour the egg yolk mixture gently over the egg whites and carefully fold together until just blended (too much handling will cause the egg whites to lose their volume).

5. Divide the batter between the 2 pans and bake for 35 to 40 minutes, or until the cake is firm in the center. Remove from oven and cool cakes in pans placed on racks.

6. When the cake has cooled, loosen the edges with a sharp knife and unmold. When thoroughly cool, put 1 layer on a serving platter and spread evenly with the apricot preserves. Put the second layer on top of the first.

7. In a bowl, mix the butter with the cream, vegetable shortening and vanilla. Stir in enough confectioner's sugar to give the frosting a good spreading consistency.

8. Spread the sides and top of the cake with some of the frosting, making sure it is smooth.

9. Divide the remaining frosting—tint ⅔ yellow and ⅓ green with the food coloring. Put the yellow frosting into a pastry bag and, using a star tip, press small rosettes of frosting around the bottom and top edges of the cake. Make large swags of rosettes on the sides of the cake using the star tip.

10. Use the remaining frosting in the bag to make the roses. Cover a flower nail with a small square of foil and pipe out a center petal, then surround it with larger and larger petals to resemble a rose. Remove the rose (with the foil) from the flower nail and put it in the freezer. Repeat this process until the yellow frosting is used up.

11. After cleaning the pastry bag (make sure it's completely dry), put the green frosting in the bag and, using the leaf tip, pipe out a circle of green leaves 1 inch in from the edge of the top of the cake, touching each other at the widest part of the leaf.

12. When you're ready to serve, remove the roses from the freezer and quickly strip off the foil. Put the roses on top of the cake within the circle of leaves to resemble a bouquet.

HOMEMADE ICE CREAM

When making ice cream in an electric ice cream machine, follow the manufacturer's directions. If you're making ice cream in metal ice cube trays (without the cube divider), freeze the ice cream until it's frozen 1 inch in from the edge of the pan. Scrape into a bowl and beat with an electric mixer until fluffy. Put the ice cream back in the freezer and freeze until hard.

When making ice cream in a hand cranked freezer, put the ice cream mixture into the inner canister, filling it only ⅔ full to allow for expansion. Pack crushed ice and rock salt (use 5 parts ice to 1 part salt) around the canister. Make sure the inner canister has the dasher in place and that the lid is on tight to keep the salted water from leaking into the ice cream.

The first 5 minutes, crank very slowly, then crank more vigorously until the crank is hard to turn. Ice and salt should be added from time to time as the ice melts. Pack the ice and salt over the top of the canister and let stand to harden the ice cream. Remove the canister carefully, wipe it off and remove the lid. Pull out the dasher and store the covered canister in the freezer until you are ready to eat the ice cream.

VANILLA ICE CREAM

Makes 1 quart

1 cup light cream
1 cup heavy cream
½ cup milk
⅔ cup sugar
1 teaspoon vanilla extract or 1 vanilla bean
dash salt

1. Mix all the ingredients together, chill and freeze as directed above.

FRENCH VANILLA ICE CREAM

Makes 1 quart

2 cups heavy cream
1 vanilla bean (Step 1) or 1½ teaspoons vanilla extract (Step 2)
⅔ cup sugar
4 egg yolks
1 cup milk
dash salt

1. In a saucepan, heat the cream, vanilla bean and sugar in a double boiler over barely simmering water. Beat the egg yolks, milk and salt and add to the cream. Cook until thickened or until the mixture coats a spoon. Remove the bean, slit open the pod and scrape the seeds into the cream.

2. Chill the cream for 2 hours. If using vanilla extract, add it now. Freeze as directed above.

Fruit Ice Cream. Mix 1½ cups peeled and mashed peaches, apricots or bananas (or whole berries), ½ cup sugar and 1 tablespoon fresh lemon juice. Fold into the cream and freeze.

Almond Ice Cream. Fold ½ cup sliced toasted almonds and ½ teaspoon almond extract into the cream and freeze.

Chocolate Ice Cream. Melt 2 squares (2 ounces) semisweet chocolate and mix with ½ cup water. Let it cool, then fold into the cream and freeze.

Coffee Ice Cream. Mix ¼ cup water with 2 tablespoons instant coffee, fold into the cream and freeze.

Peppermint Ice Cream. Omit the sugar in the recipe, fold ¾ cup crushed peppermint sticks into the cream and freeze.

Liqueur Ice Cream. Fold ½ cup of the desired liqueur, such as Amaretto or crème de cassis into the cream, then freeze.

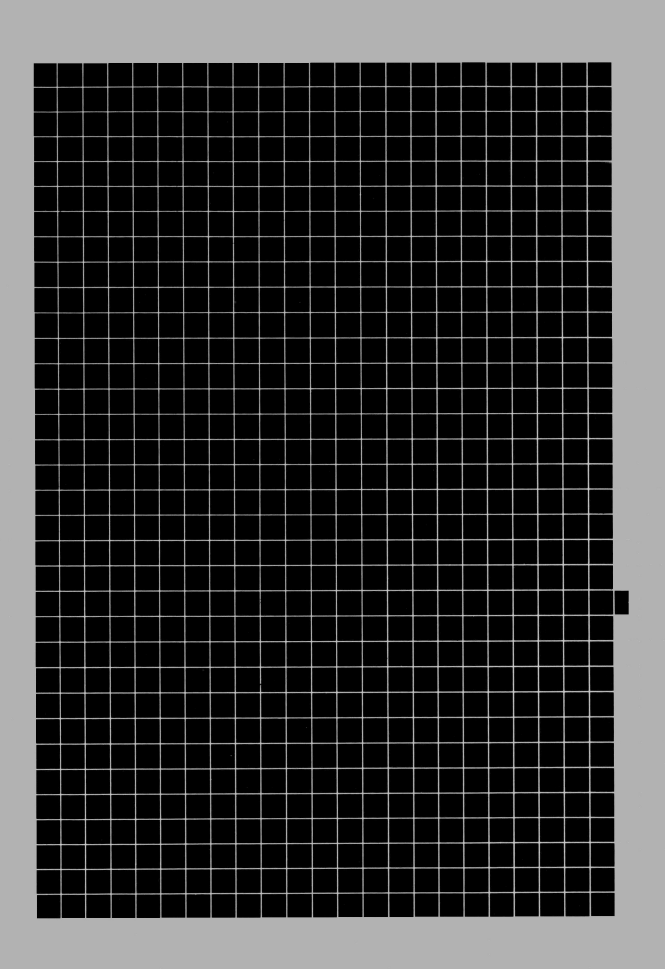

III.

FEASTING

Big-Deal Dinners

□□□□

The major part of this book (until now) has been devoted to meals and parts of meals that can be assembled rapidly and with a very light hand. A typical menu might be a small first course of pasta primavera, a quickly sautéed scaloppini with mushrooms, fresh asparagus with mustard sauce and a raspberry ice.

Sometimes, however, there's an urge to do it up the old way—a giant production whose preparation is at least half the fun. Holidays are the obvious times for such major investments, so we present the New American Thanksgiving and Christmas dinners, which can, of course, be used interchangeably or to celebrate any day at all. Here, too, are other dinners whose every detail is worked out for you.

French Dinner

THE MENU
Serves 8

Jambon Persillé
(Ham with Parsley in Aspic)

Gigot d'Agneau Farci
(Stuffed Leg of Lamb)

Haricots Blancs et Tomates
(White Beans and Tomatoes)

Asperges à la Sauce Moutarde
(Asparagus with Mustard Sauce)

Assorted Cheeses with French Bread

Tartes aux Poires
(Pear Tarts)

Always relying on local and seasonal ingredients, French cooking is the simply sophisticated prodigy of its peasant forebears. As a matter of fact, the epicurean extreme of rigidly complicated sauces and elaborately rich pastries has given French food a bad name it doesn't deserve. In all great French food preparation, a simple truth prevails: a dish depends on the freshness and integrity of its ingredients (an idea that is, not surprisingly, central to the New American Cuisine as well). As prime examples, this menu draws from Burgundy, land of wine-dark sauces and stews, and the hearty cuisine of Brittany and Normandy.

STRATEGIES
This dinner for 10 should be served in a succession of shining courses. The first is the ham with parsley in sparkling aspic, cut into thin slices and adorned with tiny, crisp cornichons. The ham should be made a day ahead to make sure it's firmly jellied and easy to slice.

The stuffed leg of lamb is accompanied by tender white

313

turkey with melted butter. Unless the turkey is marked "self-basting," prepare to brush it every 30 to 40 minutes with ½ cup melted butter during cooking. Cover the top of the bird loosely with a piece of foil to keep the breast from drying out and put the turkey in the oven. There are too many variables in a large bird to give an exact formula for roasting time. A 15- to 18-pound stuffed bird will take anywhere from 3½ to 4½ hours. You should start checking at 3½ hours. A meat thermometer stuck in the thickest part of the thigh meat, without touching a bone, should read 170° to 180°F. The leg should move up and down easily, and when the skin at the thigh joint is punctured, the juices should be clear.

5. While the turkey is roasting, put the giblets in a saucepan. Stick the onion with the cloves and add it to the saucepan with the other seasonings. Add 3 cups water and bring to a boil over high heat. Remove any scum that rises to the top, reduce the heat, cover the pan and simmer for 1 hour, or until the giblets are tender. Remove the meat from the stock and let it cool. Strain the stock and hold it in reserve for the gravy. Take the meat off the neck bone and chop it along with the liver, heart and gizzard if you want giblet gravy. Set aside.

6. When the roast is done, remove it to a platter and put it in a warm place to settle for 15 to 20 minutes before carving (see page 135).

7. Pour off all but ½ cup of the fat from the pan. Place the pan on a burner over medium heat. Add the flour and cook, stirring constantly, for 4 to 5 minutes. Stir in the brown stock and giblet stock and deglaze the pan, scraping up all the browned particles in the pan. Stir in the Madeira. Check the seasoning and add salt and pepper if needed. Stir in the chopped giblets and heat through. When ready to serve, pour into a sauce boat.

CRANBERRY AND WINE SAUCE

1 pound fresh cranberries
2 cups sugar
2 cups port wine
½ teaspoon ground cinnamon
½ teaspoon freshly grated nutmeg
½ teaspoon ground cloves

1. Wash the cranberries in a colander and pick out any stones, leaves and spoiled berries.

2. In a 3-quart saucepan, combine the berries, sugar and wine. Bring to a boil over high heat, stirring to dissolve the sugar. Lower the heat slightly and let boil, uncovered, until the berries begin to pop their skins, not more than 4

to 5 minutes. Stir in the spices, remove from the heat and pour into a serving bowl or oiled mold. Let cool, then refrigerate until ready to serve. Loosen edges with the tip of a knife, tap to loosen and unmold.

BRUSSELS SPROUTS AND CHESTNUTS

2 pounds chestnuts
2 pounds Brussels sprouts
½ cup butter
salt
freshly ground black pepper

1. The first step in peeling chestnuts is cutting slits or crosses through the tough outer shell on the flat side of the nuts. While you are scoring the chestnuts, bring a pot of water to a rolling boil. Drop in the scored chestnuts and let boil 4 to 5 minutes. Remove them from the pot, a few at a time, and peel both the outer and inner skins. If any of the inner skins are hard to remove, throw the chestnuts back in the pot and simmer again until the skin loosens. Warm chestnuts peel easily; cold ones do not. Put the peeled chestnuts in a large saucepan. Add water to cover and simmer 20 minutes, or until cooked.

2. Trim the Brussels sprouts, remove the tough outer leaves and wash. Place in a saucepan with water to cover. Add 1 teaspoon salt and bring to a boil over high heat, lower the heat slightly and simmer, uncovered, for 15 to 20 minutes, or until tender.

3. Drain vegetables and toss with butter, salt and pepper.

APRICOT GLAZED YAMS

8 large yams
½ teaspoon salt
½ cup butter
grated rind of 1 lemon
1 teaspoon freshly grated nutmeg
1 12-ounce jar apricot preserves

1. Scrub the yams and put them in a large saucepan with enough water to cover and the salt. Bring to a boil over high heat, lower the heat slightly and boil, covered, for 15 to 20 minutes, or until the yams can be pierced with a fork but are still firm. Drain and cool. Peel the yams and cut into large chunks. Cover and refrigerate until ready to glaze and serve.

2. In a heavy skillet, melt the butter over medium heat. Stir in the lemon rind, nutmeg and preserves. When the preserves are melted, add water, 1 teaspoon at a time, until the glaze is the consistency of heavy cream.

3. Add the yam pieces and stir gently until they are all coated with glaze and piping hot, about 8 to 10 minutes. Serve in a warm dish.

PUMPKIN-MINCEMEAT PIE

1 recipe Basic Pastry (see page 267)
1 cup prepared mincemeat
1 16-ounce can pumpkin or 2 cups fresh pumpkin purée
1 13-ounce can evaporated milk or 1⅔ cups light cream
3 eggs, well beaten
¾ cup firmly packed light brown sugar
1 teaspoon ground cinnamon
1 teaspoon freshly ground nutmeg
1 teaspoon ground cloves
1 cup heavy cream
¼ cup sifted confectioner's sugar
½ teaspoon freshly ground nutmeg

1. Preheat the oven to 350°F. Roll out the pastry to fit a 10-inch pie pan. Put the dough in the pan and flute the edges, making a high rim all around. Spread the mincemeat evenly across the bottom of the pastry shell.

2. In a large bowl, combine the pumpkin, milk, eggs, sugar and spices. Beat until well blended and smooth. Pour into the pie shell over the mincemeat.

3. Bake in the middle of the oven for 1 hour, or until the filling has set and the top is puffed and brown. Cool on a rack but don't cut until it is at room temperature. (The puff will fall, but that's to be expected.)

4. Just before serving, whip the cream in a chilled bowl with the confectioner's sugar and nutmeg.

Note. For plain pumpkin pie, omit the mincemeat.

Christmas Celebration

THE MENU
Serves 8

Roast Goose with Sausage-Apple Stuffing

Wild Rice with Mushrooms

Julienne of Vegetables

Chestnut Mousse in a Meringue Shell with Chestnuts in Rum

Christmas Pudding with Hard Sauce

Even the colors of a Victorian Christmas feast are rich and inviting, like an oil painting of a Dickensian holiday from our childhoods. Modern cooking methods and techniques have taken much of the pain and lots of the time out of preparing a meal like this. And although it isn't a half-hour special, much can be done ahead, with finishing touches at the last minute. It's a dinner to celebrate and remember for a long time—and not because of days spent over a hot stove.

To accommodate the best of the past with our current appetites and tastes, we simplified the menu. Desserts are the sugar plums of Christmas fantasy, so we make room for them by eliminating appetizers and bread. We offer two desserts—a chestnut mousse and an English Christmas pudding. A medley of crisp vegetables replace creamed onions and turnips and, yes, even the salad. The Christmas goose with sausage-apple stuffing can't ask for much more than wild rice and a lusty Burgundy wine.

STRATEGIES
The Christmas pudding and the chestnuts in rum should be made well ahead to let the flavors marry. Hard sauce, too, will keep for several days. The chestnut mousse can be made ahead and kept chilled. The meringue shell will hold for a week if you store it in an airtight container in a cool, dry place. Putting the two together is a simple, last-minute job. Christmas Day, the timing must be worked around the goose, which cooks for 4 hours and must stand for at least 30 minutes to allow the meat to firm and the juices to settle before carving. Its preparation should be started at least 5 hours before dinnertime. If the vegetables are trimmed and sliced early, getting the meal on the table will take less than 45 minutes.

ROAST GOOSE WITH SAUSAGE-APPLE STUFFING

Goose is a rich-tasting, succulent, dark-meat bird that revels in a full-bodied flavorful stuffing. Sausage, onion, giblets and apple are the traditional combination, and that's all it takes to fill the bird. The glaze is a twentieth-

century shortcut: a can of frozen concentrated orange juice thinned with port wine and spiked with Dijon mustard. Luscious bunches of green and purple grapes and chicory leaves make a festive, opulent garnish.

1 12- to 14-pound goose
salt
freshly ground black pepper
2 pounds bulk breakfast sausage
2 large onions, chopped
4 large tart cooking apples, peeled, cored and diced
1 6-ounce can frozen orange juice concentrate
½ cup port wine
2 tablespoons Dijon mustard
purple and green grapes

1. If the goose is frozen, let it defrost completely before cooking. Remove the giblets and wash the goose under cold water and pat dry. Rub both inside and out with salt and pepper.

2. In a saucepan, cover the giblets and the neck with 3 cups water. Bring to a boil, reduce the heat and simmer, covered, until tender—about 30 to 35 minutes. Drain and chop the giblets. Chop the meat from the neck and discard the bones.

3. Preheat the oven to 350°F. In a large heavy skillet, fry the sausage meat over medium heat until brown and crumbly. Spoon off excess fat, push the meat to the sides of the pan and add the onions, apples and chopped giblets and neck meat. Sauté over medium heat for 5 minutes. Remove from heat, mix well and cool until you can handle it.

4. Just before the goose is ready to be roasted, lightly pack the sausage mixture into the goose and truss it with string or skewers (see page 120). Line a shallow roasting pan with foil—this makes cleaning up the glaze easy—and put the stuffed goose on the pan's rack. Roast for 3½ to 4 hours, or until the goose is tender (the legs will move up and down easily).

5. Defrost the orange juice concentrate. In a bowl, mix it with the wine and mustard. During the last hour of roasting, baste the goose every 15 minutes with the orange juice mixture. Let the goose stand for at least 30 minutes before carving. Serve it on a heated platter garnished with chicory and bunches of purple and green grapes.

WILD RICE WITH MUSHROOMS

1 pound wild rice
8 cups Chicken Stock (see page 58)
⅓ cup Cointreau or Triple Sec
1 teaspoon salt
½ cup butter
½ pound fresh mushrooms, sliced

1. Rinse the rice several times in cold water, removing any foreign particles. In a heavy 4-quart saucepan, combine the rice, stock, Cointreau, salt and all but 2 tablespoons of the butter. Bring to a boil, lower the heat, cover tightly and simmer for 30 to 35 minutes, or until liquid is absorbed.

2. In a skillet, melt the remaining butter over medium heat. Sauté the mushrooms for 3 to 4 minutes and toss with the cooked rice. Garnish with parsley and serve in a warm bowl.

JULIENNE OF VEGETABLES

1 bunch carrots, cut into thin 2-inch strips
4 yellow squash, cut into thin 2-inch strips
4 zucchini, cut into thin 2-inch strips
⅓ cup butter
1 teaspoon chopped fresh or ¼ teaspoon dried thyme
1 teaspoon chopped fresh or ¼ teaspoon dried chervil
1 small onion, peeled and grated
salt
freshly ground black pepper

1. Steam the carrot strips for 10 minutes. Add the yellow and green squash and steam another 5 minutes. Toss immediately with the herbs, onion and salt and pepper to taste and serve in a warm dish.

CHESTNUT MOUSSE IN A MERINGUE SHELL

Chestnuts are traditional to Christmas and so are rich sweetmeats. If you were to have one dessert a year, this might well be the choice. Give yourself plenty of time to put together the mousse in meringue shells. It is as easy as pie but does require some patience and dexterity to make the meringue shell as decorative as it is delicious. The chestnut spread is made in France and can be found in gourmet and specialty shops.

Christmas Pudding with Hard Sauce, Chestnut Mousse in a Meringue Shell with Chestnuts in Rum, Roast Goose with Sausage-Apple Stuffing, Wild Rice with Mushrooms and Julienne of Vegetables

1 cup dark rum or brandy
2 envelopes unflavored gelatin
1 17½-ounce can chestnut spread (crème de marron)
3 cups heavy cream
6 egg whites at room temperature
½ teaspoon cream of tartar
2 cups sugar

1. Choose a 2-quart mold for the mousse. (We use a melon-shaped one.) Line a baking sheet with foil and outline the bottom of the mold in the center of it. This will be the pattern for making the meringue shell fit the mousse.

2. To make the mousse, mix the rum with the gelatin in a small saucepan. Stir over low heat until the gelatin is completely dissolved. In a large mixing bowl, stir this mixture into the chestnut spread and let it cool to room temperature. Whip the cream until it forms soft peaks and fold it into the chestnut-gelatin mixture. Carefully pour this mousse into the mold, cover and chill until firm—at least 6 hours.

3. To make the meringue, beat the egg whites until foamy. Add the cream of tartar and continue beating until the mixture is stiff but not dry. Beat in the sugar gradually, 1 tablespoon at a time, so that the egg whites do not break down and the mixture is stiff and glossy.

4. Preheat the oven to 200°F. Using about ½ the meringue mixture, spread a ¾-inch layer over the mold pattern outlined on the foil-covered cookie sheet. This is the base that will hold the mousse. Put the remaining meringue in a pastry bag with a large blunt tip and press out a series of rosettes around the edge of the meringue base. Make sure that the rosettes are on the outer edge and will not interfere with the unmolding of the mousse in the center. Bake the meringue for 1 hour, or until hard to the touch. (If it starts to brown, the oven is too hot and you should turn it down.) Use a potholder to prop the oven door open a crack to let the moisture escape. Cool the meringue in the oven.

5. When ready to serve, put the meringue shell on a serving platter. (The foil can be pulled from the meringue easily.) Dip the mousse mold in lukewarm water for a few seconds, tap it to loosen the edges and invert it onto the meringue shell. Garnish with chestnuts in rum.

CHESTNUTS IN RUM

Makes 6 pints

A sauce for the chestnut mousse that also goes with ice cream and simple cakes. A good gift, too.

4 pounds fresh chestnuts, shelled (see page 314)
12 cups water
3 pounds dark brown sugar
3 cups dark rum
1 orange, thinly sliced
¼ cup chopped crystallized ginger

1. In a large saucepan, bring the chestnuts and water to a boil over high heat, lower the heat, cover and simmer for 10 minutes. Remove the chestnuts, 1 at a time, from the water and strip off the skin while they're still warm. Put the peeled chestnuts in a saucepan, cover with water and cook, covered, until chestnuts are easily pierced—about 30 to 35 minutes, depending on the size of the chestnuts.

2. Mix the remaining ingredients in a large saucepan and bring to a boil. Boil gently for 5 minutes. Add the chestnuts and again bring to a boil. Remove from the heat.

CHRISTMAS PUDDING

Makes 1 4-quart pudding

The English couldn't have Christmas without this legendary steamed pudding, redolent with spirits and fruit. It includes everything from the traditional suet and stout to dark rum, raisins, candied fruit and almonds. It can be stored in foil to let the flavors develop and, of course, makes a wonderful gift.

1 cup flour
1 teaspoon baking powder
½ teaspoon salt
8 slices stale dry white bread with crusts, grated
2 teaspoons pumpkin pie spice
1 pound dark brown sugar
½ pound ground suet
4 eggs
⅔ cup barley wine or sherry wine (barley wine is an old English wine sold in some liquor stores)
⅔ cup stout
¼ cup dark rum
1¼ pounds dried currants
½ pound raisins
½ pound golden raisins
1 cup finely chopped mixed candied fruits
1 large green cooking apple, peeled, cored and chopped
½ cup chopped almonds
rum

1. In a large mixing bowl combine all the ingredients except the fruits, almonds and rum. Mix until well blended. Fold in the fruits and nuts, cover the bowl and let stand at room temperature for 2 hours.

2. Preheat the oven to 350°F. Grease a round-bottomed 4-quart ceramic or other heat-proof bowl and line it with a single layer of cheesecloth. (Or you can use 2 2-quart bowls.) Pack the bowl with the pudding mixture and cover the top with greased aluminum foil.

3. Set the bowl in an open pan deep enough to hold 2 inches of water. Bake the pudding in its pan of water for 4 hours, refilling the water from time to time as necessary. (The 2 smaller puddings will take only 3 hours; they can bake in the same pan of water as long as the bowls do not touch.)

4. Let the pudding cool in its bowl. Use the cheesecloth to remove it. Wrap the cooled pudding first in fresh cheesecloth that has been dipped in rum, then in aluminum foil. The pudding will keep at room temperature for weeks. You can sprinkle with more rum from time to time. To serve, remove the foil and heat the pudding for 30 minutes in a steamer or over a double boiler. Cut in thin wedges and top with hard sauce.

HARD SAUCE

½ pound softened sweet butter
1 pound confectioner's sugar
1 tablespoon rum, brandy or vanilla extract

1. In a large bowl, combine all the ingredients and beat until fluffy. Chill for at least 2 hours, or until hard.

Cold Summer Supper

THE MENU
Serves 4

Chicken Pesto Salad

Vegetable Stuffed Shells with Dill Dressing

Smoked Mozzarella with Oil and Black Pepper

Chilled Asparagus (see page 220)

French Bread with Chive Butter (see page 79)

Sorbets (see page 240)

Hot summer nights call for cold, light dinners—light colors, textures and tastes. The best of such meals can be made from seasonal produce without a long stint in the kitchen.

Pesto is usually associated with linguine, but it makes a fine dressing for composed salads and chicken. Instead of the expected crudités, let fresh raw vegetables make their appearance as a chopped filling for pasta shells, all bound together with a dill dressing. Smoked mozzarella is made almost saladlike with fine golden olive oil and cracked black pepper. Steamed, chilled asparagus tastes fine with or without the dill dressing that's used for the pasta salad.

STRATEGIES

The joy of the feast is twofold—in its summery green color and its total do-ahead nature. All of the marketing can be done a day or more in advance, with the exception of the bread. Poach the chicken and make the pesto the day before. Put a thin film of olive oil on top of the pesto and it won't turn dark.

Toss the chicken pesto salad several hours before the meal. The shells can be cooked a day ahead and, for optimum freshness, stuffed that morning. The chive butter can be blended the day before, and the sorbets can be frozen then, too. The mozzarella is a fast, last-minute operation.

CHICKEN PESTO SALAD

Cold chicken pesto is a long way from the obligatory chicken salad of ladies' luncheons of yore. Poach a stewing hen the day before (page 121) or, if you don't have time, poach two whole chicken breasts the morning of the meal. Allow at least 2 hours for the chicken to chill in the sauce.

2 pounds skinned and boned chicken breasts
salt
freshly ground black pepper
2 cups Chicken Stock (see page 58)
1 recipe Pesto (see page 187)
2 cups shelled fresh raw peas
pine nuts for garnish
leaf lettuce

1. Sprinkle the chicken breasts lightly with salt and pepper. Put them in a skillet and add the stock. Cover and simmer gently for 20 to 25 minutes, or until cooked. Let the chicken cool in the stock.

2. Cut the cooled chicken into 1½-inch chunks and put them in a bowl. Stir in the pesto sauce. Chill, covered, for 2 hours.

3. When ready to serve, toss the chicken and pesto again to coat the chicken. Garnish with peas and additional pine nuts. Serve on lettuce leaves.

VEGETABLE STUFFED SHELLS WITH DILL DRESSING

2 teaspoons salt
16 jumbo shells (about 6 ounces)
1 cup chopped raw broccoli
1 cup shredded raw zucchini
½ cup chopped mushrooms
¼ cup sliced scallions
salt
1 cup heavy cream
2 tablespoons fresh lemon juice
2 tablespoons chopped fresh dill

1. Bring 3 quarts of water to a rolling boil in a large pot. Add 2 teaspoons salt and the shells. Boil until tender but still firm, about 12 to 15 minutes. Drain and cover the shells with cold water in a large bowl.

2. In a large bowl, mix the vegetables and salt to taste. Let stand for 1 hour, then drain.

3. In a blender or food processor, combine the cream, lemon juice and dill and process a few seconds, then stop. Process another few seconds and see if the dressing has thickened slightly (if you overprocess, you will have lemon butter), then salt to taste. By hand, whip the sauce with a whisk until it thickens.

4. Drain the shells. Mix half of the dressing with the drained vegetables. Stuff the shells. Spoon the remaining dressing over the stuffed shells and serve.

SMOKED MOZZARELLA WITH OIL AND BLACK PEPPER

1 pound smoked mozzarella
⅓ cup olive oil
½ clove garlic, crushed
1 teaspoon black peppercorns, cracked

1. Cut the mozzarella into ¼-inch-thick slices and put the slices on a serving platter.

2. In a small bowl, mix the oil, garlic and pepper. Pour over the mozzarella and leave at room temperature for 1 hour before serving.

Counterclockwise from top: **Chicken Pesto Salad, Smoked Mozzarella with Oil and Black Pepper, Vegetable Stuffed Shells with Dill Dressing and Chilled Asparagus (see page 220)**

Fritto Misto

THE MENU
Serves 4

Seafood Fritto Misto

*Black Olives, Pimentos, Anchovies, Capers,
Red Onion Rings and Radishes*

Italian Bread

Cold Lemon Soufflé

Fritto misto means "mixed fry" in Italian, and it stirs up reminiscences of soft Mediterranean summer nights. The lacy, crisp batter seals in the freshness of moist fish and shellfish.

Served with lots of lemon halves and heaping bowls of antipasto—pimentos, oil-cured black olives, anchovies, red onion rings, radishes with sweet butter—and fresh ground loaves of bread, fritto misto makes a memorable meal.

Deep-fat frying should be done in small batches, so put an electric fryer where guests can fend for themselves. You could start the first-round and keep it hot in the oven for a few minutes until everyone is ready. A chilled rosé or dry white wine complements fritto misto. A chilled, soothing lemon soufflé is just the right ending.

STRATEGIES
Make the cold lemon soufflé the day before. The antipasto ingredients can be bought a day or two ahead, but the fish and bread must be absolutely fresh. The batter needs to chill 2 hours, so make it ahead. Some of the fish will need shelling, and if you use octopus or squid you'll need to do some precooking (see page 113).

Use part olive oil for the cooking fat for flavor; the proportion is a matter of taste. Remember the cardinal rule for deep-fat frying: never overcrowd the pan or the foods will fry unevenly. Use paper towel for draining the cooked fish unless you have a tempura pan with a wire draining rack.

Fritto Misto uses the freshest seafood available—sole, halibut, shrimp, lobster, clams, octopus and squid. Start off with a vegetable antipasto.

SEAFOOD FRITTO MISTO

2 egg yolks, beaten
3 tablespoons olive oil
¾ cup cold white wine
1 cup sifted all-purpose flour
1 teaspoon salt
3 pounds assorted fish and shellfish—choose 3 or 4 from the following: filets of sole, halibut, sea scallops, squid (see page 113); shelled and deveined shrimp (see page 108); rock lobster tails, cut in half lengthwise (see page 105); shucked clams (see page 110); sliced, cooked octopus; tiny smelts or fresh sardines.
olive oil and vegetable oil
lemon wedges

1. To make the batter, mix the beaten egg yolks with the 3 tablespoons oil in a bowl, then slowly add the wine, stirring constantly.

Cold Lemon Soufflé

2. Add the flour to the egg-wine mixture, stirring constantly, then mix in the salt. Chill the batter for at least 2 hours.

3. Pre-cook the squid and cut into rings; pre-cook the octopus and slice the tentacles. Cut the fish into bite-size pieces and shell the shrimp. Remove the lobster tail meat and cut into pieces. Keep the fish and shellfish chilled until ready to cook.

4. In a deep frying pan or wok, heat the oil to 375° F (use a candy thermometer to check the temperature). Put the bowl containing the batter in a larger bowl filled with ice. Coat the fish pieces in the batter, drain off excess, then drop the fish into the hot oil. Fry small pieces 3 to 4 minutes, larger ones 6 to 8 minutes, turning once to cook both sides. The cooked fish should be lightly browned. Drain briefly and serve with lemon wedges.

COLD LEMON SOUFFLE

1¼ cups lemon juice
1 cup sugar
2 envelopes unflavored gelatin
4 eggs, separated
1 cup heavy cream
rind of 1 large lemon, slivered
¼ cup water

1. In a saucepan, mix the lemon juice, ½ cup of the sugar, gelatin and egg yolks. Stir over low heat until the gelatin is dissolved. Remove from heat and let cool to room temperature in a large bowl.

2. Prepare a 1-quart soufflé dish by making a collar of aluminum foil around the top. This will add about 2 inches to its height. Lightly oil the inside of the foil collar and tie it tight with string.

3. Whip the egg whites until stiff and set aside. Whip the cream until it holds peaks. Fold the egg whites first, then the whipped cream into the lemon mixture. Carefully spoon this mixture into the soufflé dish. Chill in the refrigerator for at least 4 hours or overnight.

4. In a small heavy saucepan, mix the lemon rind, water and remaining sugar. Bring to a boil over high heat, lower the heat to medium and continue to boil slowly until the syrup is thick—about 5 to 6 minutes. Spoon out the rind, spread on wax paper and separate the slivers. Cool the candied lemon rind before using it to garnish the soufflé.

5. When ready to serve the soufflé, remove the collar and add the candied lemon peel around the edge.

The Essential Stewpot

No cooking is more elemental and satisfying than tossing succulent ingredient after ingredient into a bubbling, aromatic caldron. Be the results an elegant ragout or a thick country soup, they are the outcome of rich ethnic traditions developed by generations of cooks.

Stews can be prepared two ways. Browned stews offer richness from the deglazed cooking juices after all the ingredients have been browned. The other method adds cooking liquids to uncooked ingredients and lets the whole dish simmer, releasing flavors during cooking. Fish and veal are good candidates for the latter method; red meat takes well to the first.

Some stews benefit from "aging" in the refrigerator; day-before preparation gives them a chance to marry and deepen flavors. Chili and Burgundian stew are good examples. Others, like bouillabaisse and paella, cook quickly—taking less than 1 hour from first chopping to the table. These should be served as soon as they are ready; fish especially will toughen with an overly long heated wait.

The rest of the meal is easy: salad, bread, a simple dessert. Serving is equally relaxed: ladle at the table, straight from the pot or a big tureen. Check the Index for more ideas.

JAMBALAYA

Serves 8 to 10

Jambalaya is a Cajun triumph, a culinary verification of the 200-year-old cultural identity of a group of Americans whose heartland is now Louisiana. Their ancestors were Frenchmen who, in the 1700s, settled in an area of Canada then called Acadia (now Nova Scotia). When the English took over Canada, the Acadians refused to swear allegiance to the English flag and stop speaking French, so in 1755 the English deported them. And they, like so many others, brought their rich heritage with their pots and pans.

Cajun cooking is country cuisine and often very spicy. Cajuns cook rabbit and squirrels, gizzards and livers, as well as native fish, crawfish and many one-pot meals, rice, beans and all. Next to gumbo, jambalaya is the best-known Cajun food. With a salad of Bibb and escarole, cucumbers and red onions, warm sourdough bread and ice cold beer, the feast is on.

¼ cup butter
1 pound andouille or other smoked sausage, sliced
½ pound smoked ham, cut into small pieces
¼ cup flour
3 medium white onions, finely chopped
4 scallions, chopped
1 green pepper, chopped
4 cloves garlic, minced
4 ripe tomatoes, peeled and chopped, or 2 cups canned tomatoes, drained and chopped
1 bay leaf, crumbled
1½ teaspoons chopped fresh or ½ teaspoon dried thyme
¼ teaspoon cayenne pepper
1 teaspoon freshly ground black pepper
3 cups Brown or Chicken Stock (see pages 57 and 58)
1 cup diced cooked chicken
2 cups uncooked long-grain rice
2 pounds raw shrimp, peeled and deveined (see page 108)
salt

1. In a 5-quart frying pan or Dutch oven, melt the butter and sauté the sausage and ham until lightly browned.

2. Stir in the flour and add the onions, scallions, green pepper and garlic and sauté over medium heat until the vegetables are soft and the flour is lightly browned, about 6 to 10 minutes.

3. Stir in the rest of the ingredients except the shrimp and salt. The liquid should just cover the contents; add more

stock if needed. Bring to a boil, cover the pan tightly, lower the heat and simmer for 25 to 30 minutes, or until all the liquid is absorbed. Add the shrimp and continue to cook until the shrimp are pink, about 5 minutes. Taste for salt and serve.

CHILI CON CARNE

Serves 4 to 6

Chili con carne is part of our food heritage. Soul-warming kettles of this pungent stew made their debut when home was the range. Venison, buffalo and beef were the chief throw-ins, and free-growing chilies and close-at-hand seasonings added spice.

The settling of the frontier marked the close of an era. Thankfully, chili survived, though not unscathed. Some complain that we've diluted its pure beginnings. We contend that our culinary horizons have widened as tomatoes, onions, green peppers, celery and, yes, red pinto beans (originally served on the side) found their way into our pots.

Make the chili a day or two ahead and let the seasoning develop. Then heat it up slowly and serve with ice-cold beer, a salad that stands on its own (romaine, Bibb lettuce and escarole) and a plump loaf of sourdough bread.

1½ pounds ground beef (or 1½ pounds boneless lean chuck cut into ½-inch cubes)
1 medium onion, chopped
1 clove garlic, minced
1 green pepper, seeded and chopped
2 tablespoons chili powder
½ teaspoon paprika
2 cups Brown Stock (see page 57)
2 cups pinto beans, cooked (optional)
salt
freshly ground black pepper

1. In a heavy skillet or Dutch oven, sauté the meat over high heat until brown and crumbly. Push the meat to the sides of the pan and add the onion, garlic and green pepper. Sauté until the onion is golden and the green pepper soft—about 5 minutes. Spoon out any excess fat.

2. Add the spices and stock. Turn up the heat and bring to a boil, then lower the heat and cover. Simmer 30 to 40 minutes, or until the stew is slightly thickened. (Cook longer, about 1 hour, if beef is cubed.)

3. Add the beans, season to taste with salt and pepper and simmer another 5 minutes. Ladle into soup bowls and sprinkle sweet, mild, delicate flavor.

Shrimp, smoked ham, rice and sausage are the basics of a hearty Cajun Jambalaya.

MOUSSAKA

Serves 6 to 8

Politics aside, the hospitality of the Middle Eastern table has retained its warmth and ritual. Today these rituals still give us a feeling of warmth and continuity, a link with a rich, ongoing heritage.

Middle Eastern cuisine is probably the oldest in the world. Lamb and wheat have been staples there for some nine thousand years. We don't know who introduced the use of garlic, eggplant or olives to the region, but a prototype of pita, flat Arab bread, was found in an ancient Egyptian tomb. Travel and trade made such New World foods as tomatoes and peppers staples in the sixteenth century.

To complement the moussaka, serve pita bread and scented mint tea.

3 medium eggplants
salt
olive oil
2 large onions, chopped
1 clove garlic, chopped
1½ pounds ground lamb
1 tomato, peeled and chopped
½ cup tomato paste
3 tablespoons chopped parsley
salt
freshly ground black pepper
¼ cup butter
¼ cup flour
2 cups milk
dash grated nutmeg
2 egg yolks

1. Cut the unpeeled eggplant into ½-inch-thick slices. Generously sprinkle both sides of the slices with salt and let them stand on a large platter or in a colander for 30 minutes to allow the bitter juices to drain.

2. In a large skillet, heat the oil over medium heat. Pat the eggplant slices dry and briefly sauté them, turning once, until brown on both sides. Drain on paper towel.

3. In a separate skillet, sauté the onions and garlic in olive oil over medium heat until the onions are golden. Add the ground lamb and sauté until brown. Drain the excess fat from the cooked lamb. Add the tomato, tomato paste and parsley and mix well. Add salt and pepper to taste. Simmer for about 15 minutes, or until the lamb is cooked and the liquid is absorbed.

4. Preheat the oven to 375°F. To prepare the sauce, melt the butter in a saucepan over medium heat. Add the flour and cook for 1 minute, stirring constantly.

5. Add the milk and cook, stirring constantly, until the mixture simmers and thickens. Add the nutmeg.

6. In a small bowl, beat the egg yolks. Stir in a little of the sauce (to keep the eggs from cooking), then add this mixture to the sauce. Season to taste with salt and pepper.

7. In a buttered 13×9×2-inch baking pan, alternate layers of eggplant and meat mixture, ending with the eggplant. Spoon the white sauce on top and bake for 45 minutes. The top should be brown. Let the moussaka stand 10 minutes before serving.

CHOUCROUTE GARNIE
Alsatian Sauerkraut Stew

Serves 4

Choucroute *means sauerkraut and* garnie *refers to the accompaniment of sausages, strong, lusty flavors of garlic, onions and other vegetables. The joy, at least part of it, in this stew is the small amount of preparation that goes into it. All the ingredients can be bought ahead. The actual preparation time is very little, considering the heft of the pot. The entire meal can be put together in less than an hour.*

Serve the choucroute garnie with thick slices of black bread, bowls of red or white radishes and plenty of sweet butter.

2 tablespoons corn oil
2 medium onions, sliced
2 cloves garlic, finely chopped
1 tart apple, peeled, cored and chopped
1 carrot, thinly sliced
2 pounds sauerkraut, drained and rinsed with cold water
1 teaspoon caraway seeds
1 cup dark beer
¼ cup gin
1 pound Canadian bacon or smoked ham, cut into ½-inch-thick slices
4 knockwurst, bratwurst or kielbasa, cut into 2-inch pieces, sweet or hot Italian sausage or smoked sausage links

1. In a large saucepan, heat the oil and sauté the onion, garlic, apple and carrot until they are lightly browned, about 5 to 6 minutes.

2. Add the sauerkraut, caraway seeds, beer and gin. Cover and simmer for 10 minutes. Add the meats, cover and simmer, stirring occasionally, for 25 to 30 minutes.

Bouillabaisse is served as two courses—soup and entrée.

BOUILLABAISSE
Mediterranean Seafood Stew

Serves 6

Bouillabaisse, the fish stew native to Marseilles, has long been the subject of a culinary controversy over which version is really authentic. Some contend it's not the real thing unless fish indigenous to the Mediterranean— rascasse, lophius and rouget—are used. But as any fisherman's wife knows, the ingredients depend on the catch of the day, as long as there is a combination of fatty, oily fish, whitefish and shellfish. What distinguishes a bouillabaisse from other fish stews are the seasonings— saffron, garlic, tomatoes, onions and herbs native to Provence, in southern France.

It is served as two courses. For the first, the broth is served in large flat bowls over slices of French bread browned in olive oil with a spoonful of rouille, a hot pepper and garlic sauce, served on top. For the second course, the fish is served in the same bowl with more fried French bread and rouille. Boiled potatoes and a good chilled white wine are all that's needed to round out the meal.

The stew will take a little over 15 minutes to cook, so start the rouille first. Once the fish stew is ready to serve, thin the rouille with some of the hot fish broth and your first course is ready.

⅓ cup olive oil
2 cloves garlic, chopped
4 tomatoes, peeled, seeded and chopped
2 onions, chopped
2 leeks, sliced
2 tablespoons chopped fresh parsley
1 teaspoon crumbled saffron threads
¼ teaspoon crushed fennel seeds
1 bay leaf
1½ teaspoons chopped fresh or ¼ teaspoon dried thyme
1½ teaspoons chopped fresh or ½ teaspoon dried summer savory
3-inch strip orange rind
1 eel (about 1½ pounds), cut into 1½-inch pieces
2 pounds whole firm fish (mackerel, cod, bass, haddock or red snapper), cleaned, scaled (see page 97) and cut into 1½-inch slices—heads, tails, bones and all
1 cup dry white wine
2 lobsters (1 pound each), cut into pieces (see page 105)
2 pounds whole whitefish (sole, flounder, mullet or whiting), cleaned, scaled and cut into 1½-inch slices— heads, tails, bones and all
salt
freshly ground black pepper

1. In a heavy-bottomed 4-quart kettle or Dutch oven, heat the oil over medium heat and sauté the garlic, tomatoes, onions, leeks and parsley for 5 minutes.

2. Add the saffron, seeds, herbs, orange rind, eel, firm fish and wine to the kettle with enough water to submerge the fish. Cover, turn up the heat and bring to a boil. Uncover and boil over medium high heat for 8 minutes.

3. Add the lobster and tender fish pieces and continue to boil for another 8 minutes, or until the lobster is red and the fish tender. Season to taste with salt and pepper and serve—first the broth, then the fish.

ROUILLE

1 small red bell pepper, seeded and coarsely chopped
1 small green pepper, seeded and coarsley chopped
1 4-ounce can sweet green chilies, drained
1 4-ounce jar pimento, drained
3 cloves garlic
⅓ cup olive oil
¼ cup dry bread crumbs
Tabasco sauce
salt
½ cup bouillabaisse broth

1. Purée all the ingredients except the Tabasco, salt and broth in a blender or food processor. Season with Tabasco and salt and let stand at least 30 minutes at room temperature to marry the flavors. When the bouillabaisse is ready, thin the rouille with ⅓ cup broth and serve.

FRIED BREAD

1 loaf French bread
olive oil

1. Slice the bread into ½-inch-thick pieces.

2. Heat ¼ inch oil in a heavy skillet until it starts to haze (cloud and barely smoke). Arrange a single layer of bread in the skillet, brown on one side, turn and brown the other side. Keep the browned bread warm in a 200°F oven while frying other batches.

CASSOULET

Serves 6

Whenever a food tradition is handed down from generation to generation, controversy emerges. And so it is with the cassoulet, a provincial meal of beans and meats from southwestern France.

Debates rage on: should it be duck or goose; pork or lamb? What type of duck, goose, pork or lamb? The only points of agreement are that cassoulet should have the best white beans and should stew for as long as possible.

1 pound dried Great Northern or navy beans
6 cups water
1 onion, studded with 2 cloves
bouquet garni (see page 26)
1 teaspoon salt
1 5- to 6-pound goose or duck
salt
freshly ground black pepper
½ pound slab bacon or salt pork, cut into 1-inch pieces
1 pound garlic sausage, sliced
¼ cup butter
1 onion, minced
2 cloves garlic, chopped
3 tomatoes, peeled and chopped
2 cups dry bread crumbs
¼ cup melted butter

1. Soak beans in water to cover overnight. Drain beans and put in a large saucepan. Add water, whole onion, bouquet garni and 1 teaspoon salt. Simmer, covered, for 1½ hours, or until beans are tender. Drain and reserve the liquid.

2. Preheat the oven to 350°F. Sprinkle the goose or duck with salt and pepper and roast in a roasting pan for 1½ to 2 hours, or until the legs can be moved up and down easily.

Cool and reserve the fat in the roasting pan. Cut into serving-size pieces or remove skin and pull meat from bones in large pieces.

3. In a skillet, fry the bacon and sausage in butter until pieces are brown. Add onion and garlic and sauté for another 5 mintues. Add tomatoes and ½ cup of the reserved bean-cooking liquid and simmer 20 minutes.

4. Preheat the oven to 275°F. Put ½ the beans with bouquet garni in a 4-quart casserole. Top with bacon and sausage mixture and goose. (Add the reserved goose fat; it will flavor and enrich the beans.) Top with remaining beans. Add enough of the reserved bean liquid to cover.

5. Cover and bake for 2 hours. Sprinkle top with crumbs mixed with melted butter. Bake, uncovered, for 2 hours more, or until top is brown and crusty. Remove bouquet garni before serving.

BURGUNDIAN BEEF STEW

Serves 4 to 6

A tapestry of colors and fragrances, nothing in the world rivals the richness of a wine harvest in Burgundy. The holiday spirit is alive in the harvest feast. The stew (called a potée in France), a simple boiled dinner of pork, beef and sausage with root vegetables, cabbage, flageolets (small dried green beans) and herbs, is the essence of warmth and serious, simple food.

You can prepare the stew a day or two ahead. Time allows the flavors to marry and the fat to congeal for easy removal. Be careful not to overcook the stew when reheating—the vegetables and beans will get mushy.

After warming the stew, serve it in 2 courses—the broth followed by a warmed platter of meat and vegetables. A Dijon mustard sauce for the meat and French bread complement this delicious, filling meal.

½ cup diced slab bacon
2 medium onions, chopped
2 stalks celery, chopped
2 carrots, sliced
2 leeks, chopped
1 small yellow turnip, diced
1½ pounds boneless lean fresh pork shoulder
1½ pounds boneless lean beef, chuck or bottom round
1 1-pound kielbasa (Polish sausage), cut into 2-inch lengths
bouquet garni of 2 sprigs fresh parsley, 3 tablespoons celery leaves, 1 sprig fresh or ½ teaspoon dried thyme, 1 bay leaf, tied in cheesecloth
8 cups Brown Stock (see page 57)
2 large potatoes, peeled and quartered

Burgundian Beef Stew can be prepared a day or two ahead.

1 small green cabbage, quartered
2 cups cooked, dried or canned flageolets, drained
salt
freshly ground black pepper

1 In a large stew pot or Dutch oven, fry the bacon pieces over medium high heat until crisp. Remove and drain on paper towel. Reserve crisp pieces.

2. Add the onions, celery, carrots, leeks and turnip to the hot fat and sauté about 5 minutes.

3. Add the pork, beef, sausage, and bouquet garni to the pot and add stock to cover. Bring to a boil over high heat, skim off any surface foam, then lower the heat. Cover the pot and simmer gently for 1 to 1½ hours, or until the meat is tender. Skim off any excess fat.

4. Add the potatoes and cabbage. Cover the pot and simmer an additional 10 minutes, or until these vegetables are tender. Add the flageolets and simmer another 5 to 10 minutes, or until they are heated through. Discard the bouquet garni and season to taste with salt and pepper. The stew can be served immediately. Pour the

broth into a warm tureen and put the meat and vegetables on a warm platter. Slice the meat and sprinkle the vegetables with crisp bacon.

5. If you won't be serving the stew for a day or two, reduce the cooking time of the last batch of vegetables to 5 minutes. Remove the pot from the stove and allow it to cool away from the heat. When it is lukewarm, refrigerate the stew. Remove any congealed fat. Reheat, covered, by bringing to a boil over medium heat, then lowering the heat and simmering for 10 minutes.

MUSTARD SAUCE

Makes 1 cup

1 cup Crème Fraîche (see page 250)
1 tablespoon Dijon mustard
1 tablespoon fresh lemon juice
2 tablespoons chopped chives
salt

1. In a bowl, combine all the ingredients, adding salt to taste. Chill until ready to serve.

CARBONNADES A LA FLAMANDE
Flemish Stew with Beer

Serves 6

This Flemish beef stew is characterized by its full-bodied heartiness—a direct benefit of its beer-based sauce. As with a wine-based stew, the alcohol cooks off and the rich mellowness remains. Bacon, onions and mustard round out Belgium's national dish; sugar and lemon give it a hit of a sweet-sour piquancy. Serve with a green salad, a dark bread such as pumpernickel and plenty of chilled beer.

3 pounds boneless beef chuck, cut into 1½-inch chunks
salt
freshly ground black pepper
flour
6 slices bacon
3 tablespoons butter
4 large onions, sliced
2 cups dark beer
1½ tablespoons Dijon mustard
2 teaspoons sugar
1 tablespoon lemon juice
1½ teaspoons chopped fresh or ½ teaspoon dried thyme

1. Sprinkle the beef with salt and pepper and dredge in flour. In a heavy skillet or Dutch oven, fry the bacon over medium high heat until crisp. Remove the bacon, drain on paper towel, and set aside.

2. Add the butter to the bacon drippings and brown the beef on all sides, still over medium to high heat. Don't crowd the pan—sauté the beef in batches, removing the browned pieces to a warm plate.

3. When all the beef has been browned and set aside, lower the heat to medium and sauté the onions until translucent and golden—about 8 minutes. Return the beef to the pan and add the remaining ingredients. Bring to a boil over high heat, reduce the heat, cover tightly and simmer for 1½ hours, or until the beef is tender. If necessary, season again with salt and pepper.

4. Serve the stew sprinkled with the crumbled bacon. Dark bread and beer are traditional accompaniments.

A salad of chopped vegetables *(top)* accompanies lamb stew on a bed of couscous.

COUSCOUS LAMB STEW

Serves 8

Couscous is North Africa's pasta, a staple as basic as the potato. It refers to either the cracked wheat grain or a stew served with it. In North Africa (where it is the national dish of several countries) the stew can be based on seafood, vegetables, fish, poultry or lamb. Ours celebrates lamb, with plenty of vegetables for variety's sake.

Serve with small bowls of pine nuts, light and dark raisins, yogurt spiked with chopped mint, crumbled feta cheese and pita bread. Melon and dried fruits such as figs and apricots make an appropriate dessert.

2 cups couscous
1 teaspoon salt
4 pounds boneless lamb, cut into 1-inch cubes
salt
freshly ground black pepper
⅓ cup olive oil
2 large onions, sliced
2 medium zucchini, sliced
2 cloves garlic, chopped
2 green peppers, chopped
2 tomatoes, chopped and juices drained
1 large eggplant, chopped
4 cups Brown Stock (see page 57)
1 6-ounce can tomato paste
¼ cup fresh lemon juice
1 teaspoon turmeric
salt
freshly ground black pepper
1 20-ounce can chick peas

1. In a large bowl, mix the couscous and the salt. Add water a little at a time, using your fingers to make sure that every grain is moistened. Keep adding water and mixing until it is all crumbly and damp—no lumps.

2. Sprinkle the lamb with salt and pepper to taste. In a *couscousière* or large stock pot, heat the oil and brown the lamb. Add the onions, zucchini, garlic, peppers, tomatoes and eggplant to the pot. Stir in the stock, tomato paste, lemon juice and turmeric. Season with salt and pepper to taste. Cover the pot and heat until the stew begins to simmer.

3. Put the couscous in the top part of a *couscousière* or in a metal colander placed in the stock pot above the stew. Lower the heat and simmer the stew for 1 hour or until the lamb is tender. From time to time, uncover and stir the grain to keep it fluffy. During the last 15 minutes, add the chickpeas to the stew and season with salt and pepper, if necessary.

PAELLA

Serves 4 to 6

Like many traditional foods, the ingredients that give character to the Spanish paella vary according to the region it comes from. Inland, you'll find the hearty rice meal thick with vegetables, meat, game, poultry and sausages. Nearer the shore, the mélange includes seafood.

The simplest versions of paella mix rabbit, beef and ham or chicken, veal and sausage with the ever-present saffron rice, onions, garlic, peppers and tomatoes. A more extravagant version is rich with lobster, mussels, shrimp and clams, chicken, duck, ham and sausage. The finishing stroke: artichoke hearts, peas and capers.

For all the glorious options, the basic cooking method is the same. The meat and seafood are cut into small pieces for quick cooking and, if necessary, browned before the other ingredients are added. The seasonings and rice are sautéed in olive oil; then stock is added and the rice is baked like any pilaf until tender.

Paella takes its name from the large, round, two-handled iron pan it's cooked in. The paella pan looks like a flat-bottomed wok, and if you don't have a paella pan, a wok can be substituted for it (or use a large heavy skillet). In Spain, enormous paellas are sometimes cooked outdoors over wood fires, which makes a crust of browned rice in the bottom of the pan. Should your paella turn out the same way, don't worry—the crust is considered a delicacy.

Paella should be served as soon as it comes out of the oven. If put on hold for too long, the fish will get rubbery and the rice dry. You can do all the chopping and browning ahead and start with Step 5, 40 to 45 minutes before feasting begins. The actual cooking and arranging will take about 10 minutes; the baking, 25 to 30.

A meal in itself, paella is well accompanied by a salad of arugula, Bibb lettuce and watercress, tossed with oil, vinegar, salt and freshly ground pepper. Remember loaves of fresh, coarse bread and a bottle of dry white wine.

1 1½-pound lobster
½ pound hot or mild Italian sausage
¼ cup olive oil
1½ pounds small chicken pieces, such as thighs, drumsticks or breast halves
½ pound smoked ham, cubed
1 medium onion, chopped
1 green pepper, seeded and chopped
1 large tomato, peeled, seeded and chopped
1 clove garlic, minced
3 cups uncooked long-grain rice
4 cups Chicken Stock (see page 58)
½ teaspoon salt
¼ teaspoon crumbled saffron threads
12 littleneck clams
12 mussels, cleaned and scrubbed (see page 110)
1 pound raw shrimp, shelled and deveined (see page 108)
1 cup fresh or frozen peas
¼ cup pimento strips

1. With a cleaver or heavy knife, chop off the tail section of the lobster and cut it, shell and all, into 1-inch-thick slices. Cut off the large claws. Remove and discard the stomach and intestinal vein found in the body section, then quarter the body section, shell and all. Set aside and preheat the oven to 400°F.

2. In a small skillet (not the paella pan), brown the sausages over medium high heat for 5 to 6 minutes per side. Drain on paper towel and discard the sausage fat. Let sausages cool, then cut into ½-inch slices.

3. In a paella pan, large heavy skillet or wok, heat the olive oil over medium high heat. When it begins to smoke, add the chicken pieces and brown them evenly, about 10 minutes, turning frequently. Remove the chicken pieces and set aside.

4. Brown the ham in the paella pan and set aside.

5. Sauté the onion, green pepper, tomato and garlic in the paella pan, adding olive oil if necessary, until the onion is soft and the tomato liquid has evaporated. Push the vegetables to the side of the pan, add the rice, and sauté gently for 5 minutes.

6. Add the stock, salt and saffron. Stirring constantly, bring to a boil over high heat. At the first rolling bubbles, remove the pan from the heat. Arrange the chicken, sausage and ham on top of the rice, distributing evenly

7. Put the pan on the lower rack of the oven. If you're using a wok, put it on its ring so it won't burn. Bake, uncovered, stirring occasionally, for 20 to 25 minutes, or until the liquid has been absorbed and the rice is tender. Add lobster, clams and mussels (hinge side down so they can open), shrimp, peas and pimentos. Push down into rice and bake covered for another 10 minutes, or until shells open. Serve immediately.

Late-Night Suppers

There's always a special sense of camaraderie when friends gather around a communal table—especially in the middle of the night. After the theater or other people's parties, something more than a midnight snack is a fitting end to an evening (or start to an early morning). The solution: the late-night dinner— delightful, simple to serve and, ultimately, relaxing for everyone. Keep it cozy and informal, and with clever planning you can bring a select few home at eleven for midnight supper.

Welsh Rarebit

THE MENU
Serves 8

Welsh Rarebit

Broccoli, Green Beans, Carrots, Red and Green Peppers

Sesame Seed Bread

Amaretti Cookies

Pears Poached in Cognac

Welsh rarebit is a tradition from the British Isles, a simple, hearty dish whose original name, "rabbit," recalls hard times when cheese was the only "meat" on the table. If at the last minute you find that your gathering has turned into a crowd, just add more cheese and beer. Make the rarebit in batches: the fresher the rarebit, the smoother the consistency and the richer the flavor.

Welsh rarebit is usually served over toast, but we've taken it a step further for use as a sauce for raw vegetables, too. Serve it with beer and oven-toasted bread. Then, for a festive finale, pears poached in Cognac with tiny sweet cookies.

STRATEGIES

The pears can be poached the day before. The Italian cookies come in large red tins. Wash and trim the vegetables early in the day and keep crisp in ice water. Buy bread and wrap it well. Toasting the slices at the last minute will recrisp the bread. Grate the cheese. Ice plenty of beer; save one or two bottles for cooking.

When friends arrive, the only thing left to do is put the rarebit together. Welsh rarebit can be made in a saucepan on the stove or in a chafing dish at the table. It should be kept warm over very low heat.

WELSH RAREBIT

4 cups grated sharp Cheddar or Cheshire
2 tablespoons flour
½ teaspoon dry mustard
1 teaspoon sweet paprika
1 cup beer
1 teaspoon Worcestershire sauce
2 eggs
16 slices French bread or other crusty white bread, oven-toasted

Serve Welsh Rarebit with vegetables instead of toast.

1. Toss the cheese with the flour, mustard and paprika.

2. In a 2- to 3-quart saucepan or chafing dish heat the beer and Worcestershire sauce until bubbles just begin to form around the edges. You don't want the liquid to even simmer, much less boil. Add a handful of cheese and stir until it's melted. Continue stirring in the cheese, handful by handful, until it's all melted and the rarebit is smooth.

3. In a small bowl, beat the eggs. Add about 2 tablespoons of the cheese mixture to the eggs (to keep them from cooking too quickly). Add the eggs to the rarebit and stir until the mixture is glossy and smooth—a minute or so.

4. Keep the rarebit warm over a low heat. Spoon the rarebit over toasted bread or vegetables, according to individual preference.

VEGETABLES

Use 1 bunch raw broccoli, cut into pieces; 1 pound whole green beans; 4 carrots, cut into sticks; and 4 red peppers and 4 green peppers, cut into strips. Arrange on a platter and serve alongside the rarebit.

PEARS POACHED IN COGNAC

8 medium firm pears, peeled and left whole
1 cup sugar
peel from 1 lemon
1 cinnamon stick
8 whole cloves
½ cup Cognac

1. Put pears in a deep saucepan and add the sugar, lemon peel and enough water to just cover the pears. Add the cinnamon stick and cloves. Bring to a boil, lower the heat and simmer for 20 to 25 minutes, or until pears are easily pierced with a fork but still hold their shape.

2. When the pears have cooled in the sauce, stir in the Cognac and chill until ready to serve. Serve pears with poaching syrup spooned over them.

Tortellini

THE MENU
Serves 6 to 8

Tortellini

Tomato Herb Sauce

Fresh Herbs

Salsa Besciamella (see page 186)

Vegetable Sauce

*Green Salad with Vinaigrette Dressing
(see page 80)*

Italian Bread

Cantaloupe-Orange Ice with Marsala

Grapes

Tortellini, small pasta "hats" filled with chopped meat, cheese or spinach, are chewier than ravioli and more delicately shaped. They're the perfect pasta for buffet-style serving: easy to spear on a fork, with lots of little crevices to catch a delectable sauce or two.

Best of all, you can buy very good tortellini by the pound, either refrigerated or frozen, so the heart of your dinner is already halfway home. The real surprise is an assortment of sauces you "just happened to whip up" along with salad, bread and a homemade fruit ice.

STRATEGIES

Buy the tortellini (or make your own—see page 193), figuring 1 cup per person, and make the cantaloupe-orange ice the day before. You can also buy the bread and the fresh herbs the day before and keep well wrapped. Wash the grapes and chill them—at supper they can be used as a centerpiece.

Prepare the sauces the day before but cook them 5 minutes less than the recipes suggest. Cool them quickly, uncovered, to room temperature and then refrigerate until it's time to reheat them.

On the day of the gathering, wash and tear the salad greens into small pieces and store them in towels or plastic bags in the refrigerator. Prepare the dressing.

While you boil the water for the tortellini and reheat the sauces, slice the onion and toss the salad with the dressing. Be careful not to overcook the sauces; they'll lose their fresh taste. Chop the fresh herbs for the garnish.

Clockwise from top right: **Salad Vinaigrette, Tortellini with Salsa Besciamella, Tomato Herb Sauce and Vegetable Sauce and Cantaloupe-Orange Ice with Marsala**

TORTELLINI

4 pounds tortellini, fresh (see page 193) or frozen
10 quarts boiling water
1 tablespoon salt

1. In your largest cooking pot, bring the water to a rolling boil and add the salt.

2. Drop in the tortellini and boil for 10 to 12 minutes if fresh, 12 to 15 minutes if frozen. Drain and serve immediately in a heated bowl.

TOMATO HERB SAUCE

Makes about 1 quart

This sauce requires the best possible fresh tomatoes. If the sauce is overcooked, it will lose its fresh taste and some of its texture. If it seems too thin, add a tablespoon of beurre manié *(see page 142) and stir until the sauce thickens—not more than a minute or so.*

¼ cup olive oil
3 cloves garlic, chopped
10 large ripe tomatoes, peeled, seeded and chopped
1½ teaspoons chopped fresh or ½ teaspoon dried oregano
1½ teaspoons chopped fresh or ½ teaspoon dried basil
1½ teaspoons chopped fresh or ½ teaspoon dried thyme
salt
freshly ground black pepper

1. In a heavy 2-quart saucepan, heat the oil over medium heat and sauté the garlic until golden—about 5 minutes.

2. Add the tomatoes and herbs and cook over low heat, uncovered, for 10 to 15 minutes, stirring frequently. Add salt and pepper to taste and serve in a warm bowl.

FRESH HERBS

Makes about 1 cup

Fresh herbs are a seductive change from the expected grated Parmesan. You can also toss the pasta with olive oil or butter, then sprinkle the herbs on top.

4 scallions, white part only, sliced
8 sprigs fresh parsley, coarsely chopped
16 fresh basil leaves, coarsely chopped
¼ cup sliced fresh chives

1. Just before serving, slice or chop as directed and mix in a small bowl.

VEGETABLE SAUCE

Makes about 2 quarts

This is really stir-fried vegetables and can be made in a wok instead of a skillet. Be careful not to overcook.

½ cup olive oil
2 cloves garlic, chopped
1½ teaspoons chopped fresh or ½ teaspoon dried oregano
3 tablespoons red wine vinegar
1 pound green beans, cut into 1-inch pieces
4 small zucchini, cut into ½-inch pieces
1 pound fresh mushrooms, sliced
1 bunch broccoli, cut into flowerets
salt
freshly ground black pepper

1. In a large heavy skillet, heat the oil over medium heat and sauté the garlic until golden—about 5 minutes. Stir in the oregano and vinegar. Add the vegetables and stir over high heat for 5 minutes. Add salt and pepper to taste.

2. Serve hot in a warm bowl.

CANTALOUPE-ORANGE ICE WITH MARSALA

An airy confection of fruit and wine with a creamy texture and a delicate taste. Take it out of the freezer 10 minutes before serving. Slightly softened, it's easier to serve and has more flavor.

4 cups diced peeled ripe cantaloupe (2 medium melons)
2 cups orange juice
1 cup Marsala
1 cup sugar
2 egg whites at room temperature

1. Purée the melon in a blender or food processor. Pour into a bowl and stir in the orange juice, Marsala and sugar. Stir until the sugar is dissolved. Freeze until the mixture is mushy and frozen around the edges—about 1 to 2 hours.

2. Beat the partially frozen mixture with an electric beater until very smooth. This beating gives the finished ice its creamy texture.

3. In a separate bowl, beat the egg whites until they form stiff peaks. Fold the beaten egg whites into the beaten fruit ice, cover the container and freeze until hard—at least 6 hours or overnight.

New Classic Picnics

Gone are the days when a tuna sandwich, tired coleslaw and the old army blanket would be enough for an outdoor event. Now we're willing to spend a little extra time in the planning and preparation of food that's standard fare indoors but seems to acquire new tastes when brought outside.

The new classic picnic owes more to good planning than to high cost or fussiness. Baskets carry the feast and airtight containers keep the food fresh. Wood trivets from the kitchen smooth out rough terrain. A large jar becomes a soup tureen.

Our suggestions for four outdoor meals: a picnic for 6, a traditional New England clambake, a lovers' picnic and a no-cook picnic. With the obvious exception of the clambake, the cooking is all done ahead.

New England Clambake

THE MENU
Serves 12

Littleneck or Cherrystone Clams

Lobster

Corn on the Cob

Idaho Potatoes

Sourdough Bread

Salad with Garlic Dressing

Watermelon

Chilled White Wine and Beer

There is no feast more American than the clambake. A New England specialty long before the *Mayflower* landed, this method of steaming seafood and vegetables over hot stones and seaweed was devised by the Indians of the North Atlantic coast. The early Massachusetts settlers knew a good thing when they tasted it.

You don't have to live on the East Coast to hold a clambake. Most of the ingredients can be purchased from your friendly fish market. In the summer, fresh clams, fish and lobsters abound everywhere. Seaweed's a little trickier to find. Many fishermen pack their catch in seaweed, and the market will probably have some on hand or will be glad to order some for you.

STRATEGIES

The first priority is getting your order in to the fish market for the lobsters and clams (seaweed, too, if you're not going to gather your own). The refrigerator can be stocked well ahead with beer and wine—just transfer it all to ice chests or galvanized tubs. Everything but the potatoes must be absolutely fresh. Do the shopping the morning of the clambake. Wash and tear the salad greens and vegetables (store in plastic bags in an ice chest), mix the dressing in a jar with a tight-fitting lid, scrub the potatoes and cut the lemons and limes into wedges at home. The clams can be scrubbed at home and stored in pails covered with cold water until they're ready to go on the fire. Wrap the bread in aluminum foil so that it can be heated near the fire.

Here's the equipment you'll need for cooking and preparing: a covered pan to melt the butter, a serrated knife to slice the bread, a large plastic bag to toss the salad and dressing. You'll also need shovels for digging the pit, potholders or oven mitts, long-handled tongs, big plastic bags or baskets for gathering in the seaweed and a tarpaulin to keep the steam in during cooking.

Don't forget to take ice, matches, big plates, lots of napkins, forks and knives, cups or glasses and small bowls for the melted butter. If you're headed for a barren beach, take firewood along.

Arrive at the beach at least 5 hours before you plan to eat. That will give you an hour to dig the pit, collect the stones and build the fire. The fire must burn for about 2 hours before the stones are hot enough to cook on. The steaming takes about 1½ hours.

CLAMBAKE

4 bushels seaweed
1 bushel clams, scrubbed
12 2-pound lobsters
24 ears corn, silks removed but husks left on
12 Idaho potatoes, scrubbed
2 pounds butter
6 limes, cut into wedges
6 lemons, cut into wedges
salt
freshly ground black pepper

1. To protect your fire from the winds, dig a pit in the sand, 1 yard in diameter and 2 feet deep.

2. Collect approximately 50 to 60 large stones about the size of cantaloupes to line the pit. Put rocks on the bottom of the pit in an even layer.

3. Four hours before targeted eating time, start the fire. Add wood from time to time to keep it burning briskly for 2 hours. Then remove the charred wood and brush the ashes off the rocks. The rocks should be white-hot.

4. While the fire is burning, collect the seaweed and keep it wet in buckets or plastic bags. The best is rockweed— the kind with little air pockets that make it float—but any seaweed will do. The seaweed allows the water to drip on the hot rocks, creating more steam for cooking. It also adds a sea-salty flavor to everything under the tarpaulin.

5. Cover the hot rocks with 1½ bushels of seaweed. Drain the clams and put them in a wire cooker or canvas mesh bag and put it on the first layer of seaweed. (The clams, too, give out juices as they cook, which create steam and add flavor to the whole.) Next, the lobsters—either loose or in mesh bags—and another layer of seaweed, about ½ bushel. Add the corn and potatoes, then cover them with the remaining seaweed. Sprinkle the seaweed with water

A traditional New England Clambake consists of clams, lobster, corn on the cob and potatoes.

if it seems dry. Cover the whole clambake with a canvas tarpaulin large enough to be held down on the edges of the pit with rocks. Let the clambake steam for 1½ hours.

6. Approximately 30 minutes before eating time, put the foil-wrapped bread on the edge of the pit to heat up. Do the same to the butter 15 minutes later.

7. Remove the tarpaulin, push back the seaweed with a shovel (be careful, the fire and the steam it gives off will be very hot) and dig out the potatoes, corn, lobsters and clams with long-handled tongs. Give everyone a cup or bowl of melted butter for dipping, lime and lemon wedges and salt and pepper for seasoning the seafood.

Note. The only "must" in a clambake is the clams. Crabs, shrimp or any whole fish can be substituted for lobster. Chicken is frequently layered into the pit above the fish. Although corn and potatoes are almost always included, other vegetables such as onions and sweet potatoes combine well with clambake flavors. Just be sure to layer everything with plenty of seaweed.

If you can't make it to the beach, clams, lobsters, potatoes and corn can be steamed at home in a lobster steamer on the stove. Remove all but a single layer of husk from the corn and use the discards to line the bottom part of the 2-piece steamer. Add water to cover husks, layer in other ingredients in the top part of the steamer and steam over boiling water for about 1 hour, or until the potatoes are tender.

SALAD WITH GARLIC DRESSING

Robust garlic dressing is added to the bag of greens at the last minute for sand-free tossing and serving.

2 heads romaine, torn into pieces
2 heads leaf lettuce, torn into pieces
2 medium red onions, sliced
1 pint cherry tomatoes
4 cucumbers, sliced
2 cups olive oil
1 cup red wine vinegar
1 tablespoon salt
1 tablespoon sugar
1 teaspoon freshly ground black pepper
3 cloves garlic, minced

1. Put the greens and vegetables in a large plastic bag. Chill.

2. When ready to serve, shake the dressing ingredients in a jar or container with a tight-fitting lid. Add the dressing to the plastic bag and shake gently until the greens and vegetables are lightly coated.

Lawn Party

THE MENU
Serves 6

Crudités Marinated in Garlic-Basil Vinaigrette

Salmon Pâté with Melba Toast

Cold Zucchini Soup

Cold Stuffed Veal Roast with Yogurt Sauce

Brown Rice and Vegetable Salad

Fruit and Cheese

French Bread

Chilled White Wine

However elegant your outdoor meal, it's got to come together quickly. The idea after all is to get out the door. The tablecloth is a printed sheet; plates, cutlery and glasses the real thing.

STRATEGIES

Everything on the menu can be prepared the day before and spend the night in the refrigerator. The bread should be baked or purchased the day of the picnic. The fruit should probably be picked out a day ahead to be sure it will be ripe. (Overnight in a brown paper bag will take care of not-quite-ripe fruit.) Choose from peaches, pears, kiwis and apples.

The pâté, soup and yogurt sauce should be kept chilled. The same holds true for creamy cheese, and in very hot weather for all cheeses. Try a chèvre, Taleggio or a rich triple crème such as L'Explorateur.

CRUDITES MARINATED IN GARLIC-BASIL VINAIGRETTE

2 quarts assorted raw vegetables—any combination of the following: carrot sticks, celery sticks, sliced zucchini, whole scallions, button mushrooms, cauliflower, broccoli tops, whole young green beans
¾ cup olive oil
¼ cup fresh lemon juice
1½ tablespoons chopped fresh chives
1 clove garlic, mashed
salt
freshly ground black pepper
2 tablespoons chopped fresh basil (do not use dried basil)

Crudités Marinated in Garlic-Basil Vinaigrette *(center)*, Brown Rice and Vegetable Salad, Salmon Pâté and Cold Stuffed Veal Roast with Yogurt Sauce make an elegant lawn party.

1. In a shallow bowl, arrange the vegetables in groups.

2. In a small bowl, beat the oil, lemon juice, chives and garlic until thick. Add salt and pepper to taste and mix well.

3. Pour the dressing over the vegetables, cover and chill for at least 2 hours or overnight. Before you leave for your picnic, sprinkle with basil.

SALMON PATE

1 pound fresh boned salmon steak or filet or 2 7¾-ounce cans salmon, drained
1 cup dry white wine (only if using fresh salmon)
1 tablespoon pickling spice (only if using fresh salmon)
1 teaspoon salt (only if using fresh salmon)
1½ tablespoons capers, drained
1½ tablespoons lemon juice
1½ tablespoons pickle relish, drained
1 medium potato, boiled, peeled and mashed

⅛ teaspoon salt
⅓ cup melted butter
⅓ cup plain yogurt or sour cream (optional)

1. If you're using fresh salmon, put it in a skillet with the wine, pickling spice and 1 teaspoon salt. Bring it to a boil over high heat, lower the heat, cover the pan and simmer for 15 to 20 minutes, or until the salmon flakes easily (thin slices may cook faster). Let the salmon cool in the liquid, then drain. Discard the skin and bones and flake the fish into a bowl.

2. If you're using canned salmon, remove and discard any skin and bones and flake the fish into a bowl.

3. Mix the salmon with capers, lemon juice, relish, mashed potato, salt and butter. If you want a firmer pâté, pack into an oiled 4-cup terrine or mold, cover and chill for at least 2 hours or overnight.

4. For a creamier, more spreadable pâté, add yogurt or sour cream before packing into the mold and chilling.

MELBA TOAST

Crisp homemade melba toast has the perfect texture to go with the salmon pâté. We suggest using Italian or French bread, but any white or dark bread will work fine.

1. Bake ¼-inch-thick slices of fresh bread on a rack in the middle of a preheated 275°F oven until golden brown and hard—about 10 to 15 minutes. The slow oven keeps the slices from burning.

COLD ZUCCHINI SOUP

2 cups Chicken Stock (see page 58)
3 shallots, minced
1½ teaspoons chopped fresh or ½ teaspoon dried thyme
6 small zucchini (about 1¼ pounds), sliced
½ teaspoon salt
3 tablespoons dry sherry
¾ cup heavy cream
chopped fresh parsley or chives

1. In a 2-quart saucepan, bring the stock to a full boil. Add the shallots, thyme, zucchini and salt, lower the heat and simmer, uncovered, until the zucchini is tender—about 8 to 10 minutes.

2. Drain the zucchini, reserving the cooking stock and a few whole slices of zucchini. Purée the rest in a blender or food processor. Add the reserved stock and zucchini slices and blend until the slices have been chopped into small pieces and the soup is well mixed—a few seconds.

3. Stir in the sherry and cream and chill the soup, covered, for at least 2 hours or overnight. Taste for salt after the soup has chilled, and add more if desired. Serve the soup sprinkled with parsley or chives.

COLD STUFFED VEAL ROAST

Veal, lighter than beef and more flavorful than chicken, is boned, stuffed, then rolled up, roasted, chilled and sliced.

1 5- to 6-pound veal shoulder, boned, trimmed and rolled
salt
freshly ground black pepper
2 medium onions, chopped
½ cup chopped fresh parsley
¾ cup chopped fresh mushrooms
⅓ cup dry bread crumbs

1. Preheat the oven to 350°F. Unroll the roast and flatten into a sheet by pounding with a meat mallet or a rolling pin. Sprinkle lightly with salt and pepper.

2. Combine the remaining ingredients in a bowl and mix well. Add salt and pepper to taste. Spread the stuffing evenly over the flattened veal. Roll up the meat and tie it together with string at 2-inch intervals. Rub the rolled roast with salt and pepper.

3. Put the meat on a rack in a shallow roasting pan and roast for 2 hours, basting every 15 minutes with pan juices.

4. Let the roast cool, then refrigerate for at least 2 hours or overnight. Cut into ½-inch slices and serve with yogurt sauce.

YOGURT SAUCE

1½ cups plain yogurt
½ teaspoon curry powder
1½ tablespoons Dijon or Meaux mustard
1 teaspoon celery seed
1 clove garlic, minced

1. Combine all the ingredients in a small bowl, cover and chill for several hours or overnight.

BROWN RICE AND VEGETABLE SALAD

Instead of potato salad, serve nutty-tasting brown rice mixed with olives, pimentos and mushrooms.

1½ cups raw brown rice
4 cups Chicken Stock (see page 58)
1 cup mushrooms, quartered
¼ cup olive oil
¼ cup pimentos, drained and diced
1 cup (about 20) pitted black olives
2 small tomatoes, cored, seeded and chopped
2 tablespoons red wine vinegar
1½ teaspoons fresh chopped or ½ teaspoon dried oregano
1½ teaspoons fresh chopped or ½ teaspoon dried marjoram
salt
freshly ground black pepper

1. In a 2-quart saucepan, bring the rice and stock to a boil over high heat. Lower the heat, cover tightly and simmer, stirring occasionally, until the rice is tender—about 45 to 50 minutes—adding more stock if necessary.

2. In a skillet, sauté the mushrooms in oil for about 5 minutes.

3. While the rice is still hot, stir in the sauteed mushrooms and the remaining ingredients, mixing thoroughly. Add salt and pepper to taste. Let cool and then chill for at least 2 hours or overnight.

Courting Picnic

THE MENU
Serves 2

Cold Roast Chicken with Pork Stuffing

Eggplant Salad

Pickled Vegetables

Fruit and Cheese

French Bread

Chilled White Wine

STRATEGIES

Make the chicken and the salad the day before. The pickled vegetables—baby corn cobs, cauliflower, beans and pimentos come from jars at the delicatessen. All you have to do is mix them, add sliced scallions and chill. Choose some favorite cheeses and the most gorgeous ripe fruit you can find.

COLD ROAST CHICKEN WITH PORK STUFFING

1 2½-pound chicken
2 tablespoons lemon juice
¾ pound ground fresh pork
3 scallions, chopped
¼ cup fresh bread crumbs
3 tablespoons chopped fresh parsley
2 eggs, well beaten
1 teaspoon salt
1 tablespoon fresh or 1 teaspoon crumbled dried sage
¼ teaspoon freshly ground pepper
3 tablespoons butter
1 teaspoon sweet paprika

1. Preheat the oven to 450°F. Rub the inside of the chicken with lemon juice.

2. Prepare the stuffing by mixing pork, scallions, bread crumbs, parsley, eggs, salt, sage and pepper (your hands do the best job).

3. Stuff, sew or skewer the opening and truss the chicken (see page 120) and put it on the rack of a shallow roasting pan. In a small saucepan, melt the butter and mix in the paprika. Brush the melted butter over the chicken. Bake for 15 minutes, then lower the heat to 350°F and cook another 45 minutes, or until the chicken is tender.

4. Chill the chicken for at least 2 hours or overnight.

Cold Roast Chicken with Pork Stuffing and Pickled Vegetables

EGGPLANT SALAD

1 1-pound eggplant
1 medium onion, chopped
2 tomatoes, peeled, seeded and chopped
1 clove garlic, minced
½ teaspoon salt
¼ cup olive oil
2 tablespoons cider vinegar or lemon juice
1½ teaspoons chopped fresh or ½ teaspoon dried thyme
1 teaspoon chopped fresh parsley
salt
freshly ground black pepper

1. Preheat the oven to 350°F. Pierce the eggplant in several places with a fork and bake for 30 minutes, or until soft.

2. When the eggplant is cool, peel and dice it. In a large bowl, mix the diced eggplant, onion, tomatoes and garlic.

3. Mix the remaining ingredients together in a jar or bowl and toss the vegetables with the dressing. Add salt and pepper to taste. Chill for at least 2 hours or overnight.

The New Cornucopia

In a perfect example of the assimilation process crucial to the New Cuisine, we'll admit we saw the first version of this indoor picnic at a restaurant tucked into the hills above Nice in the south of France. There, in joyous celebration of local produce, glorious native vegetables and charcuterie were crammed, uncut and unadorned, into an outsize market basket and put on the unsuspecting diner's table. Mustard pots, cornichons, coarse salt and herbed mayonnaise soon followed, along with an easily

wielded knife and more cutting boards than plates. The joy was obvious and immediate—slicing off your own hunk of sausage is more fulfilling than eating someone else's prepared selection.

Best at a table of 4 or more—communal vibes buzz with the tactile delight of passing whole fennel to a friend, dipping zucchini with fingers instead of forks.

The vegetable choice is limited only by those few species that may look great whole but don't taste wonderful raw—like winter squash and potato. Include garlicky sausages, long breads or coarse, fat loaves. And consider the lovely promise of vegetable soup tomorrow.

Appendices

Freezing

There is a certain art to freezing that goes well beyond the usual rules of how long or what to freeze. It is based on a value judgment of what's worthwhile. You can freeze fresh green beans, for example, but why bother when they're available fresh year-round? Better to stash once-a-year berries; or several portions of stew for a quick meal; or butter for a puff pastry session; or egg whites because you've used the yolks in a Hollandaise.

But like all good art, you need to know the basics before dipping your brush (or wrapping the first package). Most important is the temperature of your freezer: for long-term storage it must be 0°F or less. Combination refrigerator/freezer compartments usually register 10°F. A thermometer will help you adjust the setting, or just check your ice cream: if it's hard, the temperature will be 0°F or less; soft and you can be sure it's above 10°F.

The actual wrapping is also important, since air causes freezer burn (a white film) and destroys the food's flavor. Wrap foods tightly in foil, plastic wrap or freezer paper; for long-term storage use heavy duty paper. If using freezer jars or plastic containers, remember that frozen foods expand, so leave one-half inch headspace and put a piece of foil or plastic wrap on top of the food to protect it from the air. Put the wrapped food in direct contact with the bottom or sides of the freezer for the first 12 hours for faster freezing. Then cover and freeze. Label everything with its contents, amount and date. It makes obvious sense to freeze in amounts you can use in one meal or for one use. Some cooks freeze stock, for example, in ice cube trays, so it's available cube by cube.

Most meats freeze well; a stew or meat in sauce will survive 3 months with little flavor change, although a beef steak or roast can be kept up to 8 months or longer with little deterioration in flavor. Fatty meats such as hamburger (which is best frozen in a flat shape for easier defrosting), should only be kept about 3 months. Chicken or turkey parts are good for 6 months (boned chicken breasts are an excellent emergency quick-thawing staple) and whole birds keep for 12 months. Whole ducks and geese retain their goodness for 6 months.

Fish loses some of its fresh taste when frozen, but it is still acceptable. Fish stews freeze quite well, but don't hesitate to freeze lean fish for up to 9 months; fatty fish and shellfish for 2 to 4 months.

Game can be frozen up to a year.

Vegetables should be quickly blanched in boiling water for a few minutes before freezing. Most last up to a year. Best candidates: vegetable stews or some short-seasoned vegetable you know you'll crave out of season. Packaged, frozen spinach is a perpetually useful staple, and commercially packed peas and artichoke hearts are good.

Most fruits freeze well, especially those in syrups or juice. Save space for peaches, rhubarb and berries that are only available fresh for a few precious months. To freeze berries, spread them out in a single layer on cookie sheets, freeze, then wrap tightly in plastic bags; this allows you to use 1 or 20 at a time. You can freeze a whole, unopened bag of fresh cranberries or buy frozen, unsugared, dry-packed fruits. Most fruits keep up to a year.

Breads are a joy to freeze; use a loaf slice by slice or heat crusty breads to regain their crunch. Most cakes, muffins and other baked goods change very little when frozen. It's best to freeze unfrosted cakes (freeze buttercream frosting separately). One of a freezer's best assets is keeping uncooked pastry on hand such as Basic Pastry (see page 267), Food Processor Puff Pastry (see page 275) or phyllo dough.

Sherbets, ice cream and frozen juices are obviously frozen foods to keep on hand, but think about the convenience of never running out of butter (it keeps 6 months), milk (also 6 months), cheese (except for some soft cheeses that crumble, most last up to 5 months) or stock (beef, chicken and fish are all invaluable). Egg yolks and egg whites are freezer naturals, since so many recipes call for uneven numbers of them; both keep up to a year.

Of course, there are some foods that should not be frozen because freezing destroys the crispness of many foods. They include salad greens, tomatoes, whole potatoes, raw celery, onions, peppers and grapes.

Glossary

Beyond basic cooking methods and simple terms such as "mix" or "mince," there are some culinary terms that need a brief description to understand recipe instructions. While some words are interchangeable, many have very specific meanings that affect the outcome of a recipe.

Al dente. Perfect pasta—cooked until it is firm to the touch and still slightly chewy without being tough.

Au gratin or gratinée. A simple way to dress up vegetables, meats and fish, the food is broiled or baked with a layer of bread crumbs and/or grated cheese on top until a savory, thin brown crust forms.

Bard. A method of keeping meat from drying out and adding flavor, to bard is to cover lean meats with a thin layer of fat, usually bacon or thinly sliced pork fat.

Baste. Another method for retaining and adding to a food's natural moisture and flavor, basting involves brushing or spooning moisture or fat onto the food before and during cooking. A bulb baster is useful.

Beurre manié. A classic and foolproof way to thicken soups, stocks or stews, *beurre manié* translates as equal amounts of butter and flour creamed together. It is then beaten into the liquid to be thickened and simmered.

Blanch. Also called parboiling, blanching is a brief cooking or immersion in boiling water. It removes strong flavors from foods, prepares other foods for freezing and also removes nut, fruit or vegetable skins (most notably, tomato).

Bruise. Release the flavor of foods, especially herbs and spices, by crushing them.

Caramelize. Turn sugar into a golden brown syrup by melting over low heat. It can refer to plain sugar or to the natural sugar in other foods, such as onions.

Clarify. Separate solids from a liquid. The term most frequently refers to butter when the golden oil is poured off from the whey that has settled to the bottom when the butter is melted.

Crimp. Seal a double crusted pie by pinching the edges together.

Cream. Not the dairy product, but a method of blending foods by mashing them together with a wooden spoon or a large fork against the sides of a bowl. Butter is the most commonly "creamed" food, usually with sugar or herbs.

Curdle. The undesirable effect of overcooking. When a food (usually a dairy product based sauce or custard) becomes lumpy or separated and forms curds.

Cut in. A pastry term that refers to the action in which shortening is literally cut into increasingly smaller pieces by hand, with two knives or with a pastry blender while simultaneously blending it with dry ingredients like flour.

Use cold shortening, and a coarse "meal" will soon form.

Deglaze. Add liquid to a degreased cooking pan after the food has been sautéed or roasted. While the liquid simmers all the browned particles and cooking juices are scraped up into the deglazing liquid to add flavor, color and substance to the final sauce.

Dredge. Helps food to brown easily by forming a dry coating of flour or bread crumbs on the outside before cooking.

En croûte. Food that is baked in either a pastry or a bread crust.

Filet. Refers to a piece of meat, poultry or fish that has been cut off the bone; also the action of deboning.

Flute. Decoratively finishing off the edges of a pie crust by pinching it against the edge of the pan, fluting can also mean cutting out a repeating pattern on mushroom caps or other vegetables or fruits.

Fold. Blending light, whipped foods such as egg whites or whipped cream into a heavier substance. Folding must be done carefully so as not to reduce the volume of the mixture and make it heavy. Folding is done gently with a rubber spatula by pushing the lighter food down into the heavier mixture, then raking along the bottom and up the sides again and again, gradually rotating the bowl to reach all the corners.

Glaze. Glazing coats food with a thick liquid or sauce that adds flavor or shine. Breads are glazed with egg yolks for a glossy crust; roasted birds are glazed with melted marmalade or jelly for flavor and gleam.

Julienne. A method of slicing food into long, thin, delicate strips—most commonly vegetables that are then sautéed or used as a garnish.

Marinate. Enhancing and often tenderizing the flavor of certain foods (generally meats) by immersing them in a seasoned liquid for several hours or longer. Acids such as lemon juice, vinegar and wine do the tenderizing.

Pan broil. Instead of broiling under heat, a heavy, oiled, preheated skillet is used to fry foods. The results are similar.

Parboil. Cooking in water for a few minutes to tenderize slightly such as onions, green peppers or cabbage for stuffing.

Pinch. Just that—the tiny amount of seasoning that can be held between your thumb and forefinger; an immeasurably small amount.

Proof. A baking term that describes a test to see if yeast is active (still able to make food rise).

Purée. A popular way of serving vegetables and fruits, the word technically refers to any food that has been turned into a smooth, thick consistency with a sieve, food mill, blender or food processor.

Reduce. Thickening liquid or lessening its volume by boiling, reducing also intensifies the flavors.

Roux. Similar to *beurre maníe*, a roux is a mixture of any hot fat and flour that is first cooked together and then used as a thickener in stocks, sauces or stews.

Scald. Bringing a liquid, usually milk, to just below the boiling point.

Score. Yet another way to tenderize meat or vegetables by cutting shallow slits at regular intervals; it also keeps them flat during cooking.

Steep. Tea and other dried foods such as mushrooms steep by resting in water that was first brought to a boil. Steeping hydrates the food and brings out its flavor.

Truss. Trussing keeps the wings and legs of a bird from overcooking or burning during cooking by tying them close to the body. On a large bird such as a turkey, these extremities should be released for the last segment of cooking so the meat under them can fully cook.

Measuring

LIQUID MEASURE VOLUME EQUIVALENTS

a pinch	=	slightly less than ⅛ teaspoon
a dash	=	a few drops
1 teaspoon	=	¼ tablespoon
1 tablespoon	=	3 teaspoons
2 tablespoons	=	1 fluid ounce
4 tablespoons	=	¼ cup or 2 ounces
5⅓ tablespoons	=	⅓ cup or 2⅔ ounces
8 tablespoons	=	½ cup or 4 ounces
16 tablespoons	=	1 cup or 8 ounces
¼ cup	=	4 tablespoons
⅜ cup	=	¼ cup plus 2 tablespoons
⅝ cup	=	½ cup plus 2 tablespoons
⅞ cup	=	¾ cup plus 2 tablespoons
1 cup	=	½ pint or 8 ounces
2 cups	=	1 pint or 16 fluid ounces
4 cups	=	2 pints or 1 quart or 32 ounces
1 quart	=	2 pints or 4 cups
1 gallon	=	4 quarts

SOLID FATS EQUIVALENTS

1 tablespoon		⅛ stick	½ ounce
2 tablespoons		¼ stick	1 ounce
4 tablespoons	¼ cup	½ stick	2 ounces
8 tablespoons	½ cup	1 stick	4 ounces
16 tablespoons	1 cup	2 sticks	8 ounces
32 tablespoons	2 cups	4 sticks	16 ounces

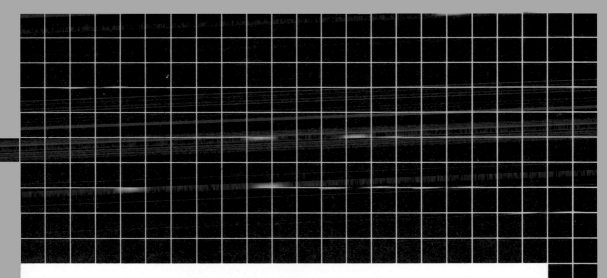

Index

□□□□

Page numbers that appear in **boldface** refer to recipe titles.
Page numbers that appear in *italics* refer to photographs.

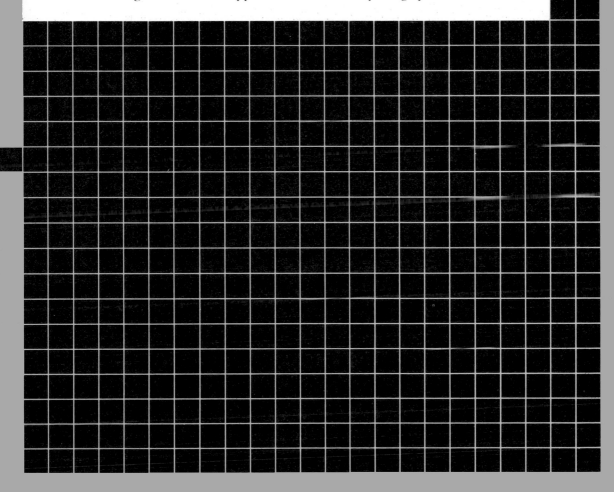

A

Acorn Squash with Apple Stuffing, **231**, *231*
agnolotti, *182*
    alla Puttanesca, **191**, *191*
    verde, *182*
Alfredo, Sauce, for pasta, **187**
allspice, 20, *21*
almonds, 19
    Cookies, Chocolate-filled, **285**
    Ice Cream, **303**
Alsatian Muenster, *278,* 280
Alsatian Sauerkraut Stew (Choucroute
    Garnie), **328**
anchovies:
    Bagna Cauda, **41**
    filets, 18
    paste, 18
    Sauce, with Broccoli and Cream,
        190
angel food cake pans, 28
angel hair pasta, *182*
    with Shrimp and Herb Sauce, *183,*
        188
    with Truffles and Sweetbreads
        (Capelli d'Angelo with Truffles
        and Sweetbreads), **176**
aniseed, 20, *21*
Antipasto, **43**, *43*
appetizers:
    Antipasto, **43**, *43*
    Artichokes, Stuffed, **219**
    Asparagus Mousse, **219**
    Asparagus with Mustard Sauce
        (Asperges a la Sauce Mou-
        tarde), **311**
    Baba Ghanoush (Eggplant
        Purée), **47**, *49*
    Bacon-Cheese Quiche, **275**
    Bagna Cauda, **41**
    Bean Salad, White, *49,* **52**
    Brie en Croûte, **42**, *42*
    Broccoli and Cheese Soufflé, **91**,
        91
    Carpaccio, *39,* **40**
    Caviar, 54
    Céleri Rémoulade, **42**
    Cheese in Crust (Cuscinetti), **273**
    Cheese Soufflé, **90**
    Cheese Tart (Quiche au Fromage),
        274

Chicken and Mushroom Soufflé,
    91
Chicken Mousse, Hot, **130**
Chicken Quenelles à la Crème,
    130, *130*
Cold Salmon Mousse, **103**, *103*
Country Pâté, **46**, *46*
Croque Monsieur, *39,* **40**
Crudités Marinated in Garlic-Basil
    Vinaigrette, **344**, *345*
Cucumber and Yogurt Salad, **47**,
    49
Curried Mushrooms with Red Bell
    Peppers, *39,* **41**
Cuscinetti (Cheese in Crust), **273**
Dolmathes (Grape Leaves Stuffed
    with Pilaf), *49,* **51**, *51*
Duck Liver Mousse with Endive,
    46
Eggplant Caviar, **49**
Eggplant Purée (Baba Ghanoush),
    47, *49*
Eggplant Salad, **347**
Eggplant Salad with Roasted
    Peppers, **223**
Eggs à la Russe, **83**
Eggs in Aspic, **85**
Endive Stuffed with Cheese, **44**
Escargots de Bourgogne (Snails in
    Butter and Garlic), **115**
Figs, Fresh, with Prosciutto, **45**
Fresh Figs with Prosciutto, **45**
Fresh Shrimp with Chive Butter,
    106
Grape Leaves Stuffed with Pilaf
    (Dolmathes), *49,* **51**, *51*
Green Beans Vinaigrette, **220**
Grilled Sweetbreads with Bacon,
    45
Guacamole, **42**
Ham with Parsley in Aspic (Jam-
    bon Persillé), *309,* **311**
Herbed Goat Cheese, *39,* **41**
Hot Chicken Mousse, **130**
Hot Shrimp Mousse with Sauce
    Aurore, **108**
Hummus, **47**, *49*
Jambon Persillé (Ham with Parsley
    in Aspic), *309,* **311**
Kibbeh, *49,* **52**
Leek and Potato Pâté, **226**, *227*
Liver Mousse, Duck, with Endive,
    46

Mozzarella, Smoked, with Oil and
    Black Pepper, **320**, *321*
Mushroom and Chicken Soufflé,
    91
Mushrooms, Curried, with Red
    Bell Peppers, *39,* **41**
Mushrooms Stuffed with Escar-
    gots, **43**
Mussels, Saffron, **110**
Mussels with Avocado Sauce, **43**
Mussels with Ravigote Sauce, **109**
New Potatoes Stuffed with Caviar,
    44
Onion and Spinach Soufflé, **91**
Onion Quiche, **275**
Pâté, Country, **46**, *46*
Pâté, Leek and Potato, **226**, *227*
Pâté Maison en Croûte, **273**, *273*
Pâté, Salmon, **345**, *345*
Phyllo Turnovers, *49,* **50**, *50*
Quiche au Fromage (Cheese
    Tart), **274**
Radishes with Butter (Radis au
    Beurre), *39,* **40**
Ratatouille, **223**
Saffron Mussels, **110**
Salmon Mousse, Cold, **103**, *103*
Salmon Pâté, **345**, *345*
Salmon, Smoked, with Horserad-
    ish Cream, *39,* **40**
Salmon Soufflé, **91**
Saucisson en Croûte (Sausage in
    Crust), **275**
Sausage in Corn Bread, **261**, *261*
Sausage in Crust (Saucisson en
    Croûte), **275**
Scallops and Shrimp with Green
    Sauce, *39,* *39*
Seviche, **104**
Shrimp, Fresh, with Chive Butter,
    106
Shrimp and Artichoke Toast, **44**
Shrimp and Scallops with Green
    Sauce, *39,* *39*
Shrimp Mousse, Hot, with Sauce
    Aurore, **108**
Smoked Mozzarella with Oil and
    Black Pepper, **320**, *321*
Smoked Salmon with Horseradish
    Cream, *39,* **40**
Snails in Butter and Garlic (Escar-
    gots de Bourgogne), **115**

Index

(appetizers cont'd.)
  Spinach and Onion Soufflé, **91**
  Spinach Timbale, **230**
  Stuffed Artichokes, **219**
  Stuffed Shells, Vegetable, with Dill
      Dressing, **320**, *321*
  Sweetbreads, Grilled, with Bacon,
      45
  Tapénade, **39**, *39*
  Taramasalata, **47**, *49*
  Tempura, **52**, *52, 53*
  Terrine, Veal, Ham and Pork, **45**,
      46
  Terrine, Vegetable, **233**
  Turnovers, Phyllo, *49*, **50**, *50*
  Veal, Ham and Pork Terrine, **45**,
      46
  Vegetable Custard, **89**, *90*
  Vegetable Quiche, **274**, *275*
  Vegetable Stuffed Shells with Dill
      Dressing, **320**, *321*
  Vegetable Terrine, **233**
  Vegetable Vinaigrette, *39*, **41**
  White Bean Salad, *49*, **52**
  Yogurt and Cucumber Salad, **47**,
      49
apples, 19, *240, 243*
  Baked, en Croûte, **270**, *270*
  Baked, with Brandy and Raisins,
      249
  Brown Betty, **300**
  and Calvados Omelet, **88**
  Calvados Soufflé, **92**
  Kuchen, *256*, **257**
  Pie, *264*, **268**
  Stuffing, Acorn Squash with, **231**,
      231
  Wine-Poached, **139**
apricots, *239*, 240
  Bread, **258**
  Glazed Yams, *312*, **314**
  Liqueur Sauce, **289**
  Sorbet, **246**, *247*
arborio, 204, *205*
artichoke, Jerusalem, *see* Jerusalem
      artichoke
artichokes, *215*, 216–218
  and Crab Meat Ravigote, **109**
  Heart Omelet, Creamed Crab and,
      88
  hearts, frozen, 19
  Oeufs au Beurre Noisette et (Eggs
      in Brown Butter with), **86**, *86*

and Shrimp Toast, **44**
Stuffed, **219**
arugula, 213, *213*
  Braised, **225**
asparagus, 213, *213*
  Asperges à la Sauce Moutarde
      (with Mustard Sauce), **311**
  Chilled, with Cold Mousseline
      Sauce, **220**, *220*
  and Ham on Puff Pastry with Sauce
      Madère, *76*, **173**
  Mousse, **219**, *220*
  Poached Egg with, *9*, **84**
aspic, 59
  beef, 59
  chicken, 59
  coating with, 59
  Eggs in, **85**
  emergency, 59
  fish, 59
  Jambon Persillé (Ham with Parsley
      in), *309*, **310**
  molding of, 59
Aurore, Sauce, **73**, *99*, 108
avocados, *215*, 216
  Bisque, **66**
  and Cucumber Soup, **66**
  Guacamole, **42**, *82*
  Salad, Chicken and, **234**
  Salad with Yogurt Dressing, **234**
  Sauce, Mussels with, **43**

B

Baba Ghanoush (Eggplant Purée), **47**,
      49
bacon, 19
  Canadian, *172*
  Cheese Quiche with, **275**
  Chicken Sauté with, **123**
  Frogs' Legs Wrapped in, **116**
  Grilled Sweetbreads with, **45**
  and Mushroom Frittata, **89**, *89*
Bagna Cauda, **41**
baked:
  Apple or Pear en Croûte, **270**, *270*
  Apples with Brandy and Raisins,
      249
  eggs, *see* eggs, baked
  Fish with Sauce Aurore, **99**, *99*
  Ham, *33*, **173**

Papaya, **250**
Potato, **295**, *295*
Spaghetti Squash, **231**
Stuffed Fish, **98**, *98*
baking, 16, *16*
baking, clay, 17, *17*
baking equipment, 28
baking pans, 28
baking pellets, aluminum, 28
baking powder, 19
Baking Powder Biscuits, **262**
baking sheets, 28
baking soda, 19
bananas, 240, *240*
  Bread, **258**
  Fritters, **249**
  Sautéed, **249**, *285*
Banh Cam (Sesame Cakes), **285**, *285*
Barbecued Spare Ribs, Jimmy's, **169**
barbecuing, *see* grilling
barley, 209
  Salad, **210**
  Soup, **60**
Basic Boiled Greens, **224**
Basic Brown Sauce (Espagnole Sauce),
      70, **75**
Basic Nut Bread, **258**
Basic Pastry, **264**, *266*, **267**
Basic White Bread, *252*, **254**, *255, 256*
basil, 20, *21*
  Pesto (Sauce), **187**, *187*
bass, sea, *94, 96*
bass, striped, *94, 96*
bay leaf, 20, *21*
beans, 18, 200–203
  Baked, New England, **203**
  black, 200, *200*
  black-eyed peas, 200, *200*
  Black-Eyed Peas with Ham, **201**
  cannellini, 200
  Cannellini Salad with Tuna, **201**
  Cassoulet, **330**
  chickpeas, 200, *200*
  Chickpea Salad, **202**
  Curried Kidney, **202**
  Dal and Tomatoes, **203**
  dried vs. canned, 200
  essentials of, 200
  fava, 200, *213*, 215
  flageolets, 200
  Flageolet Salad, **202**
  green, *213*, 215
  Green, Vinaigrette, **220**

Haricots Blanc et Tomates (White, and Tomatoes), **311**
kidney, 200, *201*
Kidney, Curried, **202**
Lentil Pilaf, **202**
lentils, 200, *201*
Lentil Soup, Cold, **68**
lima, 200, *213*, 215
Louisiana Red, and Rice, **206**
mung, 200–201
navy, 201
New England Baked, **203**
pink, *213*
pinto, 201
Red, Louisiana, and Rice, **206**
Refried (Frijoles Refritos), **203**
split peas, 201
Stewed Pinto, **203**
Soup, **62**
wax, *213*, 215
White, Salad, *49*, **52**
White, and Tomatoes (Haricots Blanc et Tomates), **311**
Béarnaise Sauce, 70, **77**, *78*
    Blender or Food Processor, **78**
Beaumont, *278*, 280
Béchamel Sauce, **70**, *70*
beef, 152–156, *152*
    aspic, 59
    Braised, with Mustard, **153**, *153*
    Brisket, **154**
    brisket cut of, *152*
    Carbonnades à la Flamande (Flemish Stew with Beer), **333**
    Carpaccio, *39*, **40**
    Châteaubriand à la Bordelaise (Filet Mignon Wrapped in Forcemeat with a Bordelaise Sauce), **154**, *155*
    Corned Beef Hash and Eggs, **298**, *298*
    essentials of, 152
    Gravy, Old-Fashioned, **297**, *297*
    ground, *152*
    and Kidney Pie, **176**
    as leftover, 32
    raw, Carpaccio, **40**
    rib, roast, whole with short ribs, *152*
    ribs, boneless roast, *152*
    ribs, short, *152*
    Ribs, Short, Braised with Horseradish Sauce, **156**
    round-bone sirloin, *152*
    serving of, 152
    Shabu-Shabu, **154**
    shank-cross cuts, *152*
    short ribs, *152*
    Short Ribs, Braised, with Horseradish Sauce, **156**
    Standing Rib Roast of, **297**, *297*
    steak, whole with short rib, *152*
    Stew, Burgundian, **330**, *331*
    stir-frying of, 13, *13*
    Stock, **57**
    tenderloin, *152*
    tournedos, *152*
    Tournedos with Bordelaise Sauce, *75*, **154**
    and Vegetables, Stir-Fried, **155**
    Vegetable Soup with, **60**
    see also steak, beef; roast beef
beef round:
    bottom, *152*
    top, *152*
Beer Bread, **257**
beets, 215, *215*
    Borscht (Soup), **66**
    Marinated, **220**
    Red Flannel Hash, **298**
    Salad, and Ham, **236**
beluga caviar, 54
Besciamella, Salsa, **186**, 338, *338*
Beurre Blanc (White Butter), **80**, *80*
    Salmon Steak with, **99**
Beurre Noir (Brown Butter), **80**
Beurre Noisette (Brown Butter), **80**
bibb lettuce, 213, *213*
Birthday Cake, **301**, *302*
Biryani, Chicken, **126**
biscuits:
    Baking Powder, **262**
    Buttermilk, **262**
    Cheese, **262**
Bisque, Avocado, **66**
black beans, 200, *200*
    Soup, **62**
blackberries, *243*, 244
black-eyed peas, 200, *200*
    with Ham, **201**
black pepper, freshly ground, *21*, 24
black peppercorns, *21*, 24
Blender Hollandaise or Béarnaise, **78**
Blender Mayonnaise, **79**
Bleu d'Auvergne, 283, *283*
blueberries, *239*
    Muffins, **294**
    Pancakes, **292**
bluefish, *94*, 96
Boiled Lobster, **104**
Boiled Rice, **205**
boiling, 14, *14*
    vegetables, 219
bok choy, *216*, 218
    Sweet and Pungent, **220**
Bolognese Sauce, **190**
Bordelaise Sauce, **75**, *75*, 154
Borscht (Beet Soup), **66**
Boston lettuce, 213, *213*
bottoni (buttons), *182*
Bouillabaisse (Mediterranean Seafood Stew), **329**, *329*
bouquet garni, 18, 26
Bourbon Sweet Potatoes, **229**
Boursault, *278*, 281
bowls, 27
brains, 174, *174*
    in Black Butter, **178**
    preparation of, 174
braised:
    Arugula, **225**
    Beef with Mustard, **153**, *153*
    Celery Hearts, **222**
    Chinese Cabbage, **222**
    Dandelion Greens, **225**
    Leeks, **226**
    Partridge, **144**
    Rice with Saffron (Risotto Milanese), **208**
    Salsify, **230**
    Short Ribs with Horseradish Sauce, **156**
    Veal Roast, **161**
    Veal Shanks (Osso Buco Milanese), **158**
braising, 14, *14*
    vegetables, 219
brandied fruits, packaged, 19
Bran Muffins, **294**, *294*
Bratchäs, 281, *283*
bread crumbs, packaged, 18
breads, 251–262
    Apple Kuchen, *256*, **257**
    Apricot, **258**
    Baking Powder Biscuits, **262**
    Banana, **258**
    Basic Nut, **258**
    Basic White, *252*, **254**, *255*, *256*
    Beer, **257**

Index

(breads cont'd.)

Brioche Loaves, **256,** *256*
Buttermilk Biscuits, **262**
Carrot Wheat-Germ, *258,* **260**
Cheese, *258,* **260**
Cheese Braid, **254,** *256*
Cinnamon Rolls, *256,* **257**
Cranberry-Orange, **258**
for croutons, 19
flours in, 252
freezing and defrosting of, 252, 351
French, **256,** *256*
Fried, **330**
glazes of, 252
Herbed, **254,** *256*
Irish Soda, **260**
Katchapuri with Salmon, **257**
Popovers, **262**
Prosciutto and Onion, **260**
quick, 258–262
quick, essentials of, 258
rising process of, 252
Rye, *256,* **257**
Sausage in Corn, **261,** *261*
Sicilian Pizza, *256,* **257**
Skillet Corn, **261**
sticks, 19
Wheat-Germ, *258,* **260**
Whole-Wheat Health, **256,** *256*
yeast, 252–258
yeast, essentials of, 252
Brie en Croûte, **42,** *42*
Brie de Meaux, *278,* **280**
Brillat-Savarin, *278,* **281**
Brin d'Amour, **283,** *283*
Brioche Loaves, **256,** *256*
Brisket, 152, **154**
broccoli, 215, *215*
Anchovy and Cream Sauce, **190**
and Cheese Soufflé, **91,** *91*
rabe, *216*
steamed, Hollandaise on, 77
steaming of, 12, *12*
broiled:
Fish Steaks, **99**
Squab with Raspberry Vinegar Sauce, **140**
Squid, **113**
broiling, 15, *15*
Brown Butter (Beurre Noir or Beurre Noisette), **80**
Brownies, **300**

Brown Rice and Vegetable Salad, *345,* **346**
Brown Rice Salad, **207**
Brown Sauce, Basic (Espagnole Sauce), 70, **75**
Brown Stock, **57**
Brussels sprouts, *216,* 218
and Cauliflower with Cream Sauce, **222,** *222*
and Chestnuts, *312,* **314**
Bucheron, *278,* 281
buckwheat groats, *see* kasha
bulghur wheat, 18, 209
Kibbeh, *49,* **52**
Bundt pans, 28
Buñuelos, **286**
Burgundian Beef Stew, **330,** *331*
Burgundy, Eggs in, *83,* **84**
butter, 19
Beurre Blanc (White), **80,** *80*
Beurre Noir (Brown), **80**
Beurre Noisette (Brown), **80**
Chive, **79,** *79*
Clarified, **79**
freezing of, 351
butter beans, *see* lima beans
Butterflied Leg of Lamb, **166**
Buttermilk Biscuits, **262**

C

cabbage:
Chinese, 215
Chinese, Braised, **222**
green (head), 215, *215*
red, 215, *215*
savoy, 215, *216*
shredding of, 31, *31*
Steamed, and New Potatoes, **221,** *222*
Stuffed Savoy, **221**
Cabécou, *278,* 281
Caerphilly, **283,** *283*
Cajun:
Jambalaya, **326,** *327*
Rabbit, **145,** *146*
Shrimp Etouffée, *106,* **107**
cake pans, 28
cakes:
Birthday, **301,** *302*
Chocolate Mousse, **287**

freezing of, 351
layers, baking of, 16, *16*
Sesame (Banh Cam), **285,** *285*
see also tortes
cake testers, 28
calamari, *see* squid
calculated cooking, 32–33, *33*
Calvados:
Chicken with Cream and, **125,** *125*
Roast Goose with Fennel and, **139**
calves' liver, *see* liver, calves'
Camembert, *278,* 280
canisters, 28
cannaroni regati, *182*
canned ingredients, 18–19
cannellini beans, 18, 200
Salad with Tuna, **201**
cantaloupe, *240,* 244
Orange Ice with Marsala, *338,* **340**
Cantonese Lobster, **105**
capelli d'angelo (angel hair), *182*
Shrimp and Herb Sauce, **188**
with Truffles and Sweetbreads, **176**
capellini, *182*
capers, 18, 20, *21*
capon, *see* chicken
caraway seed, 20, *21*
Carbonnades à la Flamande (Flemish Stew with Beer), **333**
cardamon, 20, *21*
Carpaccio, *39,* **40**
Carp roe, Taramasalata, **47,** 49
carrots, 19, 213, *213*
julienne technique for, 31, *31*
Julienne of Vegetables, **316**
Wheat-Germ Bread, *258,* **260**
casserole cookware, 28
casseroles, *see* stews
Cassoulet, **330**
Castello, **283,** *283*
cauliflower, *215,* 216
and Brussels Sprouts with Cream Sauce, **222,** *222*
Cream of Any Vegetable Soup, **59**
caviar, 18, 54, *54*
beluga, 54
Eggs with Sour Cream and, **83**
lumpfish and whitefish, 54
New Potatoes Stuffed with, **44**
osetra, 54
pressed or broken, 54

red, 54
sevruga, 54
cayenne pepper, *21,* 24
celeriac (celery root), *216,* 218
Salad, and Tomato, **235**
Céleri Rémoulade, **42**
celery, 19, *215,* 216
Cream of Any Vegetable Soup, **59**
Hearts, Braised, **222**
celery root, *see* celeriac
celery seed, 20, *21*
cellophane noodles, 18
Chasseur, Sauce, **79,** *129*
Châteaubriand à la Bordelaise (Filet
Mignon Wrapped in Force-
meat with a Bordelaise Sauce),
154, *155*
Chaumes, *278,* 280
cheese, 19, 278–283, *278, 283*
Baked Eggs with, **85**
Biscuits, **262**
Braid, **254,** *256*
Bread, *258,* **260**
Brie en Croûte, **42,** *42*
and Broccoli Soufflé, **91,** *91*
Croque Monsieur, *39,* **40**
Cuscinetti (in Crust), **273**
Endive Stuffed with, **44**
essentials of, 278–280
firm, 280
freezing of, 351
Fresh Figs with Prosciutto, **45**
Gruyère Omelet, **87**
hard, 280
Herbed Goat, *39,* **41**
listing of, 280–283
Pears Stuffed with, **284,** *284*
Phyllo Turnovers, *49,* **50,** *50*
purchasing of, 278
Quiche, with Bacon, **275**
Quiche au Fromage (Tart), **274**
Scrambled Eggs au Poivre, **87**
semisoft, 278
soft, 278
Soufflé, **90**
storing of, 278
Tart (Quiche au Fromage), **274**
Welsh Rarebit, **337,** *337*
see also specific cheeses
Cheesecake, Ricotta, **272,** *272*
cherries, 239–240, *239*
Pie, **268,** *269*
chervil, 20, *21*

chestnuts:
and Brussels Sprouts, *312,* **314**
Mousse in a Meringue Shell, **316,**
316
Purée, **223**
in Rum, *316,* **318**
Chèvre Cendré, **283,** *283*
Chevron, *278,* 281
chicken, 119–132
and pie, 59
and Avocado Salad, **234**
Basic Broiled, **121**
Basic Roast, **120,** *120*
Biryani, **126**
breasts, 128–132
Breasts, Cold Cutlets with Herb
Mayonnaise, **128**
breasts, fileting of, *128*
Breasts with Ginger Sauce, *8,* **129**
Breasts, Poached, **131**
Breasts Sautéed with Hunter's
Sauce, **129**
breasts, skinning and boning of,
128
Breasts, Suprêmes au Chasseur
(Sautéed with Hunter's Sauce),
129, *129*
broiler, 119, *119*
broth, 18
buying of, 120
capon, 119, *119*
clay baking of, 17, *17*
Cold Roast, with Pork Stuffing,
347, *347*
Coq au Vin, **124,** *125*
with Cream and Calvados, **125,**
125
Cream Gravy for, **127**
cutlets, *see* breasts
cutting up, *122*
essentials of, 119–120
freezing, 351
Fried, Herb Batter, **127**
Fried, Southern, **127**
frozen, 19, 351
fryer, 119, *119*
Herb, **121**
Herb Batter Fried, **127**
Herbed, **121**
Hot Mousse, **130**
Lemon, **121**
Liver Mousse with Endive as variation, **46**

Livers, Baked Eggs with, **85**
Marinated, **121**
Mousse, Hot, **130**
and Mushroom Soufflé, **91**
with Olives, **126**
Pesto Salad, **319,** *320*
Pie, Phyllo, **131**
Pie, and Sausage, **274,** 275
Poule au Pot (Poached), **121**
Provençale, **123**
pullet, 119, *119*
roaster, 119, *119*
and Sausage Pot Pies, **274,** *275*
Sauté with Bacon, **123**
Sauté with Herbs, and White Wine,
123, *124*
Sauté with Mushrooms, **123**
Sauté with Pancetta, **123**
Sauté with Salt Pork, **123**
Sautéed Breasts with Hunter's
Sauce (Suprêmes au Chaus-
seur), **129**
sizes of, 119
Soup, **58**
and Sorrel Salad, **131**
Southern Fried, **127**
stewing, 119, *119*
Stew with Couscous, **126**
Stir-Fry Green, **129**
Stock, **58**
Storing of, 120
suprêmes, *see* breasts
Tortillas, **131**
types of, 119, *119*
Quenelles à la Crème, **130,** *130*
Vegetable Sauté, **123**
chickpeas (garbanzo beans), 18, 200,
200–201
Hummus, **47,** *49*
Salad, **202**
chicory, 19, *213*
Child, Julia, 9
Chili con Carne, **326**
chilies, 18
Chive Butter, **79,** *79*
with Shrimp, Fresh, **106**
chives, *21,* 22
chocolate, 19
Almond Cookies filled with
(Tuiles aux Amandes), **285**
Brownies, **300**
Chip, Cookies, **298**
Dipped Fruits, **246**

(chocolate cont'd.)
Filling, **287**
Hot Mocha Soufflé, **92**
Ice Cream, **303**
Mousse Cake, **287**
Soufflé, **92**
Torte, with Orange, **271**, *271*
chopping, 30–31, *30–31*
chopping boards, 27
chops, lamb, *162*
Herb Garlic, **166**
Sesame, **166**
chops, pork, *169*
Stuffed, **170**
stuffing of, 170, *170*
chops, veal, *156*
Sautéed with Cream Sauce, *160*,
161
with Vegetable Sauce, **161**
Choucroute Garnie (Alsatian Sauer-
kraut Stew), **328**
Chowder, Seafood, **66**
Christmas celebration, 315–319
Chestnut Mousse in a Meringue
Shell, **316**, *316*
Chestnuts in Rum, *316*, **318**
Christmas Pudding, *316*, **318**
Hard Sauce, *316*, **319**
Julienne of Vegetables, **316**, *316*
menu for, 315
Roast Goose with Sausage-Apple
Stuffing, **315**, *316*
strategies for, 315
Wild Rice with Mushrooms, **316**,
316
chutney, 18
cinnamon, *21*, 22
Cinnamon Rolls, *256*, **257**
Cinnamon Toast, **295**
Cioppino, San Francisco, **66**
clams, 18, *94*, 96
Clambake, **342**, *342*
on the Half Shell, **111**
hard-shell, *94*, 96
juice, 18
preparation of, *110*
soft-shell, *94*, 96
White Sauce, **188**
Clarified Butter, **79**
clay baking, 17, *17*
cloves, *21*, 22
cocktail party recipes, 43–45
Endive Stuffed with Cheese, **44**

Fresh Figs with Prosciutto, **45**
Grilled Sweetbreads with Bacon,
45
Mushrooms Stuffed with Escar-
gots, **43**
Mussels with Avocado Sauce, **43**
New Potatoes Stuffed with Caviar,
44
Shrimp and Artichoke Toast, **44**
Cocoa, 19, **295**
Coconut Milk and Peas, Shrimp with,
109
Coeur à la Crème, **284**
coffee:
frozen, 19
Hot Mocha Soufflé, **92**
Ice Cream, **303**
Mousse, Frozen with Amaretto-
Orange Sauce, **289**
coffeepots, 28
colanders, 28
Cold Cucumber Soup, **66**, *66*
Cold Lemon Soufflé, **324**, *324*
Cold Lentil Soup, **68**
Cold Mousseline Sauce, **220**, *220*
Cold Poached Trout with Watercress-
Lime Sauce, **101**
Cold Roast Chicken with Pork Stuffing,
347, *347*
Cold Salmon Mousse, **103**, *103*
Cold Stuffed Veal Roast, *345*, **346**
cold summer supper, 319–321
Chicken Pesto Salad, **319**, *320*
menu for, 319
Smoked Mozzarella with Oil and
Black Pepper, **320**, *320*
strategies for, 319
Vegetable Stuffed Shells with Dill
Dressing, **320**, *320*
Cold Tomato Sauce, **194**
Cold Zucchini Soup, **346**
collard greens, *216*
combination pastry, 264
comfort foods, 291–303
Almond Ice Cream, **303**
Apple Brown Betty, **300**
Baked Potato, **295**, *295*
Beef, Standing Rib Roast of, **297**,
297
Birthday Cake, **301**, *301*
Blueberry Pancakes, **292**
Brownies, **300**
Chocolate Chip Cookies, **298**

Chocolate Ice Cream, **303**
Cinnamon Toast, **295**
Cocoa, **295**
Coffee Ice Cream, **303**
cookies, *299*
Corned Beef Hash and Eggs, **298**,
298
Custard, **301**, *301*
Flan, **300**
French Toast, **292**, *292*
French Vanilla Ice Cream, **303**
Fruit Ice Cream, **303**
Gravy, Old-Fashioned Beef, **297**,
297
homemade ice cream, *264*, 303
Liqueur Ice Cream, **303**
Mashed Potatoes, **297**, *297*
Muffins, Blueberry, **294**, *294*
Muffins, Bran, **294**, *294*
Muffins, Corn, **294**, *294*
Oatmeal, **292**, *292*
Oatmeal Cookies, **298**
Pancakes, **292**
Peach Cobbler, **300**
Peanut Butter Cookies, **299**
Peppermint Ice Cream, **303**
Red Flannel Hash, **298**
Rice Pudding, **301**, *301*
Stewed Tomatoes, **297**, *297*
Vanilla Ice Cream, **303**
conchiglie (seashells), *182*
containers, lidded, 28
cookies, *299*
Buñuelos, **286**
Chocolate Chip, **298**
Chocolate-filled Almond (Tuiles
aux Amandes), **285**
Oatmeal, **298**
Peanut Butter, **299**
Pine Nut, **284**
Sesame Seed, **284**
cooking techniques, 12–17, *12–17*
cookware, 27, 28
Coq au Vin, **124**, *125*
cord, 28
coriander, *21*, 22
corn, 213, *213*
Cornbread, Sausage in, **261**, *261*
Cornbread, Skillet, **261**
corned beef:
Hash and Eggs, **298**, *298*
Red Flannel Hash, **298**
cornichons, 18

Corn Muffins, **294,** *294*
corn oil, 18
cornstarch, 19
Coulommiers, *278,* 280
Country Pâté, **46,** *46*
Country Risotto, **209**
courting picnic, 347, *347*
    Cold Roast Chicken with Pork
        Stuffing, **347,** *347*
    Eggplant Salad, **347**
    menu for, 347
    strategy for, 347
couscous, 18, 209
    Chicken Stew with, **126**
    Lamb Stew, **333,** *333*
    Milk and Honey, **209**
    Pilaf, **209**
cowpeas, *see* black-eyed peas
crab, *94,* 97
    with Artichoke Ravigote, **109**
    blue-shelled, *94,* 97
    Creamed, and Artichoke Heart
        Omelet, **88**
    dungeness, *94,* 97
    shelling of, *106*
    and Shrimp Boil, **105**
    and Shrimp Gumbo, **65,** *65*
    and Vegetable, Peking, **106**
crackers, 19
cranberries, 239, *239*
    Orange Bread, **258**
    Stuffed Game Hens, **133**
    and Wine Sauce, *312,* **314**
cream, 19
Creamed Crab and Artichoke Heart
    Omelet, **88**
Cream Gravy, **127**
Cream of Any Vegetable Soup, **59**
Cream Sauce (Sauce Crème or Sauce
    Supreme), **70**
Crème Anglaise, peaches with, **247**
Crème Fraiche, 19, **250**
Creole Tripe, **178**
crêpes:
    for Crepiere, **288**
    German Pancake, **289**
Crepiere, **288**
Crevettes en Folie ("Extravagant"
    Shrimp), **108**
Croque Monsieur, *39,* **40**
Crown Roasts of Lamb, **166**
Crudités Marinated in Garlic-Basil
    Vinaigrette, **344,** *345*

crusts, *see* pastry
cucumbers, *215,* 216
    and Avocado Soup, **66**
    seedless, *215*
    slicing of, 30, *30*
    Soup, Cold, **66,** *66*
    and Yogurt Salad, **47,** *49*
currants, 239, *239*
curry:
    Kidney Beans, **202**
    Mushrooms with Red Bell Pep-
        pers, *39,* **41**
    powder, *21,* 22
    Turkey, **136**
    Vegetable Kari, **232**
Cuscinetti (Cheese in Crust), **273**
Custard, **301,** *301*
    for Crepiere, **287**
    Flan, **300**
    Vegetable, **89,** *90*
cutting equipment, 27

D

Dal and Tomatoes, **203**
Dandelion, Braised, **225**
dandelion greens, 216
Danish Stuffed Calves' Heart, **175**
dates, 245
demi-glace, 56, 58
desserts:
    Almond Cookies, Chocolate-filled,
        285
    Almond Ice Cream, **303**
    Apple Brown Betty, **300**
    Apple Calvados Soufflé, **92**
    Apple Pie, **268**
    Apple Tart, Upside-down, **286,**
        286
    Apples, Baked, with Brandy and
        Raisins, **249**
    Apples en Croûte, Baked, **270,**
        270
    Baked Apples or Pears en Croûte,
        270, *270*
    Baked Apples with Brandy and
        Raisins, **249**
    Baked Papaya, **250**
    Banana Fritters, **249**
    Bananas, Sautéed, **249**
    Birthday Cake, **301,** *302*
    Brownies, **300**

Buñuelos, **286**
    Cake, Birthday, **301,** *302*
    Cake, Chocolate Mousse, **287**
    Cantaloupe-Orange Ice with
        Marsala, *339,* **340**
    cheese, 278–283
    Cheesecake, Ricotta, **272,** *272*
    cheeses, list of, 280–283
    Cherry Pie, **268,** *269*
    Chestnut Mousse in a Meringue
        Shell, **316,** *317*
    Chocolate Chip Cookies, **298**
    Chocolate Dipped Fruits, **246**
    Chocolate-filled Almond Cookies,
        285
    Chocolate Ice Cream, **303**
    Chocolate Mousse Cake, **287**
    Chocolate-Orange Torte, **271,** *271*
    Chocolate Soufflé, **92**
    Christmas Pudding, **318**
    Cobbler, Peach, **300**
    Coeur à la Creme, **284**
    Coffee Ice Cream, **303**
    Coffee Mousse, Frozen, with
        Amaretto-Orange Sauce, **289**
    Cold Lemon Soufflé, **324,** *324*
    cookies, *see* cookies
    Crepiere, **288**
    Custard, **301,** *301*
    Figgy Pudding, **288**
    Flan, **300**
    French Vanilla Ice Cream, **303**
    Fresh Fruit Compote, **245**
    Frozen Coffee Mousse with
        Amaretto-Orange Sauce, **289**
    Frozen Fruit Ice (Sorbet), **246,**
        247
    Fruit Compote, Fresh, **245**
    Fruit Ice Cream, **303**
    Fruit Purée, **246**
    Fruit Tart, **248**
    fruits, *see* fruit
    Fruits in Cassis, **245**
    Fruits in Cider, **245**
    German Pancake, **289**
    Grand Marnier Soufflé, **92**
    Ice Cream, Homemade, *see* Home-
        made Ice Cream
    Lemon Soufflé, Cold, **324,** *324*
    Lemon Soufflé, Hot, **92**
    Liqueur Ice Cream, **303**
    Mango with Ricotta Cream, **250**
    Meringue with Fruit, **248,** *249*

Index

(desserts cont'd.)

Meringues, Poached, with Fruit Purée, **248**

Mincemeat-Pumpkin Pie, *313,* **315**

mousse, *see* mousse

Oatmeal Cookies, **298**

Orange-Cantaloupe Ice with Marsala, *339,* **340**

Orange-Chocolate Torte, **271,** *271*

Papaya, Baked, **250**

Peach Cobbler, **300**

Peaches with Crème Anglaise, **247**

Peanut Butter Cookies, **299**

Pear Tarts (Tartes aux Poires), *309,* **311**

Pears en Croûte, Baked, **270,** *270*

Pears, Poached in Cognac, **338**

Pears Stuffed with Cheese, **284,** *284*

Pecan Pie, **268**

Peppermint Ice Cream, **303**

pies, *see* pies

Pine Nut Cookies, **284**

Poached Meringues with Fruit Purée, **248**

Pudding, Christmas, **318**

Pudding, Figgy, **288**

Pudding, Rice, **301,** *301*

Pumpkin-Mincemeat Pie, *313,* **315**

Rice Pudding, **301,** *301*

Ricotta Cheesecake, **272,** *272*

Rum Mince Pie, **268**

Sautéed Bananas, **249**

Sesame Cakes (Banh Cam), **285,** *285*

Sesame Seed Cookies, **284**

Sorbet (Frozen Fruit Ice), **246,** *247*

soufflé, *see* soufflé

Tarte Tatin (Upside-down Apple Tart), **286,** *286*

Tartes aux Poires (Pear Tarts), *309,* **311**

Torte, Walnut, **286**

Tuiles aux Amandes (Chocolate-filled Almond Cookies), **285**

Vanilla Ice Cream, **303**

Vanilla Soufflé, **91**

Walnut Torte, **286**

Dijon mustard, 18

dill, *21, 22*

Dressing, on Vegetable Stuffed Shells, **320,** *320*

Popovers, **262**

Seafood Salad, **104**

dinners, big-deal, 307–324

Christmas celebration, 315–319

cold summer supper, 319–321

French, 308–311

fritto misto, 323–324

Thanksgiving feast, 312–315

Dipping Sauce, for Tempura, **52**

Dolmathes (Grape Leaves Stuffed with Pilaf), *49,* **51,** *51*

dolmathes techniques, *51*

Dôme de Chèvre, *278,* 281

dressing:

Dill, **320**

Garlic, **344**

Vinaigrette, **80**

see also sauces

dried fruits, 19

Drunken Fish, **103**

duck, *119,* 136–139

description of, 136

essentials of, 136

Liver Mousse with Endive, **46**

wild, 142–143, *143*

Wild, Roast, **139**

Wild, Roast Mallard, **142**

duckling, 136–137

Breast, with Mangoes, **138**

Broiled, **138**

essentials of, 136

Roast, **136**

Vietnamese, *137,* **138**

Dutch ovens, 27

E

eel, *113,* 114

description of, 114

Jellied Mold, **114**

eggplant, *215,* 216

Baba Ghanoush (Purée), **47,** *49*

Caviar, **49**

Moussaka, **328**

Salad, **347**

Salad with Roasted Peppers, **223**

Sauce, with Zucchini, **189**

Stuffed, **223**

eggs, 19, 81–92

in Aspic, **85**

Baked, with Cheese, **85**

Baked, with Chicken Livers, **85**

Baked, with Cream, **85**

Baked, Florentine, **85**

Baked, with Tomatoes and Cream, *72,* **85,** *85*

Corned Beef Hash and, **298,** *298*

essentials of, 82

freezing of, 351

Fried, **86**

fried, au Beurre Noisette (in Brown Butter), **86**

fried, au Beurre Noisette et Artichauts (in Brown Butter with Artichokes), **86,** *86*

Fried, Mexican, **86**

Fried, Oriental, **86**

frittata, *see* frittatas

Hard-Boiled, *82,* **83**

Hard-Boiled, with Guacamole, **42,** *82*

Hard-Boiled, with Mayonnaise Vinaigrette, *82,* **83**

Hard-Boiled, à la Russe, *82,* **83**

Hard-Boiled with Sour Cream and Caviar, *82,* **83**

Mollet, **82**

Poached, **83**

Poached, with Asparagus, **84**

Poached, Benedict, **84**

Poached, in Burgundy, *83,* **84**

Poached, in Patty Shells, **276**

Portugaise, **84**

Scrambled, **87**

Scrambled, with Mushrooms and Peppers, **87**

Scrambled, au Poivre, **87**

Scrambled, with Smoked Salmon in Brioche, *86,* **87**

Soft-Boiled, **82**

soufflés, *see* soufflés

Vegetable Custard, **89,** *90*

whites, frozen, 19

eggs, omelet, *see* omelets

electronic kitchen, 8

emergency pastry, 264

Emmenthaler, 281, *283*

en Croûte (in crust):

Baked Apples, **270,** *270*

Baked Pears, **270,** *270*

Brie, **42,** *42*

Saucisson, **275,** *275*

endive:
  Belgian, *216,* 218
  Duck Liver Mousse with, **46**
  Stuffed with Cheese, **44**
English Farmhouse, 281, *283*
Epoisses, *278,* 280
equipment, cooking, 27–28, *29*
escargots:
  de Bourgogne (Snails in Butter
    and Garlic), **115**
  Mushrooms Stuffed With, **43**
  see also snails
escarole, 19, 213, *213*
Escoffier, Auguste, 69
Espagnole Sauce (Basic Brown Sauce),
  70, **75**
"Extravagant" Shrimp (Crevettes en
  Folie), **108**

F

fagiola beans, *see* cannellini beans
fava beans, 200
fennel, *21, 22, 216,* 218
  au Gratin, **224,** *224*
  Roast Goose and Calvados with,
    139
  Sautéed, **224**
feta, 283, *283*
fettuccine, *182*
  verde, fresh, *182*
figs, 239, *239*
  Figgy Pudding, **288**
  Fig Jam, **250**
  Fresh, with Prosciutto, **45**
Filet Mignon, Wrapped in Forcemeat
    with a Bordelaise Sauce
    (Châteaubriand à la Borde-
    laise), *152,* **154,** *155*
fines herbes, 26
  Omelet with, **87**
first courses, 37–54
  see also appetizers
fish:
  aspic, 59
  Baked, with Sauce Aurore, **99,** *99*
  Baked Stuffed, **98,** *98*
  Bouillabaisse (Mediterranean Sea-
    food Stew), **329,** *329*
  Broiled, Steaks, **99**
  broiling of, 15, *15*

Cold Poached Trout with Water-
    cress-Lime Sauce, **101**
dressing and fileting of, *97*
Drunken, **103**
freezing of, 351
freshwater, *94,* 96
Grilled, with Herbs, **101**
Grilled, Wrapped in Dried Fennel,
  101
Herbed Baked, **99**
as leftover, 32
à la Meuniere (Sautéed in Butter),
  100
Mousse, Cold Salmon, **103**
Paupiettes of Lemon Sole, **102**
Poached in Macôn Wine, **102**
Poached Salmon with Green
  Sauce, **100,** *100*
Poached Trout, **101**
Poached Trout with Ravigote
  Sauce, **101**
Poached Trout with Velouté Sauce,
  101
Salmon Mousse, Cold, **103,** *103*
saltwater, *94,* 96
Sautéed in Butter (Fish à la
  Meuniere), **100**
Seviche, **104**
Stock, **58**
Stuffed Filets, *73*
Stuffed Filets with Mushroom and
  Wine Velouté Sauce, **99**
Tapénade, **39,** *39*
Tempura, **52,** *52, 53*
Whole Small Baked, **98**
  see also specific fish and seafood
flageolets, 18, 200
  Salad, **202**
Flan, **300**
Flemish Stew with Beer (Carbonnades
  à la Flamande), **333**
flounder, *94, 96*
flour, 19
  all-purpose enriched, 252
  gluten, 252
  hard-wheat, 252
  specialty, 252
  stone-ground whole-wheat, 252
  unbleached, 252
  whole-wheat, 252
fluting, 31, *31*
Fontina d'Aosta, *278,* 280
food processing equipment, 28

Food Processor Hollandaise or Béar-
  naise, **78**
Food Processor Mayonnaise, **79**
Food Processor Puff Pastry, **275**
Forcemeat, Filet Mignon Wrapped in,
  154
forks, wooden, 27
freezing, 351
French Bread, **256,** *256*
French dinner, 308–311
  Asperges à la Sauce Moutarde
    (Asparagus with Mustard
    Sauce), **311**
  Gigot d'Agneau Farci (Stuffed Leg
    of Lamb), *309,* **310**
  Haricots Blanc et Tomates (White
    Beans and Tomatoes), **311**
  Jambon Persillé (Ham with
    Parsley in Aspic), *309,* **310**
  menu for, 308
  strategies for, 308–309
  Tartes aux Poires (Pear Tarts), *309,*
    311
French-fried potatoes, 15, *15*
French Toast, **292,** *292*
French Vanilla Ice Cream, **303**
Fresh Figs with Prosciutto, **45**
Fresh Fruit Compote, **245**
Fresh Herbs, *338,* **340**
fresh ingredients, 19
Fresh Shrimp with Chive Butter, *79,*
  106
Fresh Tomato Sauce, **186,** *187*
Fresh Tomato Soup, **62**
fried:
  Bread, **330**
  Chicken, Herb Batter, **127**
  Chicken, Southern, **127**
  Eggs, *see* Eggs, Fried
  Octopus with Pesto, **114,** *114*
  Okra, **226**
  Rutabaga, **229,** *229*
  Zucchini with Green Peppercorn
    Butter, **232**
Frijoles Refritos (Refried Beans), **203**
Frittatas, **89**
  Mushroom and Bacon, **89,** *89*
  Potato and Ham, *33,* **89**
  Sausage and Pepper, **89**
  Zucchini and Onion, **89**
fritto misto dinner, 323–324
  Cold Lemon Soufflé, **324,** *324*
  menu for, 323

Index

(fritto misto cont'd.)
  Seafood, *323,* **324**
  strategies for, 323
Fritters, Banana, **249**
frogs' legs, *113,* 116
  preparation of, 116
  Wrapped in Bacon, **116**
Frozen Coffee Mousse with Amaretto-
  Orange Sauce, **289**
frozen ingredients, 19
fruit, 237–250
  brandied, 19
  Cantaloupe-Orange Ice with
    Marsala, *338,* **340**
  in Cassis, **245**
  Chocolate Dipped, **246**
  in Cider, **245**
  Compote, Fresh, **245**
  Crème Anglaise, with Peaches,
    247
  Crème Fraîche for, **250**
  dried, 19
  essentials of, 239–245
  Fig Jam, **250**
  freezing of, 351
  Frozen Fruit Ice (Sorbet), **246,**
    246
  Ice Cream, **303**
  with Meringue, **248,** *249*
  Peaches with Crème Anglaise, **247**
  in Port Wine, **245**
  Purée, **246,** *246*
  Purée with Poached Meringues,
    248
  Sorbet (Frozen Fruit Ice), **246,**
    247
  Tart, **248,** *287*
  in White Wine, **246**
  see also specific fruits
fruit vinegar, 18
frying, 15, *15*
fusilli:
  longo, *182*
  spindles, *182*
  verde, *182*
  wheels, *182*

G

game, 141–147
  essentials of, 142
  freezing of, 351

hens, *see* Rock Cornish game hens
  see also specific game
garbanzo beans, *see* chickpeas
garlic, 19, *21,* 22, 215, *215*
  -Basil Vinaigrette, **344**
  chopping of, 30, *30*
  Dressing, Salad with, **343**
  Herb Lamb Chops, **166**
  Oil and Parsley Sauce, **185**
  peeling of, 31, *31*
  Vinaigrette, **80**
Gazpacho, **68**
gelatin, 19
German Pancake, **289**
German Style Pork Back Ribs, **170**
Gigot d'Agneau Farci (Stuffed Leg of
  Lamb), *309,* **310**
ginger, *21,* 22
  Marinade, for Grilled Flank Steak,
    153
  Sauce, with Chicken Breasts, *8,*
    129
Glazed Parsnips, **228**
Glazed Yams, Apricot, **314**
Glaze, Mustard, with Roast Game
  Hens, **132**
glossary, 353–354
gnocchi, *182*
Goat Cheese, Herbed, **41**
Goat Cheese Salad, Warm, **235**
goose, *119,* 139–140
  essentials of, 139
  Roast, with Fennel and Calvados,
    139
  Roast, with Sausage-Apple Stuffing,
    315, *316*
  Wine-Poached Apples for, **139**
gooseberries, 239, *239*
Gorgonzola, 281, *283*
Gouda, *278,* 280
grains, 209–210
  Chicken Stew with Couscous, **126**
  Couscous Lamb Stew, **333,** *333*
  Couscous Pilaf, **209**
  Kasha, **210**
  Milk and Honey Couscous, **209**
  Tabbouleh with Romaine Leaves,
    210
Grana Padano, 281, *283*
Grand Marnier Soufflé, **92**
grapefruit, *240,* 244
Grape Leaves Stuffed with Pilaf
  (Dolmathes), *49,* **51,** *51*

grapes, 239, *239*
gratin dishes, 28, 219
Gratte-Paille, *278,* 280
gravy:
  Cream, **127**
  Old-Fashioned Beef, **297,** *297*
Greek Salad, **236**
green beans, *213,* 215
  Vinaigrette, **220**
green horseradish *(wasabi),* 112
Green Mayonnaise, **79**
green peppercorns, *21,* 24
Green Rice, **206**
greens:
  Basic Boiled, **224**
  chicory, 19, *213*
  collard, *216*
  dandelion, *216*
  Dandelion, Braised, **225**
  mustard, 213, *216*
  with Pot Liquor, **225**
  see also lettuce; spinach; kale
Green Sauce, Poached Salmon with,
  100, *100*
Gremolata, **158**
grilled:
  Fish with Herbs, **101**
  Fish Wrapped in Dried Fennel,
    101
  Flank Steak, **152**
  Flank Steak with Ginger Marinade,
    153
  Lamb Shanks, **167,** *167*
  Scallops, **111**
  Sweetbreads with Bacon, **45**
grilling, 16, *16*
ground veal, *156*
Gruyère, 281, *283*
Guacamole, **42,** 82
Gumbo, Shrimp and Crab, **65,** *65*

H

ham, 19
  Asparagus and, on Puff Pastry with
    Sauce Madère, *76,* **173**
  Baked, **173**
  and Beet Salad, **236**
  Black-Eyed Peas with, **201**
  butt end, *172*
  country, *172*
  Croque Monsieur, *39,* **40**

fresh, *169*
hocks, *172*
how to cook, *172*
imported canned, 18
Jambon Persillé (with Parsley in Aspic), *309,* **310**
and Leeks au Gratin, *33,* **173**
and Lentil Soup, **63**
and Potato Frittata, **89**
shank end, *172*
Veal and Pork Terrine with, **45,** *46*
whole, *172*
see also prosciutto
hamburgers, grilling of, 16, *16*
Hard-Boiled Eggs, *82,* **83**
Hard Sauce, *316,* **319**
Haricots Blancs et Tomates (White Beans and Tomatoes), **311**
hash:
Corned Beef, and Eggs, **298,** *298*
Red Flannel, **298**
Hazan, Marcella, 9
hearts:
beef, 174, *174*
Calves', Danish Stuffed, **175**
preparation of, 174
hens, Roasted Game, *74*
see also Rock Cornish game hens
Herb Batter Fried Chicken, **127**
Herb-Cheese Popovers, **262**
Herbed Baked Fish, **99**
Herbed Bread, **254,** *256*
Herbed Goat Cheese, *39,* **41**
Herbed Saffron Rice, **206**
Herbed Vinaigrette, **80**
herbes de Provence, 26
Herb Garlic Lamb Chops, **166**
herbs, 20–26, *21*
chopping of, 31, *31*
Fresh, *338,* **340**
Homemade Pasta with, **185**
jars of, 28
mincing of, 31, *31*
pots of, 28
Sauce, and Shrimp, **188**
Sauce, Tomato, *338,* **340**
vinegar, 18
in vinegar, *25*
Hiyashi Somen, **197**
Hoisin sauce, 18
Hollandaise Sauce, **77,** *77*
Blender or Food Processor, **77,** *77*
Homemade Ice Cream, *265,* **303**

Homemade Pasta, **184,** *184*
honey, 19
honeydew melon, hors d'oeuvres, *see* cocktail party recipes
horseradish, 18, *21,* 22
Cream, with Smoked Salmon, **40**
Sauce, for Braised Short Ribs, **156**
wasabi (green), 112
Hot Chicken Mousse, **130**
Hot Mocha Soufflé, **92**
Hot Shrimp Mousse with Sauce Aurore, **108**
and Sour Prawn Soup, **63**
Hummus, **47,** *49*
Hunter's Sauce (Sauce Chasseur), **76,** *129*

I

iceberg lettuce, 213, *213*
Ice Cream, Homemade, *264,* **303**
Almond, **303**
Chocolate, **303**
Coffee, **303**
freezing of, 351
French Vanilla, **303**
Fruit, **303**
Liqueur, **303**
Peppermint, **303**
Vanilla, **303**
Indonesian Pork Sate, **172**
ingredients:
fresh, 19
frozen, 19
in packages, cans and jars, 18–19
produce, 19
innards, 174–178
essentials of, 174
how to cook, *174*
see also brains; hearts; kidneys; liver; sweetbreads; tongue; tripe
Irish Soda Bread, **260**

J

Jambalaya, **326,** *327*
Jambon Persillé (Ham with Parsley in Aspic), *309,* **310**
Jam, Fig, **250**
Japanese Noodle Salad, **197**

jarred ingredients, 18–19
jars:
glass, 28
herb, 28
spice, 28
Jellied Eel Mold, **114**
jellyroll sheets, 28
Jerusalem artichoke, *216,* 218
with Lemon, **225**
Jimmy's Barbecued Spareribs, **169**
juice, freezing of, 351
Julienne of Vegetables, *316,* *316*
Julienne of Vegetables Omelet, **88**
julienne technique, 31, *31*
juniper berries, *21,* 23

K

kale, 213, *216*
Kasha, 209, **210**
and Lentils, **210**
and Noodles, **210**
Katchapuri with Salmon, **257**
Kibbeh, *49,* **52**
kidney beans, 18, 200, *201*
Curried, **202**
kidneys:
beef, 174, *174*
and Beef Pie, **176**
lamb, *174,* 174
pork, 174
preparation of, 174
and Sweetbreads en Brochette, **176,** *177*
veal, 174
kiwi fruit, *243,* 244
as garnish, *133*
Meringue with Fruit, **248,** *249*
knives, 27
sharpening of, 30, *30*
kohlrabi, *216,* 218
in Cream Sauce, **225**
kosher (coarse) salt, 18
Kuchen, Apple, *256,* **257**
kumquats, *243,* 244

L

ladles, 27
Lait de Chèvre, *278,* 281
lamb, 162–167

Index

(lamb cont'd.)
breast of, *162*
chops, *162*
Chops, Herb Garlic, **166**
chops, loin, *162*
chops, rib, *162*
Chops, Sesame, **166**
chops, sirloin, *162*
crown roast, *162*
Crown Roasts of, **166**
essentials of, 162
ground, *162*
how to cook, 162
Kibbeh, *49*, **52**
Korma (Stew), **164**
leg of, *162*
Leg of, Butterflied, **166**
leg of, carving of, *165*
leg of, Frenched, *162*
Leg of, Stuffed (Gigot d'Agneau Farci), *309*, **310**
Moussaka, **328**
rack, *162*
riblets, *162*
roasting of, 17, *17*
Saddle of, with Pink Peppercorns, **164**
shanks, 162
Shanks, Grilled, **167**, *167*
shoulder arm chops—round bone, *162*
square-cut shoulder, *162*
steaks, leg, *162*
Stew, **164**
Stew, Couscous, **333**, *333*
stew cuts of, *162*
Stuffed Riblets, **165**
Langres, *278*, 280
lasagne:
baking of, 16, *16*
Vegetable, **193**
last courses, 277–289
See also cheeses *and* desserts
lawn party, 344–346, *345*
Brown Rice and Vegetable Salad, *345*, **346**
Cold Stuffed Veal Roast, *345*, **346**
Cold Zucchini Soup, **346**
Crudités Marinated in Garlic-Basil Vinaigrette, **344**, *345*
Melba Toast, **346**
menu for, 344
Salmon Pâté, **345**, *345*

strategies for, 344
Yogurt Sauce, *345*, **346**
leeks, *216*, 218
Braised, **226**
Cream of Any Vegetable Soup, **59**
Ham and, au Gratin, *33*, **173**
Pie, Yam and, **232**
and Potato Pâté, **226**, *226*
lemon rind, *21*, 23
lemons, 19, *240*, 243–244
Chicken, **121**
Jerusalem Artichoke with, **225**
rind, *21*, 23
Soufflé, **92**
Soufflé, Cold, **324**, *324*
lentils, 18, 200, *201*
Kasha and, **210**
Pilaf, **202**
Soup, and Ham, **63**
Soup, Cold, **68**
lettuce:
bibb, 213, *213*
Boston, 213, *213*
chicory, 213, *213*
iceberg, 213, *213*
loose leaf, 213, *213*
red-leaf, 213, *213*
romaine, 213, *213*
L'Explorateur, *278*, 280
lima beans, 200
Pasta e Fagiola Salad, **195**, *195*
limes, 19, *240*, 244
linguine, *182*
Pasta Primavera, **189**
with Squid and Peas, **113**
verde, *182*
Liqueur Ice Cream, **303**
liquid measure volume equivalents, 355
Livarot, *278*, 280
liver, calves', 174–175, *174*
Sautéed with Port and Juniper Sauce, **175**
liver, chicken:
Baked Eggs with, **85**
Mousse with Endive, **46**
loaf pans, 28
lobster, *94*, 96–97
Boiled, **104**
Cantonese, **105**
Clambake, **342**, *342*
Salad, **104**
shelling of, *105*

Locatelli, 281, *283*
loose leaf lettuce, 213, *213*
Louisiana Red Beans and Rice, **206**
lumache, *182*
lumpfish caviar, 54
lumpfish roe, 18
Lyonnaise, Potatoes, **228**

M

macaroni, *see* pasta
maccheroni alla chitarra, *182*
mace, *21*, 23
Madère, Sauce, **76**, *76*, 173
main course, from leftovers, 32
Mallard Duck, Roast, **142**
mangoes, *243*, 245
Duckling Breast with, **138**
with Ricotta Cream, **250**
Marinade, Ginger, for Grilled Flank Steak, **153**
Marinara Sauce, **186**
Marinated Beets, **220**
Marinated Chicken, **121**
marjoram, *21*, 23
Mashed Potatoes, **297**, *297*
Mayonnaise, **78**
Blender or Food Processor, **79**
Green, **79**
Sauce Remoulade, **79**
Vinaigrette, Eggs with, *82*, **83**
measuring, 355
measuring cups, 27
measuring equipment, 27
measuring spoons, 27
meat, 149–178
Chile con Carne, **326**
freezing of, 351
Paella, **334**
Phyllo Turnovers, *49*, *50*, **51**
Tempura, **52**, *52*, *53*
see also specific meats; innards
Mediterranean Seafood Stew (Bouillabaisse), **329**, *329*
Melba Toast, **346**
melons, *240*, 244
in Cassis, **245**
menus, 305–348
meringue:
with Fruit, **248**, *249*
Poached, with Fruit Purée, **248**

Shell, with Chestnut Mousse, **314,** *314*

Mexican Eggs, **86**

mezze, 47–52

    Baba Ghanoush, **47,** *49*

    Cucumber and Yogurt Salad, **47,** *49*

    Dolmathes (Grape Leaves Stuffed with Pilaf), *49,* **51**

    Eggplant Caviar, **49**

    Hummus, **47,** *49*

    Kibbeh, *49,* **52**

    Phyllo Turnovers, *49,* **50**

    Taramasalata, **47,** *49*

    White Bean Salad, *49,* **52**

milk, 19

    freezing of, 351

    and Honey Couscous, **209**

mincemeat:

    Pumpkin-Mincemeat Pie, *312,* **315**

    Rum Mince Pies, **268**

mincing, 31, *31*

Minestrone, **60**

mint, *21, 23*

Miso (Soybean Soup), **63**

mixers, electric, 28

mixing bowls, 27

mock puff pastry, 264

molds, 28

Montrachet, *278,* 281

Mornay Sauce, **72,** *72,* 158

Moussaka, **328**

mousse:

    Asparagus, **219,** *220*

    Cake, Chocolate, **287**

    Chestnut, in a Meringue Shell, **316,** *316*

    Duck Liver, with Endive, **46**

    Frozen Coffee, with Amaretto-Orange Sauce, **289**

    Hot Chicken, **130**

    Salmon, Cold, **103,** *103*

    Shrimp, Hot, with Sauce Aurore, **108**

Mousseline Sauce, Cold, **220,** *220*

mozzarella cheese, 19, *278,* 280

    Smoked, with Oil and Black Pepper, **320,** *320*

Muenster, Alsatian, *278,* 280

muffins:

    Blueberry, **294,** *294*

    Bran, **294,** *294*

    Corn, **294,** *294*

muffin tins, 28

mung beans, 200–201

mushrooms, *215,* 216

    and Bacon Frittata, **89,** *89*

    Chicken Sauté with, **123**

    and Chicken Soufflé, **91**

    Cream of Any Vegetable Soup, **59**

    Curried, with Red Bell Peppers, *39,* **41**

    dried, 18

    fluting of, 31, *31*

    Phyllo Turnovers, *49,* **50,** *50*

    Sauce (Sauce aux Champignons), *70,* **73,** 99

    Scrambled Eggs with Peppers and, **87**

    Stuffed with Escargots, **43**

    truffles, 216

    Wild Rice with, **316,** *316*

mussels, *94,* 96

    with Avocado Sauce, **43**

    preparation of, *110*

    with Ravigote Sauce, **109**

    Saffron, **110**

    Sauce, with Shrimp and Wine, **189**

mustard, *21, 23*

    Braised Beef with, **153,** *153*

    Dijon, 18

    Glaze, on Roast Game Hens, **132**

    Sauce, for Asparagus, **311**

    Sauce, for Burgundian Beef Stew, **331**

    Vinaigrette, **80**

N

Nantua Sauce, **72,** *72*

navy beans, 201

    New England Baked Beans, **203**

nectarines, *239,* 240

New American Cuisine, characteristics of, 8–9

New Cabbage and Steamed Potatoes, **221,** *222*

new cornucopia, *348, 348*

    sausage, *348, 348*

    vegetables, *348, 348*

New England Baked Beans, **203**

New England Clambake, 342–344, **342,** *343*

    Clambake, **342,** *342*

    menu for, 342

    Salad with Garlic Dressing, **344**

    strategies for, 342

New Larder, 18–19

New Potatoes Stuffed with Caviar, **44**

New York Cheddar, 281–283, *283*

Niçoise, **235,** *235*

noodles:

    cellophane, 18

    Kasha and, **210**

    Spaetzle, **196,** *196*

    Stir-Fry Pork with Zucchini and, **171**

noodles, Oriental, 196–197

    Hiyashi Somen, **197**

    Japanese Salad, **197**

    ramen, 196

    soba, 196

    somen, 196

    Thai Crisp Fried, **197**

    udon, 196

nori (seaweed), 112

Nouvelle Cuisine, 8–9

nutmeg, *21, 23*

nuts, 19

O

Oatmeal, **292,** *292*

    Cookies, **298**

ocean perch, *94,* 96

octopus, 113–114, *113*

    description of, 113

    Fried, with Pesto, **114,** *114*

    preparation of, 113

    Vinaigrette, **114**

oils:

    corn, 18

    Garlic and Parsley Sauce, **185**

    olive, 18

    peanut, 18

    sesame, Oriental, 18

    vegetable, 18

    walnut, 18

Oka, *278,* 280

okra, *216,* 218

    Fried, **226**

    Rice and, **207**

    Stewed, and Tomatoes, **228**

Old-Fashioned Beef Gravy, **297,** *297*

olive oil, 18

olives, 18
   Chicken with, **126**
Olivet Foins, *278, 280*
Omelets, **87,** *88*
   with *Fines Herbes,* **87**
   Gruyère, **87**
   Puffed, Apple and Calvados, **88**
   Puffed, Creamed Crab and Artichoke Heart, **88**
   Puffed, Julienne of Vegetables, **88,** *88*
   Puffed, Raspberry and Rum, **88**
   Sour Cream and Watercress, **87**
   Vegetable, **87**
onions, 19, 215, *215*
   Bermuda, 215
   Bread, Prosciutto and, **260**
   chopping of, 30, *30*
   Cream of Any Vegetable Soup, **59**
   pearl, 215
   Quiche, **275**
   red, 215, *215*
   shallots, 215, *215*
   Soup, **60**
   Soup, Cream of Any Vegetable, **59**
   Soupe Soubise, **60**
   Spanish, 215, *215*
   and Spinach Soufflé, **91**
   Sweet and Sour, **228**
   yellow, 215
   and Zucchini Frittata, **89**
oranges, 19, *240,* 243
   Cantaloupe-Orange Ice with Marsala, *338,* **340**
   rind, *21, 23*
oregano, *21, 23*
Oriental Eggs, **86**
Oriental noodles, *see* noodles, Oriental
osetra caviar, 54
Osso Buco Milanese (Braised Veal Shanks), **158**
oysters, *94,* 97
   on the Half Shell, **111**
   preparation of, *110*
   and Scallops Pie, **276**
   Stew, **65**

P

packaged ingredients, 18–19
Paella, **334**

Paglia e Fieno (Straw and Hay), **188,** *188*
Paillard of Veal with Sage and Prosciutto, **158**
Pancakes, **292**
   Blueberry, **292**
   German, **289**
Pancetta, Chicken Sauté with, **123**
pans, 27
papaya, *243,* 244
   Baked, **250**
paprika, *21,* 23
Parisienne, Sauce, **74,** *74,* 132
Parmesan cheese, 19
Parmigiano-Reggiana, 281, *283*
parsley, *21,* 24
   Jambon Persillé (Ham with, in Aspic), *309,* **310**
   Sauce, with Oil and Garlic, **185**
parsnips, *216,* 218
   Glazed, **228**
   Stir-Fried, **228**
Partridge, Braised, **144**
pasta, 18, 179–197
   agnolotti, *182*
   Agnolotti alla Puttanesca, **191,** *191*
   agnolotti verde, *182*
   boiling of, 14, *14*
   bottoni (buttons), *182*
   Broccoli, Anchovy and Cream Sauce, **190**
   cannaroni regati, *182*
   capelli d'angelo (angel hair pasta), *182*
   Capelli d'Angelo, with Shrimp and Herb Sauce, *183,* **188**
   Capelli d'Angelo with Truffles and Sweetbreads, **176**
   capellini, *182*
   Clam Sauce, White, **188**
   cold, 194–195, 320
   Cold Tomato Sauce, **194**
   conchiglie (seashells), *182*
   definition of, 182
   e Fagiola Salad, **195,** 195
   fettuccine, *182*
   fettuccine verde (fresh), *182*
   Fresh Tomato Sauce, **186,** *186*
   fusilli (spindles), *182*
   fusilli (wheels), *182*
   fusilli longo, *182*

fusilli verde, *182*
gnocchi, *182*
Herb, Homemade, **185**
Hiyashi Somen, **197**
Homemade, **184,** *185*
ingredients of, 182
Japanese Noodle Salad, **197**
Lasagne, Vegetable, **193**
as leftover, 32
linguine, *182*
linguine verde, *182*
lumache, *182*
maccheroni alla chitarra, *182*
making, techniques, *183*
Marinara Sauce, **186**
Mussels, Shrimp and Wine Sauce, **189**
Oriental, *see* noodles, Oriental
Paglia e Fieno (Straw and Hay), **188,** *188*
penne, *182*
pennette, *182*
penne verde (quills), *182*
Pesto (Basil Sauce), **187,** *187*
preparation of, 183
Primavera, **189**
Puttanesca Sauce, **190**
Ravioli with Spinach Stuffing and Cheese Sauce, **192,** *192*
rigatoni, *182*
salads, 194–195
Salsa Besciamella, **186**
Sauce Alfredo, **187**
Sauce Bolognese, **190**
sauces, 185–189
Scallop and Spinach Salad, **194,** *194*
Shells, Vegetable Stuffed with Dill Dressing, **320,** *320*
Shrimp and Herb Sauce, **188**
Spaetzle, **196,** *196*
spaghettini, *182*
Spinach, Homemade, **185**
Straw and Hay (Paglia e Fieno), **188,** *188*
Stuffed, 182, 191–193, 320
tagliarini, *182*
tagliarini verde, *182*
tagliatelle, *182*
Thai Crisp Fried Noodles, **197**
Tomato, Homemade, **185**
Tomato Herb Sauce, *338,* **340**

Tomato Sauce, Cold, **194**
Tomato Sauce, Fresh, **186**, *186*
Tortellini, *182*, **193**, *338*, **340**
types of, 182
Vegetable Lasagne, **193**
Vegetable Salad, **194**
Vegetable Stuffed Shells with Dill Dressing, **320**, *320*
White Clam Sauce, **188**
Whole-Wheat, Homemade, **185**
ziti, *182*
Zucchini and Eggplant Sauce, **189**
pastry, 263–276
Bacon-Cheese Quiche, **275**
Baked Apples en Croûte, **270**, *270*
Baked Pear en Croûte, **270**, *270*
Basic, 264, *266*, **267**
Chicken and Sausage Pot Pies, **274, 275**
Chocolate-Orange Torte, **271**, *271*
combination, 264
Cuscinetti (Cheese in Crust), **273**
emergency, 264
essentials of, 264
Food Processor Puff, **275**
freezing of, 351
mock puff, 264
Onion Quiche, **275**
Pâté Maison en Croûte, **273**, *273*
Patty Shells, Poached Eggs in, **276**
Pie, Apple, *264*, **268**
Pie, Beef and Kidney, **176**
pie crust, *see* Basic Pastry
pies, *see* pies
puff, 264
Puff, Asparagus and Ham on, with Sauce Madère, *76*, **173**
Puff, Food Processor, **275**
puff, frozen, 19
Quiche au Fromage (Cheese Tart), **274**
Ricotta Cheesecake, **272**, *272*
Salmon Stuffed Trout en Croûte, **272**
Saucisson en Croûte (Sausage in Crust), **275**
Scallops and Oyster Pie, **276**
tart, 264
Torte, Chocolate-Orange, **271**, *271*
Vegetable Quiche, **274**, *275*
pastry bags, 28

pastry boards, 28
pastry brushes, 28
pastry scrapers, 28
pastry tips, 28
pâté, 45–46
canned, 18
Country, **46**, *46*
Duck Liver Mousse with Endive, **46**
Leek and Potato, **226**, *226*
Maison en Croûte, **273**, *273*
Quail on Toast with, **144**
Salmon, **345**, *345*
Veal, Ham and Pork Terrine, **45**, *46*
Vegetable Terrine, **233**
pâtés and terrines, 45–46
Paupiettes of Lemon Sole, **102**
peaches, *239*, 240
Cobbler, **300**
with Crème Anglaise, **247**
Peanut Butter Cookies, **299**
peanut oil, 18
pears, 240–243, *240*
Baked, en Croûte, **270**, *270*
Poached in Cognac, *337*, **338**
Stuffed with Cheese, **284**, *284*
Tartes aux Poires (Tarts), *309*, **311**
peas, *213*, 215
frozen, 19
Shrimp with Coconut Milk and, **109**
snow, *213*, 215
with Squid and Linguine, **113**
Pecan Pie, **268**
peeling, 31, *31*
Peking Crab and Vegetables, **106**
penne, *182*
verde (quills), *182*
pennette, *182*
pepper:
black, freshly ground, 24
cayenne, 24
white, 24
peppercorns:
black, 24
green, 24
pepper flakes, *21*, 24
Peppermint Ice Cream, **303**
peppers:
bell, *215*, 218

chili, *215*, 218
Red Bell, with Curried Mushrooms, *39*, **41**
Roasted, Eggplant Salad with, **223**
roasted red, 18
and Sausage Frittata, **89**
Scrambled Eggs with Mushrooms and, **87**
sweet, *215*, 218
perch, ocean, *94*, 96
persimmons, *243*, 245
Pesto (Basil Sauce), **187**, *187*
with Fried Octopus, **114**, *114*
frozen, 19
Salad, Chicken, **319**, *320*
pheasant, 142, *143*
with Chartreuse, **142**
Stew, **142**
phyllo dough, frozen, 19
Phyllo Pie, Chicken, **131**
phyllo techniques, 50
Phyllo Turnovers, *49*, *50*, **50**
pickling spice, *21*, 24
picnics, 341–348
courting, 347
lawn party, 344–346, *345*
new cornucopia, 348, *348*
New England clambake, 342–344
pie crust, *see* Basic Pastry
pie pans, 28
pies:
Apple, *264*, **268**
Beef and Kidney, **176**
Cherry, **268**, *269*
Chicken Phyllo, **131**
Pecan, **268**
Pot, Chicken and Sausage, **274**, *275*
Pumpkin-Mincemeat, *312*, **315**
Rum Mince, **268**
Scallop and Oyster, **276**
Yam and Leek, **232**
see also quiche
pike, walleye, *94*, 96
Pilaf, **206**
Couscous, **209**
Dolmathes (Grape Leaves Stuffed with), *49*, *50*, **51**
Lentil, **202**
Rice and Okra, **207**
pimento, *21*, 24
Pineapple Sorbet, **246**, *247*

pineapples, *240, 243*
Pine Nut Cookies, **284**
pine nuts, 19
pinto beans, 18, 201
    Frijoles Refritos (Refried Beans),
      203
    Stewed, **203**
Pipo Crem', 281, *283*
pizza cutters, 27
pizzas, Sicilian, *256,* **257**
plantain, *243, 244*
plastic bags, 28
plums, 239, *239*
poached:
    Chicken (Poule au Pot), **121**
    Eggs, **83**
    Eggs in Patty Shells, **276**
    Eggs with Asparagus, **84**
    Meringues with Fruit Purée, **248**
    Salmon with Green Sauce, **100,**
      100
    Shad Roe with Wine Sauce, **115**
    Trout, **101**
    Trout, Cold, with Watercress-Lime
      Sauce, **101**
    Trout with Ravigote Sauce, **101**
    Trout with Velouté Sauce, **101**
poaching, 12, *12*
pomegranates, *243,* 245
pompano, *94, 96*
Pont-l'Eveque, *278, 280*
Popovers, **262**
    Dill, **262**
    Herb-Cheese, **262**
poppy seeds, *21,* 24
porgies, *94, 96*
pork, 169–173
    Back Ribs, German Style, **170**
    bacon, *see* bacon
    blade roast, *169*
    breakfast sausages, *169*
    Broth, **103**
    center loin roast, *169*
    Chicken Sauté with, **123**
    chops, blade, *169*
    chops, rib, *169*
    Chops, Stuffed, **170,** *170*
    chops, stuffing of, *170*
    Country Pâté, **46,** *46*
    country ribs, *169*
    essentials of, 169
    ground, *169*
    ham, *see* ham

how to cook, *169*
    Indonesian Sate, **172**
    Jimmy's Barbecued Spareribs, **169**
    as leftover, 32
    picnic shoulder, *169*
    preparation of, 169
    prosciutto, *see* prosciutto
    ribs, country, *169*
    Ribs, Back, German Style, **170**
    rib roast, *169*
    Roast Loin with Sauce Robert, **171,**
      171
    salt, *169*
    sausage, *see* sausage
    smoked, *172*
    sparerib cuts of, *169*
    Spareribs, Jimmy's Barbecued,
      169
    square-cut shoulder, *169*
    Stir-Fry, with Zucchini and
      Noodles, **171**
    Stuffing, with Cold Roast
      Chicken, **347,** *347*
    tenderloin, *169*
    Veal and Ham Terrine with, **45,** *46*
    see also bacon; ham; prosciutto;
      sausage
Portugaise, Eggs, **84**
potatoes, 19, 213, *213*
    Baked, **295,** *295*
    Clambake, **342,** *342*
    Cream of Any Vegetable Soup, **59**
    frying of, 15, *15*
    and Ham Frittata, **89**
    Idaho, 213, *213*
    and Leek Pâté, **226,** *226*
    Lyonnaise, **229**
    Mashed, **297,** *297*
    new, 213, *213*
    New, and Cabbage, Steamed, **221,**
      222
    New, Stuffed with Caviar, **44**
    Pâté, Leek and, **226,** *226*
    russet, 213
    Salad, **228**
    sweet, *see* sweet potatoes
Pot Cheese, *278, 280*
Pot Pies, Chicken and Sausage, **274,**
    275
pot roast, braising of, 14, *14*
Poule au Pot (Poached Chicken), **121**
Pouligny-Saint Pierre, *278,* 281
poultry, 117–140

cutting up, *122*
freezing of, 351
as leftover, 32
see also specific poultry
Prawn Soup, Hot and Sour, **63**
preparation techniques, 30–31,
    30–31
preserves, 19
Primavera, Pasta, *8,* **189**
produce, 19
prosciutto:
    Fresh Figs with, **45**
    and Onion Bread, **260**
    Paillard of Veal with Sage and, **158**
    Soubise, Sweetbreads and, **178**
Provolone, 281, *283*
pudding:
    Christmas, *316,* **318**
    Figgy, **288**
    Rice, **301,** *301*
puffed omelet, *see* omelet, puffed
pullet, 119
Pumpkin-Mincemeat Pie, *312,* **315**
Purée, Eggplant (Baba Ghanoush),
    47, *49*
Purée, Fruit, **246,** 248
Puréed Turnips and Chestnuts, **231,**
    232
puréeing, vegetables, 219
Puttanesca Sauce, **190**

Q

quail, 143–144, *143*
    Roast, **143**
    Sautéed, **144**
    on Toast with Pâté, **144**
Quenelles, Chicken, à la Crème,
    130
quiche:
    Bacon-Cheese, **275**
    au Fromage (Cheese Tart), **274**
    Onion, **275**
    Vegetable, **274,** *275*
quiche pans, 28
quick breads, 258–262
    Apricot, **258**
    Baking Powder Biscuits, **262**
    Banana, **258**
    Basic Nut, **258**
    Buttermilk Biscuits, **262**
    Carrot Wheat-Germ, *258,* **260**
    Cheese, *258,* **260**

Cranberry-Orange, **258**
essentials of, 258
Irish Soda, **260**
Popovers, **262**
Prosciutto and Onion, **260**
Sausage in Corn, **261**, *261*
Skillet Corn, **261**
quinces, *243, 244*

R

rabbit, *143, 145 147*
    Cajun, **145**, *146*
    in Red Wine, **146**
    Stew, **145**
racks, 28
Raclette, 281, *283*
Radis au Beurre (Radishes with Butter), *39,* **40**
radishes, 213, *213*
raspberries, 239, *239*
    as garnish, *129*
    Purée, **246**, *246*
    and Rum Omelet, **88**
Raspberry Vinegar Sauce, with Broiled Squab, **140**
Ratatouille, **223**
Ravigote Sauce, **74**, *74,* 132
    Poached Trout with, **101**
    Roast Game Hens with, **132**
Ravigote Sauce, Cold, with Mussels, **109**
Ravioli with Spinach Stuffing and Cheese Sauce, **192**, *192*
Reblochon, *278*, 280
red caviar, 54
Red Flannel Hash, **298**
red-leaf lettuce, 213, *213*
red snapper, *94,* 96
    Baked Stuffed, **98**, *98*
    poaching of, 12, *12*
Refried Beans (Frijoles Refritos), **203**
rhubarb, 245
ribs, *see specific meats*
rice, 204–209
    American, 204, *204*
    Arborio, 18, 204, *205*
    basmati, 204
    Boiled, **205**
    Braised, with Saffron (Risotto Milanese), **208**
    brown, 18, 204, *204, 205*

Brown, and Vegetable Salad, *345,* **346**
Brown, Salad, **207**
Chinese sweet, *205*
converted, 204, *204*
Country Risotto, **209**
Eggs Portugaise, **84**
Green, **206**
Herbed Saffron, **206**
Indian, *205*
instant, 204
as leftover, 32
long-grain, 18, 204, *204, 205*
Louisiana Red Beans and, **206**
and Okra, **207**
Paella, **334**
Pilaf, **206**
polished Carolina, 204
Pudding, **301**, *301*
Risotto Milanese (Braised Rice with Saffron), **208**
Saffron, **206**
Seafood Risotto, *208*
short-grain white, 204
Steamed, **205**
Stir-Fry of, and Vegetables, **207**
Vegetable Soup with, **60**
wild, 18, 204–205, *204*
Wild, with Mushrooms, **316**, *316*
Wild, Steamed, **207**
rice wine vinegar (*su*), 112
ricotta, *278*, 280
    Cheesecake, **272**, *272*
    Cream, with Mango, **251**
rigatoni, *182*
ring molds, 28
Risotto Milanese (Braised Rice with Saffron), **208**
roast beef:
    boneless rib, *152*
    clay baking of, 17, *17*
    Standing Rib Roast, **297**, *297*
    whole rib with short ribs, *152*
roasted game hens, *74*
Roast Goose with Sausage-Apple Stuffing, **315**, *316*
roasting, 17, *17*
Roast Loin of Pork with Sauce Robert, **171**, *171*
Roast Turkey with Sausage-Cornbread Stuffing, **312**, *312*
Roast Veal with Tuna Sauce (Vitello Tonnato), **159**, *159*

Robiola, *278*, 280
Rocamadour, *278, 281*
Rock Cornish game hens, *119,* 132–133
    Broiled Split, **132**, *133*
    Cranberry Stuffed, **133**
    essentials of, 132
    Roast, with Mustard Glaze, **132**
    Roast, with Ravigote Sauce, **132**
rolling pins, 28
Rolls, Cinnamon, *256,* **257**
romaine, 19, 213, *213*
    Tabbouleh with, **210**
Roquefort, 283, *283*
rosemary, *21, 24*
Rouille, **329**
roux:
    dark brown, 65, *65*
    white, 70
Royal Provence, *278, 281*
rulers, 28
Rum and Raspberry Omelet, **88**
Rum Mince Pies, **268**
rutabaga, *213,* 215, *216*
    Fried, **229**, *229*
Rye Bread, *256,* **257**

S

Saddle of Lamb with Pink Peppercorns, **164**
saffron, *21, 24*
    Mussels, **110**
    Rice, **206**
sage, *21, 25*
St. André, *278,* 280
salad greens, 19
    see also greens; lettuce
salads, 233–236
    Avocado and Chicken, **234**
    Avocado, with Yogurt Dressing, **234**
    Barley, **210**
    Beet and Ham, **236**
    Brown Rice, **207**
    Brown Rice and Vegetable, *345,* **346**
    Cannellini, with Tuna, **201**
    Chicken and Avocado, **234**
    Chicken and Sorrel, **131**
    Chicken Pesto, **319**, *320*

Index

(salads cont'd.)
Chickpea, **202**
Eggplant, **347**
Eggplant, with Roasted Peppers, **223**
Flageolet, **202**
with Garlic Dressing, **344**
Greek, **236**
green, 233, *234*
Ham and Beet, **236**
Japanese Noodle, **197**
from leftovers, 32
Lobster, **104**
Niçoise, **235**, *235*
pasta, 194–195
Pasta e Fagiola, **195**, *195*
Potato, **228**
preparation of, 233
Scallop and Spinach Pasta, **194**, *194*
Scallop and Vegetable, **111**
Seafood, Dill, **104**
Seviche, **104**
Squab, **140**
Tabbouleh with Romaine Leaves, **210**
Tomato and Celeriac, **235**
Tuna Pasta, **195**, *195*
vegetable, 233–236
Vegetable and Brown Rice, 345, **346**
Vegetable Pasta, **194**
Warm Goat Cheese, **235**
White Bean, *49*, **52**
salmon, 18, *94*, 96
Katchapuri with, **257**
Mousse, Cold, **103**, *103*
Pâté, **345**, *345*
Poached, with Green Sauce, **100**, *100*
Smoked, with Horseradish Cream, *39*, *40*
Smoked, with Scrambled Eggs in Brioche, **87**
Soufflé, **91**
Steak with Beurre Blanc, *80*, **99**
Trout Stuffed with, en Croûte, **272**
Salsa Besciamella, **186**, 338, *338*
salsify, *216*, 218
Braised, **230**
Sautéed, **230**

salt, 26
kosher (coarse), 18
sandwiches, Croque Monsieur, *39, 40*
San Francisco Cioppino, **66**
sardines, 18
sashimi, 112
saucepans, 27
sauces, 69–80
Alfredo, **187**
Amaretto-Orange, Frozen Coffee Mousse with, **289**
Apricot Liqueur, **289**
Aurore, **73**, *99*, 109
Avocado, Mussels with, **43**
Bagna Cauda, **41**
Béarnaise, *70*, **77**, *78*
Béchamel, **70**, *70*
Besciamella, **186**, *338*
Beurre Blanc (White Butter), **80**, *80*
Beurre Noir (Beurre Noisette; Brown Butter), **80**
Blender Hollandaise or Béarnaise, **78**
Blender Mayonnaise, **79**
Bolognese, **190**
Bordelaise, **75**, *75*, 154
brown, 75–76
butter, 79–80
aux Champignons (Mushroom), *70*, **73**, 99
Chasseur (Hunter's), **76**, *129*
Chestnuts in Rum, *316*, **318**
Chive Butter, **79**, *79*
Clam, White, **188**
Clarified Butter, **79**
Cold Tomato, **194**
Cranberry and Wine, *312*, **314**
Cream (Sauce Crème; Sauce Supreme), **70**
for Crepiere, **288**
Dipping, for Tempura, **52**
egg, 77–79
Espagnole (Basic Brown), *70*, **75**
essentials of, 70
Food Processor Hollandaise or Béarnaise, **78**
Food Processor Mayonnaise, **79**
Fresh Tomato, **186**, *186*
Garlic Vinaigrette, **80**
Green Mayonnaise, **79**
Hard, *316*, **319**

Herbed Vinaigrette, **80**
hoisin, 18
Hollandaise, **77**, *77*
Hunter's (Chausseur), **76**, *129*
Madère, **76**, *76*, 173
Marinara, **186**
Mayonnaise, **78**
Mayonnaise, Blender or Food Processor, **79**
mères, 70
Mornay, **72**, *72*, 158
Mussels, Shrimp and Wine, **189**
Mushroom and Wine (aux Champignons), *70*, **73**, 99
Mustard, **331**
Mustard Vinaigrette, **80**
Nantua, **72**, *72*
Oil, Garlic and Parsley, **185**
Paglia e Fieno (Straw and Hay), **188**
Parisienne, **74**, *74*
pasta, 185–189
Pesto (Basil), **187**, *187*
Raspberry Vinegar, with Broiled Squab, **140**
Ravigote, **74**, *74*, 132
Ravigote, Cold, **109**
Rémoulade, **79**
Robert, **76**, *171*
Rouille, **329**
Salsa Besciamella, **186**, *338*
Sate, Indonesian Pork, **172**
Sherry Cream, **249**
Shrimp and Herb, **188**
Supreme (Cream), **70**
Tabasco sauce, 18
Tomato, Cold, **194**
Tomato, Fresh, **186**, *186*
Tomato Herb, *338*, **340**
Tuna, with Roast Veal (Vitello Tonnato), **159**, *159*
Vegetable, *338*, **340**
Velouté, *73*, *73*, **101**
Vinaigrette Dressing, **80**
vinaigrettes, 80
Watercress-Lime, for Cold Poached Trout, **101**
white, 70–74
White Clam, **188**
Worcestershire sauce, 18
Yogurt, *345*, **346**
Zucchini and Eggplant, **189**

Sauerkraut Stew, Alsatian (Choucroute Garnie), **328**
sausage:
    breakfast, *169*
    and Chicken Pot Pies, **274,** *275*
    in Corn Bread, **261,** *261*
    in Crust (Saucisson en Croûte), **275**
    meat, frozen, 19
    new cornucopia, *348, 348*
    and Pepper Frittata, **89**
    Saucisson en Croûte (in Crust), **275**
    Stuffing, with Apple, *315,* **316**
    Stuffing, with Cornbread, **312,** *312*
sautéed:
    Bananas, **249,** *285*
    Calves' Liver with Port and Juniper Sauce, **175**
    Chicken Breasts with Hunter's Sauce (Suprêmes au Chasseur), **129,** *129*
    Fennel, **224**
    Salsify, **230**
    Veal, *72*
    Veal Chops, **161,** *161*
    Venison Steaks, **147**
sautéing, *13, 13*
    vegetables, 219
savory, *21,* 25
scales, 27
scallions, 215, *215*
scallops, *94,* 97
    Grilled, **111**
    and Oyster Pie, **276**
    and Shrimp with Green Sauce, **39,** *39*
    and Spinach Pasta Salad, **194,** *194*
    and Vegetable Salad, **111**
scrambled eggs, *see* eggs, scrambled
sea bass, *94,* 96
seafood, 93–116
    Bouillabaisse (Stew, Mediterranean), **329,** *329*
    Chowder, **66**
    Clambake, **342,** *342*
    Dill Salad, **104**
    essentials of, 95–97
    Fritto Misto, *323,* **324**
    Paella, **334**
    risotto, 208
    San Francisco Cioppino, **66**

Seviche, **104**
storage of, 95–96
    see also fish; shellfish *and specific seafood*
seasonings, 20–26, *21, 25*
sesame:
    Cakes (Banh Cam), **285,** *285*
    Lamb Chops, **166**
    oil, Oriental, 18
sesame seed, *21, 25*
    Cookies, **284**
Seviche, **104**
sevruga caviar, 54
Shabu-Shabu, **154**
shad roe, *113,* 115
    Poached, with Wine Sauce, **115**
    preparation of, 115
shallots, 19, *21,* 25
    peeling of, 31, *31*
    see also onions
shellfish, *94,* 96–97
    Clambake, **342,** *342*
    clams, preparation of, *110*
    Crab, Peking, and Vegetables, **106**
    crab, shelling of, *106*
    Crab and Shrimp Boil, **105**
    Crab Meat with Artichoke Ravigote, **109**
    Crevettes en Folie ("Extravagant" Shrimp), **108**
    Fresh Shrimp with Chive Butter, **106**
    Grilled Scallops, **111**
    Hot Shrimp Mousse with Sauce Aurore, **108**
    as leftover, 32
    Lobster, Boiled, **104**
    Lobster, Cantonese, **105**
    Lobster Salad, **104**
    lobster, shelling of, *105*
    mussels, preparation of, *110*
    Mussels with Ravigote Sauce, **109**
    oysters, preparation of, *110*
    Oysters or Clams on the Half Shell, **111**
    Peking Crab and Vegetables, **106**
    Saffron Mussels, **110**
    Scallop and Oyster Pie, **276**
    Scallop and Shrimp with Green Sauce, **39,** *39*
    Scallop and Spinach Pasta Salad, **194,** *194*

Scallop and Vegetable Salad, **111**
Scallops, Grilled, **111**
Shrimp with Coconut Milk and Peas, **109**
shrimp, deveining of, *108*
Shrimp Etouffées, **107,** *107*
Shrimp "Extravagant" (Crevettes en Folie), **108**
Shrimp, Fresh, with Chive Butter, *79,* **106**
Shrimp Mousse, Hot, with Sauce Aurore, **108**
shrimp, shelling of, *108*
sherbets, freezing of, 351
    see also sorbets
Sherry Cream Sauce, **249**
Short Ribs, Braised, with Horseradish Sauce, **156**
shredding, 31, *31*
shrimp, *94,* 96
    and Artichoke Toast, **44**
    with Coconut Milk and Peas, **109**
    and Crab Boil, **105**
    and Crab Gumbo, **65,** *65*
    Crevettes en Folie ("Extravagant"), **108**
    deveining of, *108*
    Etouffée, **107,** *107*
    Fresh, with Chive Butter, *79,* **106**
    Mousse, Hot, with Sauce Aurore, **108**
    Sauce, and Herb, **188**
    Sauce, with Mussels and Wine, **189**
    and Scallops with Green Sauce, **39,** *39*
    shelling of, *108*
Sicilian Pizza, *256,* **257**
Skillet Corn Bread, **261**
skillets, 27
slicing, 30, *30*
smelt, *94,* 96
Smoked Mozzarella with Oil and Black Pepper, **320,** *320*
smoked pork, 172
    see also specific varieties
Smoked Salmon with Horseradish Cream, *39,* **40**
snails (*escargots*), *113,* 115
    in Butter and Garlic Sauce (Escargots de Bourgogne), **115**
    Mushrooms Stuffed with Escargots, **43**

Index

(*snails cont'd.*)
    preparation of, 115
Soft-Boiled Eggs, **82**
Sole, Paupiettes of Lemon, **102**
solid fats equivalent, 355
Sorbet (Frozen Fruit Ice), **246,** *247*
sorrel:
    Chicken and, Salad, **131**
    Cream of Any Vegetable Soup, **59**
soufflé dishes, 28
soufflés:
    Apple Calvados, **92**
    Broccoli and Cheese, **91,** *91*
    Cheese, **90**
    Chicken and Mushroom, **91,** *91*
    Chocolate, **92**
    Cold Lemon, **324,** *324*
    Grand Marnier, **92**
    Hot Mocha, **92**
    Lemon, **92**
    Lemon, Cold, **324,** *324*
    Mocha, Hot, **92**
    Salmon, **91,** *91*
    Spinach and Onion, **91,** *91*
    Vanilla, **91**
soups, 55, 59–68
    au Pistou, 20
    Avocado and Cucumber, **66**
    Avocado Bisque, **66**
    Barley, **60**
    Beef Vegetable, **60**
    Black Bean, **62**
    Borscht (Beet), **66**
    Chicken, **58**
    cold, 66–68
    Cold Cucumber, **66,** *66*
    Cold Lentil, **68**
    Cream of Any Vegetable, **59**
    Cucumber, Cold, **66**
    Fresh Tomato, **62**
    Gazpacho, **68**
    Ham and Lentil, **63**
    Hot and Sour Prawn, **63**
    from leftovers, 32
    Lentil, Cold, **68**
    Lentil and Ham, **63**
    Minestrone, **60**
    Miso (Soybean), **63**
    Onion, **60**
    Oyster Stew, **65**
    Prawn, Hot and Sour, **63**
    San Francisco Cioppino, **66**
    Seafood Chowder, **66**

    Shrimp and Crab Gumbo, **65,** *65*
    Soubise, **60**
    Soybean (Miso), **63**
    Summer Squash, **62**
    Tomato, Fresh, **62**
    Turkey, **136**
    Vegetable, **60,** *60*
    Vegetable Beef, **60**
    Vegetable, Cream of Any, **59**
    Vegetable Rice, **60**
    Winter Squash, **62**
    Zucchini, Cold, **346**
sour cream, 19
    Eggs with Caviar and, **83**
    and Watercress Omelet, **87**
Southern Fried Chicken, **127**
Soybean Soup (Miso), **63**
soy sauce, 18
Spaetzle, **196,** *196*
spaghetti, *see* pasta
spaghettini, *182*
Spareribs, Jimmy's Barbecued, **169**
spatulas, 27
spinach, 213, *213*
    Homemade Pasta, **185**
    and Onion Soufflé, **91**
    pasta, Paglia e Fieno (Straw and
        Hay), **188,** *188*
    Ravioli Stuffed with, and Cheese
        Sauce, **192,** *192*
    and Scallop Pasta Salad, **194,** *194*
    Timbale, **230**
split peas, 201
spoons, wooden, 27
spring-form pans, 28
squab, 140, *143*
    Broiled with Raspberry Vinegar
        Sauce, **140**
    essentials of, 140
    Salad, **140**
squash:
    acorn, *215,* 218
    Acorn, with Apple Stuffing, **231,**
        231
    Baked Spaghetti, **231**
    butternut, *216,* 218
    Hubbard, 218
    pattipan, *216,* 218
    Soup, Summer, **62**
    Soup, Winter, **62**
    spaghetti, *216,* 218
    Spaghetti, Baked, **231**
    turban, 218

    yellow, *215,* 218
    yellow, Julienne of Vegetables,
        316, *316*
    see also zucchini
squid, 113, *113*
    Broiled, **113**
    description of, 113
    with Linguine and Peas, **113**
    preparation of, 113
Standing Rib Roast of Beef, **297,** *297*
steak, beef:
    Béarnaise on grilled sirloin, *78*
    boneless chuck, *152*
    Châteaubriand à la Bordelaise,
        154, *155*
    chuck, *152*
    filet mignon, *152*
    flank, *152*
    frozen, 19
    Grilled Flank, **152**
    Grilled Flank with Ginger Mari-
        nade, **153**
    porterhouse, *152*
    shell, *152*
    sirloin, *152*
    skirt, *152*
    T-bone, *152*
    whole rib with short rib, *152*
Steamed Rice, **205**
Steamed Wild Rice, **207**
steaming, 12, *12*
    vegetables, 219
stew, 325–334
    beef, *152*
    Bouillabaisse (Mediterranean
        Seafood), **329,** *329*
    Burgundian Beef, **330,** *331*
    Carbonnades à la Flamande
        (Flemish, with Beer), **333**
    Cassoulet, **330**
    Chicken, with Couscous, **126**
    Chili con Carne, **326**
    Choucroute Garnie (Alsatian
        Sauerkraut), **328**
    Couscous Lamb, **333,** *333*
    Jambalaya, **326,** *327*
    Lamb, **164**
    Lamb Korma, **164**
    from leftovers, 32
    Moussaka, **328**
    Oyster, **65**
    Paella, **334**
    Pheasant, **142**

Rabbit, **145**
veal, *156*
Stewed Okra and Tomatoes, **228**
Stewed Pinto Beans, **203**
Stewed Tomatoes, **297**, *297*
Stilton, **283**, *283*
stir-fry:
 Beef and Vegetables, **155**
 Green Chicken, **129**
 Parsnips, **228**
 Pork with Zucchini and Noodles, **171**
 of Rice and Vegetables, **207**
 Vegetable Sauce, *338*, **340**
stir-frying, 13, *13*
 vegetables, 219
stocks, 55, 56–59, *57*
 aspic, 59
 Beef (Brown), **57**
 Chicken, **58**
 emergency (chicken, fish and beef), 58
 essentials of, 56
 Fish, **58**
 freezing of, 351
 frozen, 19
 making, techniques for, *57*
 Turkey, **136**
 White, **56**
storage bins, 28
Straw and Hay (Paglia e Fieno), **188**, *188*
strawberries, *239*, 240
 as garnish, 133
 with raspberry purée, *246*
 Sorbet, **246**, *247*
striped bass, *94, 96*
stuffed:
 Artichokes, **219**
 Breast of Veal, **161**
 Eggplant, **223**
 Fish Filets, **73**
 Fish Filets with Mushroom and wine Velouté Sauce, **99**
 Grape Leaves (Dolmathes), **51**, *51*
 Game Hens, Cranberry, **133**
 Leg of Lamb (Gigot d'Agneau Farci), **310**
 Pears, with Cheese, **284**, *284*
 Pork Chops, **170**, *170*
 Savoy Cabbage, **221**
 Shells with Dill Dressing, Vegetable, **320**, *320*

Trout en Croûte, Salmon, **272**
stuffing:
 Apple, with Acorn Squash, **321**, *321*
 Pork, with Roast Chicken, **347**, *347*
 Sausage-Apple, with Roast Goose, **315**, *316*
 Sausage-Cornbread, with Roast Turkey, **312**, *312*
su (rice wine vinegar), 112
sugar:
 brown, 19
 granulated, 19
Sukiyaki, *see* Shabu-Shabu
Summer Squash Soup, **62**
suppers, late night, 335–340
 tortellini, 338–340
 Welsh rarebit, 337–338, *337*
Supreme, Sauce (Cream Sauce), **70**
Suprêmes au Chasseur (Sautéed Chicken Breasts with Hunter's Sauce), **129**, *129*
sushi, 112
 description of, 112
 Pressed, **112**
 Rolled, **112**
 Shaped, **112**
 Vinegared Rice for, **112**
Sweet and Pungent Bok Choy, **220**
Sweet and Sour Onions, **228**
Sweet and Sour Tongue, **178**
sweetbreads, *174*, 175
 Capelli d'Angelo with Truffles and (Angel Hair Pasta with Truffles and), **176**
 Grilled, with Bacon, **45**
 and Kidneys en Brochette, **176**, *177*
 preparation of, 175
 and Prosciutto Soubise, **178**
sweet potatoes, 213, *213*
 Bourbon, **229**

T

Tabasco sauce, 18
Tabbouleh with Romaine Leaves, **210**
tagliarini, *182*
 verde, *182*
tagliatelle, *182*
Taleggio, *278*, 281

tangerines, *243, 244*
tape measures, 28
Tapénade, **39**, *39*
Taramasalata, **47**, *49*
tarragon, *21*, 25
tart pans, 28
tarts:
 pastry, 264
 aux Poires (Pear), *309*, **311**
 Tatin (Upside-down Apple), **286**, *286*
tea:
 black (fermented), 19
 green (unfermented), 19
 herbal, 19
 spiced, 19
techniques and basics, 12–33
Tempura, 52, **52**, *52, 53*
terrines, 28, 45–46
 Veal, Ham and Pork, **45**, *46*
 Vegetable, **233**
 see also pâté
Tête de Moine, 281, *283*
Thai Crisp Fried Noodles, **197**
Thanksgiving feast, 312–315
 Apricot Glazed Yams, *312*, **314**
 Brussels Sprouts and Chestnuts, *312*, **314**
 Cranberry and Wine Sauce, *312*, **314**
 menu for, 312
 Pumpkin-Mincemeat Pie, *312*, **315**
 Roast Turkey with Sausage-Cornbread Stuffing, **312**, *312*
 strategies for, 312
thermometers, 27
thread, heavy sewing, 28
thyme, *21*, 26
timers, 27
toast, 19
 Cinnamon, **295**
 French, **292**, *292*
 Melba, **346**
 Shrimp and Artichoke, **44**
tomatoes, *215*, 216
 Baked Eggs with Cream and, **85**, *85*
 beefsteak, *215*, 216
 and Celeriac Salad, **235**
 cherry, *215*, 216
 Cream of Any Vegetable Soup, **59**
 Dal and, **203**

Index

(tomatoes cont'd.)
- Eggs Baked in, *72*
- Haricots Blanc et Tomates (White Beans and), **311**
- Herb Sauce, *338, 340*
- hot-house, *215,* 216
- Italian plum, *215,* 216
- Pasta, Homemade, **185**
- paste, 18
- Sauce, Cold, **194**
- Sauce, Fresh, **186,** *187*
- sauce, frozen, 19
- Sauce, Herb, *338,* **340**
- Soup, Cream of Any Vegetable, **59**
- Soup, Fresh, **62**
- Stewed, **297,** *297*
- Stewed Okra and, **228**
- White Beans and (Haricots Blanc et Tomates), **311**
- whole Italian plum, 18

tongs, 27

tongue, *174,* 175
- fresh, *174,* 175
- lamb, 175
- pickled, 175
- pork, 175
- preparation of, 175
- smoked, *174,* 175
- Sweet and Sour, **178**

tools, 27

Tortellini, *182,* **193,** 338, *338*

Tortellini supper, 338–340, *338,* **340**
- Cantaloupe-Orange Ice with Marsala, *338,* **340**
- Fresh Herbs, *338,* **340**
- menu for, 338
- strategies for, 338
- Tomato Herb Sauce, *338,* **340**
- Vegetable Sauce, *338,* **340**

tortes:
- Cassis Mousse, **290**
- Chocolate-Orange, **271,** *271*
- Walnut, **286**

tortillas:
- Chicken, **131**
- Mexican Eggs, **86**

tournedos, *152*
- with Bordelaise Sauce, *75,* **154**

tripe, *174,* 175
- Creole, **178**
- preparation of, 175

trout, *94, 96*

Cold, with Watercress-Lime Sauce, **101**

Poached, **101**

Poached, with Ravigote Sauce, **101**

Poached, with Velouté Sauce, **101**

Stuffed with Salmon, en Croûte, **272**

truffles, 216
- Capelli d'Angelo with Sweetbreads and (Angel Hair Pasta with Sweetbreads and), **176**

Tuiles aux Amandes (Chocolate-filled Almond Cookies), **285**

tuna, 18
- Cannellini Salad with, **201**
- Pasta Salad, **195,** *195*
- Tapénade, **39,** *39*
- Vitello Tonnato (Roast Veal with Sauce), **159,** *159*

turkey, *119,* 134–136
- Basic Roast, **134,** *134*
- carving of, *135*
- Curry, **136**
- essentials of, 134
- Roast, with Sausage-Cornbread Stuffing, **312,** *312*
- Soup, **136**
- Stock, **136**
- storage of, 134

turmeric, *21, 26*

turnips, *213,* 215
- Puréed, and Chestnuts, **231,** *232*

Turnovers, Phyllo, **50,** *50*

twine, 28

U

ugli fruit, 245

Upside-down Apple Tart (Tarte Tatin), **286,** *286*

V

Vacherin Fribourgeois, 281, *283*

Vanilla Ice Cream, **303**

Vanilla Soufflé, **91**

veal, 156–162, *156*
- boneless leg roast, *156,* 159
- Boneless Shoulder Roast, *156,* **161**
- breast of, *156,* **161**

chops, *156*

Chops, Sautéed, **161**

Chops with Cream Sauce, **161,** *161*

Chops with Vegetable Sauce, **161**

Cold Stuffed Roast, *345,* **346**

essentials of, 156

ground, *156*

Ham and Pork Terrine with, **45,** *46*

how to cook, *156*

leg steak, *156*

Marengo, **162**

Osso Buco Milanese (Braised Shank), **158**

Paillard of, with Sage and Prosciutto, **158**

rib chops, *156*

rib roast, *156*

Roast, Braised, **161**

Roast, Cold Stuffed, *345,* **346**

roast, cuts, 156

Roast, Shoulder, **161**

Roast, with Tuna Sauce (Vitello Tonnato), **159**

sautéed, *72*

sautéing of, 13, *13*

scallopini, frozen, 19

Scallopini in Wine, **158**

scallops, *156*

shank, *156*

shoulder, *156*

Shoulder Roast, **161**

stew, *156*

Stuffed Breast of, **161**

Terrine, with Ham and Pork, **45,** 46

Vitello Tonnato (Roast, with Tuna Sauce), **159,** *159*

vegetable oil, 18

vegetables, 211–236
- Antipasto, **43,** *43*
- aromatic, used in stocks, 56
- Bagna Cauda, **41**
- and Beef Soup, **60**
- Chestnut Purée, **223**
- Chicken Sauté, **123**
- cooking techniques, 219
- Cream of Any Vegetable Soup, **59**
- Crudités Marinated in Garlic-Basil Vinaigrette, **344,** *345*
- Custard, **89,** *90*
- essentials of, 213–218
- freezing of, 351

Gazpacho, **68**
Julienne of, **316,** *316*
Kari, **232**
Lasagne, **193**
as leftovers, 32
new cornucopia, *348, 348*
Omelet, **87**
Omelet, Julienne of, **88**
Pasta Salad, **194**
Peking Crab and, **106**
pickled, *347*
Puréed Turnips and Chestnuts,
 231, *232*
Quiche, **274,** *275*
Ratatouille, **223**
Salad, and Brown Rice, *345,* **346**
Salad, Scallops and, **111**
Sauce for Tortellini, *338,* **340**
Sauce, with Veal Chops, **161**
Soup, **60,** *60*
Soup, Cream of Any, **59**
Soup, Rice and, **60**
Stir-Fried Beef and, **155**
stir-frying of, 13, *13*
Stir-Fry of Rice and, **207**
Stuffed Shells with Dill Dressing,
 320, *320*
Tempura, **52,** *52, 53*
Terrine, **233**
Vinaigrette, *39,* **41**
for Welsh rarebit, *337,* **338**
Yam and Leek Pie, **232**
 see also specific vegetables
Velouté Sauce, **73,** *73*
venison, *143,* 147
 Roast, **147**
 Sautéed Steaks, **147**
vermouth, dry, 19
Vietnamese Duckling, *137,* **138**
Vinaigrette Dressing, **80**
vinegars:
 fruit, 18
 herb, 18
 su (rice wine), 112

wine, 18
Vitello Tonnato (Roast Veal with Tuna
 Sauce), **159,** *159*

___

W

walleye pike, *94, 96*
walnut oil, 18
walnuts, 19
Walnut Torte, **286**
Warm Goat Cheese Salad, **235**
wasabi (green horseradish), 112
water chestnuts, 18
watercress, 213, *213*
 Cream of Any Vegetable Soup, **59**
 -Lime Sauce, Cold Poached Trout
 with, **101**
 and Sour Cream Omelet, **87**
watermelon, *240, 240*
Welsh Rarebit supper, 337–338, **337,**
 337
 menu for, 337
 Pears Poached in Cognac, *337,*
 338
 strategies for, 337
 Vegetables, *337,* **338**
Wheat-Germ Bread, Carrot, *258,* **260**
whisks, 27
White Bean Salad, *49,* **52**
White Beans and Tomatoes (Haricots
 Blancs et Tomates), **311**
White Butter (Beurre Blanc), **80,** *80*
White Cheshire, 281, *283*
White Clam Sauce, **188**
whitefish, *94, 96*
whitefish caviar, 54
white pepper, *21,* 24
White Stock, **56**
Whole Small Baked Fish, **98**
Whole-Wheat Health Bread, **256,** *256*
wild duck, 142–143, *143*
 Roast, **139**
 Roast Mallard, **142**

Wild Rice with Mushrooms, **316,** *316*
wine:
 Burgundy, Eggs in, *83,* **84**
 dry white, 19
 Fish Poached in, **102**
 -Poached Apples, **139**
 red, 19
 Sauce, Cranberry and, *312,* **314**
 Sauce, with Mussels and Shrimp,
 189
wine vinegar, 18
Winter Squash Soup, **62**
wok cookery, 13, *13*
 see also stir-fry
Worcestershire sauce, 18

___

Y

yams:
 Apricot Glazed, *312,* **314**
 and Leek Pie, **232**
yeast, 19, 252
yeast breads, *see* breads
yogurt, 19
 and Cucumber Salad, *47,* **49**
 Dressing, with Avocado Salad, **324**
 Sauce, *345,* **346**

___

Z

ziti, *182*
zucchini, *215,* 218
 Cream of Any Vegetable Soup, **59**
 and Eggplant Sauce, **189**
 Fried, with Green Peppercorn
 Butter, **232**
 Julienne of Vegetables, **316,** *316*
 Minestrone, **60**
 and Onion Frittata, **89**
 Soup, Cold, **346**
 Stir-Fry Pork and Noodles, **171**